planning • environment • cities

Series Editors: Yvonne Rydin and Andrew Thornley

The context in which planning operates has changed dramatically in recent years. Economic processes have become increasingly globalized and economic fortunes have fluctuated. Administrations in various countries have not only changed, but old ideologies have been swept away and new ones have tentatively emerged. A new environmental agenda has prioritized the goal of sustainable development, requiring continued action at international, national and local levels.

Cities are today faced with new pressures for economic competiveness, greater accountability and participation, improved quality of life for citizens, and global environmental responsibilities. These pressures are often contradictory and create difficult dilemmas for policy-makers, especially in the context of fiscal austerity.

In these changing circumstances, planners, from many backgrounds, in many different organizations, have come to re-evaluate their work. They have to engage with actors in government, the private sector and non-governmental organizations in discussions over the role of planning in relation to the environment and cities. The intention of the *Planning, Environment, Cities* series is to explore the changing nature of planning and contribute to the debate about its future.

This series is primarily aimed at students and practitioners of planning and such related professions as estate management, housing and architecture as well as those in politics, public and social administration, geography and urban studies. It comprises both general texts and books designed to make a more particular contribution, in both cases characterized by: an international approach; extensive use of case studies; and emphasis on contemporary relevance and the application of theory to advance planning practice.

D0168981

planning • environment • cities

Series Editors: Yvonne Rydin and Andrew Thornley

Published

Philip Allmendinger
Planning Theory (2nd edn)

Chris Couch
Urban Planning: An Introduction

Ruth Fincher and Kurt Iveson
Planning and Diversity in the City: Redistribution, Recognition and Encounter

Cliff Hague, Euan Hague and Carrie Breitbach
Regional and Local Economic Development

Patsy Healey
Collaborative Planning (2nd edn)

Patsy Healey
Making Better Places: The Planning Project in the 21st Century

Simon Joss
Sustainable Cities: Governing for Urban Innovation

Ted Kitchen
Skills for Planning Practice

Ali Madanipour
Urban Design, Space and Society

Peter Newman and Andrew Thornley
Planning World Cities (2nd edn)

Michael Oxley
Economics, Planning and Housing

Yvonne Rydin
Urban and Environmental Planning in the UK (2nd edn)

Mark Tewdwr-Jones
Spatial Planning and Governance: Understanding UK Planning

Geoff Vigar, Patsy Healey and Angela Hull with Simin Davoudi
Planning, Governance and Spatial Strategy in Britain

Iain White
Environmental Planning in Context

Forthcoming

Luca Bertolini: **Planning the Mobile Metropolis**
Jon Coaffee and Peter Lee: **Urban Resilience: Planning the Shock-Proof City**
Ed Ferrari: **GIS and Planning for the Built Environment**

Other titles planned include

Comparative Planning
Planning History
International Planning

Planning, Environment, Cities
Series Standing Order ISBN 978–0–333–71703–5 hardback
Series Standing Order ISBN 978–0–333–69346–9 paperback
(*outside North America only*)

You can receive future titles in this series as they are published. To place a standing order please contact your bookseller or, in the case of difficulty, write to us at the address below with your name and address, the title of the series and the ISBN quoted above.

Customer Services Department, Macmillan Distribution Ltd,
Houndmills, Basingstoke, Hampshire, RG21 6XS, UK

Urban Planning

An Introduction

Chris Couch

macmillan education   palgrave

First published 2016 by
PALGRAVE

Palgrave in the UK is an imprint of Macmillan Publishers Limited, registered in England, company number 785998, of 4 Crinan Street, London, N1 9XW.

Palgrave Macmillan in the US is a division of St Martin's Press LLC, 175 Fifth Avenue, New York, NY 10010.

Palgrave is a global imprint of the above companies and is represented throughout the world.

Palgrave® and Macmillan® are registered trademarks in the United States, the United Kingdom, Europe and other countries.

ISBN 978–1–137–42757–1 hardback
ISBN 978–1–137–42756–4 paperback

This book is printed on paper suitable for recycling and made from fully managed and sustained forest sources. Logging, pulping and manufacturing processes are expected to conform to the environmental regulations of the country of origin.

A catalogue record for this book is available from the British Library.

A catalog record for this book is available from the Library of Congress.

Printed in China

Contents

List of Figures

List of Tables

Preface

Some years ago, Macmillan Education was kind enough to publish my book *Urban Renewal: theory and practice* (Couch, 1990). The book was quite successful and I was invited to produce a second edition but the time never seemed right and then other priorities intervened. So, although I have since written extensively on many planning topics I never returned to this book. However, in recent years my teaching has included some introductory courses to planning students at the University of Liverpool. In undertaking this task it has constantly struck me that, whilst there are some excellent text books that I recommend to students, too many others are out-of-date, only partially relevant, or too sophisticated to be introductory texts. If you want a book that directly fits the needs of your course, the solution, as every university lecturer will tell you, is to write it yourself. Urban planning is a broader concept than that of urban renewal but I did feel that there remained sufficient in the structure and some of the general ideas in the original book that I could develop into a new and broader text covering the wider spectrum of the modern urban planning agenda.

Thus the purpose of this book is to introduce readers to a discussion about urban problems and their solutions, including ideas about what can be done to make urban areas more sustainable, efficient and equitable, and how the planning system can contribute to achieving these goals. The range of urban problems and policy responses to be considered here are those that are likely to be found in the urban planning documents of almost any city in the developed world: environmental sustainability; economic development; the role of town and city centres; housing provision; neighbourhood renewal; urban design; conservation; mobility and accessibility. The book is intended as an introductory text in urban planning for students on undergraduate planning courses and those on postgraduate 'conversion' courses in planning. But it is also aimed at students in other disciplines, such as the social sciences or the built environment professions, who might be taking a single module in planning or who are merely interested in the topic. It is also hoped that the text will be of interest to the general reader who wants to learn more about the functioning of towns and cities and the nature of urban planning.

Acknowledgements

I would like to thank the following for their knowledge and advice concerning urban planning in various countries and case studies: Hermann Bömer (Universität Dortmund), Wolfgang Börstinghaus (Stadt Flensburg), Pamela Ewen (TAYplan), Peter Geraghty (Southend-on-Sea Borough Council), Helen Hooper (WDR & RT Taggart), Jeen Kootstra and Paul Vreeken (Gemeente Utrecht), Bernd Kötter (Stadt Dortmund), David Leslie (Edinburgh City Council), Janet O'Neill (O'Neill Associates), Sean Tickle (Rolfe Judd), Rene Van der Lecq (Ruimte Vlaanderen) and Frank Weijzen (Gemeente Den Haag).

The photographic credits go to Daniel Couch (Paris), Matthew Cocks (China), Charles McCorkell (Dublin) and WDR & RT Taggart (Belfast). All other photographs were taken by the author. Thanks also go to Thomas Couch for computing advice and special thanks to Anna Couch for preparing the drawn maps and illustrations.

I would like to acknowledge the support of all my colleagues at the University of Liverpool, particularly Peter Batey, Olivier Sykes and Matthew Cocks (now at the University of Birmingham), for their advice and useful suggestions on earlier drafts of the manuscript. I would also like to thank Stephen Wenham at Palgrave for commissioning the book and to the series editors, Yvonne Rydin and Andy Thornley, for their constructive comments. Nevertheless the errors and omissions in this text remain entirely my own responsibility. Finally and most importantly, I would like to thank my wife, Lynda, for putting up with me working on the book and taking up far too many evenings and weekends doing so over the past year.

Note: Online sources were accurate to the best of our knowledge at the time of going to press.

The author and publishers would like to thank DACS and Faber & Faber Limited for kindly granting permission to reproduce part (b) of Figure 1.5.

Introduction

Urban development and planning

As urban areas have grown and become ever more complex systems of interconnected activities, so the unfettered interplay of market forces has proved insufficient to avoid increasing inefficiencies in urban development and form. Without some element of planning, growing cities would probably sprawl ever further into the surrounding countryside and declining cities would see valuable urban land abandoned. Both would result in inefficient patchworks of fragmented urbanism, difficult and expensive to service and inequitable in their impacts on the economies of firms and the life chances of individuals. Environmental degradation and natural resource depletion would go unchecked. Today, across the developed world virtually all governments recognize the importance of urban planning in ensuring efficiency and equity in the use of land and other resources. Planning is seen to support economic growth by ensuring the availability of developable land and by coordinating the provision of infrastructure (highways, utilities, etc.). It also plays a key role in the protection and conservation of the natural, built and historic resources and environments. Furthermore, a well planned urban area contributes to the development of inclusive communities and the opportunity to live in attractive, safe and healthy neighbourhoods (DCLG, 2012).

Some economists argue that the justifications for public policy and state intervention in society (expenditure and regulation) can be divided into two basic categories: legitimation and accumulation. The former requires that the state provides defence and police functions and social policies designed to protect society from both external and internal threats, to avoid public unrest or maintain social harmony. The accumulation function of the state is more complex but more directly related to supporting economic activity and growth. Here the state provides social capital, that is to say, all the commonly owned infrastructure upon which the economic system depends, including social investment (e.g. in education) and physical capital investment (e.g. transportation and utility networks) (O'Connor, 1973). Thus the justification for state-led urban planning becomes apparent. The accumulation function might include the planning of transportation and utilities networks or planning the use of land to maximize the efficiency of urban structure and form. It can also be used to justify state intervention in urban regeneration processes which the private sector finds difficult, such as land reclamation and

1

land assembly. Environmental and heritage protection and enhancement are also legitimized as social physical capital investment (increasingly so in the age of the competitive city) but might also be seen in part as necessary social expenses incurred in the maintenance of social harmony.

For neo-classical economists, urban planning can be justified in various circumstances (Mills and Hamilton, 1984; Balchin et al., 1995; Evans, 2004). The first of these is the divergence between private and social costs in production and consumption. The social costs of an activity are those costs borne by society as a whole, as distinct from private costs – those that are reflected in the market price of goods and services. The private costs of, say, chemical production would be the costs to the firm in terms of labour, materials and energy used in production, whereas the social costs would include the burden of pollution, traffic congestion and so forth caused by this production. Thus it can be argued that an important reason for state intervention (planning) is to deal with the gap between private and social costs, whether by regulation, taxation or subsidies.

A second reason for urban planning is to deal with market imperfections. There are many imperfections in land and property markets. These can include: inertia amongst producers or consumers in responding to changes in market conditions; lack of knowledge about aspects of the workings of the market; the distorting effects of monopoly or monopsony power; the immobility of factors of production; inequalities of income or wealth amongst consumers. The state may intervene to ease these difficulties and distortions in order to improve the functioning of the market, for example, increasing the supply of land zoned for a particular use, regulating monopolies and encouraging competition, or speeding up planning decisions.

Thirdly, some elements of urban development are essential but difficult or impossible for the market to provide. These include much of the physical infrastructure of cities such as streets, utilities, social control and protection services, urban landscaping and parks. Since each individual or firm desires to consume only some (very small and varying) proportion of these elements, it is impractical for market transactions to take place efficiently. In these circumstances it is logical for some common agency, usually the state, to plan and produce such infrastructure and services.

Fourthly, merit goods may be provided by the state because political value judgements have been made that certain groups of people should have these goods or services regardless of their ability to pay or indeed their own personal desires in the matter: classic examples include education and health care for children. Given that a market economy inevitably produces great divergences in income levels and the ability to pay for goods and services, it is often argued that a further reason for state intervention is to redress some of the imbalance created by 'helping those least able to compete in the market' to do so, or at least to obtain the basic necessities of modern life. Certainly transfer payments through the state and state subsidies (e.g. housing demand subsidies) are typical ways in which the state seeks to achieve such aims.

Thus, each of these – the desire to provide social or physical capital investment that cannot be efficiently achieved by the market; to alleviate market imperfections; to deal with the social costs of economic activity; or to avoid social unrest – is a potential reason for the state to intervene in urban areas and engage in urban planning.

The process of urban planning

Although planning is a relatively new subject for academic study, it has built up a considerable body of theory that informs contemporary discourse and practice. This theory is frequently sub-divided into two categories: theories 'of' and 'in' planning. The distinction was made by Andreas Faludi who identified: (a) theories of planning, concerned with procedural issues in planning and methods and processes of decision making, that is, how plans were made; and (b) theories in planning, concerned with the substantive content of plans, that is, what planners were trying to achieve by making plans (Faludi, 1973).

Through the first half of the twentieth century theories of planning were mainly based around the relatively simple but robust view that evolved from Geddes's (1915) idea that plan making should follow a linear process of 'survey – analysis – plan'. At this stage more controversy was being generated by theories in planning where there was a strong distinction between the modernists and those who favoured more traditional approaches to the design of cities. By the 1960s procedural theories of planning were embracing the work of McLoughlin (1969) and Chadwick (1971) with their view of the city as a system of interconnected parts, in which the outcomes of any intervention (planning policy) would lead to impacts across the whole system. In order to understand fully the impact of policy decisions, planning would require a much higher level of data gathering and analysis than hitherto.

Under this model, urban planning had to be both comprehensive (taking account of all the interconnections between different parts of the urban system) and rational (scientific and dispassionate). This of course proved to be impossible. In the first place, gathering and analysing such vast quantities of data on the urban system and the interlinkages between policy areas was impossible, and it was wrong to assume that planners had the level of power and control over the environment that McLoughlin's approach required. Two alternative approaches offered a way out of this problem. Lindblom (1973) suggested that in reality it was impossible to be comprehensive, so policy makers took the best possible decisions within the limitations of their own knowledge and resources, and subsequent decisions simply had to take on board previous decisions and their outcomes. In other words, policy making was 'disjointed' and moved forwards in incremental stages, with each round of decision making adjusting to the changes made by the previous round. In another alternative, Etzioni (1973) suggested a 'mixed-scanning' approach whereby most of the urban system would be monitored with a 'light touch', gathering only limited data and subjecting it to no more than routine monitoring. Only if this monitoring identified some abnormality in the system (such as a sudden rise in unemployment) would there be a need for more detailed investigation.

In the second, place urban planning was neither wholly scientific nor dispassionate. Because planning was concerned with the allocation of resources and affected the use and value of land, it was evidently a political process that would, at different times and places, operate to the benefit of some groups in society and at a cost to others. There was no universal 'public interest' that was served by planning. Following this line of argument, through the 1970s and 1980s a series of commentators debated the purposes and political economy of planning, exploring in whose interests the system really operated (see, for example, Harvey, 1973; Pickvance, 1976; Harloe, 1977).

Recognition of the political nature of urban plans and planning decisions leads naturally on to the idea that in any democratic society local inhabitants and other stakeholders should have the opportunity to contribute to and participate in these processes (Taylor, 1998). Through the 1960s a number of factors supported moves towards greater public involvement in planning decisions. In the USA the impacts of social conflict and the civil rights movement were leading to more participatory forms of urban governance. In the UK and elsewhere in Europe there seemed to be a widening gap between the ambitions of urban planners and politicians for large scale urban renewal and transportation projects and the desires of an increasingly socially mixed urban population for more gradual approaches to urban investment involving housing improvement, area renovation and the protection of heritage. Central and local governments were also beginning to realize that participatory forms of planning were not only more equitable but could bring more knowledge to bear on problems and so improve the quality of decision making. By the 1970s a number of countries had legislated to facilitate public participation in urban planning and area regeneration.

During the 1990s, Healey (1997) and others saw urban planning as something more collaborative, drawing on social and political theory to propose an approach that recognizes the fragmented nature of institutional decision making, and adopting a more negotiated and consensus seeking style of planning. Whilst this model represents the most plausible analysis of the planning process in the early twenty-first century, as is evident from the case studies in later chapters of this book, it is not without its critics who question, for example, the potential for creating consensus out of conflict (Rydin, 2003; Lord, 2012). Campbell and Fainstein suggest that because planning claims to be able to predict the consequences of its actions:

> Planners need to generalize from prior experience if they are to practice their craft. In their day-to-day work, planners may rely more on intuition than explicit theory; yet this intuition may in fact be assimilated theory. In this light, theory represents cumulative professional knowledge. (2003, p. 2)

This would seem to emphasize the importance of experience and perhaps the 'collective knowledge' that arises from collaboration.

The debate over the approaches, procedures, purposes and political economy of urban planning stretches back to the 1980s, prompting some to suggest that discussion of the normative goals of planning (that is, theories in planning) are being neglected (Taylor, 1998). Indeed, in 2002, Talen and Ellis proposed that 'the construction of a theory of good city form [should] be rescued from its marginalized position in the ambiguous subfield of urban design and elevated to an equal rank with process-oriented theories of planning' (quoted in Ferreira et al., 2009, p. 37).

The urban planning agenda

Whilst not excluding discussion of theories of planning, this book is more concerned with what planners are trying to achieve in terms of 'good city form'. It focusses more on making 'calculations about "what should be done", not just about "how it is done"' (Fincher and Iveson, 2008, pp. 4–5). In so doing the discussion draws upon the history of urban change and planning, contemporary theories in planning and experiences and examples from professional planning practice. Many previous planning text books published in the UK adopted a narrow UK-specific approach to the discussion of planning issues, policy and practice. Planning practice is becoming increasingly internationalized and there is a growing recognition of the similarity of issues facing urban planners in many different cities and countries, particularly in the developed world. This text takes a broad view, drawing upon urban theory, policies and practice from a number of countries, particularly in Europe, as appropriate. It tries to avoid over-reliance on local knowledge or parochial assumptions in order to understand the nature of planning issues and solutions.

Planning takes place on a number of scales and in many contexts, and various compound nouns have emerged to describe the activity concerned. These include: 'regional planning', 'city-regional planning', 'metropolitan planning', 'town planning', 'city planning', 'urban planning', 'neighbourhood planning', 'village planning' and 'rural planning'. Whilst such terms provide an indication of the focus of planning in each case, these distinctions are seldom precise and there is often considerable overlap in their meaning and scope.

The words contained within the title of this book – urban planning – are intended to let the reader know that its main focus of concern is the urban area, ranging from large agglomerations to free-standing cities and smaller towns, and the different dimensions of urban planning from the city-region, through the city scale down to the planning of districts, neighbourhoods, individual sites and buildings. And it is important to recognize the limits of this book: issues of national or regional planning or rural planning or theories of planning are not discussed in any depth except where these topics are important to the discussion of urban planning.

Another set of terms refer to 'land use planning', 'spatial planning', 'physical planning', 'community planning' and so forth, with each term suggesting a slightly different set of concerns. Again there is frequently a lack of clarity or agreement about their precise meaning. The term 'spatial planning' represents an attempt to suggest a form of planning that is more positive and comprehensive than 'traditional land use planning' or 'physical planning'. But in the author's opinion this is unfair because planning has always comprised two elements: a positive element proposing a preferred form of development and a so-called negative element controlling or regulating development. Both are as old as the modern idea of planning itself. Development cannot be controlled without some notion of the goal against which it is being measured. Whilst, from early in the nineteenth century, German cities engaged in 'Town Extension Planning' to establish a preferred pattern of development, they also imposed controls to ensure its achievement. In France a distinction is frequently made between 'l'urbanisme prévisionnel' (forward planning), which includes the forecasting and response to urban change through the provision of regulatory plans, and 'l'urbanisme opérationnel' (operational planning), which is concerned with implementing urban change through planning, designing and implementing projects. In the UK some distinction has been made between urban planning and urban regeneration, with the latter having more positive connotations although in reality it is simply one element of the former. Thus, there has always been a positive, proactive side to urban planning. There is more strength in the argument that the range of concerns of planners – the planning agenda – has broadened and become more comprehensive, more holistic, over the years, moving gradually from its early nineteenth century concern with towns and cities as physical entities to embrace wider economic, social and environmental issues.

The Royal Town Planning Institute (RTPI) uses a simple publicity slogan to define planning: 'mediation of space – making of place'. These words capture the essence of the subject. They confirm that there are two broad elements in planning: one about control and management, the other about creativity. In the first, planning is concerned with mediating or determining the use of land and buildings in the face of the competing wishes of different individuals and groups in society: not just the interests of land owners, but also those of neighbours and the wider community at large; not just examining financial gains and losses but including consideration of wider social costs and benefits; not just in the short run but taking a longer term perspective as well. The second element of planning is about visioning, designing and implementing development and change in the physical fabric of towns and cities. This ranges from the design and construction of new cities, as in the UK after the Second World War or in early twenty-first century China, to urban extensions, the redesign or redevelopment of parts of existing cities, the redevelopment of obsolete housing areas, the creation of new squares and green spaces, and the redesign of streets to make them safer and pleasanter places.

However, there are more elaborate definitions and descriptions. In their *Founding Charter* the European Council of Spatial Planners (ECTP-CEU) state that:

> Town Planning ... is concerned with the promotion, guidance, enhancement and control of development in the constantly changing physical environment in the interest of the common good but respecting the rights of the individual ... It is both a management and a creative activity ... Town Planning is rarely an independent process; it must take account of external decisions. It works through and negotiates with the decision making mechanisms of society's political institutions and public and private sectors. Public participation is an indispensable element in the process. By virtue of its direct involvement with people and their day to day activities, Town Planning inevitably has strong political overtones. (ECTP-CEU, 1985, Annex A)

Perhaps the important points here are that the physical, socio-economic and political environment within which planning takes place is constantly changing, so planning has to evolve. Solutions that worked at one time or in one place may not work in another. The ECTP-CEU also highlight the involvement of stakeholders and the importance of negotiation in reaching decisions, and thereby confirm the political nature of the activity.

In their explanation of what planning is, the American Planning Association (APA) and Planning Institute Australia (PIA) both stress normative goals for the profession:

> a dynamic profession that works to improve the welfare of people and their communities by creating more convenient, equitable, healthful, efficient, and attractive places for present and future generations....It helps them find the right balance of new development and essential services, environmental protection, and innovative change. (APA, 2014)

> Planners are professionals who specialise in developing strategies and designing the communities in which we live, work and play. Balancing the built and natural environment, community needs, cultural significance, and economic sustainability, planners aim to improve our quality of life and create vibrant communities. (PIA, 2014)

In the UK, the Quality Assurance Agency for Higher Education's *Subject Benchmark Statement for Town and Country Planning*, whilst recognizing that diversity is an important characteristic of planning, defines a number of core principles. Planning is seen as: concerned with relationships between society and space; being integrative; managing processes of change through deliberate and positive actions; requiring appropriate administrative and legal frameworks for implementing action; involving the allocation of limited resources; and requiring the study, understanding and application of a diverse set of multidisciplinary knowledge (Quality Assurance Agency for Higher Education, 2008, paras 2.1–2.7).

The complexity of planning activities makes it clear that planning is seldom the task of a single person. It invariably involves many different skills both within and beyond the planning profession and considerable data gathering and analysis across a range of subject areas, so that one of the planner's key roles is that of coordinating and synthesizing the actions of other professionals into a coherent and optimal response to a problem. Although the core of urban planning might be summarized as that branch of urban governance concerned with the development and use of land, it is clear from the above definitions that its scope goes beyond this to embrace wider issues of social, economic and environmental policy. The boundaries of the profession become almost impossible to define.

Urban areas are constantly evolving: either expanding, contracting or undergoing internal restructuring in response to economic and social pressures or changes in international, national or local policy. In the developed economies of Europe contemporary patterns of urbanization and the structures of towns and cities have emerged over many centuries, with great accelerations in change following the industrial revolution and after each of the two world wars. In many countries the rate of growth slowed in the latter half of the twentieth century, but since the millennium some countries and some cities, especially capital cities, have again experienced a period of rapid growth as a result of both local and international inward migration that itself is the result of changing economic, social or political pressures.

Localities with a rising level of economic activity may experience increased urbanization and the intensification of land and building use. In localities undergoing a downturn in economic activity such change is likely to lead to a reduction in densities, land and building vacancy and dereliction. Furthermore, there will be public utilities, transportation infrastructure and social facilities to be provided, adapted, expanded, contracted or replaced in response to these changing demands.

In all developed countries, over the period since the industrial revolution, governments have, with varying degrees of enthusiasm and sophistication, increasingly made attempts to intervene in these processes of urban development and change in order to achieve social objectives that are not met by the workings of the land and property markets. Whether for public health reasons, for military purposes or in response to social pressures, from the nineteenth century governments typically began to control the design of streets and utility networks, to set minimum standards for housing, and later to control the use of land, together with the location and intensity of development. Governments also became involved in urban development in other ways, such as overcoming market imperfections and undertaking physical capital investment themselves, for example by undertaking (unprofitable) highway and utility investment in order to unlock locations for (profitable) property development. There might also be new or uncertain markets where state action was required before investor confidence could be established, for instance in stimulating urban regeneration in economically marginal locations.

If the state is going to intervene in the evolution and development of urban areas, if it is to indulge in urban planning, it raises the question of what should be the goals of such intervention. What is good urban form? Whilst such a discussion is the focus of much of the rest of the book, it is worth pausing for a moment to remember that these questions are political and there are disagreements about even the most basic ideas of good city form.

Amongst the early 'seers' in town planning, Ebenezer Howard's solution to the problems of the nineteenth century city was to build low density 'garden cities', merging the best features of town and country. However, a few years later, Le Corbusier proposed the use of modern technology to increase urban densities, to build high and free up the ground for circulation and enjoyment (Hall, 1975).

Responding to the role that cities could play in contributing to sustainable development, the European Commission in its *Green Paper on the*

Urban Environment (CEC, 1990) called for European cities to become more compact and socially inclusive, with higher densities, mixed uses, less reliance on the motor vehicle, with better management and protection of built, natural and cultural resources and heritage (CEC, 1990, part 5). Much of the subsequent conventional wisdom of urban theory in planning and urban planning practice has been written in this same vein.

In their report *Towards an Urban Renaissance* Richard Rogers and his colleagues on the Urban Task Force supported this view, saying that:

> Towns and cities should be well designed, be more compact and connected, support a range of diverse uses within a sustainable urban environment which is well integrated with public transport and adaptable to change. The process of change should combine strengthened democratic local leadership with an increased commitment to public participation. (Urban Task Force, 1999, p. 5)

Broadly supporting these aspirations for the city, the journalist Paul Mason identifies the key qualities of his perfect city. These include the idea that the city's 'finance sector has to be big enough to mobilise global capital and local savings but not so big that the global elite runs things' and with a democratic political culture. It must have bicycles and trams. It must be happy with its historic architecture and should have entire neighbourhoods designed around 'hipster' economics, typically containing vintage clothes shops, a micro-brewery, independent coffee bars and workshops for creative micro-businesses. The city has to have theatres, not just big ones, and a 'massive ecosystem' of gay, lesbian and plain old sleazy hangouts. It must be 'ethnically mixed and tolerant and hospitable to women' (Mason, 2014, p. 7).

However, not everyone agrees with Mason's ideas about the future city. Adams and Watkins (2002) summarize the arguments of a number of writers who are sceptical about the benefits and achievability of the compact city. Breheny raises particular doubts about the acceptability of urban compaction, at least in the UK. Using evidence from previous studies he suggests that 'people aspire to the very opposite of the compact city ... there is a clear clash between the high density aspirations of the compactionists and the desires of local communities to protect their quality of life' (Breheny, 1997, p. 216). Williams (2004) provides further evidence of a limited demand for urban renaissance and the gap in attitudes to urban living between planners and households. And in the USA there are a number of voices expressing doubts about the merits of the compact city:

> Any reversal of urban-development patterns is bound to be extremely costly, if not impossible. People do not want cities that look like New

Urbanist dreams, and they certainly cannot afford them. (Gordon and Richardson, 2000)

Surveying people who worked in Liverpool (the higher density core city of the Merseyside conurbation with many of the attributes admired by Mason) but who lived in Wirral (a lower density, more suburban adjoining borough), positive views were found in relation to Liverpool as a place for work, shopping and leisure but strongly negative views on the city as a place to live (Nevin, 2001). Even this small sample of views is sufficient to suggest that there is unlikely to be consensus about the types of city and urban form that should be the goal of urban planning.

In 2012 the UK Coalition Government stated in its *National Planning Policy Framework* (NPPF) that:

> The Government is committed to ensuring that the planning system does everything it can to support sustainable economic growth. Planning should operate to encourage and not act as an impediment to sustainable growth ... local planning authorities should plan proactively to meet the development needs of business and support an economy fit for the 21st century. (DCLG, 2012, paras 19 and 20)

This suggests a more limited role for planning and raises questions about what happens when the goal of environmental sustainability conflicts with that of (sustainable) economic growth. And different pressure groups each have differing ambitions for the planning system. In response to Kate Barker's *Review of Land Use Planning* (2006), the UK's National Federation of Builders (NFB) commented:

> We hope that this latest review will concentrate on delivering policies that will release more land for development. There have been too many restrictions, over and above greenbelt. Unless these are either removed or simplified, it will be impossible to identify land for additional housebuilding in areas of high demand, particularly in the South of England. (NFB, 2006)

This is clearly a view that does not perceive benefit in the notion of the compact city.

The point is that there are a number of different political ideological views on the goals of the planning system and many different factions of society, each with their own agenda, who wish to see planning orientated towards their particular needs and desires. And of course, discussion is not only confined to the goals of planning but also to the means. Is it better to encourage and facilitate or to restrict and control? Should policy be implemented through direct spending by the state or by influencing the market to achieve the desired goals? Is it better to influence the market by regulation, taxation or subsidy? Or is advocacy and negotiation a better way forward? This book considers these concerns in the context of different aspects of the urban planning agenda.

The structure of the book

So, how should a book about theories in urban planning be organized? Looking across the structure of planning courses at different universities it is possible to see that programmes and therefore core text books can be structured in a number of ways. Some courses are structured around the different scales of planning, with individual modules dealing with planning at national, regional, local and neighbourhood levels. This can work well in developing students' understanding about the interconnections between policy fields at different scales. On the other hand, there is always the danger that the treatment of each policy field might lack depth. Another approach is to use the planning process as a structuring device, with modules on problem identification, option generation, plan making and implementation. Again, this is a legitimate approach but the emphasis is very much on decision making processes and theories of planning. A third approach is to use policy fields to structure the planning course. Here the course structure would closely reflect that of a typical development plan with modules on economic development, housing, transport and so forth. The structure of this book adopts this third approach, particularly because it allows for a strong focus on theories in planning and discussion of the goals of urban planning in different policy fields. But no structure is perfect and the danger to taking this approach is that connections between policy fields can be lost. One of the key features of urban planning is the necessity to look at the interactions between policy fields and to produce and implement horizontally and vertically integrated solutions. Hence, although the main thrust of this book is to consider individual policy fields in turn, it is also necessary to begin with some chapters that consider the historical evolution of the whole planning agenda, the contemporary goals of planning and the nature of planning systems.

The first three chapters explain the evolution of planning, institutional frameworks and the contemporary goals of planning. Chapter 1 explores the history of urban change since the industrial revolution and the planning response to urban problems as they emerged, that is, how the planning agenda has evolved over the years. Whilst the chapter considers the early development of urban areas, it quickly moves to an examination of the changing city in the nineteenth century – for it is in this period that the story of modern urban planning really begins. This is followed by a detailed description of key stages in the evolution of modern urban planning systems and policies through the twentieth and into the twenty-first centuries.

Chapter 2 considers the nature of government and governance systems before describing the nature of planning systems in a variety of countries. Whilst the emphasis is in contrasting the experience of different European countries, the nature of urban planning in the USA, China and Australia as also considered. The chapter then goes on to explore the implementation of urban planning at different scales from the city-region to the neighbourhood and individual site. This is done through a series of case studies that draw upon planning practice in Germany, Belgium and the UK. Chapter 3 considers the notion of sustainable development and the contemporary goals of urban planning. A number of key issues are examined, including population trends, urbanization and urban sprawl, global warming and climate change, natural resource depletion and energy issues, before discussing the emergence of sustainable policy responses at international, national and local levels. This is followed by case studies of contemporary practice, including experiences from the cities of Copenhagen and Freiburg.

Subsequent chapters look in more detail at each of the key policy fields of urban planning. Each chapter includes some analysis of trends, the nature and causes of problems, consideration of the issues facing planners, and discussion of planning methods and solutions at various scales from the city-region to the neighbourhood. In each chapter substantial use is made of experiences and examples from planning practice as well as academic discourse.

Thus, Chapter 4 examines the nature and structure of urban economies and the drivers of economic growth and change before considering how local economic development strategies are prepared. Urban planning responses are explored, including both land use planning and the transformation or regeneration of urban areas to accommodate new forms of economic activity. Baltimore and Dortmund provide detailed cases studies of urban transformation. One dimension of the urban economy that requires special attention is the changing nature of urban centres and their retail, civic and cultural functions, which is discussed in Chapter 5. Drawing upon examples from Liverpool, London, Paris and elsewhere, the chapter explores contemporary practice in planning urban centres and the control of retail and commercial development.

Chapter 6 considers the nature of urban housing markets and the contribution of urban planning in housing supply, the issue of housing regeneration and the socio-economic problems involved in neighbourhood renewal. There is a discussion of general and specific housing requirements and their measurement, as well as questions of what and where to build and how to stimulate housing investment. This is followed by an examination of the issues surrounding housing obsolescence and the policy choices between area redevelopment and renovation. The design and building of large new housing areas is examined through case studies from China and the Netherlands, whilst the renovation of outworn neighbourhoods draws on experiences from Gateshead in north-east England and Dublin in Ireland.

Chapter 7 deals with placemaking and conservation in urban planning. The chapter begins with some discussion of image, character and aesthetic quality in urban places. This is followed by an examination of contemporary policies for urban design, green infrastructure and urban conservation that draws upon examples of practice from the UK, France and Poland. Mobility, accessibility and the impact of transportation systems and infrastructure are the concerns of Chapter 8. Having established the nature of the issues, the chapter draws upon examples of contemporary practice to examine methods of planning for accessibility, mitigating the impact of mobility, and best practice in the use of road space and the design of streets. Finally, Chapter 9 offers some conclusions about the evolving urban planning agenda and the nature, limitations and future of urban planning.

In each of these chapters the discussion is informed by both contemporary theory and views from professional practice, and draws upon examples and case studies of planning policy and implementation from towns and cities across a number of different countries. The majority of examples and case studies are drawn from a selected range of countries: notably the UK, Ireland, France, Germany, the Netherlands, Belgium, Denmark and Poland, with some mention of urban planning in the USA, China and Australia. This is not to deny that there is much of interest to be written about many other countries, but in this book the purpose of looking at urban planning internationally is less to do with accumulating detailed knowledge about each country and more about illustrating that urban planning takes place in different socio-economic, political and institutional contexts. Sometimes these contexts are very important in shaping location-specific planning solutions, but at other times planning solutions are more universal, regardless of context. Readers will also find that repeated references are made to some cities, especially Dortmund, Dundee, Liverpool, London, Paris, Rotterdam and York. This too has a purpose: to provide examples of planning practice from different types of city in different locations, partly because these are interesting cities from a planning perspective and partly, of course, because of the limitations of the author's own knowledge and experience.

Using this approach, it is hoped that the book goes some way towards developing the reader's knowledge and understanding of the aims and objectives of contemporary urban planning. And by using a large number of examples and case studies the voice of planning practice will come through and so strengthen the links between theory and practice and illustrate the difficulties and compromises that form part and parcel of the planners' job in, as the Royal Town Planning Institute puts it, the mediation of space and the making of place.

Chapter 1

The Evolution of Urban Change and Planning

Introduction

Before considering the nature and purposes of contemporary urban planning it is important to understand the foundations upon which the modern city and modern planning systems have been built. Understanding this history is important for a number of reasons. First, anyone who is making a claim to be a professional in any subject, including urban planning, might reasonably be expected to know something of the origins and evolution of their own profession. Second, an understanding of history allows the professional planner to learn from the achievements of earlier generations – how places have been created and how the use of space has been mediated – and from their mistakes. Much of urban policy is devised through what is known as 'incremental adaptation', that is to say, taking a previous or existing solution and applying it, perhaps in modified form, to some new problem. In order to engage in this form of policy making it is necessary to know and understand the nature of previous rounds of urban planning and design – to know what worked well, why and how it worked and in what circumstances.

This chapter therefore provides an introduction to the history of urban areas and their planning. The discussion explores the evolution of urban problems as they were perceived at different points in time and the nature of the planning response at that time. For the reasons outlined below, the chapter concentrates on the last two centuries, drawing upon a range of experiences and examples from planning practice in the UK, continental Europe and North America, to provide a rounded and international view of urban change and planning.

The chapter starts with a brief mention of the early development of urban areas but the main discussion begins with a look at the industrial revolution and its impact on urbanization before considering the structure and dynamics of the industrial city. It then explores the justifications for state intervention in urban growth and change and the origins of modern town planning in the late nineteenth and early twentieth centuries. This is followed by a chronological discussion of the subsequent evolution of urban change and planning in the developed

15

world. Key periods of change are identified, including the inter-war period, the Second World War and its impacts on urbanization and planning, the shift from modernism to postmodernism in urban policy in the 1960s, the emergence of the post-industrial city and growing concern for environmental issues and sustainable development. The chapter concludes with some discussion of major trends and issues in the mid-2010s.

The early development of urban areas

Where should we start? The earliest urban societies appear to have emerged in Mesopotamia and the Indus valley, with Uruk in Mesopotamia being perhaps the world's first city, dating from around 5,000 BC. Further cities developed in later classical civilizations: to some extent in ancient Egypt (Memphis, Thebes) and particularly in Greece during the first millennium BC, where the 'city-states' (such as Athens, Corinth and Sparta) represented a new form of socio-political organization. Cities also developed in the early civilizations of Central and South America and South-east Asia. Whilst much of this urbanization was organic, many early cities show traces of having been planned, to at least some degree. There was frequently a separation of land uses. Often architectural or locational prominence was given to civic and religious buildings. In many cities urban form was defined by a planned grid of streets, and city boundaries were defined by walls or fences. Indeed, Hippodamus of Miletus (498–408 BC) has been called 'the father of town planning' for his work in designing the layout of numerous Greek cities, for example, the port city of Piraeus near Athens.

Planned and well organized towns were a particular feature of the Roman civilization in Europe. Typically these walled cities were laid out as a grid-iron defined by two major streets: the east–west Decumanus (typically a main military route) and the north–south Cardo (a kind of high street), intersecting at the main forum or market-place. Streets were usually paved and drained. Many modern European cities can trace the Roman origins of contemporary street patterns: for instance, the modern city centre of Chester (UK) almost exactly fits the ancient Roman layout of the city. The centres of French cities such as Lyon, Arles and Nîmes not only show clear evidence of Roman street patterns but also contain many preserved structures from the period, including temples, arenas and other civic buildings. But these ancient cities were planned within the context of command and slave-based economies. They are primarily of modern planning interest for their architecture and physical structure, rather than for any lessons that might inform our understanding about the functioning or planning of the contemporary city.

In the post-Roman period urban life in Europe dwindled for a number of generations, and it was only in medieval times that a process of reurbanization began in earnest. With a gradual increase in inter-regional trading, proto-industrial activity and the emergence of stronger forms of governance, the medieval city began to grow. But few showed the degree of formal organization found in the classical city. Most of these places developed slowly and organically with little regulation and no comprehensive planning. It was only later, as towns grew larger and more complex, that governments began to impose regulations on development, often to improve hygiene, to control the risk of fire, or for military purposes.

Whilst few towns developed according to any sort of plan, there were some notable exceptions. From the twelfth to the fourteenth centuries fortified 'bastide' towns were developed for purposes of colonization and control in North Wales and South-west France. The planned development of Londonderry (Derry) in Northern Ireland after 1613 had a similar purpose. There were other emerging commercial and political reasons for establishing new towns, as exemplified by the creation of the port of Le Havre (1517) at the mouth of the River Seine, the trading city of Zamość in Poland (1580) and the ducal capital of Neustrelitz in Mecklenburg (1733). Sometimes disaster forced planned reconstructions such as the rebuilding of many Sicilian cities in the new 'baroque' style after the 1693 earthquake, or Lisbon after a similar event in 1755. There was some planning of city expansion in a few central European cities, often under royal patronage, for example in Berlin from the end of the seventeenth century with the development of Dorotheenstadt and Friedrichstadt. Similarly, at the beginning of the nineteenth century, Maxvorstadt became the first planned expansion of Munich, developed in a 'classical' style. In many European cities, the removal of city walls provided scope for substantial urban development projects. In Paris, demolition of the former Charles V and Louis XIII walls at the end of the seventeenth century permitted construction of the 'grands boulevards', well before the later 'Haussmann' redevelopments. Vienna's Ringstrasse is another fine example, developed after 1857 as a broad, green boulevard to accommodate expansion of the central city. It contains grand private residences as well as new civic buildings, including the parliament, town hall, university, state opera and a number of museums.

Colonial expansion, notably by Britain, France and Spain, did lead to many planned settlements in the 'new world' of North America, South Asia and later in Australia and parts of Africa. From the beginning the form of most North American cities was controlled through the imposition of a rectangular grid of streets and building blocks. However, such planned interventions were rare in the UK: even after the Great Fire of

London (1666), despite competing plans for the comprehensive rede-sign of the city, redevelopment was predominantly organic and subject only to regulation rather than a planning regime. Indeed, despite the examples mentioned above, until at least the nineteenth century, the majority of the expansion and internal restructuring and redevelop-ment of most European cities was organic, unplanned and uncoordi-nated, with little concern for the social costs of individual actions. (For further reading about urban planning in the pre-industrial period, see: Korn, 1953; Hiorns, 1956; Mumford, 1961; Stewart, 1964; Morris, 1979.)

However, it was with the coming of the industrial revolution that we see the emergence of the contemporary city with all its social, economic, political and environmental complexity and, in many cases, a period of expansion that was exponentially greater than anything seen before. It was this combination of complexity and speed of change that dramati-cally increased the need for state intervention to tackle the combined challenges of accommodating economic development, housing rapidly expanding urban populations, providing efficient movement systems, and maintaining public order, health and safety. In other words, to plan and manage the city. Thus in this book, which is about the goals and means of contemporary urban planning, the discussion of urban change and planning begins not with pre-history, nor with the early develop-ment of the European city, but with the industrial revolution.

The changing city in the nineteenth century

The industrial revolution was a period of economic growth and acceler-ated industrial productivity brought about by increased industrial investment combined with rapid technical and social innovation. These processes emerged in the Midlands and North of England in the second half of the eighteenth century, some decades before similar trends became visible in other European countries. There were a number of reasons why the UK became the first industrialized nation. In comparison with its continental competitors the country possessed a relatively stable political system that supported a free market, entrepreneurialism and free movement of labour. The country was well endowed with raw mate-rials, including coal and water as sources of power and a comparatively good transport system. There were economies of scale that resulted from its dense and growing population that provided a large home market for goods. Furthermore, this market was supplemented by a growing colo-nial empire (Hobsbawn, 1968; Ashton, 1997; Allen, 2009). In conse-quence, as shown in Figure 1.1, the UK was urbanizing faster than its competitors.

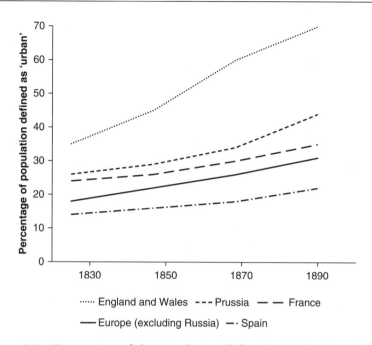

Figure 1.1 *Proportion of the population defined as 'urban' in selected European countries, 1825–1890*

Source: Based on approximate data from Hohenberg and Lees (1985), Figure 7.2.

The industrial revolution had both direct and indirect effects on the development of towns and cities with a number of different types of urbanization taking place. Primary urbanization created new workplaces, providing space for basic economic activity (i.e. industries that exported goods or services and brought income from other locations), and housing for workers and their families. The historic origins of many pre-industrial towns lie in the functions of trade and exchange. These were the basic economic activities that drove the development of market towns and places of transhipment such as ports. Liverpool, Rotterdam or Antwerp, for example, can trace their origins to such functions. Extractive industries, by their nature, have to be located where the raw materials are found and so stimulate the urbanization in their locality. Mining settlements, such as those in Tyneside, South Yorkshire, Wallonia, Silesia and the Ruhr basin are typical examples. In the nineteenth century coal provided the major source of power for industrial production, so many of these towns became locations for iron and steel production and heavy engineering.

The textile industry also depended upon good supplies of water and coal. The earliest textile mills were dependent upon water power and located in upland areas such as the Pennine towns of northern England. Later, as steam power became more important, coalfield locations were preferred, such as Manchester and the surrounding towns in Lancashire (cotton); Leeds, Bradford and West Yorkshire (woollens); Lille-Roubaix-Tourcoing (cottons, linens). Many other forms of manufacturing also provided the basic raison d'être for urban growth. But service industries can provide an economic base. A major stimulus for the growth of Cambridge in England lies in the foundation of the university in the thirteenth century. It could even be argued that much of the City of London's economic wealth results from the export of financial services across the world. A number of free-standing capital cities such as Washington, Canberra or Brasilia can identify government as their basic activity.

A secondary wave of urbanization followed as these basic industries and their workers had to be supported by a range of secondary or non-basic economic activities. These might include investment in infrastructure, ancillary industries, financial, legal and other professional services. Those who worked in the basic industries needed housing, food, clothing, education, religion and leisure. All of these activities employed additional workers generating additional income and fostering further growth, none of which would have occurred in that location without the existence of the basic industry. At later stages of development the provision of local governance, health care and education can all be seen as elements of secondary urbanization.

An upward spiral of tertiary urbanization can also be identified, based upon the larger markets, agglomeration economies and comparative advantages that emerged with the growth of these industrial and commercial centres. Competition between firms forces them to continuously seek reductions in the costs of production and increases in productivity. One of the ways in which this can be achieved is through economies of scale: increasing the volume of production so as to bring down the average costs. The larger the market the more economies of scale could be achieved, and the larger the city the more attractive a location it became for local service providers. Additionally, some cities were able to develop because they had specific locational advantages over other cities: a sheltered harbour, a river crossing, access to raw materials or proximity to markets.

With industrial growth and urbanization came an expanding middle class of managerial and professional workers with rising spending power. This accelerated the process of suburbanization, perhaps more so in the UK than any other European country, as the middle classes sought to buy themselves out of the disease-ridden inner cities to the fresh air of the periphery. But not all the wealth and income generated in these towns was spent locally. Whilst the aristocracy had been visiting spas and the seaside for health cures and enjoyment since the eighteenth century, it was in the nineteenth century that the middle classes, growing in numbers and benefitting from improved transport systems, began to visit spa and seaside towns. This led to a very different form of urbanization, not based upon production but on consumption. In these leisure towns the dominant land uses were residential development, hotels, spas, casinos, ballrooms, parks and gardens.

The social mix would be different too, with low representation of working classes and a high preponderance of the affluent middle classes and the elderly. Bath, Cheltenham and Harrogate were amongst the most well known of the English spas. But there were many examples across Europe, including Vichy in France, Baden Baden in Germany, Karlovy Vary (Karlsbad) and Mariánské Lázně (Marienbad) in the Czech Republic. Brighton is often credited with being the first seaside resort in the UK, with the patronage of the Prince Regent from the 1780s. Other resorts followed, especially along the south-east coast. But it was again the coming of the railway and the advent of paid holidays that saw the rapid growth of seaside resorts in the mid-nineteenth century. In Germany the Baltic coast became a popular destination. In France resorts accessible to Paris sprang up along the Normandy coast, including Cabourg and Deauville which became favourites amongst the Parisian elite. The later development of the Côte d'Azur on the Mediterranean coast was by contrast facilitated through investment from northern Europe as wealthy British, Germans and Russians fled their cold winters in search of a pleasanter environment.

In the UK, the growth of London can be distinguished as a separate and distinct type of urbanization based upon its sheer scale, history, cultural and political dominance. London developed rapidly during the nineteenth century as the expanding national economy required ever greater and more sophisticated financial services, over which the City of London had a huge comparative advantage compared with other cities. This growing and more complex economy required more and better central government, which led to the growth of ever larger offices of state around Parliament in Westminster. London was also the country's dominant port and had its own industrial base and agglomeration economies, including a phenomenal concentration of middle class and aristocratic wealth and spending power which far surpassed those of any other British city. The only other European city that could make a similar claim to a unique position in the urban hierarchy was Paris. Throughout most of its history Paris has dominated the French national economy and political and cultural life. Today, with a metropolitan area population of around 12.0 million, it is nearly six times larger than the next biggest city (Lyon). No other European city has in recent times achieved the scale and international importance of London or Paris. Only Moscow comes near. Perhaps Berlin and Vienna might have continued to grow from their early twentieth century status to this level of importance had it not been for the turn of history.

The structure and dynamics of the industrial city

Not only were these processes of urbanization characterized by an expansion of the urban area, they also saw increases in the intensity of land use and the restructuring of earlier phases of urbanization. Within these urbanization processes, market forces were beginning to lead to significant restructuring of the urban realm and the renewal of transitional areas. As the size of urban areas grew, so did competition for the best located sites, usually the most central areas. The effect of this competition was to bid up the price of land. As land prices rose so the intensity of land use increased, whether for production or housing purposes, so as to maximize profits. Sites that were being used sub-optimally (e.g. those containing low building densities or low value land uses) would tend to be cleared and rebuilt at higher densities. This applied in industrial and commercial areas where small scale workshops might be replaced with larger multi-storey premises, or in housing areas where early industrial cottages might be replaced with more profitable higher density housing developments. Housing might also be replaced by more profitable industrial or commercial uses on better located more central sites.

Indeed, deterioration in working class housing conditions was one of the most significant outcomes of the early industrial revolution. The search for employment forced many households to leave the agricultural economy and migrate towards the growing towns and cities. Industrialists were constantly seeking to limit wages in order to provide a source of finance to invest in new technology to maintain their competitive position and levels of profit. Faced with a surplus of labour, industrialists were able to keep wages low and in consequence many working class households could afford only meagre rents. Except for a few rare examples of employer-built housing, urban growth in the UK was organic and the rate and type of housing construction was dependent upon demand. In order to achieve a profit from housing provision, developers maximized density and kept the size and quality of dwellings to a minimum (Gaudie, 1974; Burnett, 1986). Thus, in the industrializing towns and cities, the new factories were surrounded by a sea of dense and very poor quality housing development in which unhealthy and degrading living conditions became the norm. It is noteworthy that the state took many years to intervene in this situation. In the UK at least, a dominant economic philosophy of 'laissez-faire' made governments reluctant to become involved in the workings of the housing market. Systems of local governance were very restricted in terms of their capacity or desire to intervene. The power and leverage of the working class to promote change was severely limited by lack of industrial, political or legal power, and until the middle of the nineteenth century there was a very low level of knowledge and understanding about the relationship between housing conditions, public health and life expectancy.

In addition to market pressures, a second major force for urban restructuring was the expansion of the service sector. As trade and industry developed, an ever increasing range and sophistication of economic infrastructure was required: trade needed banking facilities, insurance, transportation agents, legal services and a host of other ancillary services. It also required more and better central and local government regulation and support. These changes led to a growth in office employment that began in earnest in the eighteenth century mercantile period but accelerated during the nineteenth century. Many offices, because of their close economic linkages with one another and the need for personal contacts, desired the most accessible central area locations. Because of their very high levels of profit per unit of area compared with other land-using activities, they tended to be able to outbid and replace other uses in such locations.

A related trend was the growth of the middle class and the rise in their aggregate spending power, some of which could be spent on luxury goods, clothing and other household items, so stimulating the development of more substantial retail areas within the nineteenth century city. The profit obtainable per unit of area from retailing was greater than almost any other land use except offices, and because of the need for accessibility (especially for comparison shopping) shops tended to gravitate towards the city centre. So there were two land uses, offices and shops, which were frequently complementary occupants of the same parcel of land. While shops required a street level entrance, office users were often content with upper floors. Hence these multi-storey developments could yield tremendous economic power and easily displace previously established but less profitable land uses.

Another important factor in the development and renewal of the nineteenth century city was the coming of the railway. The impact of this revolutionary form of transport was so great as to be difficult to imagine today. The physical construction of the railways through existing urban areas and the construction of mainline stations and termini within city centres caused immense destruction of property and forced the exodus of thousands of inhabitants and countless businesses. According to Cherry (1972) 1,275 people in 255 'cottages' made way for Manchester Central station and 6,142 people in 443 tenements were displaced in the building of Glasgow St Enoch's station. The railway reordered the pattern of accessibility within the city, enhancing land values and stimulating new land uses such as hotels and warehousing near important stations and reducing the value of property adversely affected by the intrusion of smoke, grime, noise and smell associated with railway lines, goods yards and engine sheds.

As urban areas grew they also tended to sprawl, particularly with the coming of improvements in urban transportation from the mid-nineteenth century onwards. Technological changes and increases in the efficiency of urban transport systems enabled greater distances to be travelled for the same cost, thus enabling cities to spread over a larger area without economic loss. If a city maintained the same level of population and economic activity but covered a larger physical area then the density of development would fall. As densities fell so the average rent from economic activity or housing per unit of area would fall (i.e. rental income would become more thinly spread) with central and inner area rents falling and peripheral rents rising. Whilst the total aggregate value of all land rent in the city would remain the same (because the level of population and economic activity had not changed) it would be spread over a larger area, so allowing businesses and inhabitants to each occupy more space without additional cost. Figure 1.2 illustrates these relationships.

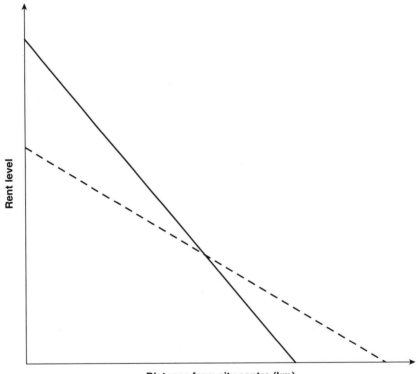

—— City without transport improvements   – – City with transport improvements

Figure 1.2   *The effect of transport improvements on the distribution of urban land values*

Source: C. Couch, 2016.

Until the early twentieth century improvements in transportation occurred mainly along the radial routes of tramways or suburban railways, leading to a tendency for cities to follow a star-shaped pattern of expansion. Later, however, the impact of the motor vehicle was to accelerate these trends considerably, filling in the gaps between the points of the star and extending rapidly outwards the boundary of the urban area. The advent of the motor bus and increasing ownership of motor cars permitted the development of suburban housing estates. The emergence of the motor lorry and electrical power enabled industry to vacate many traditional inner city locations for new peripheral industrial estates on cheaper land which was more accessible to regional highway systems; their former locations becoming 'zones of transition' seeking alternative land uses.

Only in the city centres were different forces at work. Service sector employment increased throughout much of the twentieth century. In many city centres this led to an expansion and intensification of the use of land for offices until decimated by the IT revolution at the end of the century. Similarly, for much of the twentieth century, the city centre remained the primary location for comparison goods retailing. In spite of suburbanization the city centre remained the most accessible part of the city, the focus of rail, bus and road networks, and the point where the potential market for such goods was at its peak. It was only from the middle of the century in North America and a little later in Europe that there was any significant decentralization of this type of retail activity. Figure 1.3 summarizes these processes of urban development and change in the nineteenth century industrial town.

The origins of modern town planning

Apart from indirect involvement, for example in infrastructure provision, and despite some appalling urban problems, the desire of the state to intervene in urban areas and their development was relatively weak until the middle of the nineteenth century. While there was limited enthusiasm for urban planning on the part of the state, a few local landowners and entrepreneurs took a keen interest in planning the expansion of towns.

New Lanark, founded by David Dale in 1795 and developed by his son-in-law Robert Owen, is one of the first modern examples of an enlightened entrepreneur providing an industrial village for the workers in his cotton mill. As became typical of such paternalistic endeavours, decent affordable housing was constructed in a village that included schools, health care and opportunities for adult education. Although New Lanark became famous throughout Europe, few followed its developers' example. One entrepreneur who did, albeit some years later, was

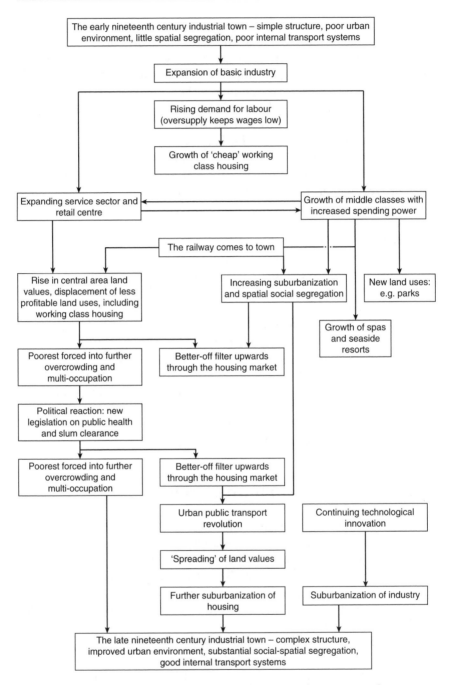

Figure 1.3   *Urban development and change in the nineteenth century industrial town*

Source: C. Couch, 2016.

Sir Titus Salt, a Bradford mill owner, who developed the village of Saltaire. Moving his expanding mill business from Bradford to a new site adjoining the River Aire and railway line a few miles north at Shipley, Sir Titus created a complete industrial village. In addition to some 800 well-built houses, the village included an 'institute for recreation and education', parkland, allotments, a hospital and alms-houses. The whole development represented a harmoniously planned and integrated settlement of high architectural quality.

Later in the century, two other philanthropic entrepreneurs were to have a significant impact on the design of British towns. In 1887 William Lever purchased 23 hectares of land near Bromborough Pool in Cheshire to accommodate his expanding soap manufacturing enterprise. Adjoining the new factory he developed 'Port Sunlight', a planned village of cottages and associated amenities for his workers. The design was a departure from the type of urban form being created in British cities at

(a)   (b)

Figure 1.4   *Contrasting styles of housing development in (a) Saltaire and (b) Port Sunlight*

Source: C. Couch, 2016.

Note: The rather austere urban style of Saltaire is in marked contrast to the more suburban and greener environment created at Port Sunlight 40 years later.

that time, moving away from long rows of terraced houses towards a more informal townscape of low density groups of cottages in a variety of vernacular styles in a green landscape that brought the feel of the countryside into the town (see Figure 1.4). Similarly, in 1879 the Cadbury brothers moved their expanding chocolate factory from central Birmingham to a conveniently situated greenfield site four miles south of the city. A decade or so later they began development of what became known as 'Bournville' – a model village of low density, high quality cottage-style houses with large gardens in an extensively landscaped setting. Both developments had been influenced by the 'arts and crafts' movement and concerns about the poverty of the natural environment within the nineteenth century city. Both were to be very influential in shaping the subsequent 'garden cities' movement.

The first significant state interventions in urban development in the UK took the form of regulatory Acts of Parliament. With emerging knowledge about the causes and epidemiology of diseases such as cholera and typhoid, the Public Health Act 1848 established Local Boards of Health with the aim of improving urban water supply, sewerage and street cleansing and provided a framework for local by-laws to improve the quality of housing. The Public Health Act 1875 set even higher standards regarding water supply, sewerage, streets and housing, while the Artisans and Labourers Dwellings Improvement Act of the same year gave local authorities powers to deal with insanitary areas through slum clearance and re-housing programmes. Unfortunately this 'planned' redevelopment still received no housing subsidy, so the rents of new properties in these 'improvement areas' were frequently beyond the means of dispossessed tenants. Also there was an inevitable time-lag between clearance and rebuilding, so whilst sanitation was improved, the immediate impact of these schemes was of limited benefit to those living in the worst housing conditions.

The end of the nineteenth century saw the beginnings of a literature on town planning. In 1889, Camillo Sitte wrote *Der Städtebau nach seinen künstlerischen Grundsätzen* (*City Planning According to Artistic Principles*), in which he defined a set of principles for urban design and aesthetics in town planning. Joseph Stübben's *Der Städtebau* (*City Planning*) (1890, republished 1907) advocated a unified approach to planning both the outward extension of towns and the improvement of their inner areas (Sutcliffe, 1981).

Perhaps the most influential figure in the early history of the town planning movement in the UK was Ebenezer Howard. The late 1890s was a period of growing concern about urban social conditions: the slum conditions in which many still lived; the paucity of new cheap urban housing; the monotonous environment and lack of greenery in many cities. Howard was not a professional architect or engineer but he had an interest in land reform and social improvement. In 1898 he published his book *Tomorrow: A Peaceful Path to Real Reform* (republished in 1902 under the title *Garden Cities of Tomorrow*). He took forward the ideas for new communities developed by Owen and others and combined them with the concept of land reform – communal ownership of land and the notion of moving the working classes out of the high density central cities to lower density suburban settlements. He proposed to dismantle the existing conurbations and replace them with groups of smaller, separate but socially and economically integrated 'garden cities' built at low densities and incorporating large areas of green space. Howard illustrated his ideas with a number of diagrams. He used the idea of three magnets to show the best and worst features of town dwelling and countryside living in the first two magnets and how, in the third magnet, a hybrid area of town-country might combine the best of both worlds: economic and social opportunity combined with a pleasant environment. Further diagrams showed in stylized form how a new central city and a series of satellite towns could be combined into an integrated whole that had the agglomeration economies of a big city but the environmental amenity of a small town (see Figure 1.5). Whilst the communal ownership of land was a key feature in Howard's vision for the garden city it was mainly their physical characteristics that became Howard's legacy.

Howard's ideas were taken up with some enthusiasm and in 1899 the Garden City Association was formed. Its secretary, Thomas Adams, was a key figure in broadening support for the idea and was later to be influential in setting up the Town Planning Institute. By 1903 a company, First Garden City Ltd, had been established to develop a pilot garden city. Land was purchased at Letchworth, some 35 miles north of London, and a master plan was designed by two architects, Raymond Unwin and Barry Parker. By 1907 the town had a population of 5,000 and was designed to eventually grow to 32,000 (Cherry, 1972). Unwin was a theorist as well as an architect and in 1909 he published one of the first British text books on the subject, *Town Planning in Practice: an introduction to the art of designing cities and suburbs* (Unwin, 1909).

The movement also took off in other countries. In Germany a similar 'garden city association' was founded in 1902 with the aim of developing self-contained (living and working), socially mixed, green cities. A number of projects were developed, including Karlsruhe-Rüppur and several settlements in the Ruhr – of which Margarethenhöhe in Essen is one of the most well known.

Around the same time in the USA the City Beautiful movement was flourishing. Again in reaction to the poor state of the nineteenth century city, this movement proposed the beautification of cities, 'civic virtue' and a harmonious urban society. The movement was influential in the

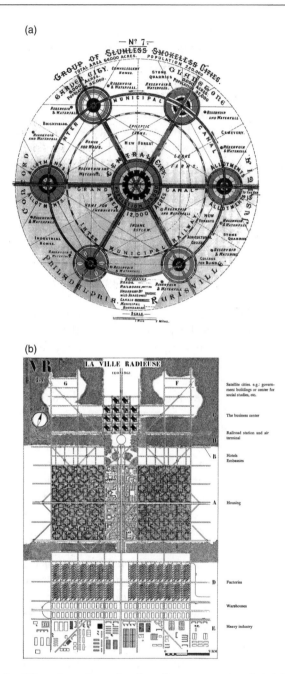

Figure 1.5   *Theories of good urban form contrasted. (a) Ebenezer Howard's Garden City and (b) Le Corbusier's* Ville Radieuse

Sources: (a) Reproduced from Howard (1898); (b) Reproduced from Le Corbusier (1935). © FLC/ADAGP, Paris and DACS, London 2015

redesigning of a number of central city areas in the USA including Chicago, Washington DC and districts in Pittsburgh, Philadelphia. The movement was even influential as far afield as Australia.

With the founding of the Federation of Australia (1901) it was decided to develop a purpose-built capital city for the new nation. The site for this new city was to be at Canberra, approximately midway between Sydney and Melbourne. A planning competition was held and won by the architect Walter Burley Griffin from Chicago. Griffin's proposals integrated many new ideas in town planning, architecture and landscape design. Influenced by the 'city beautiful' movement, his bold design incorporated grand axes, vistas and landmarks as well as emerging modernist ideas about land use zoning and the creation of neighbourhoods. And unlike many other competitors, his plan was adapted to the topography and natural landscape of the area (Freestone, 2010).

In searching for the origins of regulatory town planning we should perhaps look to Germany, for city authorities began to intervene in the planning of new settlements much earlier there than elsewhere. As long ago as 1794 the Prussian *Allgemeine Landrecht* (general territorial code) permitted the state to 'limit the use of private land in the common interest' and to reserve land for new roads.

> The *Allgemeine Landrecht* thus codified the practice of town-extension planning. In doing so it put a powerful tool of environmental control into the hands of the urban authorities well in advance of the period of sustained urban growth. (Sutcliffe, 1981, p. 11)

Through the first period of rapid urbanization in Germany, between the 1830s and the 1870s, town extension planning, including the laying out of streets and the provision of utilities, became a normal activity across many of the country's fast growing cities. By the latter part of the nineteenth century German cities were regularly using town extension plans to set out grand designs for new suburbs with broad main streets and generous public spaces. By contrast, in the UK it was left to the market to determine the shape of urban growth. However, this did not mean that urban conditions were necessarily any better in Germany. Initially, extension planning did little to control the intensity of land use. High land values in many German cities pushed up housing densities to excessive levels and multi-storey blocks of depressing *mietskaserne* (rental barracks) became common. In terms of controlling and improving the environment of existing towns, the Public Health Acts in the UK were more advanced and more effective than anything in Germany at that time, and British developers became quite adept at building low rise terraced housing which generally provided a better residential environment than their German equivalent. However, what the German system did give that country was a cadre of professional architects and engineers skilled in town planning long before such a body of expertise emerged in the UK (Sutcliffe, 1981).

By the beginning of the twentieth century a number of voices were arguing that German-style town extension planning should supersede the British tradition of piecemeal intervention (Sutcliffe, 1981). But it was not until 1909 that the Housing, Town Planning, Etc. Act was passed. The Act permitted urban authorities to prepare town planning schemes for peripheral areas that were about to be developed. These plans could set out the layout of roads, zone land for industrial and residential development, determine development densities and dwelling types, and identify sites for public buildings and open space. Two of the earliest plans to be approved were in Birmingham: one for Quinton, Harborne & Edgbaston and the other for East Birmingham.

Most French cities grew at only a modest pace during the first half of the nineteenth century and there was little enthusiasm for intervention in the poor environmental conditions experienced in many urban areas. However, in response to a combination of rising concerns about public health, waves of social unrest and a growing feeling that the cities needed modernizing to operate on more efficient and competitive lines, central government began to encourage the larger urban authorities to engage in ambitious civic improvement programmes. There was a need to improve circulation and access around the cities, particularly to the new railway stations, and it was considered more cost effective to insert new water supply and sewerage networks as part of new street systems. The visual order of the city could be improved, and such large scale investments had significant beneficial economic multiplier effects (Sutcliffe, 1981). Whilst the most famous of these city improvement programmes was carried out in Paris under the direction of Georges Haussmann, Prefect of the Seine Département, similar work was undertaken in many other cities, including Lyon, Marseille, Bordeaux and Lille. At first these programmes concentrated only on acquiring land for the streets and buildings that would comprise the new thoroughfares and did little to improve conditions in the older neighbourhoods behind. Indeed, as with the British experience of area improvement, 'by displacing numerous poor tenants they tended to increase overcrowding and physical deterioration in slums nearby' (Sutcliffe, 1981, p. 133).

The foundations of national planning and housing policy were established in the Netherlands by the Housing Act 1901. The Act responded to the often poor, prevailing urban housing conditions by empowering municipalities to establish building regulations controlling the quality of housing; recognizing and financing building associations to develop new housing to meet social needs; and requiring large and growing municipalities to prepare extension plans (Vandevyvere and Zenthöfer, 2012).

Amongst the developments that followed was H.P. Berlage's plan for Amsterdam South in which he tried to develop a model for twentieth century housing with a formal layout, less dense and greener than the older city but recognizing that: 'The building of dwellings is becoming a work of mass production. The block building must be used again, and to an even greater extent than formerly, to provide a solution' (Berlage, quoted in Gideon, 1967, p. 801).

This new activity of town planning was initially dominated by municipal surveyors, engineers and architects but gradually a new profession began to emerge. In 1909 William Lever sponsored a Chair and Department of Civic Design at the University of Liverpool and from 1910 its journal, *Town Planning Review*, provided a forum for scholarly debate. By 1914 in the UK the Town Planning Institute had been formed 'to advance the study of town-planning' and 'to secure the association, and to promote the general interests of those engaged or interested in the practice of town-planning' (http://www.rtpi.org.uk/about-the-rtpi/, accessed 20.5.2015).

A major step forward in codifying theory about the process of town planning came from Patrick Geddes, an Edinburgh sociologist. In his 1915 book *Cities in Evolution* he argued that a plan for a geographical region must start with a survey of that region and the human activities that take place therein. These characteristics and relationships must be analysed before a plan can be drawn up. This simple dictum 'survey – analysis – plan' still lies at the core of planning process theory.

Thus by the time of the First World War a number of ideas had emerged about new urban forms to replace the insalubrious nineteenth century city, and several countries had basic planning legislation that would permit municipalities to determine the location, structure, land use and density of areas of new urbanization.

The inter-war period

Across many European countries, housing construction and slum clearance was effectively brought to a halt by the outbreak of the First World War. Some parts of Belgium and north-eastern France suffered terrible war damage. In the UK the necessity of tackling the acute housing shortage left by four years of virtual inactivity was of critical political importance. During the war the Government established the Tudor Walters Committee to consider the design and standards to be adopted in future council housing provision (Tudor Walters Committee, 1918). Strongly influenced by the town planner Raymond Unwin and the ideas of the garden cities movement, the committee recommended the building of generously proportioned traditionally constructed houses in low density, well landscaped cottage estates. The Housing, Town Planning, Etc. Act, 1919 (Addison Act) provided local authorities with a substantial level of subsidy to kick-start a programme of mass public sector housing construction on a scale never previously seen. By the mid-1920s, spurred on by rising demand and falling development costs, this programme was being complemented by an increasingly vigorous programme of speculative private housebuilding, especially in the more prosperous regions of the South-east and Midlands. The inter-war period saw record numbers of dwellings completed and a dramatic fall in the densities at which they were built.

On the European continent a different solution was being proposed. In 1922 Le Corbusier, a Swiss architect working in France, published his ideas for a *Ville Contemporaine* (later refined as the *Ville Radieuse*, 1935) which would use modern construction techniques to create a high rise, high density alternative to the garden city. These were plans for a much bigger city than Howard had ever envisaged. People would live in a more compact urban environment of high rise towers in order to free up the ground for circulation and landscaped parkland. In the *Ville Radieuse* (Radiant City) a high density would be maintained across the city with commerce accommodated in tall office towers to the north and industry to the south, so spreading the journey to work and making the best use of the transport system (see Figure 1.5 above). Standardization of designs, prefabrication and mass production were all seen as part of an 'efficient' solution to deliver mass housing in the 'machine age'. These 'modernist' approaches to city design were being taken up by other European architects, such as the German Mies van der Rohe with his 1927 Weissenhof Housing Settlement in Stuttgart (Gideon, 1967; Ward, 1994).

So there emerged two fundamentally different approaches to city form: the UK favoured Howard's low rise, low density garden city, whilst in many cities in continental Europe, Le Corbusier's high rise, high density modernist alternative was being implemented.

But there was a third utopia that was influential in the USA: the idea of the Broadacre City put forward by the architect Frank Lloyd Wright, comprising an extremely low density city in which each family would be given one acre (around 4,000 m²) of land on which to build a home. In this vision of suburbia, freed from the evils of the city, a new form of community could grow. Although offering some intellectual legitimacy to the suburbanization of US cities, the idea was later strongly criticized by writers such as Jane Jacobs (Fishman, 1982).

Advances were also being made in the Netherlands. The *General Extension Plan of Amsterdam* (1934), developed by Cornelis van Eesteren and Theo van Lohuizen of the city's Department of Public Works, used the scientific approach to plan making that had been proposed by Geddes two decades earlier. The plan was based upon inputs from a number of specialist professions. Surveys were undertaken and data analysed in order to determine forecasts of population and housing need. The plan reflected careful consideration of the social needs of the population and the medium density layout preserved the natural aspect of the River Amstel's banks and the rural belt around the city (Gideon, 1967).

In the late 1920s Clarence Perry, an American sociologist, had taken the garden city model further by devising the concept of the 'neighbourhood' as a spatial unit for planning the development of residential areas. This would typically accommodate a population of sufficient size to support a primary school, local shops and community facilities (3,000–5,000 people housed at a density of 25–30 dwellings per hectare) so that no one was more than a 10-minute walk from the school and local centre, with through traffic kept to the periphery (Ward, 1994). This simple idea was taken up in a number of North American developments in the period and formed the basis for the planning and design of much UK 'new town' development after the Second World War.

In the UK, the relatively weak planning legislation of the inter-war period did little to contain the rapid process of urban sprawl. In Figure 1.6(a), the vertically hatched area equates approximately to the amount the area of London expanded between 1919 and 1939. Fuelled by heavily subsidized low density council house building, profitable speculative private house building, and the suburbanization of industry, particularly in the new manufacturing sectors such as motor vehicle and electrical goods production, many cities sprawled rapidly during this period. The rate of transfer of land from agricultural to urban use in England and Wales increased from 9,100 ha per annum between 1922 and 1926 to 25,100 ha per annum from 1931 to 1939 (Ward, 1994).

Sprawl became a major planning concern in England, particularly the issue of 'ribbon development': building houses in the countryside along each side of major roads. This practice saved house builders some money but restricted the development of back land areas, raised concerns about traffic congestion and road safety, was visually unattractive and made it difficult to provide community services. In this regard at least the planning system was strengthened through the passing of the Restriction of Ribbon Development Act, 1935. For the rest, urban sprawl remained almost beyond control until after the Second World War.

Urban planning during and after the Second World War

In the face of growing problems of uneven regional development and urban sprawl, support for the idea of a stronger planning system had been growing in the UK throughout the 1930s. Eventually in 1937 the Government established the Royal Commission on the Distribution of

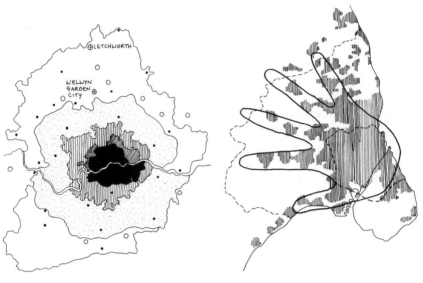

(a) Abercrombie's Greater London   (b) Copenhagen Finger Plan (1947)
          Plan (1944)

**Figure 1.6   *Different approaches to metropolitan planning.
(a) Abercrombie's Greater London Plan (1944) and (b) Copenhagen
Finger Plan (1947)***

Source: Drawn by A.L. Couch. Based upon original plans in *The Greater London Plan*
(1944) and the Copenhagen Finger Plan (1947).

Note: The Greater London Plan restricts outward expansion and forces additional growth
into satellite towns beyond the green belt, whereas the Copenhagen Finger Plan allows for
the continuous outward growth of the city along public transport routes.

the Industrial Population, under the chairmanship of Sir Montague
Barlow, to examine Britain's regional and urban planning problems.

The *Barlow Report* was important for many reasons, not least its
innovative and detailed analysis of regional economic and demographic
trends. One of its key findings was that for much of the inter-war period
employment in London and the Home Counties had been growing at
nearly twice the national average while employment in much of the
North, Scotland and South Wales had been growing at only a fraction of
this rate and even declining in some areas. The inevitable outcome of
this imbalanced growth was a strain on the housing and social systems
in the South-east, increasing urbanization in that region and growing
congestion. On the other hand, the infrastructure and social capital of
northern towns and cities was underused. The *Report* concluded that
this imbalance constituted a real national economic disadvantage which
should be rectified through restrictions on industrial investment in the

London area coupled with incentives to encourage investment in more needy areas – though committee members failed to agree on the extent of such measures. The problems of unplanned growth and sprawl of large cities were also recognized (Barlow Commission, 1940).

The late 1940s saw the repair and reconstruction of war-damaged property across many towns and cities in north-west Europe. In some cities, particularly those with a strong architectural heritage, such as St Malo in France or Warsaw's Stare Miasto (Old Town), the approach was to recreate the past: rebuilding the pre-existing streets and buildings as exactly as possible. In many other places the approach was more pragmatic. For example, many of the German cities in the badly damaged Rhine-Ruhr agglomeration kept much of the pre-existing system of streets and blocks with their inherited utility networks and land ownership patterns, but replaced damaged or destroyed buildings with cheaper new designs.

In a few instances the opportunity was taken to completely redesign the city, usually along modernist lines that emphasized a vision of an attractive, efficient, future-orientated city. Many of these were based upon plans that had been drawn up in the wartime era and were surprisingly innovative in planning terms. For instance, Abercrombie and Watson's 1944 plan for the reconstruction of Plymouth city centre was to transform the historic medieval street pattern into a beaux arts vision of functionality: wide straight boulevards lined with modernist buildings. Donald Gibson's 1945 plan for Coventry city centre provided an incredibly detailed three-dimensional statement that similarly put great emphasis on producing an attractive modern townscape that bore little relationship to the pre-war morphology of the area. The centre of Le Havre was completely rebuilt after the war on a precise grid pattern planned and designed by Auguste Perret. In Rotterdam the redevelopment of the city centre stressed functionality and opened up a new pattern of broad streets and open spaces, including the acclaimed Lijnbaan, one of the first purpose-built pedestrianized shopping streets (McCarthy, 1998).

A combination of the need to rebuild bomb-damaged areas, to respond to long-standing concerns about slum housing and urban congestion and to implement some of the ideas contained in the *Barlow Report* led to the preparation of two important plans for the post-war development of London. The extent of the planning agenda at this time can be seen in the *County of London Plan*, prepared by Patrick Abercrombie and James Forshaw for the London County Council (an area roughly equivalent to today's inner London Boroughs) in 1943. It set out plans for the redevelopment and reconstruction of London, including proposals for dealing with traffic congestion, slum housing, deficiencies in open space provision, non-conforming uses and urban sprawl.

The following year Abercrombie and his team completed a plan for the whole London city-region: *The Greater London Plan* (1944). Taking on board the findings of the *Barlow Report* the plan was based upon the assumption that the population of the city-region would be stabilized. The strategy envisaged four rings around the capital (Figure 1.6(a)). In the innermost ring the proposals were in accordance with the recently completed *County of London Plan*: slum clearance, removal of non-conforming uses and reconstruction of war-damaged areas. In the second ring, which mainly comprised the post-1919 suburban areas, little change was proposed. In the third ring was the countryside immediately surrounding the existing built-up area: a 'green belt' which was to be protected from further development. In the fourth or outer country ring, taking some inspiration from the garden cities' ideals, there would be a series of satellite or 'new towns' built to accommodate up to a million people 'overspilt' from the planned reconstruction of the inner ring.

Faced with similar problems, planners in Denmark came up with a different solution for the development of Copenhagen. According to the 1947 Finger Plan for Copenhagen, the city was to develop along five axes, or fingers, following commuter railway lines from the city core to the periphery. Between the fingers green wedges would provide space for agriculture and recreation.

Whilst, over time, London's 'green belt' has been protected against development to a surprising extent, there have been consequences, particularly in inflating property values at the edge of the city and in creating long journeys to work for those forced to commute back to the capital from expanding towns in the outer country ring. It has been argued that an alternative system of green wedges and fingers of development based upon high quality public transport corridors might have proved a more efficient design.

The post-war period

Following Abercrombie's proposals, The New Towns Act, 1946 was put in place to facilitate the building of 'new towns' in the UK. The initial concern was to accommodate overspill population from central London (Stevenage, Harlow, Crawley), but new towns were eventually designated to accommodate overspill from other cities, including Birmingham (Redditch), Liverpool (Runcorn and Skelmersdale) and Glasgow (East Kilbride), and as economic 'growth points' in declining regions such as the North-East (Peterlee, Newton Aycliffe) and South Wales (Cwmbran). The early new towns were intended to be as self-contained as possible, with little commuting back to the mother city, providing not only social housing but also employment, commercial and social facilities for their residents. Most were planned on the neighbourhood principle, with a clear separation of land uses, well designed road systems and generous landscaping.

Whilst the new towns programme eventually accommodated as much as 5 % of the UK population it did not achieve the scale of contribution its advocates had originally intended. Although the notion of self-containment had been reasonably well sustained in the early years this gradually changed as, from the 1970s, an increasing proportion of the housing was built by or sold into the private sector, outward commuting increased and the close relationship between home and workplace broke down. A further comment on the new town plans was their lack of flexibility. Neighbourhoods had been designed for the lifestyles of the 1950s in which many women were housewives and most children went to local schools. Both town and neighbourhood centres were designed for a retail and leisure economy that has long since passed into history. Road systems have struggled to accommodate the growth in traffic and did not always provide convenient routes for walking, cycling or public transport.

Nevertheless, the UK new towns programme was internationally influential and a number of other countries developed their own versions of the planned new town. In France under a 1965 plan for the development of the Paris region, a number of new towns were designated, including Cergy-Pontoise, Évry and Marne la Vallée, although these tended to be developed at higher densities with more high-rise accommodation and were never as self-contained as their UK equivalents. The Netherlands also developed new towns, notably at Lelystad and Almere. Lelystad was to be the service centre for the newly reclaimed Flevoland polder, while Almere provided overspill housing for the expanding Amsterdam city region.

The UK new towns programme was soon complemented by a system of 'expanded towns' under the Town Development Act, 1952. This provided for agreements between local authorities to accommodate overspill population from an 'exporting' city to be rehoused in an 'importing' town or district. Although less well funded than the new towns programme the scheme did have the advantage of using some existing facilities within the overspill town and providing new residents with immediate access to a fully fledged town, rather than having to wait a number of years for adequate schools, shops and leisure facilities to arrive, as new town populations did. The London County Council entered into many such overspill agreements (for example, Ashford, Andover, Basingstoke, Swindon).

One of the biggest advances in the evolution of the UK planning system was the passing of the Town and Country Planning Act, 1947. This Act established a comprehensive planning system across the whole country. County and County Borough Councils (major cities) were to be the local planning authorities with a duty to prepare a development plan for their area and powers to make additional plans at larger scales as necessary. County Development Plans (at a scale of one inch to the mile, approximately 1:50,000) would identify population and employment targets for individual settlements, transport and utility routes, environmental protection and mineral extraction zones. Town Maps (at a scale of 6 inches to the mile, approximately 1:10,000) showed detailed land use zonings for specific parcels of land. In areas where rapid change was anticipated, such as town centres or slum clearance areas, a Comprehensive Development Area (CDA) Plan allowed planners to specify the precise layout of streets and the disposition and form of individual buildings.

In the immediate post-war years it was anticipated that much of the new development in the UK would be undertaken by the state and in accordance with these plans. Nevertheless the act included provision for local planning authorities to enforce the development plan upon private developers through a system of development control. As time went by and a growing proportion of development was undertaken by the private sector, this became the primary mechanism for the implementation of development plans. But there was a further and more controversial part of the Act. Zoning agricultural land for residential development could increase its value many times over and it was felt inappropriate for individual land owners alone to benefit from such unearned income, when some of the costs of that development (for example, provision of schools and social services) had to be borne by the community. The Act therefore made provision for this increase in value (known as betterment) to accrue to the state. Unfortunately this had the side effect of diminishing the profit on land development and according to some thereby slowed down the rate of private development in the post-war era (Hall and Tewdwr-Jones, 2011).

In other countries similar legislation was emerging, for example the French Code de l'Urbanisme et de l'Habitat dates from 1954, and by 1958 that country had introduced a two-tier system of strategic (Schéma directeur) and local (Plan d'occupation des sols) plans, a decade before the introduction of such a system in the UK (Punter, 1989).

From modernism to postmodernism in urban planning

The pressures to control urban sprawl and improve design were very influential on urban renewal policies. Attention was again returning to the business of relieving overcrowding and poor housing conditions in the major cities. The UK Government wanted to see a faster rate of housing completions and a higher density of development. The apparent solution was to build high-rise housing using industrialized building techniques. In the early 1950s the London County Council had completed the Roehampton Estate, one of the first high-rise developments in the country. Set in parkland in south-west London the estate won design accolades and 'legitimized' high-rise housing in the eyes of many other local authorities. To encourage this form of housing, in 1956 the Government changed the housing subsidy arrangements to encourage high-rise building.

However, the experience of high-rise housing in use turned out to be far from satisfactory. Building costs were more than expected and after a few years it became apparent that the cost of maintenance and management costs were higher than traditional housing, and the schemes did not save as much land as expected. Many schemes proved unpopular with tenants, especially families. An economic crisis in 1967 saw subsidy arrangements reversed and high-rise housing quickly fell out of favour as a form of social housing provision. In May 1968 a gas explosion in Ronan Point, a tower block in Newham, led to the progressive collapse of one side of the block and caused a number of deaths. The media and political opinion rapidly turned against further high-rise construction. Across much of continental Europe, however, high rise accommodation was viewed differently and continued to be provided in large quantities as an efficient way of providing mass housing. In western Europe, France in particular favoured large scale high rise social housing estates, and in the state-socialist economies of Eastern Europe industrially produced multi-storey apartment blocks were the norm.

In the UK local authorities began to move away from large scale clearance programmes towards rehabilitation and area improvement. Clearance was proving increasingly expensive as well as imposing unnecessary social costs on local communities. Under the Housing Act, 1969 the idea of General Improvement Areas was established. In these areas local authorities would improve the public realm (traffic management, amenities and environmental improvements), while homeowners received enhanced subsidies for the refurbishment of individual dwellings (Gibson and Langstaff, 1982). Through the next two decades these programmes were taken up with enthusiasm across most cities with the effect the majority of pre-1919 urban dwellings benefitted from some form of subsidized improvement and their useful life extended by many years. Other countries also began to move away from slum clearance towards area improvement, notably the Netherlands where the cities of Amsterdam and Rotterdam were setting international standards for their participatory approaches to regeneration and the design quality of their physical solutions (Stouten, 2010).

Concern at the poor quality of much post-war planning and development was not confined to high-rise housing. In 1955 Ian Nairn published his book *Outrage* which castigated those in authority for producing an increasing degraded physical environment:

[I]f what is called development is allowed to multiply at the present rate, then by the end of the century Great Britain will consist of isolated oases of preserved monuments in a desert of wire, concrete roads, cosy plots and bungalows … the more complicated our industrial system, and the greater our population, the bigger and greener should be our countryside, the more compact and neater should be our towns. (Nairn, 1955, pp. 365 and 368)

This sounds like an early plea for sustainable development. In 1956 the UK Civic Trust was founded to campaign for better design and conservation in the built environment. In 1958 Sir John Betjeman, Nikolaus Pevsner and others founded the Victorian Society for the preservation and appreciation of Victorian architecture and art. Cities had expanded quickly during the nineteenth century and much of this Victorian heritage remained, indeed dominated many cities, but until then had been unappreciated and unprotected from demolition. Official thinking was not yet in tune with the Society's objectives and two important buildings were quickly lost: Euston Station in 1961 and the City of London Coal Exchange in 1962. However, the battle to save buildings such as these stirred public awareness and support for the idea of conserving more of our built heritage began to grow.

In the USA Jane Jacobs, a journalist from New York City, wrote a highly influential critique of the modernist/rationalist approach that had characterized American city planning in the post-war period: *The Death and Life of Great American Cities* (1961). She argued that this approach, which forced the separation of land uses and replaced vibrant, if 'run-down', neighbourhoods with mono-functional 'housing projects' (housing estates), was draining the life out of American cities. In her view urban planning needed a greater level of understanding of how neighbourhood economies actually worked and needed to show greater respect for the communities that lived in them. She stressed the importance of high population densities, permeable neighbourhoods and variety in property types and rent levels to support vibrant local economies and communities.

Urban conservation was coming onto the planning agenda. In France in 1962 the Loi Malraux permitted the designation of secteurs sauvegardés (safeguarded areas) in which areas of historic interest or aesthetic quality could be protected, restored or enhanced. And in 1967 the UK Civic Amenities Act introduced the concept of Conservation Areas. These were to be 'areas of special architectural or historic interest, the character or appearance of which it is desirable to preserve or enhance'. They provided a stricter regime of development control than elsewhere and allowed for enhancements to be carried out. The Government commissioned studies in four historic towns (Bath, Chester, Chichester and York) to examine how conservation would work and what it might achieve. Looking at York, Lord Esher proposed five new planning objectives for the city:

- the commercial heart should remain alive and competitive;
- decay, traffic congestion and noise should be eliminated;
- conflicting land uses should be removed;
- the historic character should be enhanced;
- new buildings should be of the highest architectural quality. (Esher, 1968)

This was a new way of looking at cities, a postmodern way of planning that protected and enhanced the existing environment and sought to create a city centre that was vital and human in character. It was a contingent approach based upon the careful analysis of local problems rather than imposing an exogenous design philosophy upon the area.

Building on these experiences the *European Charter on Architectural Heritage* which emerged from the 1975 European Architectural Heritage Year did much to establish built heritage protection and conservation as part of the international urban planning agenda.

There were also growing environmental concerns. The World Wildlife Fund, one of the first international organizations to be concerned with research, conservation and restoration of the natural environment, was founded in 1961, and in 1962 Rachel Carson published *Silent Spring*, a book which identified the detrimental effects of pesticides on the environment, especially birdlife. In 1967 the super tanker *Torrey Canyon* ran aground off the Scilly Isles, spilling its cargo of oil into the English Channel, and in 1969 a blow-out from an off-shore oil well opposite Santa Barbara in California released more than 80,000 barrels of crude oil into the sea. Both events devastated marine life over huge areas and raised questions about the environmental costs of industrial production. By the late 1960s the environmental cause was being taken up by a broader range of individuals and organizations. Friends of the Earth was established in 1969, initially as an anti-nuclear protest group, and Greenpeace, with its goal of ensuring 'the ability of the Earth to nurture life in all its diversity', was founded in 1971. In 1970 the United States Environmental Protection Agency was formed. In 1972 the global think-tank Club of Rome published *The Limits to Growth*, which identified the natural resource limits to and consequences of continued population and economic growth (Meadows et al., 1972). Soon after, Fritz Schumacher published *Small is Beautiful* (1973) in which he argued that the modern economy was unsustainable because of the failure of economics to recognize the non-renewable character of natural resources.

By the late 1960s, it was becoming clear that the UK planning system created by the Town and Country Planning Act, 1947 was proving cumbersome in its implementation and inflexible in accommodating the changing priorities in urban policy. A particular stumbling block was the requirement that all development plans had to be approved by central government. In response, the Town and Country Planning Act, 1968 proposed a two-tier system of strategic 'structure plans' containing general policies for the development of counties or county boroughs (which still required ministerial approval) and tactical, more detailed 'local plans' for smaller areas (which could be approved locally subject to conformity with the higher level plan). Under this Act, local planning authorities were required to survey local social and economic conditions while facilitating public participation in the plan making process became a legal requirement. These changes were to move town and country planning from being a technical profession towards a more social science-based profession. Planning theory was increasingly recognizing the interconnectedness of the elements of regional and urban economies: dwellings, workplaces, transport networks, and so on in a new 'systems' view of planning (McLoughlin, 1969; Chadwick, 1971).

Growing political concern about poverty and what became known as 'urban deprivation' was leading the UK Government towards an 'urban' policy that would be distinct from existing departmental interests in housing, health, social services, town planning, transportation and so on. Some experience was coming from the USA where the civil rights movement highlighted the deprivation of poor, mainly black, populations in the inner cities. In the UK inner city riots provided the final catalyst for change (Atkinson and Moon, 1994). In July 1968 the Government announced a new 'urban programme' providing modest subsidies towards social projects and community facilities in areas of urban deprivation (Gibson and Langstaff, 1982). Shortly afterwards a second programme of action-research Community Development Projects was established in a dozen areas, providing government-funded action towards community development and research (undertaken by academic teams) into the nature and causes of the problems faced by these communities. Whilst these programmes had limited success on the ground, they began to assemble a useful body of knowledge on patterns and processes of deprivation (Loney, 1983). Later, in 1972, the Government appointed consultants to undertake large scale Inner Area Studies into the causes of deprivation in inner city communities in Birmingham, Lambeth and Liverpool (Shankland, 1977). Further knowledge was emerging from the production of urban structure plans as the major cities reported on surveys of social and economic conditions in their areas.

Post-industrial change and planning

By 1974 a combination of overseas events including the effects of the 1973 Arab–Israeli war plunged western Europe into recession. The competitiveness of British industry was already in decline and the mid-1970s saw a series of industrial closures, a growing tendency for firms to transfer production abroad and rising unemployment resulting in swathes of urban dereliction. Other countries suffered too, but not yet to the same extent as the old industrial regions of the UK.

Urban economic regeneration rapidly became a major political issue. The UK Government set out new aims for urban policy that recognized the structural economic causes of urban deprivation and the adverse impact of urban sprawl and population loss on the inner cities. The proposed solutions lay in central and local government partnerships and increased public funding for the inner cities (DoE, 1976). However, this approach proved short-lived. The Labour Government lost power to Margaret Thatcher's Conservatives in May 1979. Under this new regime there was a gradual centralization of power combined with a marginalization of the role of local authorities and the local planning system. There was an increasing emphasis on 'property-led' urban regeneration via 'urban development corporations' and 'enterprise zones' and a growing role for the private sector in urban development and regeneration.

The Conservative Government was faced with recession and industrial restructuring on a massive scale. Their view was that recovery could only come from growth within the private sector of the economy. State controls, especially planning, needed to be relaxed in order to give private enterprise the flexibility to make quick market-responsive investment decisions. But there was another element to their thinking: the growing area of redundant and underused land, especially in inner urban areas, constituted waste of potentially high value property assets and a real economic resource. In some areas the scale of the problem was so vast that only public intervention could return such land to a state where the private sector could begin to think about reinvestment.

The Local Government, Planning and Land Act, 1980 paved the way for Urban Development Corporations (UDCs) which were to be funded by and responsible to central government and given substantial funds as well as extensive development and planning powers. Their purpose was to promote regeneration by reclaiming derelict land and buildings, providing infrastructure and facilitating industrial and commercial development, social facilities and housing. Fourteen UDCs were established across Britain in this period. There is little doubt of their generally impressive record in stimulating investment and economic regeneration, although there has been some criticism of their streamlined decision making, the lack of local democratic control and the emphasis on entre-preneurialism and property-led regeneration activity. But, according to Imrie and Thomas, this analysis tends to underplay the complexity and multi-layered nature of the UDCs' activities and the degree to which they were embedded with local communities and policy makers (1999).

One of the first and most well known of the UDCs was the London Docklands Development Corporation (LDDC). Between 1981 and 1998 it was responsible for the redevelopment of 2,000 hectares of derelict docklands and urban blight stretching nearly 10 km west–east from the edge of the City of London, through Wapping, Limehouse, the Isle of Dogs, the former Surrey and Royal Docks to Beckton. Over its lifetime it claimed to have achieved £1.86 billion of public investment and £7.7 billion private sector investment (a leverage ratio of 1 to 4.14). Its work included the reclamation of over 760 hectares of derelict land, provision of 144 km of new or improved roads and construction of the initial phases of the Docklands Light Railway. By 1998 some 85,000 people worked within its designated area (www.lddc-history.org.uk/lddcachieve/index.html, accessed 1.11.2014).

By the end of the decade there was in the UK a backlash against the marginalization of local planning authorities, both from the property development sector, who welcomed the certainty provided by strong, clear plans from local authorities, and from residents concerned about losing control over unwanted development 'in their backyard'. However, more important was the emerging concern for the environment that saw planning as a central tool in creating sustainable development.

Growing international concern about the impact of growth and industrialization on the world's environment had led the United Nations to establish the World Commission on Environment and Development (Brundtland Commission). The report that emerged is generally regarded as one of the most important advances in our understanding of the subject and provided us with the most commonly used definition of sustainable development: 'development that meets the needs of the present without compromising the ability of future generations to meet their own needs' (Brundtland, 1987). The *Report* particularly commented on the interlocking nature of the crisis:

> Until recently, the planet was a large world in which human activities and their effects were neatly compartmentalized within nations, within sectors (energy, agriculture, trade), and within broad areas of concern (environment, economics, social). These compartments have begun to dissolve. This applies in particular to the various global 'crises' that have seized public concern, particularly over the past decade. These are not separate crises: an environmental crisis, a devel-opment crisis, an energy crisis. They are all one. (ibid., para. 11)

In a chapter on 'the urban challenge' the Commission noted that the world of the twenty-first century would be largely urban, with the fastest growth occurring in the cities of developing countries, many of which would struggle to provide the necessary urban infrastructure, services and shelter. In the industrialized countries many cities would face problems of deteriorating infrastructure, environmental degradation and inner city decay. The Commission suggested that governments would need to develop explicit settlement strategies to guide the process of urbanization. These might include taking pressure off the largest urban centres by building up smaller towns and cities. It also recommended that there should be a decentralization of power and resources to city governments, 'which are best placed to appreciate and manage local needs' (ibid., paras 71–74).

The Commission proposed an international conference to discuss their conclusions and the need for future action. This was the United Nations Conference on Environment and Development, or 'Earth Summit', held in Rio de Janeiro in 1992. The importance of the meeting is indicated by the fact that attendance included 118 heads of state/government. The outcome was *Agenda 21*, which aimed to prepare the world for the twenty-first century, with proposals for:

- the socio-economic dimensions of sustainable development (tackling poverty, improving health, changing consumption patterns);
- conservation of natural resources (protecting fragile environments, conserving biodiversity, reducing pollution and managing waste);
- strengthening the role of major groups in decision making (including stakeholder organizations, under-represented and minority groups);
- means of implementation (including science, technology transfer, education and financial mechanisms).

In the chapter 'Promoting Sustainable Human Settlement Development' the Conference concluded that:

> In industrialized countries, the consumption patterns of cities are severely stressing the global ecosystem while settlements in the developing world need more raw material, energy, and economic development simply to overcome basic economic and social problems. (United Nations, 1992, para. 7.1)

Analysing these problems across the world, *Agenda 21* called for governments in all countries to provide adequate shelter for all, to improve human settlement management (urban governance), to promote sustainable land use planning, integrated provision of environmental infrastructure, sustainable energy and transport systems (ibid., para. 7.5).

Recognizing that the best starting point for much action towards sustainable development was at the local level (two-thirds of their proposals required local action), *Agenda 21* called on local authorities to draw up, in collaboration with local communities, their own Local Agenda 21 (LA21) strategies. These were to include a vision statement, action plan and implementation mechanisms to better focus local policies towards sustainable development.

Within Europe the notion of sustainable urban development was addressed in the European Commission's *Green Paper on the Urban Environment* (CEC, 1990), which recognized a series of problems facing European cities: increasing amounts of brownfield land, urban sprawl, the pollution of urban environments, the loss of built heritage and the loss of nature from the city. Whilst the root causes of these problems lay in macro-level socio-economic trends and events, urban planning was also seen to be at fault: inflexible planning rules that frustrated a city's ability to develop in a dynamic and organic manner and too much emphasis on planning for development, sometimes at the expense of the environment and the quality of life of inhabitants (CEC, 1990). Instead the Commission proposed:

- more compact, higher density, mixed use cities;
- better urban design and protection of urban and rural heritage;
- reuse of derelict land and buildings and revitalising existing city areas
- more and better public transport with less reliance on the car;
- better management of natural resources, energy and waste in urban development (ibid, part 5).

The late 1980s also saw a rise in interest in what became known as the 'new public health', a recognition that, long after the sanitary campaigns of the nineteenth century, the characteristics of cities were still very important in determining public health (Ashton, 1989). This recognition led to the World Health Organisation (WHO) establishing the 'Healthy Cities' programme. A healthy city was defined as one:

> that is continually creating and improving those physical and social environments and expanding those community resources which enable people to mutually support each other in performing all the functions of life and developing to their maximum potential. (WHO, 1998)

It was evident that there was a clear role for planners to take this agenda on board in shaping a healthy environment, to work with other professionals to understand health and environment linkages and to create partnerships to tackle the challenges to human health and fitness raised by issues such as heavy traffic, pollution, noise, violence, social isolation, deprivation, alcohol and substance abuse. Overlapping with the sustainable development agenda, many cities subsequently began to include these new health concerns in formulating their development plans.

By the early 1990s many European and American town and city centres were beginning to show severe signs of decline and decay. Declining urban populations, changing employment patterns, deteriorating environmental conditions, rising traffic congestion and the growth of out-of-town competition were combining to adversely affect the economy of urban centres. In the post-industrial economy, cities were increasingly finding that they had to complete for footloose economic growth. Local environmental quality and the existence of vital and vibrant centres became important elements of urban competitiveness. Reurbanization and the revitalization of urban centres became important elements in the planning agenda. This agenda built on the regeneration experience of the previous decade to develop more compact, sustainable cities.

The European Commission's *European Spatial Development Perspective* (CEC, 1999) continued the development of sustainable urban policy along similar lines to those outlined in the *Green Paper* nine years earlier. Policies included the promotion of integrated transport and communication networks, the conservation of natural and cultural heritage, the preservation and deepening of local and regional identities in an age of globalization. One key advance was the idea of 'polycentric development': a multi-centred and balanced urban system which strengthened partnerships between nearby cities and between urban and rural areas. It was argued that:

> The concept of polycentric development has to be pursued, to ensure regionally balanced development, because the EU is becoming fully integrated in the global economy. Pursuit of this concept will help to avoid further excessive economic and demographic concentration in the core area of the EU. (CEC, 1999, p. 20)

Five urban planning goals were seen to be of particular importance to the sustainable development of towns and cities:

- control of the physical expansion of towns and cities;
- mixture of functions and social groups (and the avoidance of social exclusion);
- wise and resource-saving management of the urban ecosystem (particularly water, energy and waste);
- better accessibility through means of transport that are both effective and environmentally friendly;
- conservation and development of the natural and cultural heritage. (CEC, 1999, p. 22)

In the UK the Government commissioned a task force led by Lord Rogers to identify the causes of urban decline and to establish a vision for the future of cities, based around design excellence, social wellbeing and environmental responsibility. Their report was published as *Towards an Urban Renaissance* (Urban Task Force, 1999). In line with European thinking, it proposed that cities should be compact, well connected and well designed, and support a diverse range of uses in a sustainable and adaptable urban environment. The report was in large measure accepted by the government and became policy under a White Paper published the following year (DETR, 2000).

Matters that had been of concern to the Barlow Commission seventy years earlier again reared their heads in the new millennium: growing concerns about surplus social capital in the North and an overheating economy, urban sprawl, congestion and housing shortage in the South-east. Combining aspirations for sustainable development, meeting housing needs and tackling social exclusion the UK Government published a new programme *Sustainable Communities: building for the future* (ODPM, 2003). The aim was to create sustainable communities with flourishing local economies; strong leadership and social engagement; safe, healthy and green local environments; efficient use of land and provision of amenities; good public transport, community infrastructure, services and amenities; a mix of decent homes of different types and tenures; cultural diversity and a sense of place. The programme set out a series of policies to tackle these interrelated problems through investment, designation of new growth areas in the South-east, better regional and local planning, protection of green belts, and sustained action on urban regeneration.

By 2007, the countries of the European Union had agreed the *Leipzig Charter on Sustainable European Cities*. This document called for greater use of integrated urban development policy approaches, which should:

- describe the strengths and the weaknesses of cities and neighbourhoods based upon an analysis of the current situation;
- define consistent development objectives for the urban area and develop a vision for the city;
- coordinate the different neighbourhood, sectoral and technical plans and policies, and ensure that the planned investments will help to promote a well balanced development of the urban area;
- coordinate and spatially focus the use of funds by public and private sector players;
- be coordinated at local and city-regional level and involve citizens and other partners. (CEC, 2007)

The *Charter* also called for special attention to be paid to deprived neighbourhoods within the context of the city as a whole, pursuing strategies for upgrading the physical environment, strengthening the local economy and local labour market policies, adopting proactive education and training policies for children and young people, and promoting efficient and affordable urban transport.

In the early twenty-first century climate change was becoming a matter of significant concern to governments across the world. A role for the planning system in climate change mitigation and adaptation was being developed. In 2010 the UK Town and Country Planning Association (TCPA) and Friends of the Earth (FOE) published *Planning for Climate Change: guidance and model policies for local authorities* on behalf of the Planning and Climate Change Coalition (TCPA and FOE, 2010). This document argued that:

> Spatial planning can make a major contribution to tackling climate change by shaping new and existing developments in ways that reduce carbon dioxide emissions and positively build community resilience to problems such as extreme heat or flood risk. (TCPA and FOE, 2010, p. 2)

Serious socio-economic problems were also emerging. In the context of the post-2008 economic crisis, the European Commission was becoming concerned that the European model of sustainable urban development that had developed over the previous twenty years was under increasing threat. There were a number of challenges. Some cities were increasingly affected by rapid demographic changes caused by migration, ageing populations, shrinkage or suburbanization. Economic growth was faltering across Europe, especially in the former industrial cities and non-capital cities in central and Eastern Europe. The links between economic growth, employment and social progress were weakening, pushing a larger proportion of the population out of the labour market or towards low skilled, low paid jobs. Growing income disparities were emerging, with increasing social polarization and segregation. And urban sprawl continued to be seen as one of the main threats to sustainable territorial development and the protection of urban ecosystems. (CEC, 2011)

In response the Commission set out a number of objectives for the future of urban planning. These included:

- creating more resilient and inclusive urban economies – turning diversity into an economic asset – exploiting the potential of socio-economic, cultural, generational and ethnic diversity as a source of innovation;

- creating a socially cohesive city, developing social innovation, adapting the city's economic and social life to an ageing population, attracting the young and making room for children, combating spatial exclusion and energy poverty with better housing;
- adopting a more holistic approach to environmental and energy issues – recognizing that many components of the natural ecosystem are interwoven with those of the social, economic, cultural and political urban system, making mobility sustainable, inclusive and healthy;
- recognizing the importance of maintaining thriving and dynamic small and medium sized cities to promote more spatially balanced territorial development, avoiding rural depopulation and urban drift. (CEC, 2011)

Conclusions

Figure 1.7 summarizes the evolution of planning thought and the planning agenda. Our concern with urban development and urban planning starts with the industrial revolution and its impact on towns and cities. The UK was the most rapidly urbanizing country in the late eighteenth and early nineteenth centuries and it is here that the impacts of industrialization were most keenly felt. The evolving pattern of urbanization through this period was shaped principally by economic trends and pressures rather than any state intervention. Although town extension planning had existed in Germany since the late eighteenth century, it was a long time before UK urban policy followed suit. Instead, the UK gradually developed public health and housing legislation that established development criteria which began to improve urban conditions and create a distinctive and efficient urban structure.

The profession of 'town planning' emerged early in the twentieth century with the founding of professional organizations, academic programmes of instruction and a growing body of literature and professional discourse. In the first half of that century the majority of planners were, in terms of their original training, architects, surveyors or civil engineers. At that time planning was principally concerned with land use and the physical structure of cities. The goals of planning were, in the words of Sir Patrick Abercrombie, to achieve in a city: 'beauty, health and convenience' (Abercrombie, 1933, p. 104); that is to say, a visually attractive, healthy and efficient urban environment. In the UK in particular the ideas of the garden cities movement were very influential on planning and development. However, the modern movement, which was already very influential in continental Europe, began to influence British approaches to the rebuilding of cities after the Second World War.

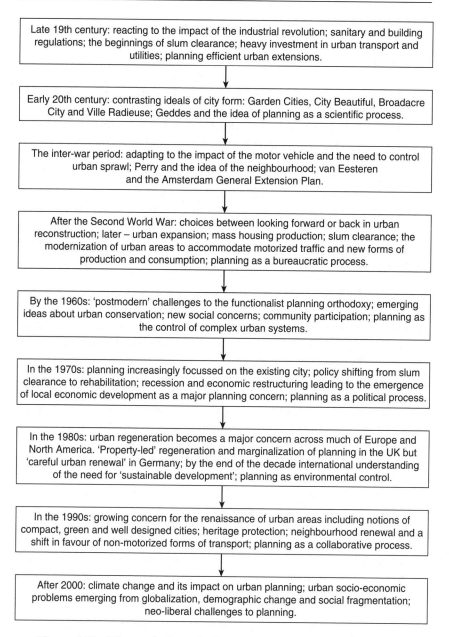

Late 19th century: reacting to the impact of the industrial revolution; sanitary and building regulations; the beginnings of slum clearance; heavy investment in urban transport and utilities; planning efficient urban extensions.

Early 20th century: contrasting ideals of city form: Garden Cities, City Beautiful, Broadacre City and Ville Radieuse; Geddes and the idea of planning as a scientific process.

The inter-war period: adapting to the impact of the motor vehicle and the need to control urban sprawl; Perry and the idea of the neighbourhood; van Eesteren and the Amsterdam General Extension Plan.

After the Second World War: choices between looking forward or back in urban reconstruction; later – urban expansion; mass housing production; slum clearance; the modernization of urban areas to accommodate motorized traffic and new forms of production and consumption; planning as a bureaucratic process.

By the 1960s: 'postmodern' challenges to the functionalist planning orthodoxy; emerging ideas about urban conservation; new social concerns; community participation; planning as the control of complex urban systems.

In the 1970s: planning increasingly focussed on the existing city; policy shifting from slum clearance to rehabilitation; recession and economic restructuring leading to the emergence of local economic development as a major planning concern; planning as a political process.

In the 1980s: urban regeneration becomes a major concern across much of Europe and North America. 'Property-led' regeneration and marginalization of planning in the UK but 'careful urban renewal' in Germany; by the end of the decade international understanding of the need for 'sustainable development'; planning as environmental control.

In the 1990s: growing concern for the renaissance of urban areas including notions of compact, green and well designed cities; heritage protection; neighbourhood renewal and a shift in favour of non-motorized forms of transport; planning as a collaborative process.

After 2000: climate change and its impact on urban planning; urban socio-economic problems emerging from globalization, demographic change and social fragmentation; neo-liberal challenges to planning.

Figure 1.7 *The evolution of planning thought and the planning agenda*

For many countries the 1950s was a period of reconstruction, planning for urban extensions and accommodating the growth of traffic. However, within a decade a new postmodern philosophy was emerging, challenging the orthodoxies of functionalist land use and transportation planning, and calling for more sensitive, people-friendly approaches that restrained the growth of urban traffic and conserved urban heritage and environments. By the late 1960s social issues were coming onto the urban planning agenda, ushered in through lessons from the civil rights movement in the USA and a growing understanding of social deprivation and social unrest in the UK and Europe. It was from this time that social scientists started to enter the profession in large numbers, eventually in many countries coming to outnumber those planners who had a background in the built environment professions.

Economic change, restructuring and the decline of many traditional urban economies through the 1970s and 1980s brought the issue of local economic development and regeneration onto the urban planning agenda. In some countries, especially the UK, this also brought political challenges to the role of the profession, questioning whether planning assisted or frustrated economic growth. But by the late 1980s there was a new challenge: the world was waking up to the immense environmental damage and inequalities brought about by unrestrained economic growth. Following the Brundtland report there were calls for a more sustainable approach to development that would meet 'the needs of the present without compromising the ability of future generations to meet their own needs' (Brundtland, 1987). By 1990 the European Commission and many national governments had responded, recognizing the importance of the aim and the key role that planning could play in its achievement. Within the planning agenda natural resource management, energy conservation, compact cities, sustainable communities, greening the city, reducing the need for travel, shifting modal split away from the motor vehicle, good urban design and heritage conservation became ever more important objectives.

By the millennium the impact of climate change was becoming clearer and this served to strengthen recognition of the importance of sustainable environments. A number of key cities, such as Copenhagen and Freiburg (see Chapter 3), were leading new approaches in this regard. However, 2008 brought a severe and lingering economic crisis, plunging many countries into recession. Coinciding with a period of international migration and conflict in some regions of the world, there were growing social pressures in many cities, leading some to call for a strengthening of social inclusion objectives in urban planning. But the perceived need to stimulate economic growth again led to right-wing political challenges to the role and benefits of planning, threatening to put short term economic gain ahead of long term environmental and social costs: the very opposite of the Brundtland definition of sustainable development.

Chapter 2

Governance and the Implementation of Planning

Introduction

Urban planning is essentially a part of the process of governing cities, that is to say, part of the formal institutions and processes through which the state (whether central or local) exercises authority, makes and implements policies to influence or determine the conduct of society. In the vast majority of developed countries government is by democracy, in the sense that the population at large influences and shapes the decisions of government through selecting representatives to make decisions (elections) or directly making decisions (referenda). As discussed in Chapter 1, urban planning emerged as an element of urban government in many western countries around the beginning of the twentieth century. The range and scope of government concerns with urban matters has subsequently evolved and expanded, so that today's urban planning agenda is vast and complex with many overlapping and potentially competing objectives.

Since the 1990s many commentators have discussed the shift from government to what they refer to as 'governance', and this has important implications for urban planning. The notion is that as societies have become more complex, as cities and regions have become more interconnected, as economies have become more globalized, as the private sector of the economy has become more powerful, and as new policy challenges have emerged (such as climate change or demographic change), so there has emerged a need for more flexible and inclusive mechanisms for public decision making. John (2001) distinguishes governance from government as follows. Government tends to be hierarchical, with central government in direct control, containing few institutions, using relatively closed procedures to make routinized policy decisions, based upon representative democracy. In contrast, governance tends to be more decentralized and fragmented, based upon many and shifting institutions depending on the problem concerned, using extensive networks to learn and make innovative decisions, based both on representative democracy and new forms of engagement, such as community participation.

A look at the changing way public decisions have been made in the city of Liverpool illustrates this shift and is representative of the experience of many cities. In the 1950s the local economy was largely dependent upon the port and manufacturing industry. Relationships with other cities and regions were relatively stable. Central government determined the basis for local government and local public decisions through Acts of Parliament and a degree of less formal advice. There was only one principal local public decision making institution: Liverpool City Council. The council was responsible for delivering a comprehensive range of services including town planning, housing, highways, sewerage, local public transport, education, police, welfare and children's services, and so on. Local public decision making was mainly hierarchical, based upon representative democracy and a few institutions, relatively closed and routinized. Today, many more institutions are involved in the equivalent decision making processes. A key difference is that many of these services have been passed to other agencies or privatized and fragmented. Additionally the local economy is much more intertwined with that of other regions, with the city more dependent on and vulnerable to decisions taken beyond its boundaries or control. Furthermore, the local planning authority has a 'duty to cooperate' with neighbouring authorities. There are quasi-governmental organizations such as the Environment Agency, English Heritage, the Local Enterprise Partnership (concerned with economic development across the city region) and a range of influential voluntary organizations and pressure groups. Much of the housing service is now delivered by separate housing associations or private organizations; sewerage and water supply are in the hands of a privatized utility company; local bus and rail services have been privatized to competing firms, coordinated by a city-regional passenger transport authority; police and fire services are also now administered at a city-regional level. Thus today public decision making in (or for) Liverpool has become dispersed and fragmented, based upon a network of many and shifting institutions depending on the problem concerned. These processes are still substantially led by the City Council and based upon representative democracy, but decisions today are much more likely to be arrived at through negotiation and collaboration between many agencies and institutions rather than direction from a few.

Within the context of urban governance, what exactly are the concerns of urban planning? Where are the boundaries between planning and other professions or departments of government? Internationally since the 1980s, planning systems have had to accommodate and adapt to three hegemonic changes to the context within which planning takes place: globalization, neo-liberalism and sustainability.

The private sector's constant search for increased productivity, economies of scale and the horizontal and vertical integration of production combined with rapidly reducing transportation costs has led to an ever more globalized economy. Cities, regions and nations are increasingly interconnected in terms of both production and consumption. Not only are more and more industrial companies multinational, spreading their production across a number of countries, but so is finance capital and a growing number of property development organizations. Hence, development decisions that might once have been taken locally by firms, agencies or investors with local connections and interests may now be taken thousands of miles away by decision makers solely focussed on maximizing returns on their investment. Globalization is forcing cities to compete ever more strongly to secure inward investment and is increasing the vulnerability of cities and regions to sudden upsurges or downturns in investment that are beyond their control. Planning systems have to adjust to this situation. In part this is leading towards a standardization in planning criteria across the globe, both in response to the expectations of international developers and as nations and regions seek to coordinate their responses to avoid being played off, one against the other, especially in terms of controlling environmental impacts. But it is also evident that planners in many countries are increasingly expected to consider the economic impact of planning decisions and to streamline plan making and decision taking in order to reduce disruption and delay in the development process.

Reactions against the crises and apparent lack of competitiveness of the UK and to some degree the US economies in the 1970s and 1980s led to a response that sought economic growth through privatization, deregulation and the encouragement of free trade. This economic philosophy, known somewhat pejoratively by its critics as neo-liberalism, led to challenges to the planning orthodoxy in many countries and on several fronts. One key idea is that a smaller proportion of the economic system (represented by total GDP) should be in the public sector, it being alleged that the private sector will produce the same goods and services more efficiently, so releasing resources that can be used elsewhere in the economy. In other words, less economic activity should be subject to state-led economic planning: the 'command economy'. A second idea is that economies will grow faster if they are less fettered by regulations, such as land use zoning and environmental controls. The problem with this, of course, is that markets (and measures such as GDP) do not take account of the social and environmental costs of market behaviour. Nevertheless, planning systems and regulations are being challenged by those who support this economic philosophy. The third idea – of encouraging free trade and, by extension, accepting the consequences of free trade including the loss of local producers, identities and cultures – is another challenge to the accepted planning wisdom of protecting heritage, diversity and cultural identities.

With regard to sustainable development, there is an impressive similarity between the goals of the countries and plans considered here. The differences lie not so much in their planning goals but in their starting points, the historical, socio-economic and institutional context within which plans are being produced. Thus in England, Belgium and the Netherlands, where population densities are very high, urban containment is a key priority. In low density France and Poland, for example, the loss of rural land to urbanization is less keenly felt. In the north of England, central Scotland, the Ruhr in Germany, Wallonia in Belgium, for example, urban planning takes place within the context of transforming older industrial cities to face a post-industrial future. In China the need for rapid urbanization has been a key policy driver and the legacy of communism gives the state very strong powers over implementation. In the USA the role of planning is limited by an underlying political hegemony that gives the state a far smaller role in the national economy than is common in most European countries.

Governance and planning systems in Europe

Today more than 70 % of the EU population lives in urban areas. In the post-industrial economy cities are increasingly seen as the source of future economic growth. But much of this potential growth is footloose and cities therefore have to compete with each other for a 'share of the action'. They must compete through improving comparative advantage, greater agglomeration economies, stronger place marketing, better environmental quality and living conditions to attract skilled workers, businesses and tourists. But in many cities there are also diseconomies that detract from their advantages as locations for economic activity. Cities also generate congestion, social exclusion and crime. The EU's goal for urban planning, articulated in its *Europe 2020* strategy, is 'smart, sustainable and inclusive growth' (CEC, 2010) but the challenges facing urban planners vary enormously between different cities and different countries. Some are growing while others are shrinking; some are prosperous and pleasant whilst others are beset by environmental and social deprivations. Table 2.1 shows in broad terms the different macro socio-economic contexts within which urban planners were working in the mid-2010s in different European countries.

Thus, for instance, Belgian planners were working in the context of a highly urbanized country with a high rate of national population growth, but where the economy was struggling and unemployment was high. In

Table 2.1 Population, economic conditions and planning systems in selected European countries

	Belgium	Denmark	Germany	France	Ireland	Netherlands	Poland	United Kingdom
Population	11.1m	5.6m	82.0m	65.6m	4.6m	16.8m	38.5m	63.9m
Population density 2012 (ppkm^2)	367.0	130.4	229.4	103.4	73.4	496.9	123.2	262.7
Built-up areas (2012)[1]	7.1%	2.4%	2.6%	1.7%	1.2%	4.2%	1.5%	2.3%
Population projections (projected % increase 2013–2020)	+6.3%	+3.0%	-1.7%	+3.2%	+0.4%	+1.8%	-0.5%	+4.3%
Old-age dependency (2013)[2]	26.8	27.6	31.8	27.5	18.6	25.5	20.1	26.4
GDP per capita 2013 (euros)	34,500	44,400	33,300	31,300	35,600	35,900	10,100	29,600
Average growth rate 2011–2013 (% annual change)	-0.6%	0.0%	+1.3%	+0.2%	+1.1%	-0.7%	+2.7%	+0.1%

(continued)

Table 2.1 *Population, economic conditions and planning systems in selected European countries (continued)*

	Belgium	Denmark	Germany	France	Ireland	Netherlands	Poland	United Kingdom
Unemployment rate (June 2014)[3]	8.1%	6.3%	4.8%	9.6%	11.9%	6.6%	8.6%	6.2%
Government type	Constitutional monarchy, complex federation of regions and communities	Constitutional monarchy, unitary government	Federal republic	Republic, unitary government, considerable devolution to regions and municipalities	Republic, unitary government	Constitutional monarchy, unitary government	Republic, unitary government	Constitutional monarchy, unitary government, but devolved powers to Scotland, Wales and Northern Ireland
National level planning	National infrastructure only	National planning report	National infrastructure and planning guidance	National spatial planning, directives and regulations	National Spatial Strategy	National spatial planning vision	Collaborative national strategic development planning process	National infrastructure and planning guidance

	Belgium	Denmark	Germany	France	Ireland	Netherlands	Poland	United Kingdom
Regional level planning	Regional spatial plans	Regional spatial development plans	Regional and sub-regional spatial plans;	Regional plans (SCOT)		Provincial planning vision	Regional development strategies and spatial plans	
Municipal level planning	Varies between regions	Municipal plans	Land use plans (F-plan)	Local plans (PLU)	Development plans	Municipal planning vision	Local development strategy	Local plans
Site development plans		Local plans	Building plans (B-plan)	Lotissements possible		Building plans (B-plan)	Local physical development plan	

Notes

1 Total built-up area as a share of the total surface area of land in the country.
2 The number of persons aged 65 and over expressed as a percentage of the number of persons aged between 15 and 64.
3 The number of unemployed persons as a percentage of the labour force based on International Labour Office (ILO) definition.

Sources: Based upon data from Eurostat, various tables.

contrast, Germany is a much bigger country but much less urbanized than Belgium with a higher level of old-age dependency and a declining population and, although GDP per capita was similar, the economy was growing and sustaining a lower level of unemployment. Looking further east, Poland is the most rural of these countries. It has a relatively young population but the low level of GDP per capita and high rate of unemployment appeared to be encouraging outward migration. On the other hand the Polish economy, starting from a low base after the end of the state-socialist period, was growing at twice the rate of Germany's.

Across Europe there are different systems of local government and local governance. Some countries have a federal structure whilst others are unitary. In federal countries (such as Germany, Austria, Switzerland and Belgium) sovereignty is shared between a group of regions or provinces and a central state with limited power and a relationship with the constituent regions that is usually defined in a written constitution. In most federal states central government has only limited concern with urban planning, most powers being found at the regional or local levels. In contrast, unitary states (such as France, Netherlands, Sweden, Denmark, Poland and Ireland) are governed as a single unit. Central government is supreme with regional or local administrations only exercising such powers as are delegated or devolved to them by central government. In unitary states it is common to find central governments with significant interests in urban planning and exercising strong influence over urban policy. The UK is technically a unitary state but with substantial powers devolved to Scotland and, to a lesser extent, Wales and Northern Ireland.

There is a growing convergence between planning systems and styles across Europe. Where countries have been faced with similar planning problems, be it controlling urban sprawl, urban regeneration or whatever, they have learned from each other the best solutions and planning methods to employ. They have learned through various mechanisms. As the international body of planning theory has increased, planning students in many countries have shared a more standardized planning curriculum, regardless of the location of their studies. There have been formal and informal international exchanges and visits between planners and planning agencies. There are a growing number of international planning consultancies which also act as conduits for the transfer of knowledge and techniques. The fundamental goals of planning within most countries are informed by the United Nations' commitment to sustainable development and all that that entails. And within the EU, the Commission not only has its own regional development policies and environmental regulations that impose constraints and opportunities upon national governments, it also provides a wide range of expert advice and guidance on policy formulation and implementation across these same fields. Furthermore, European ministers and officials concerned with urban planning regularly meet and debate planning issues. There are also alliances between cities of various types. For example, Eurocities is a network of major European cities whose purpose is to influence and work with EU institutions in response to shared urban problems. And there is a wealth of international comparative urban research, much of it focussed upon improving urban policies and planning. For example, the European Commission, working through the European Spatial Planning Observation Network (ESPON), commissioned an international comparative study into an issue facing many European countries: *Second Tier Cities in Europe: in an age of austerity why invest beyond the capitals?* (Parkinson et al., 2012).

Differences in countries' approaches to planning also arise because of their history, their inherited political and legal systems, institutions and cultures. There is a degree to which the planning solutions and approaches available within a country are limited by path-dependency. That is to say, their choices of action are limited by previous decisions, or more simply, history matters. Thus, in the UK with its legal system based upon common law, the context for urban plan making is different from France and other countries that have inherited a legal system is based upon Roman law. There is also an overlapping distinction between those countries that experienced administrative reforms in the Napoleonic period and those that did not.

The legal systems of many countries of continental Europe have their origins in the Napoleonic code and earlier ideas stemming from Roman law. They are based upon statutory laws (laws made by the state) which are codified with the intention of establishing clear legal frameworks within which society can operate. Such laws can only be replaced by enacting new laws. In the UK and many countries that fell under its colonial influence, common law predominates. Common law is made by judges, in courts, through the creation of precedents which influence the decisions of other judges in subsequent cases. Whilst a considerable amount of statute law has also been enacted, it is subject to interpretation and modification by judges sitting in courts.

Newman and Thornley (1996) identify various types of legal and administrative governance in Europe and have grouped countries into 'families' according to administrative type. The Napoleonic family, originating in France, Belgium and the Netherlands but permeating much of southern Europe including Italy and Spain, aims to provide clear rules for government and behaviour. There are written national constitutions and sectoral codes of rules for state intervention in urban matters. Local administrations, especially the French communes, often have substantial powers enshrined in the constitution and carry considerable political weight. The Germanic family (Germany, Austria and Switzerland) shares the notion of codification with the Napoleonic family but with stronger abstract and intellectual foundations. Government in each of these countries is based on a federal system. The system in the Scandinavian family (Denmark, Sweden, Norway and Finland) was historically based upon the old Germanic style of law but has evolved a more pragmatic, less rigid style than that of the modern Germanic states. The British family differs from all other forms of government in Europe. Based upon common law, the system is characterized by the lack of any written constitution and the doctrine of *ultra vires* which limits the scope of local government activity to that permitted by statute. This contrasts with the doctrine of general competence that is the norm in much of the rest of Europe. Finally, the East European family is not so much a grouping as a number of individual states that had to undergo a process of transformation in the post-communist era. By the 1990s some had reverted to former systems of government whilst others were evolving new approaches (Newman and Thornley, 1996). The following sections provide a brief description of different national planning systems. Whilst there are many common features, there are also considerable variations to powers, duties and styles of planning contingent upon local historical, geographic and cultural characteristics.

The British and Irish family

United Kingdom

In 2012 the UK had a population of 63.9 million with a density second only to the Benelux countries and a population growth rate amongst the highest in Europe. GDP per capita was similar to Germany's but unemployment was higher. The country is institutionally and culturally rather centralized and dominated by the influence of the capital city, London. Within the UK the modern planning system dates back to the Town and Country Planning Act, 1947, although the system was modified by further major legislation in 1968, 1990, 2004 and 2011. Whilst it was once possible to talk of a British planning system, with increasing devolution of political and legal powers to Scotland, Wales and Northern Ireland, there are significant distinctions emerging between the constituent countries of the UK.

In England central government is responsible for planning legislation, through the Department for Communities and Local Government (DCLG), and determines not only what statutory plans should be produced at each level of government but also the general aims and policy approaches to be adopted in those plans. There is currently no regional tier of government, except in London where the Greater London Authority has strategic planning powers. Between 2004 and 2010 the

Labour Government established Regional Assemblies that were required to produce regional development strategies, and Regional Development Agencies to promote regional economic development. Both were abandoned by the Coalition Government after 2010, with the economic development function being taken over by business-led Local Enterprise Partnerships (LEPs).

There are 326 local planning authorities in England, including 201 non-metropolitan (or shire) districts, 36 metropolitan boroughs (generally the larger cities) and 32 London boroughs plus the City of London. The main planning document local planning authorities are required to prepare is the Local Plan which sets out planning policies and proposals for the whole local authority area. Their content must be supported by an up-to-date evidence base and should be consistent with the principles and policies set out in the *National Planning Policy Framework* (*NPPF*) (DCLG, 2012). Local Plans may be complemented by additional 'supplementary planning documents' for specific areas or topics. Where development requires planning permission, the local planning authority must decide on the granting of such permission (development management) in accordance with the Local Plan unless material considerations indicate otherwise. Thus the system allows local planners rather more discretion in decision making than is the case in some other European planning systems.

Key strategic planning problems facing the country include rapid population growth and uneven regional development, with strong economic growth and associated congestion and housing shortage in London and the south-east, contrasted with economic stagnation and under-used social capital in some other regions. Industrial restructuring and outworn urban infrastructure has led to major problems of urban regeneration in many cities.

According to the *NPPF*, 'Local Plans are key to delivering sustainable development that reflects the vision and aspirations of local communities' (DCLG, 2012, para. 150). Local Plans are expected to set out strategic priorities and policies for the area including the delivery of homes and jobs; provision of retail, leisure and other commercial development; infrastructure for transport, telecommunications, waste management, water supply and wastewater; flood risk and coastal change management; provision of minerals and energy (including heat); provision of health, security, community and cultural infrastructure and other local facilities; climate change mitigation and adaptation; the conservation and enhancement of the natural and historic environment, including landscape (DCLG, 2012, para. 156).

One of the problems with this system is that in the absence of any higher tier regional or sub-regional plans there is a danger of a lack of coordination between plans for neighbouring districts and a difficulty in making decisions that have 'larger than local' significance (for example the location of a regional airport or the distribution of housing development). To overcome the general difficulty of strategic decision making the Localism Act, 2011, placed a 'duty to cooperate' on local planning authorities, requiring them to engage constructively with neighbouring authorities on strategic cross-boundary matters. With regard to the situation in the conurbations, the Local Democracy, Economic Development and Construction Act, 2009 (extended by the Localism Act, 2011), permitted local authorities to come together to create a 'combined authority' which could pool appropriate responsibilities and receive delegated powers from central government, particularly regarding economic development, regeneration and transport (essentially, strategic planning). By 2014 four such authorities had been created in Greater Manchester, Sheffield City Region, the North-east, and Liverpool City Region. With the intention of giving more power to local communities the Localism Act, 2011, also introduced a new level of Neighbourhood Plans, through which parishes or neighbourhood forums could set policies to determine planning applications within their areas. Neighbourhood Plans must be in general conformity with the strategic policies of the Local Plan.

The Scottish Government set out its long-term strategic ambitions and the framework for planning in Scotland in the *National Planning Framework for Scotland* which was first published in 2004 and amended in 2009 (Scottish Government, 2009). Within the spatial and policy frame provided by this document a single tier of 32 unitary local authorities prepare Local Development Plans, except in the four city-regions of Aberdeen, Dundee-Perth, Edinburgh and Glasgow where the constituent local authorities together prepare city-regional Strategic Development Plans. The system of development management is similar to England.

Planning policy in Wales is broadly the same as in England. However, one key difference is that the Welsh Government, in addition to providing planning policy guidance to its 22 constituent local authorities, has prepared a national *Wales Spatial Plan* (Welsh Government, 2004). This policy guidance and plan provide the framework within which each Welsh local authority produces their own Local Development Plan.

The situation in Northern Ireland is a little different. Formerly a function of the Northern Ireland Government, planning was devolved in April 2015 to 11 local authorities in the shape of 'community planning', which is:

a process led by councils in conjunction with partners and communities to develop and implement a shared vision for their area, a long term vision which relates to all aspects of community life and which also involves working together to plan and deliver better services which make a real difference to people's lives. (DOE, 2013, p. 1)

The community planning process will inform the preparation of a council's Local Development Plan which will give effect to the spatial aspects of the community plan (Lloyd and Peel, 2012). This is an attempt to better integrate spatial planning with a community's broader aspirations for the future of their area.

Ireland

Ireland has a population of 4.6 million. Apart from the cities of Dublin, Cork and Limerick, the country is largely rural. It is the least urbanized and has the lowest population density of any of the European countries included in this chapter. Its economy is increasingly dominated by the service sector and was hit badly by the post-2008 economic crisis. Although it has recovered well and GDP per capita is high, unemployment remains stubbornly high. It has a young population and a low old-age dependency ratio. Ireland was part of the UK until the early part of the twentieth century and in consequence the two countries retain strong similarities in terms of their legal and governance systems.

Economic growth has been uneven and the National Spatial Strategy is seeking a better balance of social, economic and physical development across the country. The Ministry for the Environment, Community and Local Government is responsible for developing planning policy and legislation. There are 88 local planning authorities including 29 county councils and a number of urban authorities of different types. Since the 1990s a system of regional planning has brought greater coordination and consistency to the work of local planning authorities and to support regional development. Each local planning authority must prepare and keep up to date a Development Plan for their area which states the authority's policies for land use and development control. More detailed Local Area Plans can be prepared for specific towns or districts where necessary.

Examples from the Napoleonic family

France

Metropolitan France (excluding overseas territories) has a population of 65.6 million and continues to grow despite economic stagnation and high levels of unemployment. It has a relatively low level of urbanization and a low overall density of population. In France, as in the UK, development and growth are spatially concentrated around the capital and other key metropolitan areas with rural depopulation a problem in some more remote regions.

It has a unitary system of government but since the 1980s substantial powers have been devolved to the 22 regions, 96 départements and 36,697 communes. In the major conurbations, the constituent communes are grouped together to form a Communauté Urbaine, the purpose of which is to provide coordinated strategic leadership and joint administration of large cities, especially when the urban area is spread over a large number of communes. For example, the Lille Métropole Communauté Urbaine, covering a total of 85 communes in the Lille-Roubaix-Tourcoing conurbation, was founded in 1967 and has a population of just over 1.2 million (of which only 20 % live in the core city of Lille itself).

The country has a long tradition of both regional and urban planning. Today the key strategic plan in most areas is the Schéma de Cohérence Territoriale (SCOT). This may be produced by a Communauté Urbaine or any other appropriate local authority area and sets out a medium to long term plan for the spatial development of its territory. All SCOTs have similar general objectives: equilibrium and balanced development; the renewal of urban areas; social mix; efficient management of land; environmental conservation and protection.

A typical SCOT will comprise three documents: a rapport de présentation that reports on current and forecast socio-economic and environmental conditions and the needs for intervention; a projet d'aménagement et de développement durable (PADD) which explains the agency's aims and objectives for each field of policy (economic development, housing, transport, environmental protection and so on) and must conform with the principles of sustainable development; and a document d'orientation et d'objectifs (DOO) which provides details of implementation, determining the broad pattern of land use, the balance between urban development and environmental protection, identifying key infrastructure investments and proposals for urban regeneration.

Below the level of the SCOT, the Plan Local d'Urbanisme (PLU) is a detailed land use planning document prepared by a commune (or group of communes) and forming the basis for development control. According to national regulations, the PLU will zone the territory into: U, existing urban areas where development will be permitted; UA, future urban areas where development will be permitted; A, rural areas where only development related to the rural economy will be permitted; N, protected areas where no development will be permitted.

Additionally, the PLU will set out regulations regarding changes of use, building lines, heights, density, design and utility requirements, as well as development constraints such as the protection of historic monuments or areas of flood risk. In France the density of development is commonly measured by the coefficient d'occupation des sols (COS), which is the amount of permitted development floorspace as a proportion of the surface area of the site. Thus a COS of 0.5 on a suburban site of 500m^2 would permit a development of up to a total of 250m^2 floorspace, whereas a COS of 1.5 on the same size of site in a town centre would allow a development of up to 750m^2. When combined with regulations about building heights and building lines, this gives French planners strong controls over the built form of development.

The development of large housing estates by speculative developers is still fairly unusual in France. On the other hand, there is quite a high proportion of self-build developments on what are known as 'lotissements', where a developer will obtain permission for an estate (usually housing but some light industrial parks are developed this way) subject to regulations about building density, design and so on. The developer will set out the site, provide access roads and utilities, then sell off individual plots (sub-divisions) to individuals who can then build the house of their dreams in conformity with the agreed design and layout regulations.

In addition to these regulatory plans, the French planning system also embraces l'urbanisme opérationnel (operational planning) concerned with implementing urban change through planning, designing, managing and implementing urban projects. A key tool is the zone d'aménagement concerté (ZAC) by which an area can be identified for comprehensive (re)development with stronger than normal powers over land acquisition, development planning and implementation.

Belgium

Belgium is a federal kingdom with 11.1 million inhabitants, a high density of population and a very high level of urbanization. The population is rapidly expanding and is divided between a Flemish-speaking community in the north and west of the country and a French-speaking community in the south and east, with a small German-speaking enclave near the eastern border. For fairly complex historical reasons the government of the country is divided between the Federal Government, responsible for foreign affairs, defence and security, national economic issues and communications (for example, postal services, railways); three language-based Communities with responsibility for cultural matters, education, personal and social services; and three Regions (Flanders, which is co-terminus with the Flemish community; Wallonia, which includes the French and German speaking communities; and the bilingual Brussels Capital Region) with responsibility for economic development, urban and regional planning, housing, energy and environmental policy. Within this structure, local government is provided through 10 provinces and 589 communes.

The planning system and the nature of planning problems vary between the regions. Flanders is the largest region. It is prosperous and growing, with a population of about 6 million people and a density of 440 ppkm², making it one of the most urbanized regions in Europe. Despite the dominance of Antwerp, Ghent and nearby Brussels, the urban structure is fragmented and sprawling. The planning system in Flanders comprises three tiers of plans: the Ruimtelijk Structuurplan Vlaanderen (Regional Spatial Structure Plan); the Provinciaal Ruimtelijk Structuurplan (Provincial Structure Plan) and the Gemeentelijk Ruimtelijk Structuurplan (Municipal Structure Plan). There are, in addition, regulations determining the physical form of development.

In contrast, Wallonia has a recent history of industrial restructuring that has deprived it of much of its former heavy industry (coal, steel, textiles) and left a legacy of brownfields and a high level of social deprivation. The regional Schéma de Développement de l'Espace Régional (SDER) is based upon the principles of sustainable development and social cohesion and is intended to provide a regional structure for development and a regional level of policy integration, urban regeneration, infrastructure improvements, protection and enhancement of regional heritage and natural resources. Within the framework provided by the SDER, local authorities develop their own urban policies and plans.

The strategic plan for the Brussels Capital Region is known as the Plan Regional de Développement Durable (PRDD) and identifies five challenges: rapid population growth putting pressure on the housing stock and services; the need for more jobs and training; environmental issues; poverty and a lack of social cohesion; developing the role of Brussels as an international city. Urban regeneration forms an important element in the planning policies of the Brussels Capital Region. The Region works in partnership with local communes within the framework of neighbourhood contracts to implement housing renewal, provision for local industrial and craft-based development, the enhancement of public spaces, and strengthening community social, cultural and sporting infrastructure.

The Netherlands

The Netherlands has a population of 16.8 million people, it is highly urbanized and has the highest population density of any of the countries discussed in this chapter. The population is relatively young and growing with a high level of GDP per capita and a relatively low unemployment rate. The Randstad conurbation (Amsterdam, Utrecht, Rotterdam and The Hague) is particularly densely populated and housing shortage has been a major problem. Climate change and rising sea levels present major environmental challenges in an area where much urban development is below or near sea level.

The country is divided into 12 provinces and 418 municipalities. Each tier of government has planning responsibilities. For many years the country had a clear hierarchical system of plans, with central government providing a national Spatial Planning Strategy, within which each province would produce a Streekplan (Regional Plan) and each municipality would produce a Gemeentelijk Structuurplan (Municipal Structure Plan) and, for previously undeveloped areas, a Bestemmingsplan (Local Land Use Plan). Deciding that the historic planning system was overly complex, a new system was introduced in 2008 with the intention of simplifying decision making and improving the effectiveness of planning. Under this system all the upper tiers of planning were replaced by national, regional and local Structuurvisie (structural visions) which set out the basic principles of spatial policy but, unlike the previous system of plans, are not legally binding on lower tiers of government. A further difference is that municipalities must prepare and keep up-to-date a Bestemmingsplan for the whole of their area. These changes were intended to increase the flexibility of policy makers to respond to change and enhance the general power of local government, thus following in a similar direction to changes in the English planning system since 2010 (Schmitt, 2013).

Germany: an example from the Germanic family

Germany has a population of 82.0 million. The density of population and GDP per capita are similar to the UK but the unemployment rate is lower. Unlike the UK or Netherlands, Germany suffers from a declining population, particularly in the area of former East Germany where housing surplus and a lack of economic growth are serious problems. In the Ruhr and elsewhere industrial restructuring has led to major problems of urban regeneration.

Germany is a federal country divided into 16 constituent states (Länder). These vary considerably in size from the city-states of Berlin, Hamburg and Bremen to large sprawling regions such as Bavaria (centred on Munich) and North-Rhine Westphalia (NRW), the most populous state. (An amalgamation of rural Westphalia, the Ruhr industrial district and the northern Rhineland, NRW includes four of Germany's largest cities: Cologne, Düsseldorf, Essen and Dortmund.) Below the level of the Länder, local government is divided between upper-tier Kreis (counties) and lower tier Gemeinden (municipalities), except in the larger cities which are unitary Kreis-frei Stadt combining the functions of both tiers.

The planning system in Germany is hierarchical and fairly complex. Although the federal government has only limited planning powers it does offer general guidance and principles for spatial planning and has responsibility for national economic development and communications.

Apart from this the highest level of planning authority is the Land and there are significant variations in planning systems between different Länder. A look at NRW serves to illustrate the different layers and responsibilities.

The NRW Government is responsible for a Land-wide plan setting out broad development policies and proposals. Known as the Landes-entwicklungsplan Nordrhein-Westfalen (LEP NRW), it sets out a fairly generalized framework for the future spatial and urban structure of the region. However, it also contains more detailed proposals to tackle particular problems such as the overloading of the main metropolitan areas in the west (Cologne and Dusseldorf) and the need to stabilize and develop city networks in the more rural east as well as strengthening local economies and transport infrastructure across its territory. Counteracting the overloading of metropolitan areas is to be achieved through a process of 'decentralized concentration' whereby development pressures can be steered away from the conurbation cores to other parts of the agglomeration by means of 'inter-local' cooperation and collaborative planning, that is reducing densities at the centre and increasing them in the suburbs (Knapp, 1998).

The Land is divided into five Regierungsbezirk or sub-regions: Düssel-dorf, Cologne, Arnsberg (which includes the city of Dortmund), Detmold and Münster. For each sub-region a 'Regionalplan' provides a link between the LEP and the more specific detail and guidance required by municipalities preparing their own land use plans.

The Kreis and Kreis-frei stadt then prepare a Flächennutzungsplan (F-plan) for land use development in their area. Thus, the city of Dort-mund prepares an F-plan within the context provided by the Regional-plan for the Arnsberg Regierungsbezirk. The most recent at the time of writing was prepared in 2004. Legally the F-plan is a preliminary land use plan covering the next 10–15 years, binding upon the municipality but not on land owners or developers. Within the framework provided by the F-plan, detailed Bebauungsplane (binding land use plans) are prepared by the municipality to control the development of particular sites and set out precise requirements with regard to land use and built form, including building densities, building lines, heights, landscaping and access. This is the principal way in which development is controlled in the German planning system.

Denmark: an example from the Scandinavian family

Denmark has 5.6 million inhabitants of which about one-third live in the Copenhagen city-region, although the overall population density is quite low. The population is expanding and dependency ratios are average. GDP per capita is amongst the highest in Europe. Climate change and sea level rise are a particular threat to coastal cities such as Copenhagen. A related concern is keeping the country's extensive coastal areas as free from development as possible.

Following the reform of local government in 2007 a new planning system emerged. Below the central government there are now five regional councils and 98 municipalities. Under the Planning Act, which came into force in 1992 but has since been updated to reflect new concerns and administrative changes, the role of the planning system is seen as guiding and shaping the pattern of development across the country; conserving urban, rural, and coastal heritage and environments; providing protection against all form of pollution; and involving stakeholders in decision making as far as possible.

At national level, spatial planning is the responsibility of the Department for the Environment which sets government policy, prepares a national planning report every four years, directs certain initiatives, such as the updated Copenhagen Finger Plan 2007, and can veto municipal plans that contradict national interests.

Regional councils prepare regional spatial development plans which reflect the region's business development strategy and sectoral policies (for example education), and set out the general pattern and direction of development and infrastructure provision. Regions may veto municipal plans that contradict these plans.

Municipalities prepare comprehensive Municipal Plans and more detailed legally binding Local Plans. Municipal Plans establish the general structure and objectives for land use and development within the area and provide the framework for the preparation of Local Plans. The Municipal Plan typically includes policies for the amount and location of urban development and community facilities; transport and infrastructure provision; policies to control retail development and industrial location; policies for the protection of urban heritage, agricultural areas, natural landscapes, water areas and coasts. A Local Plan is required where a major development is proposed and provides detailed regulations on the use of land, density, site layout, size and form of buildings. It has similarities to the Dutch Bestemmingsplan and the German Bebauungsplan.

An unusual feature of the planning system in Denmark and elsewhere in Scandinavia is that regional and local plans have to be adopted, or amended, by the incoming administration after each regional council or municipal election.

Contemporary plans for Greater Copenhagen have evolved from the famous 'finger plan' first created in 1947. The 2007 Finger Plan was based on a directive from central government and established a growth framework that concentrates development close to the radial transportation system. The core city (central zone) is the focus for urban renaissance and regeneration where needed. Towards the periphery development is to be located where it can make use of, or strengthen, existing public transport services, whereas the more intense generators of transport demand, such as large office blocks, are expected to locate close to metro stations. Between these peripheral lines of development lie green wedges protected from development (Danish Ministry of the Environment, 2007).

Poland: an example from Eastern Europe

The Republic of Poland is a unitary state in north-central Europe with a population of 38.5 million. It is a large country with a relatively low population density. Poland is a young country with a low level of old-age dependency and although GDP per capita is low the growth rate is relatively high. It is amongst the most successful of the former state-socialist economies. After the Second World War it was a socialist state under the influence of the Soviet Union, until 1989 when it became a democratic free-market country. It joined the European Union in 2003. Administratively the country is divided into 16 voivodeship (regions), 379 powiats (counties) and 2,478 gminas (municipalities). Larger cities have county status.

The country has a long industrial history, especially in Silesia in the south and the Baltic Sea ports to the north. The capital, Warsaw, has an international reach across central and Eastern Europe in financial and other services. Key planning problems have been associated with adjusting from a state-socialist to a market economy, and this has led to some industrial restructuring and problems of urban regeneration.

Central Government is responsible for maintaining a collaborative national strategic development planning process known as Koncepcja Przestrzennego Zagospodarowania Kraju which provides a general direction for regional and urban development. The regions make comprehensive strategies for the future economic and social development of their region. Within this context they also prepare a regional spatial development plan that elaborates the direction of urban development, settlement patterns, infrastructure planning and environmental protection.

At the local level, municipalities prepare Local Development Strategies that elaborate national and regional requirements at the local level as well as setting out local spatial development plans. These local plans are expected to: survey and report on local physical planning issues and policies; establish principles for sustainable local development, land use zoning, infrastructure development, protection of natural and built environment; and identify areas for urban regeneration. At a more detailed level the Local Physical Development Plan provides the detailed planning requirements for the development of an area: typically a parcel of land where development is imminent. These plans establish the detailed physical planning requirements for development, including land use, infrastructure and access requirements, density and sub-division (EUKN, 2005).

Planning systems in the Americas, Asia and Australasia

USA

Across the majority of the USA there are three levels of government: federal, state and local. Planning systems and administrative arrangements and terminology vary from state to state and even between cities but responsibilities for urban planning generally rest with local government: counties or municipalities. In many cities a planning commission has been established in order to distance the planning and zoning process from direct political control. If there is a gap in the American planning system it is the lack of regional planning in many states. This makes such tasks as controlling urban sprawl across municipal boundaries difficult to implement.

Two other characteristics distinguish American planning. The first is the rise in the role of non-governmental organizations (NGOs) both as agencies for public action (for example in housing) and as advocates for particular social groups or political concerns (for example environmental groups such as the Sierra Club). The other is the way that planning decisions can be subject to legal challenge in a manner that is not commonly experienced in most European countries. Urban planning in the USA takes place within the context of a society where there is often a preference for market solutions to urban problems rather than state intervention. The notion of planning and state control of land use and development rights remains a contested issue, particularly where decisions might reduce the potential value of land, and is tested in the courts from time to time. 'Planning proposals must anticipate legal challenges. The threat of litigation is chilling, whatever the reason, and it is difficult to see its results, which are largely in the form of initiatives not taken' (Teitz, 2002, p. 187).

But the federal government is not without influence in city development and urban planning. Since 1965 the Department of Housing and Urban Development (HUD) has undertaken research and policy development on housing and sustainable communities and provided funding and administration for various public and social housing programmes. Similarly, since 1970, the United States Environmental Protection Agency (EPA) has had federal responsibility for protecting human health and the environment. Working in consultation with state and other agencies, it maintains and enforces national environmental standards as well as conducting research, training and environmental assessment. Through the 1956 National Interstate and Defense Highways Act the Federal Government provides the strategy and majority funding for the system of interstate highways across the country. Today this infrastructure is criticized for contributing to urban sprawl around many American cities.

American planning has a long history. From the earliest new settlements on the eastern seaboard, the majority of towns were set out with a gridiron of wide streets enclosing developable street blocks, in stark contrast to the organic growth of the post-medieval European cities with their inefficient use of land and ever-present risks of fire and disease. Many early city planners of the USA saw aesthetic beauty as an important planning goal. Though subsequently criticized for its over-emphasis on physical design, the City Beautiful movement responded to the squalor of the nineteenth century city with the idea of building cities that incorporated efficient, healthy and grandiose designs with well landscaped avenues, squares and circles, displaying fine views and lined with elegant buildings. One of the leaders of the movement was Daniel Burnham who, together with Edward Bennett, prepared one of the earliest city plans in the USA: the comprehensive 1909 Chicago Plan. Today many American cities still prepare comprehensive plans for their communities. These plans – known as 'masterplans' – provide the goals and strategies for the development of public policy in relation to transportation, public utilities, land use zoning, environmental protection, housing and community development. These are not usually legally binding documents and in most states the legal framework that permits the preparation of comprehensive plans constitutes a right given to local governments rather than a duty.

After the First World War, the emphasis in planning shifted away from aesthetics towards the control and separation of incompatible land uses and the protection of property with the introduction of zoning regulations. The Standard State Zoning Enabling Act (SSZEA) of the 1920s, prepared by the Federal Government but enacted by individual states, provided the legal basis for land use zoning. Gradually more and more cities introduced zoning regulations to control the use of land and the density and form of development. Today there are many different methods of zoning and it represents the principal means by which development is controlled in most American cities. Zoning has been criticized for encouraging urban sprawl, imposing unnecessarily rigid regulations on the use of land and discouraging the mixed uses that modern ideas about sustainable development require. In some cities zoning is also said to have been used as a tool for social exclusion, for example by excluding (cheaper) higher density housing development from affluent suburbs. One response to this has been new urbanism movement. Similar to its European counterpart – the compact city – new urbanism promotes safe, walkable, mixed use and mixed income neighbourhoods, incorporating more traditional forms of local planning, including traditional street patterns and transit-orientated development (TOD). As with the related idea of smart growth, the intention is to create a more compact, less sprawling, less car-orientated, more sustainable form of development.

The City of Baltimore provides a good example of the workings of urban planning in the USA. Here responsibility for planning lies with a Planning Commission whose duties include preparing a comprehensive masterplan for the city, land use zoning ordinances and a capital spending programme. In 2006, following an extensive process of consultation and community participation, the city published its first comprehensive plan in more than 30 years: *Live-earn-play-learn* (City of Baltimore, 2006). The plan conforms to the visions of the State of Maryland's 1992 Planning Act and is aligned with the Maryland 1997 Smart Growth Initiatives. According to the plan development is to be concentrated in suitable areas, especially existing urban areas, and sensitive areas are to be protected. The plan responds to the city's housing needs which include a changing population structure, expanding demand for condominiums and a growing commuter market, as well as supply problems associated with the ageing of the existing housing stock. It supports economic growth in port and defence related industries as well as other burgeoning employment sectors, and identifies land for commercial or industrial development near existing transportation centres, as well as investing in new transportation infrastructure. The plan also aims to enhance cultural, entertainment and natural resource amenities, improvements in schools and the expansion of higher education opportunities as tools for human, community and economic development.

In Baltimore, the zoning framework dates back to the 1970s. In the following 30 years the city saw massive socio-economic changes including the redevelopment of the waterfront; the growth of service, technology, higher education and health-related industries; the decline of heavy industry; the suburbanization of retail development; and rising concern for urban and heritage conservation. There had also been major changes in the aims of policy both at federal and local levels, including the city's new comprehensive masterplan. All of these changes had implications for the Zoning Code which was rewritten in its entirety to make it consistent with the revised policies and to expedite development management (City of Baltimore, 2006).

Summing up the American planning system, Teitz comments that:

> as it has always been, planning is still at the mercy of political currents, but it does have a strong constituency at the local and state levels. If there are serious challenges on the scene, then there are also new forms of advocacy to counter them ... The paradox of planning in America is to try to make a better collective human life in an individualistic and capitalist society. (Teitz, 2002, p. 202)

China

With 1.35 billion people, the People's Republic of China is the largest country in the world in terms of population and the second largest in land area. It is governed by the Communist Party as a single-party state. The internal governance of the country is divided between 22 provinces, 5 autonomous regions, 4 centrally controlled municipalities (the conurbations of Beijing, Chongqing, Shanghai and Tianjin) and 2 special administrative regions (the former western colonies of Hong Kong and Macau).

Following reforms in the late 1970s the Chinese economy developed and expanded as a mixed economy (which has both command and market dimensions) to become one of the most important in the world. In consequence, China urbanized quickly with the proportion of people living in urban areas rising from around 20% in 1980 to more than 50% of the population in 2010. In consequence many cities underwent tremendous growth both densifying and sprawling, with new business districts but also increasingly, protected historic areas. In addition to the expansion of existing cities, new settlements were developed, many orientated towards particular functions such as industrial settlements, university towns, commuter suburbs or migrant enclaves (Ren, 2013).

This very rapid urban expansion and urban change required new mechanisms for urban planning and new policy goals. In a very different way to the UK and European examples above, the imperatives of economic growth drove the Chinese to move from a planned economy approach that reflected political goals, to a more market-friendly approach that would facilitate growth in the market economy, including land reform and greater respect for private property rights (Tang, 1997). According to Wu (2015) contemporary planning in China is embedded in two different and potentially conflicting traditions. For much of its history the traditional urban form in China was the walled city with strong conventions regarding the pattern of streets and the location of market-places, temples and other major elements (not unlike the Roman approach to city planning). In the actual design of specific cities these principles would be adapted to the local geographical situation (feng shui). The second tradition emerged through the opening up of China to the influence of western architects and planners, initially through developments in port cities such as Shanghai, Guangzhou and Ningbo in the late nineteenth century but subsequently through the use of western designers to advise on projects and most recently through China's engagement with the international academic community and planning discourse. The result has been a degree of fusion between the two traditions. Thus, 'despite the advocacy of various modernist concepts of metropolitan structure and urban forms, Chinese society retained some of the essential characteristics of traditional rural society' (Wu, 2015, p. 20).

The principal planning legislation is contained in the 1989 City Planning Act, supported by central government guidance on plan making processes and policies. The function of urban planning is seen as controlling and influencing city development and structure to reflect the rapidly changing socio-economic and environmental needs of Chinese cities. There is a strong preference for seeing cities develop in a 'rational', ordered and coordinated manner. There are two tiers of plans: chengshi zongti guihua (urban masterplans) that establish strategic development goals and the general direction of growth; and chengshi xiangxi guihua (detailed plans), which form the basis for development control. Urban masterplans typically span a 20-year period and are comprehensive in their coverage of policy issues including: population targets; directions of growth and urban structure; transportation, utility and infrastructure systems; flood prevention and environmental protection; conservation of natural and built environments and heritage; and urban renewal. They are also expected to consider issues of feasibility and implementation. Detailed plans are intended to confirm site boundaries and control land and building use, building densities, heights, access, layout and the provision of utilities.

In addition to these two formal tiers of plan, some other advisory planning mechanisms have emerged. A number of larger cities now benefit from a shiyu guihua (city-regional plan), a type of regional plan prepared to ensure the coordination of planning and development between central core cities and the surrounding suburbs; or a chengshi tixi guihua (urban system plan) that coordinates the planning of a network of towns and cities within an urban region. And between the level of urban masterplans and detailed plans, some cities have started to use chengshi fenqu guihua (intermediate urban district plans) in order to elaborate the strategic planning principles at a more detailed level and to clarify the planning intentions for a district or neighbourhood.

Thus the modern Chinese planning system has moved from a socialist ideology to a more pragmatic approach, increasingly driven by local growth-oriented development goals, to establish a strong hierarchy of plans at different scales and a system for the control of private development (Yeh and Wu, 1999). However, one of the critical emerging themes in Chinese public policy is that of environmental protection. Whilst the urban planning system is recognized to have a key role to play in achieving a better balance between economic development and environmental conservation, this view 'challenges the presumption in favour of development and sits uneasily with the role of planning as a political tool for capital accumulation' (Xu and Chung, 2014, p. 391). Thus in China, just as in many other countries, the tensions between short and long term development goals are keenly felt.

Australia

Australia is a federal country, established in 1901 through the coming together of six formerly self-governing British colonial states. With around 23.8 million people living in a country of 7.7 million km², it is one of the world's least densely populated countries, but this belies the fact that most of the population lives in a small number of densely occupied coastal zones. Together, the ten largest cities accommodate nearly 70 % of the population, making it a highly urbanized nation.

According to Freestone (2010), as a rapidly growing colonial country, much of the early town planning was concerned with the laying out of new towns and with suburban expansion. Gradually systems of land use zoning and development control were introduced. Through the twentieth century the evolution of urban planning was strongly influenced by UK and American planning theory and practice. The 1920s saw the emergence of some early comprehensive city-wide development plans, such as Melbourne's *Plan of General Development* (1929), and by the 1930s the agenda included concerns about the management of existing cities, especially with regard to housing quality and accessibility. The post-war period brought rapid urbanization and planned decentralization which continued through the 'long boom' of the next two decades. By the 1970s economic restructuring, a growing awareness of community issues and disenchantment with functional planning were forcing changes in the established planning wisdom.

> Inner-urban freeways were abandoned or put on hold, high rise public housing programmes terminated, and new area-based planning authorities instituted ... Heritage became an increasingly important cog of the new planning agenda. (Freestone, 2010, p. 34)

As in other western countries, the 1980s saw neo-liberal challenges to the planning orthodoxy and brought about changes that enhanced the role of planning in facilitating investment and growth whilst curtailing and streamlining its role in controlling development. But by the millennium rising and inescapable concerns about environmental degradation, climate change and social tensions within cities had moved the agenda on again. Since then Australia has moved beyond the simple importation of notions of good planning from the northern hemisphere to become a country that not only exports best practice in planning, particularly across the southern hemisphere, but also makes its own distinctive contribution to planning theory.

Today, the federal government exercises power over the national economy and financial system, communications, defence and international relations. It also funds (and influences) much of the expenditure of individual states, regulates development of national environmental significance and increasingly provides strategic planning guidance and advice – as evidenced by the emergence of a 'national urban policy' statement in 2011. This policy had three strategic goals:

- to harness the productivity of Australia's people and industry, by better managing our use of labour, creativity and knowledge, land and infrastructure;
- to advance the sustainability of Australia's natural and built environment, including through better resource and risk management;
- to enhance the liveability of our cities by promoting better urban design, planning and affordable access to recreational, cultural and community facilities. (Australian Government, 2011)

State governments are responsible for such matters as local government, urban development, housing, health, education and environmental protection. The precise nature of local government and urban planning systems varies between individual states, reflecting local conditions and political preferences. In the state of New South Wales responsibility for regional planning falls within the remit of the Department of Planning and Environment. The principal legislation governing planning in the state is the Environmental Planning and Assessment Act 1979, although in 2015 this was undergoing a process of reform to reflect the changing needs of the twenty-first century – particularly seeking faster decision making whilst accommodating greater community involvement.

The state produces thematic Environmental Planning Policies, intended to guide local responses to particular planning issues, for example: by providing a consistent planning regime for infrastructure and service provision across the state; another for the provision of affordable rental housing; and another establishing a process for assessing and identifying sites for urban renewal.

The state is also responsible for Regional Growth Plans. For this purpose the state has been sub-divided into ten sub-regions, each of which will benefit from a strategic plan providing a framework for the preparation of Local Environment Plans. For example, a regional growth plan for metropolitan Sydney (covering more than 40 local council areas and over 4 million people) was published in 2014. Reflecting national policy, this plan provides direction for economic growth, environmental management and liveability and a generalized strategy for the location of development over the following 20 years.

Local Environmental Plans are prepared by local councils and provide a basis for the control of development and protection of the environment. Since 2006 the state has tried to standardize and simplify the approach to the preparation of Local Environmental Plans by introducing a standard template that requires only one district-wide plan for each local council area and a standardized system of land use zoning. In so doing the state hopes that local plan making will be speeded up and plans more easily kept up to date, be more consistent between localities, better provide land for urban development whilst better protecting and managing natural environments and cultural heritage.

Increasingly cities across the world, and Sydney is no exception, find it helpful to prepare informal plans that can guide corporate thinking beyond the constraints imposed by these statutory development plans. The city has produced a number of these plans over the years. One of the most recent is *Sustainable Sydney 2030*. This shows the relationships between different elements of the city (localities, connections and flows) and sets out a strategic vision to achieve a more sustainable city. Its purpose is to provide a set of goals that can inform the working of different departments and agencies both within and beyond the City Council itself. According to Searle (2013) this trend towards a more 'relational' style of strategic planning in Australia has the potential to facilitate greater flexibility in detailed planning in response to unforeseen changes whilst staying within the framework of the strategy.

Planning at different scales

The previous section considered the variations in planning systems between countries and showed how these can be influenced by differences in history, geography, political ideologies and socio-economic conditions. This section will provide a series of short case studies that combine the illustration of planning styles in selected countries with a look at planning at different scales. These include a regional vision for

Flanders; the Dundee-Perth city-regional plan; a municipality-wide local plan from Halton in Merseyside; a complex development proposal from York; and a detailed Bebauungsplan (building plan) from Dortmund.

A vision for an urban region: Flanders in 2050

In 2012 the Flemish Government published a green paper setting out its vision for a spatial policy plan for Flanders. This affluent region is one of the most densely populated in Europe, located at the heart of the golden triangle between Paris, London and Frankfurt, and characterized by a growing population (expected to rise from 6 million in 2012 to 7 million by 2050), a fragmented and inefficient pattern of urbanization (often described as nebular urbanity) and the challenges of maintaining economic competitiveness and social inclusion (see Figure 2.1). The high density and interconnectedness of settlements brings, despite an intense public transport system, high car dependency and traffic congestion. The region is particularly vulnerable to climate change. Not only does a rise in sea level threaten the low lying coastal areas but changing patterns of precipitation are likely to bring more inland flooding. The region's pressured open land plays a vital role in providing for flood water containment during heavy rainfall, water storage during periods of drought, maintenance of biodiversity and accommodation for local food production and recreation. Flanders consumes more than the European average of non-renewable energy and progress towards a society consuming fewer raw materials is a priority.

Within this context the Green Paper proposes a spatial vision for 2050 based on a number of interconnected objectives (Vlaamse Overheid, 2012). The first four objectives are concerned with developing Flanders as a strong regional economy:

- growing with less space – using the existing urban area more efficiently, to increase the value added (for example, in terms of output, employment or housing) of each parcel of land;
- connecting Flanders – strengthening transport connections between the key Flemish ports of Antwerp, Zeebrugge and Ghent with their hinterlands in Belgium, the Netherlands and beyond, and exploiting the potential of key passenger interchanges (Brussels National Airport and high-speed railway stations) for intensive metropolitan development;
- innovative clusters – providing for research, development and modern manufacturing activity in innovative clusters which would offer scale economies whilst adopting the principle of 'mixed use where possible, separation where necessary';
- excellent metropolitan environments in attractive urban regions – urban regions will be the drivers of economic development in Flanders

so in order to be competitive towns and cities must offer high quality, efficient, accessible and distinctive urban environments.

There are five objectives concerned with living conditions and social issues:

- recognizability and involvement – capitalizing on diversity and protecting distinctive spatial environments that give people a sense of place, belonging and ownership, whilst maintaining a balance between public and private space and avoiding inconvenience and nuisance;
- proximity and accessibility as a guiding principle – clustering human activities (home, work, play) in a balanced way to maintain accessibility whilst reducing the demand for mobility and shifting modal split away from the motor vehicle and its associated costs of infrastructure, energy and distribution;
- polycentric urban regions – to develop towns and cities as urban regions with multiple cores, each with its own character and functions, modernizing older residential areas, improving energy efficiency, increasing capacity and density where appropriate, and strengthening social cohesion;
- making choices in suburban areas – transforming fragmented landscapes and mono-functional residential environments (urban sprawl) through selective densification in more accessible areas, doing nothing in more stable areas but limiting further sprawl and avoiding this kind of urban form in the future;
- vital countryside – preventing further fragmentation and 'creeping' urbanization and protecting the countryside's capacity for the essential functions of nature, farming, biodiversity and water, whilst other human activities will be encouraged to locate in village centres rather than the countryside.

The final objectives concern the creation of resilient space:

- shockproof territories – reducing vulnerability from external shocks and threats, organizing space more efficiently to minimize waste of resources and energy, increasing the proportion of locally produced and renewable energy, better management of the water environment, reusing residual heat from local sources and consuming locally produced food;
- climate change sponge – limiting surface sealing and using open land to absorb the impacts of flooding and droughts, and using open land to reduce 'heat-island' effects in urban areas;
- guaranteeing green-blue arteries – protection of existing green spaces and watercourses to provide for water management, biodiversity and

Figure 2.1 *The fragmented pattern of urbanization in Flanders*

Source: drawn by A.L. Couch; based upon data from Engelen et al. (2005).

Note: A key ambition of the plan is to improve the efficiency of urban land use and to limit further urban sprawl.

recreation and to introduce additional green-blue arteries when planning new developments;

• room for energy transition – minimizing energy demand through spatial policies, mixing uses and densification, increasing the energy efficiency of buildings, facilitating the transfer of energy from functions producing a surplus to functions needing energy, increasing the supply of energy from biomass, wind, waste and other renewable sources (Vlaamse Overheid, 2012).

The Green Paper proposes a bold vision but climate change and the need for efficiency in resource use impose strong imperatives, and the towns and cities of Flanders have a huge potential for intensification. It is estimated that there are 100,000 hectares of underused or vacant parcels of land capable of redevelopment within the existing built-up areas. In general terms this vision represents a shift from planning for expansion to planning for transformation. This means that implementation will be more difficult than in the past. The processes of urban design will be more complex than when planning for urban expansion and the legal and economic complexities will be greater. The translation of the vision into policies, spending programmes and regulations will have to be agreed and supported by the Flemish government and then negotiated with provincial and local administrations. Those who finance, develop and manage the built environment will have to be persuaded of the benefits of new goals and new ways of working.

Planning the city-region: TAYplan

The Planning etc. (Scotland) Act of 2006 required the preparation of Strategic Development Plans for Scotland's four city-regions. One such plan was TAYplan, covering the Dundee-Perth city-region. Because the plan extended over a number of local authority areas, an independent core planning team was established, reporting to a Board and a Joint Committee of the local authorities concerned. The purpose of this strategic planning process was to prepare, review and monitor a concise and visionary strategic land use plan for the city-region. The plan was prepared within the context of the *National Planning Framework for Scotland* (Scottish Government, 2009) and itself provides a 20-year vision for the future and the framework for local councils to prepare Local Development Plans that provide more detailed policies and identify development sites.

Starting in 2009, the first year of the strategic planning process involved the preparation of an issues report followed by a 12-week consultation period. Twelve months later a draft plan was completed and a further period allowed for representations. It was then submitted to the Scottish Government in late 2011 and approved in June 2012. The aims of the plan were: to achieve sustainable economic growth; to shape better quality places; to improve the quality of life; to respond to climate change; and to minimize resource consumption.

These aims were to be achieved through identifying locational priorities for growth; responsible management of built and natural assets; and shaping better quality places through the location, design and layout of development. Specific policies covered strategic development areas, housing, town centres and energy and waste/resource management infrastructure.

The plan set out to ensure that for all types of land use the location, design, layout and density of development would be the outcome of a proper understanding of that locality and how it worked. Various factors were to be taken into account prior to development taking place. These included improving resilience to risk; minimizing resource consumption; improving transport integration, community infrastructure and waste management. Climate change mitigation focussed on locating development in major centres to reduce travel demand, and avoiding development in areas of flood risk and coastal erosion. How development enables the community to contribute to a low carbon and low resource consumption economy and zero waste were fundamental to place quality in the proposed plan.

The plan sought to protect finite resources for long term food and resource security. These required the relative importance of development location versus its resource importance to be fundamental considerations in decision making. Moving to a low carbon and zero waste economy presents business and job opportunities, for example in the development of offshore renewable energy. The plan therefore protected the port infrastructure required for its support. The focus on development in principal settlements and place quality was intended to ensure that people would want to live and invest in such places and could live more sustainable lives.

The originality of the plan lay not only in its forward thinking policy objectives but also in its style (Figure 2.2). It differed from the previous Structure Plan in having a more strategic focus and comprising only 24 pages with 8 policies and 2 proposals. Presentation was very graphical with many ideas communicated through maps, plans or diagrams, and it was accompanied by a Proposal Action Programme explaining how the plan would be delivered. The plan was prepared on time and to budget, achieved through leadership, strong project management and collaborative partnership working between the agencies concerned. This approach with strong forward planning of work and transparency with partners promoted ownership across the board and ensured understanding and recognition of the plan across the city-region. Local councils and other key agencies helped inform and shape the plan from the outset. There were workshops, elected member briefings and meetings. Communities were involved throughout by various means including media coverage, public information events, an online interactive questionnaire, and secondary school workshops.

With its focus on sustainable development and climate change mitigation and adaptation and its approach to the plan making process, TAYplan represented a model of modern strategic planning at the city-regional scale.

Planning the town and district: Halton Local Plan

Halton is a unitary authority of 120,000 people, comprising the twin towns of Widnes on the north bank of the River Mersey and Runcorn on the south bank. The towns are linked by important regional rail and road bridges and a major regional investment in a second road bridge has recently commenced. Widnes originally developed as an important centre of the chemical industry in the second half of the 19th century. Runcorn became established as a port and industrial centre following the opening of the Bridgewater Canal and later, the Manchester Ship Canal. In 1964 it was designated a new town intended to accommodate

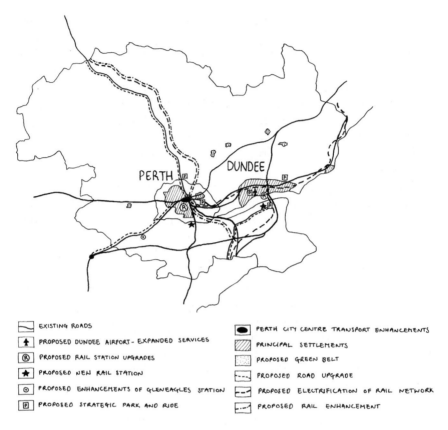

EXISTING ROADS

PROPOSED DUNDEE AIRPORT- EXPANDED SERVICES

PROPOSED RAIL STATION UPGRADES

PROPOSED NEW RAIL STATION

PROPOSED ENHANCEMENTS OF GLENEAGLES STATION

PROPOSED STRATEGIC PARK AND RIDE

PERTH CITY CENTRE TRANSPORT ENHANCEMENTS

PRINCIPAL SETTLEMENTS

PROPOSED GREEN BELT

PROPOSED ROAD UPGRADE

PROPOSED ELECTRIFICATION OF RAIL NETWORK

PROPOSED RAIL ENHANCEMENT

Figure 2.2   *TAYplan: proposals map*

Source: Drawn by A.L. Couch; based upon plans from SPDA (2012).

Note: The integrated planning of the interconnected city-regions of Perth and Dundee encourages collaboration between the constituent local authorities in the area and seeks to avoid unnecessary and inefficient competition.

overspill population from the Liverpool conurbation. In both towns industrial restructuring and decline have left a legacy of urban environmental problems and high levels of social deprivation.

The Borough of Halton faces a number of planning challenges, including the need to:

- tackle social deprivation, ageing and health issues amongst the population;
- alleviate unemployment and stimulate economic growth;
- remediate and reuse derelict and contaminated land;
- maintain and enhance local heritage assets including its waterside environments and green infrastructure;

- reduce congestion and support travel by sustainable modes;
- maintain and improve the town centres;
- respond to the threats posed by climate change and the risks of major accidents, flooding, contamination and pollution.

The Halton Local Plan was adopted in 2013 to provide an overarching strategy for future development with the objective of responding to these challenges and creating a thriving and vibrant Borough (Halton BC, 2013, para. 3.11).

The key policy (CS1) is Halton's Spatial Strategy. It set targets for the scale of development required by 2028 – 9,930 net additional dwellings; 313 ha (gross) of land for employment purposes; 35,000 m^2 of town centre retailing; 22,000 m^2 of retail warehousing – with specific location policies set out later in the document. The spatial strategy is focused around a mix of urban regeneration and limited greenfield expansion but will be largely achieved through the delivery of four 'Key Areas of Change' across the Borough where the majority of new development will be located: Ditton, South Widnes, West and East Runcorn. Only in East Runcorn will there be significant greenfield expansion. Outside of these areas the priority will be to reuse previously developed land, whilst maintaining the rural character and green infrastructure of the Borough's villages and green belt.

Housing requirements and the location of new housing are considered in some detail in the plan. The requirement was calculated in accordance with national government guidance to maintain a five-year supply of deliverable housing land. The sources of housing land supply included sites that already had planning permission or were partially completed, sites identified in previous plans, identified housing opportunities within the Key Areas of Change, other new housing or mixed-use allocations, and appropriate windfall development. The plan proposed that an average of at least 40 % of new residential development should be on previously developed land – significantly less ambitious than the previous national government target of 60 %, which was exceeded in many areas in the previous decade. A minimum density of 30 dwellings per hectare (dpha) will be sought, with 40 dpha the target in more accessible locations. On schemes of more than 10 dwellings affordable housing is to be provided at a rate of 25 % of the total residential units proposed.

Similarly, a five-year supply of employment land will be maintained, the quantity required also having been calculated in accordance with government guidance. The character and location of this supply will reflect an emphasis on Halton's economic growth potential in logistics and distribution, science and high-tech industries.

A hierarchy of town, district and local centres was defined. The two town centres – Widnes and Halton Lea (Runcorn New Town) – are to be the principal focuses for new and enhanced retail and other town centre activity. The original centre of Runcorn – the 'Old Town' – was designated as a district centre focussing on convenience, local and niche comparison and service retail and leisure uses. Other smaller local centres are to offer local convenience and service retail and complementary community facilities. Proposals for new retail or leisure developments will be subject to sequential and impact assessments. The development of new centres will be expected to consolidate and enhance the network and hierarchy of centres and not harm the vitality and viability of existing centres.

In order to achieve a reduction in the need to travel and to encourage use of sustainable transport modes, developments which generate a large number of trips will be directed into the most sustainable location available; travel plans and transport assessments will also be required. Maximum parking standards will be set to deter use of the private car. There are also specific proposals for improvements to the transport network including prioritizing public transport, walking and cycling on the existing cross-river road bridge when the new bridge is completed, reinstatement of a passenger railway service to Chester, new railway stations, park and ride facilities, new and improved pedestrian and cycle routes and facilities.

The nature of proposals for the Key Areas of Change can be considered by looking at the West Runcorn area, which includes the Runcorn Old Town centre, some older housing, underused industrial sites and dockland (Figure 2.3). It is proposed that a programme of urban regeneration will result in:

- provision of 5,200m² of additional retail floorspace in the Old Town centre;
- redevelopment of the waterfront as a residential-led mixed use regeneration incorporating more than 1,300 dwellings and a new local centre, ensuring high quality design to create a 'vibrant destination';
- an additional 26 hectares of employment land and the redevelopment and regeneration of existing employment areas across West Runcorn;
- redevelopment and modernization of the docks to further strengthen Halton's role as a centre for logistics and distribution.

This local plan is more specific than the spatial vision for the Flanders regional plan or the city-regional TAYplan both in term of quantitative targets and in specifying the location of new investment. However, the aspirations of this plan are very similar to those of the higher level plans with many policies being expressed in terms of criteria that should be met by developers rather than making more precise land use zoning or design decisions within the plan itself. In this sense the plan is very flexible. It is clear that much of the implementation will be achieved through

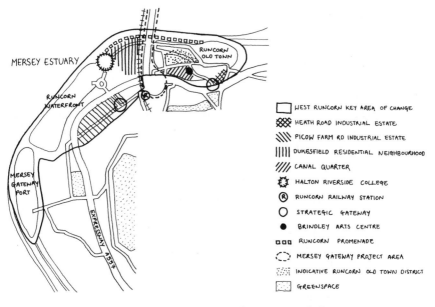

MERSEY ESTUARY

RUNCORN OLD TOWN

RUNCORN WATERFRONT

MERSEY GATEWAY PORT

EXPRESSWAY A533

☐ WEST RUNCORN KEY AREA OF CHANGE

▨ HEATH ROAD INDUSTRIAL ESTATE

⧄ PICOW FARM RD INDUSTRIAL ESTATE

|||| DUKESFIELD RESIDENTIAL NEIGHBOURHOOD

/// CANAL QUARTER

✾ HALTON RIVERSIDE COLLEGE

Ⓡ RUNCORN RAILWAY STATION

◯ STRATEGIC GATEWAY

● BRINDLEY ARTS CENTRE

▫▫▫ RUNCORN PROMENADE

⌐⌐ MERSEY GATEWAY PROJECT AREA

▦ INDICATIVE RUNCORN OLD TOWN DISTRICT

▦ GREENSPACE

Figure 2.3   **West Runcorn: key areas of change**

Source: Drawn by A.L. Couch; based upon the Halton Local Plan (Halton Borough Council, 2013).

Note: Planning at this scale provides a framework for the development and implementation of local urban regeneration programmes and projects.

negotiation between the planners, developers and a variety of other concerned stakeholders. This is very different from the more rigid specification of an optimized pattern.

Controlling development: University of York, Heslington East Campus expansion

The University of York (UK) was founded in 1964 and developed on a campus site 3 km south-east of York city centre. With the existing campus full and the university seeking to virtually double in size, it was proposed to establish a new campus about 0.5 km east of the existing university on 116 hectares of former agricultural land. The process started in 1996 when the University liaised with York City Council to secure inclusion of a new campus in the draft local plan. An outline planning application was submitted in 2004, called in by the Government, and after a public inquiry was eventually granted permission in 2007 by the Secretary of State for Communities and Local Government. The decision was controversial because the proposed site lay within the green belt. While there was broad agreement that the development of the campus would constitute inappropriate development in the green belt, the Inspector at the Public Inquiry and the Secretary of State both agreed that the very special circumstances of the case were sufficient to outweigh the limited harm that would be caused to the purposes of the green belt.

The outline planning permission was subject to 35 separate conditions. These included standard conditions that development should accord with the plans submitted at outline stage and that further approvals of reserved matters (details of the siting, design and appearance of buildings) must be obtained from the local planning authority before development was commenced. The masterplan had allocated only 65 hectares (ha) of land in the middle of the site for development and a condition of approval was that development was to be further restricted to a footprint covering no more than 23 % of this 65 ha 'inner' site, and only for 'university uses'. No development was permitted on the rest of the site. Other conditions included the submission of:

- a Detailed Design Brief;
- a Landscape Design Brief;
- a Landscape Management Plan;
- a Construction Environmental Management Plan (to minimize the impact of construction processes, including noise and traffic intrusion);
- an Environmental Site Management Plan (concerned with resource use, habitat and ecological protection);
- an Archaeological Remains Management Plan;
- a Surface Water Management Plan;
- a Foul Water Drainage Strategy;
- a Sustainable Transport Plan (to minimize traffic intrusion and support sustainable means of movement).

Additionally there were severe limits on the number of car parking spaces, requirements to monitor traffic generation and for mitigation by the University if traffic flows were more than predicted in the planning application. Further conditions protected existing water mains and sewers and required assessment of the potential for a sustainable drainage scheme. The construction details of roads, footpaths, signalling and lighting were also all subject to further approval.

As a condition of receiving planning consent the local planning authority required the University to undertake various measures to mitigate the impact of the development. (Section 106 of the UK Town and Country Planning Act, 1990 enables local authorities to negotiate contributions towards a range of infrastructure and service provision, including community facilities, green infrastructure, transport provision and affordable housing.) The most important measure was the provision of sufficient student housing on site to accommodate the anticipated growth (to avoid the expansion adversely impacting on the local housing market). Other measures included paying for certain road improvements, car parking surveys and enforcement of regulations; establishing a community forum; allowing the public permissive access to footpaths and landscaped areas of the new campus and public access to the new sports facilities to be provided on site; and making a contribution towards the education costs arising from any family housing built on site.

The Master Plan and Strategic Design Brief, as the full document was called, was produced in 2008. Its purpose was to allow the university to establish the character of the site as a whole at the start of what would be a long term development process. There were two key challenges to face: first, to create a large new 'living and learning community' in green land close to existing residential communities; and second, to create a sense of place and human identity in the whole, with each element and within the holistic identity of the University of York. The Design Brief articulated the four key building blocks of the design: the landscape; integration and connectivity; movement and access; and social and community use. It also related the planning context and the framework for the progressive implementation of the Master Plan on site, identifying key design principles that would inform the development of the site and its buildings and ensure a level of design continuity throughout the whole campus.

The cluster concept and the integration of different but complementary activities is the fundamental principle of the Heslington East Master Plan. The design, with groupings of clusters setting up a series of sequential experiences through the site, ensures that each cluster has its own architectural character, so as to avoid a relentlessly monolithic experience. Each cluster addresses uses and activities, massing and form, walking times to and around the cluster, the approach to micro-climate, connectivity with adjacent clusters and the Master Plan as a whole, views in and out and future expansion potential (BDP, 2008; O'Neill Associates, 2010). Figure 2.4 shows the proposed layout of the campus, the clusters, main access routes and connections.

Controlling development: Bebauungsplan for 'Wohnsiedlung Am Eckey', a housing development at Eving, Dortmund

The purpose of a Bebauungsplan (B-plan) is to determine, in advance of any development proposal, the land use and physical form of development that will be permitted on the site. Thus, in contrast to the UK

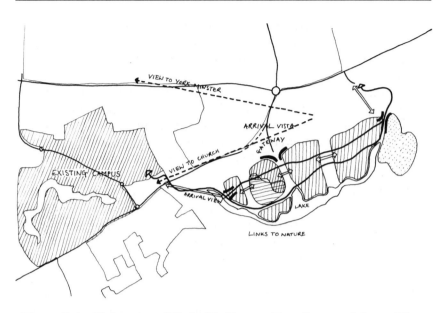

Figure 2.4   *University of York, Heslington East Campus Master Plan,
showing visual links*

Source: Drawn by A.L. Couch; based upon the 'visual links' drawing in BDP (2008), p. 19.

Note: The new campus is visually and functionally linked into urban surroundings and the
existing campus on the left of the drawing.

where the combination of rather generalized Local Plans and a reactive development control system limits the opportunities for local planning authorities to influence designs ahead of the submission of planning applications, the B-plan enables German planners to be more proactive in the planning process and can be a powerful tool for urban design.

A B-plan is prepared within the framework established by higher level plans and, unlike those plans, it is legally binding on all parties. The area covered by the plan may vary from a single building plot to a street block or occasionally a larger area. The notation used in B-plans is fairly standardized across the country. There are four main categories of land use: residential (W) – sub-divided into small, pure, general and special residential areas; mixed (M) – sub-divided into village, mixed and core areas; commercial (G) – sub-divided into commercial and industrial areas; and special areas (S). Further notation relates to the required building lines and heights, plot ratios and site occupancy as well as landscaping and the retention of existing features.

Figure 2.5 shows the Bebauungsplan Ev 148 for the Wohnsiedlung Am Eckey, a housing development at Eving in the city of Dortmund. Eving is a former mining community in the north of the city. The mine closed in the 1980s with the loss of around 5,000 jobs. During the 1990s the pit-head (a protected structure) was retained and converted into offices and the surrounding area laid out for industrial and commercial development. At the same time the district centre was rebuilt to provide modern retail and community facilities. The Wohnsiedlung Am Eckey site lies just to the west of the centre of Eving and is within 200 m of a tram stop. The site comprises backland formerly used as a sports field

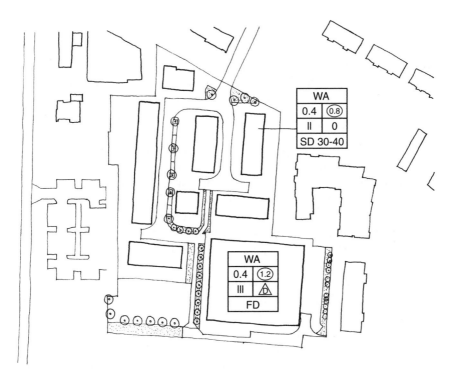

Figure 2.5   *Bebauungsplan, Dortmund, Ev 148: Wohnsiedlung Am Eckey.*

Source: Drawn by A.L. Couch; based upon a plan in Stadt Dortmund (2014).

Note: The solid line shows the building line. There would be an instruction box for each building but only two are shown here for simplicity. WA defines the use as residential; 0.4 is the site occupancy ratio; the figures 0.8 or 1.2 in the circle indicate the floor space index; the figures II and III define the acceptable number of storeys; 'o' or 'Δ' indicate the type of housing permitted (e.g. terraced or semi-detached); SD requires a pitched roof at a specified angle, FD specifies a flat roof.

and the frontage buildings are mainly two and three storey apartment blocks.

The plan emulates the existing pattern of development by requiring that the site will be used for general housing. No more than 40 % of the site is to be covered with buildings (site occupancy ratio = 0.4) and the floor space index of 0.8 implies a medium density. The plan shows the required layout of blocks, which are mostly to be two storeys in height with pitched roofs at an angle of 30° to 40°. Access, the road layout and a landscaping framework are also specified. All this gives the planners substantial control over the form of development that must be realized on the site but equally requires them to have considerable skills in detailed urban design and site planning.

Conclusions

In virtually all countries the range and complexity of stakeholders involved inevitably leads to a governance-based approach to public decision making and a collaborative style of urban planning. However, whilst this might mean that many planning decisions are taken through negotiation and consensus building it has to be recognized that there are absolute limits to this approach. There are inherent conflicts between economic growth and the environment, between the desires of the individual and the needs of society, and there are social costs of economic activity which are not borne by the market. These can only be dealt with through the sort of legal controls that are illustrated by the development management process surrounding the University of York expansion and the Bebauungsplan for housing development at Eving in Dortmund.

The role of national governments varies considerably between countries. In the UK (particularly in England) central government not only determines (and frequently changes) the shape of the planning system, it specifies the goals of urban planning in some detail, as well as influencing priorities and outcomes through state funding decisions. Whilst France is a similarly centralized state, there is a different balance of power. With the communes controlling land use and the regions having a significant financial input into urban planning, there is a more negotiated and collaborative approach. In federal countries such as Germany and the USA the central state plays a smaller role, although even here national decisions on strategic infrastructure can have a big impact on localities. It is predominantly in the smaller countries that nation-wide spatial plans are found. The complexity of larger countries, both in terms of geography and the internal structure of government, frequently prohibits such a plan. Instead, in these countries, the national government generally provides the basic legal framework for the planning system and usually offers only planning policy guidance, or sometimes direction, to lower tiers of government.

In all the countries studied here, except England, there is a regional tier of planning, interpreting and mediating national concerns and goals within the context of particular regions and in turn providing a framework for local decisions. Matters that frequently benefit from a region-wide view include major infrastructure and decisions on capital investment, the avoidance of unnecessary competition and the resolution of disputes between lower tiers of government (for example, over the location of economically beneficial or environmentally costly developments). The size and scale of regions varies between countries but they are typically either based around city-regions – the central city and its hinterland (as in Scotland with the Glasgow, Edinburgh, Aberdeen and Tayside city-regional plans); or a conglomeration of cities in close proximity – a polycentric urban region (as in the Dutch Randstad or German Ruhr, although neither is a formal planning region); or less urbanized regions with a more dispersed pattern of towns and cities (as in many French regions such as Picardie or Bretagne).

Below the regional level many countries appear to favour a two-tier system of municipal urban planning. These typically use an upper tier of planning for setting out generalized proposals for investment in infrastructure and broad policies for the control of development. Examples include the French Schéma de Cohérence Territoriale (SCOT), the Danish Municipal Plans and the Polish Local Development Strategies. Below this come more precise land use plans such as the French Plan Local d'Urbanisme (PLU). In some countries development control is based upon these area-wide land use plans. In others, such as the Netherlands and Germany, it is based on site-specific building plans (Bestemmingsplan or Bebauungsplan) that allow the municipal planners to state their preferred building form in advance of development proposals. The UK stands out because it has only a single tier of statutory municipal planning and a more flexible process of development control based upon the Local Plan (which frequently lacks precision in detailed proposals for built form) and other material considerations. In few other countries do planners have as much discretion over development control as their UK colleagues.

In all of these countries there can also be found systems of positive or proactivity planning – state-led interventions in urban areas to promote, lead or speed up urban change. These systems take different forms in different countries, although the use of arms-length quasi-autonomous agencies is common. For example, in the UK and France, new town development corporations were employed to design and build new towns in the post-war period and similar agencies are being used for that purpose in China today. The success of quasi-autonomous agencies encouraged the UK government to employ similar legislation for urban development corporations to facilitate urban regeneration in the 1980s, although they turned out to be inadequately equipped to provide the collaborative approach and local democratic accountability that the complexity of the task required. Since the 1990s the task of urban renaissance has been taken over by the more flexible and locally accountable urban regeneration companies whose task is only to 'facilitate' development. In France urban regeneration and l'urbanisme opérationnel is frequently delegated to single purpose short-life agencies, but is always under local democratic control. However, in the Netherlands and Germany these sorts of agency are less common. The development of Leidsche Rijn (Netherlands) and much of the regeneration in Dortmund (Germany) was led by the munici-palities concerned (see Chapters 6 and 7).

Chapter 3

Sustainable Development and the Goals of Planning

Introduction

This chapter starts with some consideration of the nature of various threats to the environment, including: population change; land use change, urbanization and urban sprawl; global warming, climate change and urban pollution; and natural resource depletion. This is followed by a discussion of key ideas in sustainable development, then a more specific focus on sustainable urban development, including the policies for energy, water, waste and conservation of nature. Case studies from Copenhagen and Freiburg illustrate contemporary planning practice with regard to climate change adaptation and sustainable urban development respectively. These are then followed by some concluding discussion.

> Our behaviour makes huge demands on the planet. During the 20th century, the world increased its use of fossil fuels by a factor of 12 and extracted 34 times more material resources. Demand for food, animal feed and fibre may increase by 70 % by 2050. If we carry on using resources at the current rate, we will need more than two planets to sustain us. (CEC, 2013, p. 3)

Population growth, global warming and climate change, sea level changes, land use change, urban sprawl, depletion of natural resources, loss of biodiversity and pollution of various types are each posing increasing threats to the stability environment and in particular to the urban environment.

Population change

The population of the world more than doubled over the century between 1900 and 2000 and is set to double again in the half century between 2000 and 2050. This increase in population self-evidently puts a huge strain on the world's resources and causes immense damage to the natural environment. Much of the future growth is anticipated to occur in Asia, Africa and South America. Contrastingly, the European Union (EU) projects its population (28 countries) to grow by a modest 3.6 % by 2050. Furthermore, there are considerable national variations within Europe. For example, the population of Belgium is projected to increase by more than 30 % and the UK by 20 % over this period, whereas the population of Germany is expected to decrease by around 14 % and that of Poland by nearly 10 % (see Figure 3.1).

A further issue is that these populations are also expected to age. In some countries, such as Germany which already has a relatively elderly population, the median age will rise sharply. It is remarkable that the median age of the UK population in 2050 will be less than that of Germany in 2013. In Poland, the out-migration of the young is likely to leave a residual ageing population. The Netherlands too is ageing rapidly (see Table 3.1). Not only does an ageing population put pressure on systems of health and social care, it also reshapes housing and transport

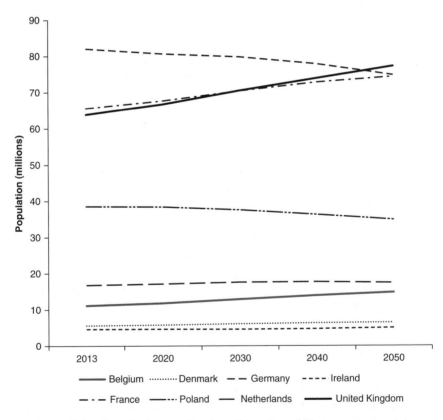

Figure 3.1   *Population projections for selected European countries*

Source: Eurostat (2013a), table proj_13npms (accessed 19.1.2015).

Table 3.1   *Projected median age of population in selected*
European countries

	2013	2050
Belgium	41.2	41.9
Denmark	41.3	43.2
Germany	46.1	50.7
Ireland	35.9	39.4
France	40.8	42.5
Netherlands	42.0	45.8
Poland	39.0	49.6
United Kingdom	39.9	42.0

Source: Eurostat (2013a), table proj_13ndbims (accessed 24.1.2015).

requirements. With a smaller proportion of the population working, the financial resources to support the changing needs of older people become more difficult to find. This is exacerbated when, as in Germany and Poland, ageing is combined with a shrinking population.

There is also considerable variation between cities, even within the same country and region. Between 2007 and 2011 the population of Liverpool grew by 5.4 % while that of the adjoining borough of Sefton fell by almost 1 %. Cologne grew by 1 % but nearby Essen shrank by 1.5 %, and in the Netherlands Eindhoven grew by nearly 3 % and Amsterdam grew by 2.2 % yet Heerlen (90 km from Eindhoven) shrank by 4.5 % (Eurostat table urb_cpop1, accessed 1.11.2014). These variations matter as growing cities face very different planning contexts from shrinking (declining) cities, as shown in Table 3.2.

Expanding cities are likely to see increasing population densities and rising housing demand, which puts pressure on the housing system to supply more dwellings if housing price inflation is to be avoided. There will also be pressure to convert more land from rural and green space to urban uses. A growing population, whether caused by natural increase or net inward migration, typically leads to a fall in the median age, increasing pressure on education services, but is likely to boost economic activity and the tax base and alleviate the provision of services for the elderly. Shrinking cities, on the other hand, are likely to experience falling population densities, a declining demand for housing, falling prices and rising vacancy, possibly leading to the fracture of previously intact communities. Brownfield areas will appear as economic activity declines. There will be surplus capacity in social capital and commercial services, although the remaining provision may not be compatible with the needs of an increasingly elderly residual population. The combination

Table 3.2 *The contrasting planning contexts typically faced by growing and shrinking cities*

Growing cities	Shrinking cities
Increasing population densities	Decreasing population densities
Rising proportion of young adults and children in the population	Rising proportion of elderly people in the population
Housing shortage, rising house prices, rising investment in housing, homelessness	Housing surplus, falling house prices, declining investment in housing, housing vacancy
Shortage of social infrastructure (utilities, schools, health care), pressure on providers to increase provision	Surplus capacity in utilities, schools, health care, difficult political decisions about closure of facilities
Shortage of commercial service provision (e.g. retailing) leading to development pressures	Surplus commercial service provision, leading to uncoordinated closures and service gaps
Strong development pressures and the urbanization of peripheral rural land	Weak development pressures and the emergence of vacant land (brownfields)
Growing income, tax base and inward investment	Declining tax base and rising dependence on external support to maintain services

Source: Adapted from Bernt et al. (2012).

of a declining population and reduced property values is likely to impact adversely on the local tax base.

Land use change, urbanization and urban sprawl

At present less than 2 % of the land area of the earth is in urban land use. However, this figure varies considerably from country to country. Some 4.1 % of the land area of the USA is defined as urban but there is huge variation from only 0.4 % in Montana and Wyoming to 27.9 % in Massachusetts and 34.6 % in New Jersey (United States Department of Agriculture, 1997). Data from the Eurostat field survey programme (Land Use/Cover Area Frame Statistical Survey, LUCAS) revealed that in 2009 4.6 % of the EU (27 countries) was covered by 'artificial areas' comprising built-up areas and unbuilt surfaced areas such as transport networks and associated areas (urban land) (Eurostat, 2009). Within the EU there was a range from 1.6 % artificial land in Finland and 1.8 % in

Sweden to 6.5 % in the UK, 12.2 % in the Netherlands and 13.4 % in Belgium. The most urbanized parts of Europe lie in northern, central and south-eastern England, the Benelux countries, the Rhine-Ruhr district of Germany, northern Italy and the Paris Basin in France. There is also a high degree of urbanization along some coastlines, including the Mediterranean coasts of France and Spain and the North Sea coast of Belgium and parts of the south-east coast of England.

However, overall the rate of urbanization (conversion of land from rural to urban uses) in Europe is very low with the average annual rate of change of urban population averaging no more than 2 % between 1950 and 1970 and falling to below 0.5 % since 2000 (UN, 2011). The mean annual urban land take for 2000–2006 in Europe as a percentage of 'artificial land' was 0.5 % (that is the urban area of Europe was increasing by 0.5 % per annum). The rate of urbanization was fastest in Albania (4.6 %), Spain (2.8 %) and Ireland (2.1 %). The slowest rate of urbanization was found in countries that were already highly urbanized, such as the UK (0.2 %) and Belgium (0.1 %) and in countries with low rates of economic growth, such as Romania and Bulgaria (both 0.1 %). This is in contrast to the global average of about 2 % per annum, although higher rates of urbanization were found in Africa (3 % per annum), China (2.85 %), India (2.47 %) and other developing countries (UN, 2011). On the other hand, the mean annual urban land take as a proportion of total urban land take in Europe was highest in the bigger developed economies of Western Europe. Between 2000 and 2006, 23.5 % of all European urbanization occurred in Spain, 12.2 % in France and 9.5 % in Germany (EEA, 2013b).

'Urban sprawl' is a term commonly used to describe patterns and processes that represent an inefficient form of urbanization. Amongst recent definitions, Peiser suggests:

> the term is used variously to mean the gluttonous use of land, uninterrupted monotonous development, leapfrog discontinuous development and inefficient use of land. (2001, p. 278)

Galster et al. suggest that the term has variously been used to refer to: '*patterns* [of urban development] … the *process* of extending the reach of urbanized areas … the *causes* of particular practices of land use, and to the *consequences* of those practices' (Galster et al., 2001, emphasis in original, p. 681). In place of this confusion they suggest that sprawl is:

> a pattern of land use [in an urbanized area] that exhibits low levels of some combination of eight distinct dimensions: density, continuity, concentration, clustering, centrality, nuclearity, mixed uses, and proximity. (Galster et al., 2001, p. 685)

Traditional urban models usually show the intensity of urban activity to be greatest in the city centre and gradually declining towards the edge of the urban area: the density gradient tends to slope downwards away from the city centre. In reality, a whole range of factors including local topography, transport routes, suburban centres and so forth will distort density gradients. Nevertheless, if the idea of a downward sloping density curve can be accepted for a moment, then, as shown in Figure 3.2, urban sprawl will always result in the density gradient becoming less steep. It is this change in the gradient of the density line that is a key defining feature of urban sprawl, distinguishing it from urban growth. Urban growth can be defined in terms of an expansion either of population or economic activity within an urban area. All other things being equal, urban growth will cause the density gradient line to shift to the right, whilst retaining the same gradient; urban

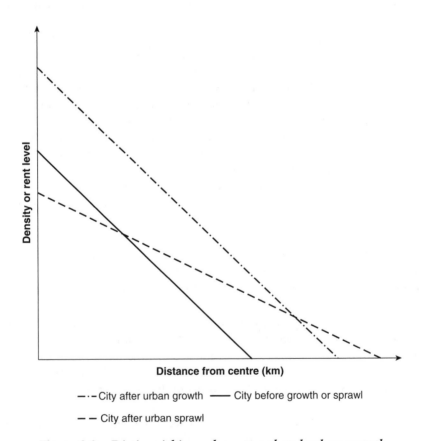

Figure 3.2   *Distinguishing urban sprawl and urban growth*

Source: Adapted from Couch et al. (2007).

sprawl will cause it to become less steep (Couch et al., 2005). This analysis leads to an important indicator of urban sprawl that can be tested empirically: changes in urban density at different distances from the city centre.

Urban sprawl has important consequences that have a direct impact on the sustainability of urban areas. Sprawl results in the unnecessary loss of productive agricultural land. Many urban areas have developed on relatively flat and well drained sites, often on good quality soil: precisely the same characteristics as the best agricultural land.

Urban sprawl causes unnecessary loss and fragmentation of natural habitats by creating barriers across movement corridors used by wildlife and reducing the available area of natural habitat below the minimum required to sustain species populations in particular locations. Although many urban areas contain substantial amounts of greenspace (ranging from parkland to sports fields and private gardens) the type of habitat they offer is different from the surrounding countryside. The proximity of urban activities can impose additional stresses on ecosystems through noise, air and soil pollution. Surface sealing and compaction of soil with loss of water permeability is a feature of urbanization and requires the development of artificial drainage systems to remove rainwater. This contributes to the risk of localized flooding in times of high rainfall. Problems are particularly severe in some coastal regions:

> The development related impacts on coastal ecosystems, and their habitats and services, have produced major changes ... The Mediterranean coast, one of the world's 34 biodiversity hotspots, is particularly affected, and the increased demand for water for urban use, competes with irrigation water for agricultural land. (EEA, 2006a, p. 31)

Urban land also tends to generate and retain more heat and be warmer than rural areas, with consequent impacts on local meteorological conditions (Figure 3.3). According to the UK Meteorological Office: 'Even where urban heat islands are not a major problem now, they could exacerbate some of the projected impacts of climate change such as heatwaves and hot summer spells (2012).

Urban sprawl and falling population densities result in growing consumption of energy, especially in relation to mobility. Car use is more prevalent, distances travelled are longer (to work, to schools, to shops and for leisure) and the lower density makes it more difficult and expensive to provide public transport. The greater distances also discourage walking and cycling. Households living in areas of sprawl thus tend to spend more time and more of their household budget travelling. This

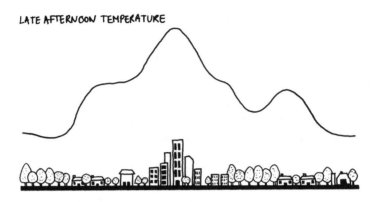

Figure 3.3   *Urban heat islands and surface sealing*

Source: Drawn by A.L. Couch.

Note: Built-up areas both generate and absorb heat whereas areas of vegetation and water dissipate heat.

increased dependence on the motor vehicle also in turn increases CO_2 emissions and contributes to global warming.

Urban sprawl also makes it more difficult and more expensive to provide utility services such as water, electricity and gas, and municipal services such as waste collection. Education, health and community services are more distant from their clientele. Retail and other commercial services are less dense, with less competition and the possibility of monopoly conditions leading to higher prices than in denser areas with more choice and competition.

Spatial social segregation is also associated with urban sprawl as more affluent families seek to live in privately owned suburban housing, whilst childless households and the less affluent are more concentrated in the inner urban areas. The European Environment Agency concludes that:

> the efficiency savings of more compact city development as compared with market driven suburbanisation can be as high as 20–45 % in land resources, 15–25 % in the construction of local roads and 7–15 % savings in the provision of water and sewage facilities. (EEA, 2006b, p. 36)

Many urban processes, notably in extractive, energy producing and manufacturing industries, lead to the pollution and contamination of the soil on which they are located. Contaminated land poses risks to human health as well as plant and animal life. As urban areas evolve some land is abandoned and left vacant or derelict for periods of time.

Much of this land is contaminated and cannot be reused without remediation. In England in 2007 there were 33,600 ha of vacant and derelict land, although this figure had improved from 41,120 ha in 2001 (DCLG, *Live Tables*, Table P302; available at: www.gov.uk/government/statistical-data-sets/live-tables-on-national-land-use-database-of-previously-developed-brownfield-land (accessed 11.6.2015)). There was also considerable variation between regions with the biggest concentrations in North-west England, Yorkshire and the Humber and the East and West Midlands. Across the rest of Europe, although the data is very patchy and definitions vary from place to place, one study estimated the amount of brownfield land in those countries for which data was available as 14,500 ha in Belgium, 30,000 ha in the Czech Republic, 20,000 ha in France, 128,000 ha in Germany, 9,000–11,000 ha in the Netherlands, 800,000 ha in Poland and 900,000 ha in Romania (Oliver et al., 2005).

Population growth, increased economic activity and urbanization are amongst the principal drivers of global warming, climate change, rising pollution and the depletion of natural resources.

Global environmental challenges

Global warming and climate change

According to the Intergovernmental Panel on Climate Change (IPCC), working under the auspices of the United Nations:

> warming of the climate system is unequivocal, and since the 1950s, many of the observed changes are unprecedented over decades to millennia. The atmosphere and ocean have warmed, the amounts of snow and ice have diminished, sea level has risen, and the concentrations of greenhouse gases have increased … Each of the last three decades has been successively warmer at the Earth's surface than any preceding decade since 1850. (IPCC, 2013, pp. 4–5)

Global warming has occurred for a number of reasons. The principal cause appears to be an increase in the amount of heat trapping 'greenhouse gases' in the troposphere, notably carbon dioxide (CO_2), methane (CH_4), nitrous oxide (N_2O) and chlorofluorocarbons (CFCs) (Figure 3.4). The amount of carbon dioxide in the atmosphere has risen by more than 30% since the early 1800s. Much of this is due to emissions from the burning of fossil fuels, such as coal and oil, for industrial and domestic heat and power and from motor vehicles. Another significant contribution comes from deforestation, whereby trees that would naturally absorb carbon dioxide emissions are lost to the ecosystem. Also, as the

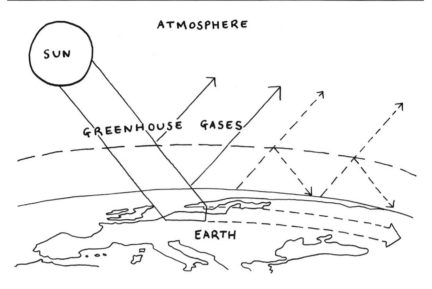

Figure 3.4 *The causes of global warming: the greenhouse effect*

Source: Drawn by A.L. Couch.

Note: Greenhouse gases trap heat, so raising the temperature of the earth's surface and atmosphere.

concentration of carbon dioxide in the atmosphere increases, more of it is absorbed into our seas and oceans and this increases their acidity which impacts on marine ecosystems with consequences for fish stocks and the food chain. Whilst methane is naturally produced from sources such as wetlands and cattle, the increased production of livestock, as well as leakage from natural gas installations, has led to a sharp rise in methane emissions. Nitrous oxide occurs naturally in the atmosphere but the volume has been increased through agricultural processes and fossil fuel combustion. Although less prevalent in the atmosphere than carbon dioxide, the impacts on global warming of methane and nitrous oxide, per unit of weight, are greater. CFC emissions come from their use as refrigerants and in aerosols, and contribute to depletion of the ozone layer in the upper atmosphere, although in recent years the use of CFCs has reduced following intergovernmental agreements.

The consequences of global warming include impacts on the climate, weather systems, sea levels, ecosystems, food production and health. Rising temperatures will lead to an expansion in the volume of the water in seas and oceans. This will be compounded by rising temperatures causing reductions in the size of polar ice caps, glaciers and sea ice. The IPCC has projected that sea levels may rise by between 26 cm and 98 cm during the twenty-first century, depending upon the projection and assumptions made (IPCC, 2013). Such a rise in sea levels will put many coastal settlements at risk of flooding by the sea, especially at times of storms, on-shore winds, low atmospheric pressure and spring tides. There will also be continuing inundation in some coastal settlements, with significant areas of land being permanently lost to the sea.

Around 100,000 km² of coastal land in the EU is less than 5 metres above sea level and vulnerable to inundation. According to the European Environment Agency:

> The most vulnerable countries are the Netherlands and Belgium, where more than 85 % of coast is under a 5 m elevation. Other countries at risk include Germany and Romania where 50 % of the coastline is below 5 m, Poland (30 %) and Denmark (22 %). In France, the United Kingdom and Estonia low coasts cover 10–15 % of the country. Eight countries, mostly in southern Europe, have less than 5 % of their coastal zones below 5 m. However, individual hot spots exist. The most significant of these is the area surrounding Venice in Italy. (EEA, 2006a, p. 42)

In the Netherlands a commission was established in 2007 (Deltacommissie) to examine the long term implications of rising sea levels. It concluded that the country should plan for a rise in the level of the North Sea of up to 1.3 metres by 2100 and at least double that figure in the subsequent century, posing a severe threat to life and the urban and agricultural economy of much of the country. The commission recommended major expenditure in strengthening sea defences as well as working with nature to broaden coastal dune systems and encourage existing beaches to expand seawards. In vulnerable areas new urban development should be subject to strict controls (Deltacommissie, 2008).

In the UK areas particularly vulnerable to sea level rise include parts of Humberside, Lincolnshire and the Wash; the Thames Estuary; south Hampshire; the Somerset Levels and lower Severn Valley; the North Wales and Lancashire coasts and the Solway estuary. In England the Environment Agency employs a range of different measures to address the flood and coastal erosion risk to communities and property, considered on a case by case basis. These measures include building flood and coastal defences, flood storage reservoirs, land management and portable defences. However, in some coastal areas increased protection may be uneconomic or undesirable for environmental reasons and some land area may have to be abandoned to the action of the sea. 'Hard choices need to be taken; we must either invest more in sustainable approaches to flood and coastal management or learn to live with increased flooding' (Pitt, 2008).

Rising temperatures are likely to lead to some areas becoming permanently hotter and experiencing less rainfall, while other areas may experience an increase in rainfall and even a fall in temperature. The ecological balance will change with some species becoming more prevalent and others declining or even becoming extinct. In consequence the nature of agricultural production may have to change in some areas and in extreme cases may have to be abandoned altogether, with clear consequences for food supply. Rising temperatures are also likely to lead to more extreme weather conditions in some places: more storms and more rapid and extreme changes in temperature. A particular consequence is likely to be inland flooding as river and drainage systems struggle to cope with storm surges. There are also potential impacts on human health as some populations are exposed to diseases not previously prevalent in their climate zone or have to cope with new extremes of heat or cold.

Different regions of Europe are likely to experience different impacts from global warming, magnifying regional differences in climate and natural resources. The Alps and Pyrenees are expected to experience shrinkage in glaciers and snow cover with consequent impacts on local ecology and economies such as the loss of winter sports tourism. Across Mediterranean lands higher temperatures, drought and increased risk of wildfires may reduce agricultural capacity and impact on other economic sectors such as summer tourism. Water shortage may also become an increasing concern across central and eastern Europe. Northern Europe, on the other hand, may benefit from reduced demand for heating and increases in certain crop yields including forestry, but may also experience increased flooding and more turbulent weather (IPCC, 2007).

Other forms of air pollution

In addition to greenhouse gases there are a number of other pollutants of the urban atmosphere. Carbon monoxide is harmful to health in high concentrations. Although naturally occurring, it can also be created through the partial combustion of fossil fuels so is often found in higher concentrations in urban areas.

Sulphur dioxide is emitted from energy production and manufacturing processes. It combines with water vapour in clouds to fall as acid rain, frequently at some distance from the original source. Thus in the 1980s it was demonstrated that a significant proportion of the acid rain that fell in southern Norway and Sweden had been borne by prevailing winds from power stations and factories in the UK. Acid rain caused immense damage to forests and the ecology of lakes and rivers. Following intergovernmental cooperation there has been a significant decrease in emissions since then.

Lead is poisonous. Formerly an additive to petrol, its removal in the 1990s resulted in a dramatic reduction in emissions. There is evidence of significant public health improvements following this change. Particulates and smoke combine with fog to cause smog and contribute to respiratory diseases. Generally the amount of particulates is decreasing but diesel engines remain a major source. In the spring of 2014 in Paris, where diesel fuel is cheaper than petrol and diesel cars are very popular, the high level of particulate emissions combined with unusually warm and still weather created a blanket of smog that settled over the city. In response the French government sought to reduce the volume of traffic by applying emergency rules that allowed only motorists with even or odd-numbered registration plates to enter Paris on alternate days; speed limits were reduced on some roads and public transport was temporarily made free.

Ozone in the stratosphere protects the earth from ultra violet radiation from the sun. Emissions of CFCs, halons and other gases cause 'holes' in the ozone layer, increasing the risk of some cancers, crop damage and animal diseases.

Natural resource depletion

Many of the world's natural resources are being depleted at an alarming rate. Some, such as the energy resources of coal, oil and gas and various minerals used in manufacturing, are finite and non-renewable. Others, such as forests, agricultural land, wild food supplies (for example fish stocks) and water can be replenished and reused so long as exploitation does not exceed the rate at which they can be restored.

According to Greenpeace USA (2014), the world will have consumed 20 % of its current coal reserves by 2030 and 40 % by 2050. It has also been forecast that global oil production will peak in 2015 and decline thereafter and that with peaking will come increased price volatility and uncertain socio-economic and political costs (Hirsch, 2005; Hallock et al., 2014). Some other reports have been a little less pessimistic. The US Energy Information Administration (EIA) has predicted that production may not peak until 2030, although the same organization is also saying that world consumption of petroleum and other liquid fuels consumption would increase by 38 % by 2040, spurred by increased demand in the developing Asia and Middle East (EIA, 2014). It has also been estimated that the world's natural gas reserves are sufficient for less than 60 years, although there are extensive non-conventional reserves of oil sands and shale gas that have the potential to extend supplies beyond this. The availability and production of a number of metals used in manufacturing, such as copper and zinc, are also likely to decline within the next generation.

Whilst these dates are somewhat arbitrary and may be adjusted according to various government regulation and market pressures, there is no doubt that oil production will start to fall within a generation. Regardless of the availability of these energy sources, it must be remembered that the burning of coal, oil and gas to produce energy emits greenhouse gases and other pollutants. Whilst the use of energy for industrial production, for transport and for heating can be made more efficient, there is little escape from the fact that societies need to become much less dependent on non-renewable energy sources and much more reliant on renewable energy.

Trees and forests are also rapidly being depleted as land is cleared for agricultural production, for urbanization or for the use of timber in manufacturing. It has been estimated that half the world's tropical forests were destroyed in the 60 years or so from 1947 (Nielsen, 2006). The depletion of forests and tree cover result in less CO_2 being absorbed and so contributes to greenhouse gas production and global warming. Removal of tree cover also affects the water cycle and increases the possibility of soil erosion and flooding. The loss of forests also reduces biodiversity as natural habitats are fractured and lost. Local populations and traditional lifestyles are also affected by deforestation.

Towards sustainable development

Sustainable development provides an integrated response to these issues of accommodating population growth and the impacts of increased economic activity and urbanization on global warming, climate change, rising pollution and the depletion of natural resources.

There are three dimensions to sustainability to be considered: environmental, economic and social. The environmental dimension of sustainable development is concerned with minimizing the impact of human activity on the climate, natural resources, habitat depletion and environmental degradation. The economic dimension is concerned with the efficient functioning of the economy to provide inclusive access to employment and equitable access to goods and services. The social dimension is concerned with the elimination of social deprivation and ensuring that society is secure, inclusive and equitable. These notions are frequently represented by the Venn diagram in Figure 3.5, in which the area of overlap between the three circles represents sustainable development in all its dimensions.

There are a number of key concepts associated with the idea of sustainability. Societies, economies and the natural environment are interdependent in both space and time, and the carrying capacity of environments within these spaces and time periods must be respected.

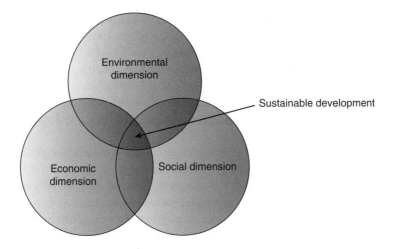

Figure 3.5 *The three interlocking circles of sustainable development*

Carrying capacity represents the amount of resource that can be taken out of the environment without causing damage, stress or long term depletion of natural resources. For example, in fishing, the industry must leave sufficient fish in the oceans for them to reproduce in adequate quantities to maintain stocks. Failure to do so will lead to their decline and eventual extinction. Where once this referred to the local environment inhabited by early civilizations, modern economies are so inter-linked that many of these relationships are world-wide. Natural resource depletion is a global challenge.

The notion of an 'ecological footprint' is closely linked to the idea of interdependence. It represents the amount of land necessary to support human activity. Thus it is a measurement of all the land required to produce the raw materials for all the food and manufactured goods and the services consumed by a given population and also to accommodate all the waste generated by that population. It is therefore a measure of the amount of biological capacity in the earth's ecosystems compared with the capacity required to support human activity. It has been estimated that the average ecological footprint per capita in the UK is 5.45 hectares – a figure that vastly exceeds the total area of land in the country.

Quality of life is an idea that goes beyond the measurement of income levels (such as GDP per capita) or wealth in terms of ownership of prop-erty and savings. It includes non-tangible public goods such as the avail-ability and quality of health care, welfare services, personal security and safety, pleasant and pollution-free environments. On some definitions it also includes the idea that all members of a society should have the opportunity to contribute to the community through a meaningful and productive life. There have been many attempts to measure quality of life, usually through composite measures of health, education, dwelling prices, crime rates and so on. One example is the 'index of multiple deprivation' devised by a UK Government study which measured seven aspects of deprivation – income, employment, health deprivation and disability, education skills and training, barriers to housing and services, crime, living environment – and aggregated the results to provide an overall measure of deprivation (or quality of life) in individual areas (ONS, 2014).

Equity is the concept of equality or fairness in economics. Equity considers the distribution of goods and services (or indeed the broader concept of the quality of life) between individuals, or social groups or spatial areas (which could be neighbourhoods, cities, regions or countries). In many societies, economic liberalization and globalization have served to widen inequalities. Not only do many argue that this is unfair and inequitable but also that concentrating too much wealth in the hands of too few in society is economically inefficient and unsustainable in the long term. Whether one believes in egalitarianism or not, most governments show broad philosophical support for the ideas of social inclusion, equality of access to basic public goods and equality of opportunities for all in society.

The precautionary principle states that where there is a possible threat of serious or irreversible environmental damage the decision should always be made on the side of caution. The idea is that if there is a suspected risk of some activity, policy or development causing environmental damage or social harm then it should not be permitted. Thus the burden of proof is on the instigator or developer to show that the proposed action, policy or development is not harmful. The concept is particularly useful in making decisions on topics where the full scientific evidence of impact is not available. Across many areas of EU law, application of the precautionary principle has become mandatory.

All economic activity can be measured in terms of private costs (borne by the market) and indirect or social costs (borne by third parties). Thus when an activity (for example, chemical production) takes place, there are private costs of production and distribution that are shown in the firm's balance sheet: the cost of land, labour, raw materials, cost of finance, transport and so forth. But there are other, indirect costs, or externalities, that are borne by third parties, such as a detrimental impact on the value of neighbouring land, or on society as a whole: costs of traffic congestion, air and ground pollution, noise pollution, depletion of natural resources. These externalities are often known as the social costs of economic activity or development. It is a key function of the planning system to measure and take account of these social costs and, in making planning decisions, look to ameliorate their impact or require compensatory payments by the developer. Thus in UK planning law, under Section 106 of the Town and Country Planning Act, 1990 (slightly modified by subsequent legislation):

> Any person interested in land in the area of a local planning authority may, by agreement or otherwise, enter into an obligation ...
>
> (a) restricting the development or use of the land in any specified way;
> (b) requiring specified operations or activities to be carried out in, on, under or over the land;
> (c) requiring the land to be used in any specified way; or
> (d) requiring a sum or sums to be paid to the [planning authority] on a specified date or dates or periodically. (Town and Country Planning Act 1990, S. 106)

A common principle in environmental law is the notion that the polluter pays. That is to say, those responsible for pollution should pay the cost of its removal or recompense society for the environmental degradation done. This gives an incentive to reduce harm and ensures that costs do not fall on society at large. Ultimately, this frequently means that it is the consumer who pays. Although externalities might have been generated through the production of goods and services, in many circumstances producers can argue that production only takes place to meet consumer demand and therefore pollution costs (for example, pollution taxes or the cost of fitting anti-pollution equipment) should be passed on to the consumer. However, in an extension to the principle, some have argued that producers should take more responsibility for their actions, even for actions that are not their direct responsibility: for example, making fast food outlets responsible for what happens even after a sale has been completed, such as removing litter from the local environment and paying for the cost of disposal of packaging; or influencing other parts of the production process, such as encouraging supermarkets to require sustainable farming methods from their suppliers.

Environmental assessment

Implementing the principle that the polluter pays requires the ability to measure the environmental impact of policies, programmes and projects. Hence in order to ensure the compliance of plans and programmes with the principles of environmental sustainability, systems of Strategic Environmental Assessment (SEA) and Environmental Impact Assessment (EIA) have been developed.

According to Fischer (2007) the rationale for SEA results from shortcomings in existing policy, plan and programme making. He considers that in too many planning systems the environment is largely considered in a reactive way and dealt with in an add-on manner, rather than treated as a core element of strategic decision making. SEA acts as an instrument for integrating environmental, social and economic aspects in order to achieve sustainable development.

SEA is carried out by the authority responsible for the production of the plan, programme or strategy and can act as a proactive tool that supports the formulation of strategic action for sustainable development. The process increases the transparency of decision making and facilitates participatory approaches to governance. SEA can set the framework for tiered decision making, helping decision makers to ask the right questions at the right time. By making these decision making processes more structured and systematic they are likely to become more efficient, benefitting the development planning process and providing a framework which will enable the EIA of individual projects to be more effectively targeted. The general principles of SEA include:

- integration (it should part of the planning process, informing rather than duplicating the assessment of planning options and alternatives);
- proportionality (it should reflect the scale and complexity of the plan);
- efficiency (it should be undertaken in an efficient manner with a focus on *significant* environmental effects of the plan.

An example taken from Dundee City Council illustrates the nature of a typical urban planning SEA.

Dundee is a medium-sized former industrial city on the east coast of Scotland which has experienced considerable economic change and population loss. However, the city has a valued historic environment and a rich natural heritage resource including internationally important species and habitats. The environment is under pressure from increasing traffic volumes and resulting air quality issues, and flood risk affects some important areas including the city centre and waterfront. The Proposed Local Development Plan (LDP) contains various policies and proposals for the city, including industrial and residential development; investments in the city centre, port and waterfront; neighbourhood renewal; conservation; and the enhancement of green infrastructure (see Chapter 7). It is these policies and proposals that were subject to SEA.

According to the SEA the main environmental trends affecting the city could be summarized as:

- *biodiversity* indicators were improving overall;
- *population* factors had stabilized;

- *human health* factors were variable with some improving and others getting worse;
- *soil* and land measures remained constant;
- *water* variables were generally stable;
- *air* and *climate factors* were variable with some improving and others getting worse;
- *the material assets* of the city were improving;
- *the cultural heritage* environment was stable or improving;
- *landscape* factors were generally improving.

Objectives were developed for each of these themes and translated into a series of environmental indicators against which the LDP strategy, policies and proposed development sites were assessed for their impacts on the environment, including effects over time, cumulative effects, secondary effects and the significance of the impact. The assessment generally found that the vast majority of policies would have a neutral or positive effect on the environment. This result is not surprising given that a key purpose of the plan was to create a quality environment, however it did result in changes to some policies. The LDP was accompanied by a technical appraisal of sites being considered for development. A number of these site-specific assessments recommended mitigation measures that would permit development to progress without significant adverse environmental impact. Such measures included, for example, the provision of landscaping to improve habitat connectivity, improvement of access links, protection of existing woodland, provision of sustainable urban drainage, protection of a listed building on or adjacent to site, the undertaking of assessments of flood risk or site contamination.

Similar in intent to SEA is the Environmental Impact Assessment (EIA). Whereas SEA is intended to be strategic and proactive, operating at the scale of whole policies, plans and programmes, EIA is concerned with the impact of individual projects. Sometimes such projects will have emerged from a wider plan or programme but this is frequently not the case, especially with private sector-led urban development or redevelopment schemes. Thus EIA is 'the process of identifying, predicting, evaluating and mitigating the biophysical, social and other relevant effects of proposed development proposals prior to major decisions being taken and commitments made' (IAIA, 2009).

EIA provides a systematic process for examining the environmental impact of proposed developments in advance of their being implemented. This process typically comprises a number of steps. The first is to screen development proposals to decide if an EIA is needed, because the process is only generally considered worthwhile in relation to major projects (in terms of scale, complexity or reach) that are likely to have significant environmental impacts. Usually only the more significant issues will be examined in depth. Typically the assessment will include some consideration of alternative proposals (in terms of scale, location, design and so on), often as a device for exploring alternative courses of action to alleviate any adverse impacts detected.

The project and its characteristics will be described and a baseline study undertaken to determine the current and likely future state of the environment without the development going ahead. Following this, the main impacts of the proposal will be identified and compared with the baseline, so that differences between the environment with and without the project (positive and negative) can be measured and evaluated for their significance. Adverse impacts will require mitigation – measures for their avoidance, reduction, remediation or compensation. An important dimension of EIA is the presentation of the findings, including a non-technical summary, in order to facilitate public consultation and participation as well as professionals from other disciplines. Decisions will then be taken on whether to allow the project to go ahead, with or without mitigating conditions, and outcomes monitored and reviewed to measure actual impacts against predicted impacts, which may then require adjustments to policy and act as a learning mechanism for future EIA (Glasson et al., 2012).

Although the use of EIA dates back to the 1960s, the EU published its first Directive requiring member countries to implement EIA only in 1985. The Directive has been updated on a number of occasions, most recently in 2014 (EIA Directive 2014/52/EU), and it requires that member countries will gradually bring in changes to the system including: considering how climate change, human health and resource efficiency can be assessed more effectively within EIA; improving the assessment process and introducing penalties for infringements (Eversheds, 2015).

The achievement of sustainable development also requires forms of governance that are collaborative, inclusive and transparent. Governance and planning systems need to be collaborative and coordinated both vertically and horizontally so that the impact of decisions on other levels of governance in other sectors and other spatial areas can be measured and taken into account in decision making. That is to say that central and regional governments need to be aware of the impact of their decisions on lower tiers of government or planning; that those concerned with, say, economic development take account of the impact of their decisions in other sectors, such as the housing or transport sectors; that those concerned with the planning of one spatial area consider the impact of their decisions upon other spatial areas; and that all consider the impact on future generations.

Greater knowledge about the internal and external operating environments of organizations invariably leads to greater efficiencies and effectiveness in undertaking the functions of the organization, be it a private firm producing goods to sell in the market or a public agency delivering a community service. This knowledge may be gained through trial and error, informal consultation, formal consultation mechanisms or scientific market research. Not to do so would be considered poor management. Yet amongst many agencies concerned with planning and the delivery of public services, there seems to be some reluctance either to consult or research client needs effectively before decisions are taken, or to monitor their effects afterwards. Thus it is evident that urban planners have to interact with their external environment in order to carry out their tasks in a proper manner. But there is a strong case for arguing that they should go further and involve the external environment in decision making.

In some senses the case has already been made and is being implemented. The very existence of governance systems or networks with overlapping responsibilities, as is now common in many cities, requires some degree of inclusivity in decision making. However, it is possible to argue that the wider inclusion of pressure groups, stakeholders and inhabitants will further improve decision making. The knowledge base for decisions is increased, a greater range of solutions may become apparent, and the acceptability of policy choices can be identified at an earlier stage. It is an important part of this process that decision making is transparent; that communities know not just what decisions are being made but how they are being made and by whom.

Sustainable urban development

Rydin (2010) has considered the role that urban development and spatial planning can play in delivering sustainable development. She identifies the dimensions of sustainable urban development as including carbon reduction, water efficiency, waste management and pollution control, nature conservation, climate change, social and economic aspects.

Carbon reduction would be facilitated by more compact urban development with better integrated transport systems. In *Towards an Urban Renaissance*, Richard Rogers and his colleagues favoured compact and well-connected cities (see Figure 3.6) in which:

> urban areas are organised in concentric bands of density, with higher densities around public transport nodes (rail, bus and underground stations), and lower densities in less connected areas. The effect of this compact layout is to establish a clear urban boundary, contain urban sprawl and reduce car use. (Urban Task Force, 1999, p. 54)

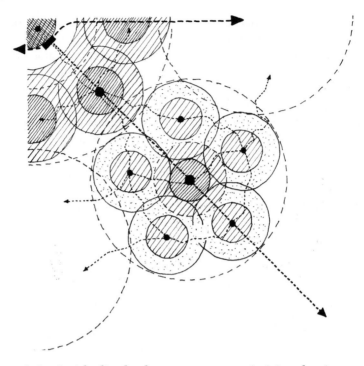

Figure 3.6 *An idealized urban structure maximizing density around public transport nodes*

Source: Drawn by A.L. Couch; based upon Urban Task Force (1999), Figure 2.1.

Note: The city is served by an integrated regional and local public transportation system. The highest density of development would be found around the most important transport hubs and urban centres, with declining levels of density at less important hubs and centres. The least accessible locations would be developed at very low densities or remain undeveloped.

Cities need to become more efficient in energy use and less reliant on non-renewable sources of energy. Urban energy use can be made more sustainable by reducing demand or shifting supply from non-renewable to renewable sources. Urban planning can make a particular contribution to reducing demand for energy use through limiting the demand for travel and shifting modal split towards the most energy efficient modes of travel (see Chapter 8), or reducing energy demand within buildings, especially for heating, cooling and lighting.

The insulation of individual buildings can minimize heat loss in winter and excessive solar heat gain in summer, thereby reducing demand for energy use in heating and ventilation systems. Local topography and micro-climates can influence the temperature within buildings. These influences can be minimized through careful choice of locations, for example avoiding building in frost hollows or exposed slopes, and by judicious landscaping, such as planting tree belts to reduce wind speed and provide shade in summer, but avoiding overshadowing in winter. Whilst summer breezes assist building ventilation, winter winds increase heat loss. Winds are smoothed over higher density low to medium rise developments, but with greater spacing and higher buildings winds are forced down and can create eddies that make outdoor spaces uncomfortable and cause heat loss from buildings (Llewelyn-Davies, 2000). Orientation can also play a significant role. The need for artificial lighting and space heating can be reduced by orientating the building to obtain maximum daylight and passive solar gain. In much of Europe this means orientating buildings' principal rooms and larger windows broadly towards the south. This typically results in an east–west street pattern (Llewelyn-Davies, 2000).

In higher density areas combined heat and power (CHP) or district heating systems can be more efficient than individual dwelling systems. But using renewable energy sources, such as wind, solar energy, hydropower, biomass and thermal energy, offers the greatest benefits. Within urban areas renewable energy may be used for electricity generation or for direct water or space heating. Wind turbines are increasingly being used to generate electricity. This may be provided through wind farms of many turbines or through individual site-specific turbines. Some countries, particularly those with strong prevailing winds, long coastlines and relatively low population densities, are particularly suited to wind energy production. Denmark is amongst the world-leaders, providing 39.1 % of the country's electricity through wind power in 2014 (Danish Wind Energy Association, 2015). But wind turbines can raise difficult planning problems, especially with regard to aesthetics and noise intrusion. Before approving such proposals, noise, safety and ecological impacts need to be considered as well as their impact on heritage and the landscape, including cumulative impacts.

In addition to passive solar heating, active solar technologies such as photovoltaics can be used to convert sunlight into electricity. Systems range from huge solar farms that feed large quantities of electricity into national networks to smaller building-mounted provisions that do no more than supplement the electricity requirements of an individual building or locality. Again, in considering such systems, planners have to consider the trade-off between the benefits of non-renewable energy and their aesthetic impact on townscapes or landscapes.

Hydroelectricity generation, in the form of harnessing river flows to generate electricity, has existed for many years. About 12 % of electricity in Scotland (1,500 megawatts) is generated through hydropower but in China the controversial Three Gorges Dam alone has the capacity to generate 22,500 megawatts of electricity. In many places there remains considerable potential for the increased use of traditional hydroelectricity generation but new forms of hydropower, such as tidal and wave power, are also beginning to make a contribution. Other renewable sources include biomass from waste materials or purpose-grown crops, either to generate electricity, for heating or to create biofuels. Geothermal energy, which exploits heat sources deep within the earth's crust, also has some potential for heating and electricity generation.

It is also important to increase efficiency in the use of water, taking only sustainable amounts from water sources and avoiding the depletion of water tables or the diversion of supplies from other areas of need. This may require market controls or regulations to limit water demand and the widespread implementation of systems for rainwater and 'grey' water recovery and reuse. 'Water Sensitive Urban Design is the process of integrating water cycle management with the built environment through planning and urban design' (CIRIA, 2013). Achieving sustainable development requires that every aspect of the water cycle – management of water demand and supply, wastewater, rainwater, watercourses and flooding – is considered concurrently and from the inception of the urban planning process.

At the city scale this is likely to mean that new development is located to avoid areas of flood risk and to minimize impacts on existing water courses and resources. Systems will be designed to capture as much rainwater run-off as possible so as to reduce pressure on drainage systems and decrease flood risk. Piped flows of captured water can be used to generate energy or diverted to irrigate green areas and crops in dry periods. Green and blue infrastructure will be designed to accommodate and direct flood waters away from residential and commercial properties in times of extreme rainfall.

In commercial and residential neighbourhoods green/blue roofs can be used to absorb and accommodate rainwater and control run-off. Soft landscaping and permeable surfaces (for example, in public spaces and car parks) reduce run-off, rainwater can be diverted to support more and healthier gardens, parks and street trees which in turn increase biodiversity and mitigate climate change and pollution. Within buildings, diverting downpipes to water butts or tanks reduces run-off and provides a source of water for non-potable uses such as toilet flushing, car washing or garden irrigation. The installation of water efficient appliances and toilets and the use of recycled water where possible can dramatically reduce water demand (CIRIA, 2013).

Urban areas need to become more self-sufficient in terms of waste management and disposal. That is to say, waste production should be minimized and, as far as possible, waste should be reused or recycled. Residual waste must be disposed of sustainably by, for example, converting waste into energy and avoiding landfill as much as possible. Waste reduction or minimization involves reducing the amount of waste produced in society through, for example, more resource efficient systems of production, producing and marketing products with less packaging or influencing patterns of consumption to prevent the creation of waste. Reuse involves using a product more than once or for more than one function: for example, glass bottles that can be returned to be refilled, and some building materials that can be retained after building demolition and reused in a new construction. In urban planning the most significant form of reuse is that of land and buildings. Increasingly, buildings that have become obsolete in one function (for example, warehousing or commercial use) are with some degree of adaptation being reused for new functions such as residential or leisure uses. Recycling involves the collection, sorting, cleaning or reprocessing of waste materials so that they can be reused either to produce the same or different products. Reuse and recycling save energy and unnecessary resource use, and avoid the financial and environmental costs of waste disposal. Recycling rates vary significantly between countries. According to the European Environment Agency, in 2010 Austria, Germany, Belgium, the Netherlands and Switzerland all recycled over 50 % of their municipal waste, whilst on average across Europe the figure was 35 % (EEA, 2013a).

Nature conservation within cities requires landscape and ecosystem protection, the maintenance and extension of green/blue networks and the incorporation of nature into urban environments and buildings (for example, green roofs). Westminster City Council in London is typical of many urban planning authorities in its approach to nature conservation. The Council's intention is to support the enhancement of open land (appearance, access, enjoyment) and the protection of sites or features of nature conservation importance. Thus the impact of development proposals on ecological habitats is carefully scrutinized and if deemed acceptable in principle, subjected to conditions and measures to mitigate any adverse effects upon nature. Open land, wildlife corridors and other sites of nature conservation importance are normally protected from development. Similarly, trees are also protected wherever they make an important contribution to the ecology, appearance or amenity of the locality. Landscaping proposals which help to create or restore wildlife habitats and their effective management are encouraged (Westminster City Council, 2007a).

Whilst today new buildings and neighbourhoods are generally being designed to achieve contemporary goals in terms of energy efficiency and sustainability, it must be remembered that much of our existing building stock was constructed to far lower standards. Given that much of this stock may last for many more decades or even centuries, especially given current policies favouring urban conservation and the reuse of buildings, 'retro-fitting' this building stock to meet modern environmental requirements becomes an important dimension of urban policy. According to the Green Building Council:

> The refurbishment of our homes and buildings is one of the greatest challenges we face to reducing carbon emissions. The majority of our existing stock requires some level of retrofit to enable us to live and work more sustainably. (UK Green Building Council, 2015)

The policy can be seen as an extension and development of the housing renovation policies that became widely used across European countries from the 1970s as a means updating sanitary provision and living conditions. Within *existing* buildings and neighbourhoods, retro-fitting for sustainability is likely to include:

- provision for micro-generation of renewable energy, including solar power;
- improvements to building insulation;
- installing smart heating/cooling and lighting systems to reduce energy demand;
- better water management and recycling systems;
- greening the space around buildings and installing green roofs and walls.

In addition to these environmental concerns there are economic and social dimensions to sustainable urban development. The economic dimension includes support for green local economic development and minimizing the environmental impacts of economic activity. The social dimension of sustainable urban development requires the development and management of inclusive communities, affordable housing and the integration of health, education and social welfare policies with spatial planning.

According to the UK Government in 2003 one of the key elements of a sustainable community is a flourishing local economy to provide jobs and wealth (ODPM, 2003). This point was reiterated by the European Commission in saying that in a period of increasing economic uncertainty many cities were failing to generate sufficient employment, especially for the young, less well qualified and marginalized social groups. The challenge was to create stronger links between economic and social development and the reduction of socio-economic polarization (CEC, 2011).

Furthermore, the growth of inter-urban and international migration, increasing diversity amongst urban populations in terms of ethnicity, culture and values, ageing populations and a widening gap between rich and poor are all leading to increased social-spatial segregation, ghettoization, isolation and loss of social cohesion. Such trends are unhelpful in seeking to create healthy, secure urban communities in which people want to live. 'The challenge for the Cities of tomorrow lies in breaking the segregation and turning the diversity into a creative force for innovation, growth and well-being' (CEC, 2011, p. 34). Or, as expressed by the UK Government in 2003, a sustainable community includes a diversity of vibrant and creative local cultures, encouraging pride and cohesion in the community; engagement and participation by local people, especially in the planning, design and stewardship of their community; an active voluntary and community sector; sufficient, decent and affordable housing; a safe and healthy local environment with good quality education, health, social and community services and facilities (ODPM, 2003).

One approach to the development of more sustainable cities, which is strongly advocated by the EU, is the use of information and communications technology (ICT) to generate 'smart' solutions to urban problems which are both 'highly efficient and sustainable on the one hand, as well as generating economic prosperity and social wellbeing on the other' (European Parliament, 2014, p. 9). It is argued that 'smart cities' are not just an innovative approach to urban problems but represent a key strategy for tackling poverty and inequality, unemployment and energy management. Proponents of the concept suggest six axes along which smart cities might develop, including:

- Governance – using open data systems and ICT to facilitate e-government, participatory decision making and co-created e-services;
- Economy – the development of e-business and e-commerce, ICT-enabled increases in productivity, advanced manufacturing and service delivery, local and global interconnectedness and flows of goods, services and knowledge;
- Mobility – ICT supported and integrated transport and logistics systems, prioritizing clean and often non-motorized options;
- Environment – ICT-enabled energy, heating and water management systems, metering, resource efficiency, waste management, pollution control and monitoring;
- People with high level e-skills – working in ICT-enabled processes, improving access to education and training, within a creative, innovative and inclusive society;
- Living – ICT-enabled life styles, behaviour and consumption, health care, healthy and safe living conditions in a culturally vibrant city (European Parliament, 2014).

Undoubtedly the implementation of these technologies and processes has the potential to improve systems of governance and the efficiency and sustainability of service provision. They may also enhance the competitiveness of 'smarter cities'. However, some of the claims for economic and social benefit may prove elusive because technological advance is unlikely to provide a panacea for the general and inevitable unevenness in the development of urban areas or the social inequalities that exist therein.

Many of these points are taken up and elaborated in various ways in the thematic Chapters 5 to 9 in discussions about the principal dimensions of urban planning: economic change and development; the changing function of urban centres; housing and neighbourhood issues; urban design and conservation; and issues surrounding mobility and accessibility. But first, two case studies illustrate the ways in which two cities – Copenhagen (Denmark) and Freiburg (Germany) – are responding to the sustainable urban development agenda.

Responding to climate change: Copenhagen Climate Adaptation Plan

Copenhagen, the capital of Denmark, is situated on the coast at sea level. With climate change likely to include higher and more unpredictable rainfall, rising sea levels and higher temperatures, the city faces a number of challenges. Whilst the City Council has established a set of priorities to respond to the dangers posed by climate change, including raising the height of sea walls to prevent inundation and expanding sewers to cope with rainwater surges, it also recognizes the need to plan to reduce its vulnerability to climate change in other ways. The purpose of the *Copenhagen Climate Adaptation Plan* is to respond to these issues. The plan takes a very long term view and aims to be flexible, have synergy with other development plans, be technically sophisticated, maintain the attractiveness of the city and contribute to green growth in the local economy.

The city changes slowly, with about 1 % of its buildings replaced annually, so by ensuring that all new buildings are adapted to climate change, the majority of the city will have been adapted within 100 years. The effects of climate change do not respect administrative boundaries so collaborative and coordinated planning is essential.

Rainfall is expected to increase by 25–55 % in winter and decrease by up to 40 % in the summer. Flooding will become more likely and the capacities of sewers and pumping stations will need to be increased. Where flooding becomes unavoidable, some measures can be taken to guide floodwater to areas such as parks and playing fields. As much rainwater as possible needs to be absorbed and cleaned locally through reducing surface sealing, providing green roofs and sustainable urban drainage systems (SUDS), thus minimizing the amount of water being drained into sewers. The municipal plan has the power to regulate how watercourses and open water areas are to be used and can specify, for example, that piped watercourses are opened or lakes enlarged to help the management of storm water. Local plans can require SUDS and, for example, the storage of storm water for some household uses.

The rising temperatures that are associated with climate change mean that the heat island effect that already exists in conurbations such as Copenhagen will be exacerbated. To combat this the plan proposes an increase in the amount of trees, green spaces and water spaces, all of which can have a cooling effect on rising temperatures. The municipal plan can designate land for green space and recreation. Through local planning the City can require new development to be designed and land-scaped to maximize shade and minimize warming. Increasing green and blue spaces and tree cover also has benefits in terms of provision of natural habitats, reducing air and noise pollution and increasing oppor-tunities for outdoor recreation and leisure.

Sea level rise is likely to have a serious impact on Copenhagen by the 2040s, so work has begun on raising the levels of sea defences. However, there are constraints: the functioning of the port has to be protected and there may be some loss of recreational opportunities. The municipal plan can exclude areas of high risk from urban development and through local planning the City can ensure that the coast remains robust and capable of withstanding higher sea levels and more powerful waves.

> Substantial investment and thorough planning are needed to meet the challenges that the changes in climate will face Copenhagen with. But by acting in time, we can minimise the expense of preventing and repairing damage, and climate adaptation can help to create green growth for Copenhagen. (Copenhagen City Council, 2011, p. 14)

Putting the whole package together: Green City Freiburg

Freiburg in southern Germany has become known as one of Europe's greenest cities. Since a successful local fight against a proposed nuclear power station in the 1970s, the city has steadily developed alternative-green strategies for its future development. A set of sustainability targets was adopted by the Municipal Council in 2009 and a 'sustainability management unit' established in 2011 to coordinate action. Not only is sustainability a key political priority but a high level of environmental awareness has been developed amongst the population. Community participation has been an important dimension of green policy making in the city. For instance citizen-led working groups identify issues in their district and propose targets for change and courses of action.

The city's sustainability targets are ambitious: in 1996 resolving to reduce carbon dioxide emissions by 25 % by 2010, updated in 2007 to a target of 40 % reduction by 2030. The focus of local climate protection policy is on energy saving and energy efficient renewable energy sources. Freiburg is one of the sunniest cities in Germany, so solar energy makes a major contribution to its energy needs, but there are also hydroelectric systems, wind turbines and other technologies such as biomass plants. Introduced in 1992, the Freiburg Energy-efficient Housing Standard for new buildings exceeded national standards for many years. But most of the housing stock already exists, so retro-fitting energy-saving measures in existing buildings is a priority. Here communication and developing understanding of the benefits amongst all stakeholders has been vital to acceptance and success. The municipality offers support to local firms for energy efficient renovation as well as training in environmental management. Much can be achieved in even the most unpromising buildings: a 16-storey residential tower dating from the 1960s was recently converted into the country's first passive high rise building at a cost of 13.4m euros. Since 2011 green energy has been offered to all residential customers and over 50 % of the city's electricity needs are met by combined heat and power generation.

With regard to mobility, the municipality's policy is to minimize the need for travel by creating a compact city, with strong neighbourhood centres, urban development along the main public transport arteries with priority for inner city development rather than suburban growth. Freiburg's transport policy promotes environmentally friendly modes of travel (walking and cycling, local public transport). Between 1982 and 1999 the proportion of bicycle traffic on inner city roads rose from 15 % to 27 % and the percentage of trips made by public transport rose from 11 % to 18 % while those by car fell from 38 % to 32 %. The building blocks of the city's transport policy have included: the development of the tram system, investing in new lines and rolling stock; developing the regional S-Bahn rail network; developing a dense network of cycle paths (from virtually none in 1970 to 420 km today); designating large parts of the city as pedestrian zones; comprehensive traffic calming in residential areas (90 % of residents live on streets with speed limits of 30 kph or lower). The city centre is a low emission zone in which high and even average polluting vehicles are prohibited.

Freiburg is one of the greenest cities in Germany. The municipal forest extends over 6,400 hectares, providing a green lung for the city, absorbing pollution and providing important recreational space, much of it subject to strict conservation policies. For more than 20 years, the city has been maintaining its green spaces along natural and ecological principles: grass is mown only twice a year and some playgrounds have been returned to their natural state. Within the streets and parks there are

50,000 trees improving the micro-climate of the city. There are 4,000 allotments, helping families supplement and enrich their diet as well as enjoy a peaceful retreat close to nature.

Watercourses, such as the River Dreisam that flows through the city, are being renaturized where practicable. The increasing use of sustainable drainage systems has allowed precipitation to be retained for reuse or allowed to seep through unsealed green spaces into the groundwater. Unnecessary artificial drainage of rainwater is being prevented by the integration of permeable surfaces and green roofs into the design of new or redevelopment building projects.

The treatment of waste is very important. The first objective is to avoid waste, for example through not using disposable drinks containers. 69 % of all waste is recycled in Freiburg. This has been made possible by the provision of a high grade, differentiated collection system and the availability of compostable waste bins for all households. Waste that cannot be recycled is incinerated to provide heat and power for use in the city.

On the economic front the city has demonstrated that the green economy creates jobs. Freiburg's Fraunhofer ISE solar research institute, committed to sustainable energy systems, employs 1,300 people. The city is also home to many other green organizations from solar factories to expert consultancies in green building and planning, education and training.

Vauban is one of the most well-known of the city's new neighbourhoods. Built on the 38 hectare site of a former military base on the outskirts of Freiburg, Vauban is a model of a sustainable new residential and mixed use neighbourhood developed to a masterplan providing homes for 5,500 inhabitants and around 600 jobs.

Planning began in the mid-1990s and most of the construction was completed between 2001 and 2014. In the 1990s the notion of sustainable development was at a relative high-point on the political and planning agenda at European, national and local levels. Internationally, *Local Agenda 21* had recently been published and in Germany innovations in sustainable urban development from the 1989 international building exhibition, Berlin IBA, and more recent Emscher Park IBA were still fresh in the mind. The origins of the masterplan lay in the actions of a pressure group, Forum Vauban, which pressed the City to acquire and develop the site of the military base in an eco-friendly way. Planning and development work was then coordinated through an inter-agency group led by the Municipality.

The layout of the area is based upon an elongated grid. A spine route, Vaubanallee, runs south-east to north-west with access roads (for loading and deliveries but no parking), and cycle and foot paths going off at right-angles to complete the grid. The spine comprises the tram

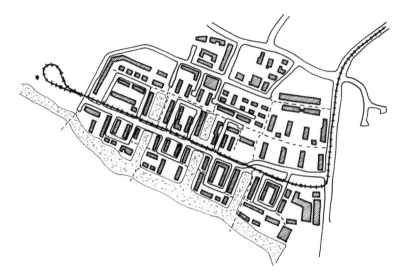

Figure 3.7   *Freiburg: Vauban*

Source: drawn by A.L. Couch; based upon the Quartier Vauban plan produced by Stadt Freiburg.

Note: The plan shows the east–west orientation of many of the residential blocks, the tram route through the central spine of the estate, the main pedestrian/cycle routes (dashed lines) and the green tongues linking to the countryside to the south.

lines, a two-lane distributor road and parallel shared cycle and foot paths (Figure 3.7). No part of the estate is more than 200 metres from a tram stop, from which there is an intensive service to the city centre about 15 minutes away. To the south a green valley runs the length of the estate with a series of green tongues extending right across the estate. Vehicle access is limited with most residents' cars being stored in three large (and expensive) multi-storey car parks on the edge of the estate. The layout favours and encourages walking and cycling over the use of the motor car. Freiburg also has a city-wide car club (car sharing) with a high concentration of members in Vauban. There is a large supermarket and neighbourhood centre at the eastern entrance to the estate and a smaller sub-centre half way along the spine road. Other facilities, such as nursery schools and children's play areas, are scattered through the estate. There is a combined heat and power plant (CHP) and district heating system. All buildings were constructed to at least low energy standard with extensive use of sustainable materials and sustainable drainage systems. About 20 % of the dwellings are built to the higher *Passivhaus* ultra-low energy building standard.

Within the framework provided by the masterplan, parcels of land were allocated to a variety of developers, leading to a range of building designs, tenures and occupation patterns. Housing cooperatives were particularly favoured in this process. For example, one of the first developers, at the end of the 1990s, was the Genova building cooperative which built two four-storey blocks comprising 36 flats of varying size to accommodate and integrate a range of different household types. The design included communal facilities and a shared semi-private garden. Future residents were actively involved in the design process. In one area the University of Freiburg developed residences for some 500 students and nearby the self-organized independent living initiative (SUSI) created some low cost and ecologically sustainable dwellings by adapting some of the former military barracks. To the east is a newer extension, known as the solar settlement, consisting of 59 entirely solar-powered dwellings that produce a positive energy balance and the ability to sell surplus energy back to the City.

The development of Vauban is impressive for the planning process, the level of community engagement, the sub-division and management of development land to encourage variety in housing design and form and for advancing the cause of ultra-low energy housing. The mobility concept seems to work well, proving a pleasant, safe, virtually car-free environment that has reduced car dependency and encouraged walking, cycling and social interaction. The inhabitants appear to be drawn from a range of income groups and household types.

Conclusions

The global population continues to increase and in many countries the nature of economic development that supports this population increase is leading to increased urbanization and the growth of cities, although it is worth mentioning that there is a substantial minority of cities, especially former industrial cities, that are currently shrinking. But at a global level, industrial production, urbanization, energy and natural resource consumption and pollution are rising. These trends are leading to natural resource and natural habitat depletion, loss of flora and fauna.

Air pollution from industrial production, energy conversion and transport systems is the principal cause of rising temperatures and less predictable weather patterns. Rising temperatures are leading to shrinkage in the polar ice caps and rising sea levels, which threaten coastal communities, especially when combined with more frequent storms. Climate change is also leading to changes in the productivity of landscapes and the population carrying capacity of different regions. Some regions and countries will become less agriculturally productive and others more so. International patterns of agriculture production will shift and some regions will become so hot and dry or suffer such unpredictable weather that they will become less habitable.

Whilst climate change requires intergovernmental action across many fronts, urban planning can play a part by reducing urban energy consumption and pollution. This can be achieved through planning more compact cities that reduce the need to travel; shifting transport modal split away from the motor vehicle towards public transport, cycling and walking; improving the energy efficiency of buildings; reusing and adapting redundant buildings and spaces for new purposes; and greening the city.

These imply planning systems that better control urban sprawl; encourage mixed uses and local service provision; investment in public transport, cycle networks and prioritizing safe pedestrian movement and access; strong regulations encouraging carbon neutral buildings; urban regeneration strategies that maximize the efficient use of existing urban land and buildings and maximize development densities around the most accessible transport nodes; and increasing the amount of green and blue infrastructure within cities.

A fundamental justification for urban planning is dealing with the social and environmental costs of development. Thus plans and planning decisions must take account of the externalities of a pattern of development or a single development proposal that may not be taken into account by the market. Furthermore, urban planning also has a responsibility to adopt the precautionary principle in decision making. Where a pattern of development or a single development proposal is likely to cause serious or irreversible environmental damage or resource loss, the decision should always be made on the side of caution.

There are social tensions within cities. Contemporary economic growth appears to be associated with growing disparities between rich and poor areas both between and within cities. There are also rising disparities in the distribution of income and wealth between different social groups: between age groups, social classes, occupation groups, indigenous and incoming populations. The growing scarcity of resources and the international population migrations resulting from conflict or climate change can only exacerbate social tensions between these different areas and groups. Again, whilst these are huge social questions that require national and international governmental action, urban planning has a role to play. A central tenet of sustainable development is equity: everyone should have an equal opportunity to obtain a good quality of life. Urban policies and planning can play an important part in this through policies that maximize equality of access to good quality living environments: to housing, health and education services, local facilities, transportation systems and green infrastructure.

Chapter 4

Economic Change, Development and Urban Planning

Introduction

There are various possible goals for urban planning with regard to local economic activity. These might include a desire to increase output per capita, to correct a skewed or unbalanced economic structure, to increase economic activity rates, to improve wage levels or tackle high unemployment. Other reasons might include underused social infrastructure or concern about the geographical balance of economic performance or contribution between regions. Which of these becomes the focus of planned intervention will be determined by the political imperatives of the public authorities concerned. But urban planning also has to deal with the social and environmental costs, the externalities, of economic development and has a responsibility to adopt the precautionary principle in making decisions about the nature and scale of economic development that should be permitted in any particular location.

This chapter will consider the structure of urban economies, the drivers of economic growth and change, planning and infrastructure provision for economic development and the transformation of areas to accommodate changes in urban economic activity. Alternative approaches and the idea of green economies will also be explored. It is in the nature of the capitalist economic system that local economies develop or grow at different rates and indeed may also decline. In growth situations the planning system is expected to make appropriate allocations of land and to ensure that the infrastructure is in place to facilitate economic development. In situations of decline, or growth rates that are deemed inadequate, a rather broader public policy effort may be required in order to manage the transformation of urban areas and to stimulate a return to local economic growth.

Before planners can intervene it is important to understand the local economy and how it is changing. The following section considers ways to measure and compare the size of the local economy, the nature of the economic base, the structure of the local economy and the components of local economic change.

The nature and structure of urban economies

The size of the local economy

The size of a local economy is typically measured as the gross domestic product (GDP) or gross value added (GVA) within its geographical boundaries. GDP is the value of the flow of goods and services produced by an economy, usually per annum. GVA is a similar measure but ignores the effects of taxation and subsidies. Obviously output is influenced by the geographical size of the area concerned so measurements of GDP per capita provide a better basis for making comparisons between areas or over different time periods. Table 4.1 compares four contrasting UK cities: London, the internationally important capital city; Liverpool, a port city and regional service centre in north-west England; Sunderland, a city on the north-east coast formerly important in shipbuilding and heavy engineering; and Cambridge, a smaller city dominated by higher education and scientific services. It can be seen that the economy of the London Region is more than twice that of the next most productive region in the table and GVA per head is nearly twice as high as in

Table 4.1   *GVA, activity rates and unemployment in four UK cities and regions, 2009*

	GVA (£ million)	GVA (£ per head)	Activity rate (%)	Unemployment rate (%)
London Region	£269,156	£35,100	75.8	7.3
Inner London	£183,880	£60,686	73.9	8.2
North-west Region	£119,079	£17,263	76.5	6.6
Liverpool	£8,667	£19,647	64.7	9.8
North-east Region	£40,369	£15,621	76.9	8.2
Sunderland	£4,905	£17,461	77.4	8.8
East of England Region	£107,209	£18,591	81.7	5.3
Cambridge	£13,606	£22,654	75.8	4.7

Source: ONS (2010) *Regional Trends No. 42*, Online tables: GVA, table 3.5 (workplace-based GVA); activity and unemployment rates, Table 9.18.

Note: Tyne and Wear conurbation – data is for Northumberland and Tyne & Wear; Cambridge data is for Cambridgeshire CC.

Liverpool or Sunderland and one-and–a-half times that of Cambridge. Looking at Inner London, with its concentration of highly paid senior professional and managerial jobs, the gap is even wider. Table 4.1 also shows how economic activity in the cities, often based on higher value tertiary employment, contributes more per head than economic activity in the regions as a whole.

A second measure of economic performance is the activity rate. This is the proportion of the population, or working age population, who constitute the labour force, that is those who are in employment, self-employed or seeking work. The activity rate for an area will vary with both the structure and performance of the local economy and with the structure of the population. The larger and more successful the economy, the higher activity rates are likely to be. Populations containing higher proportions of older people or those who find employment difficult to achieve are likely to have a lower activity rate. Within the economically active population the unemployment rate measures the proportion not currently employed but seeking work. The unemployment rate is one of the most important and politically sensitive measures of economic performance and is closely correlated with the activity rate. Clearly successful and growing economies are likely to have low unemployment rates while higher unemployment rates will be found in declining economies. Table 4.1 shows the variations that occur in activity and unemployment rates, with the east of England and Cambridge showing particularly high rates of activity and low rates of unemployment.

A closely associated concept is that of the dependency ratio. This can be measured as the ratio of the total population to the economically active population or the economically inactive population (typically pensioners and children) to the economically active population. The wage rate is the amount paid for a particular type of job. In some economic sectors, notably the public sector, wage rates are set by national pay bargaining and apply across the country. In others, especially where there are fewer national employers, wage rates will be more dependent upon local conditions of labour supply and demand. Average income levels are likely to be higher in local economies with a greater preponderance of more skilled jobs, such as managerial or professional posts. The level will be lower in areas dominated by unskilled or semi-skilled employment. Purchasing power relates to the amount of goods and services that can be purchased for a given amount of money (for example, a given wage level) in different local economies. Thus it can easily be the case that someone on a lower wage in a low cost region might be financially better off than an equivalent worker on a higher wage in a high cost region.

The nature of the economic base

Economic base analysis (sometimes known as export base analysis) is a theoretical approach to explaining local economic growth or decline in relation to the amount of goods or services the area exports to other places, that is, how much income the area earns from elsewhere. The theory divides the local economy into two parts: basic and non-basic activities.

Basic industries, or activities, provide the economic raison d'être for the existence and growth of the city. They are usually defined as those economic activities that export goods or services to locations beyond the local area and therefore bring income into the area. Without basic economic activity there is no economic reason for urbanization to take place. Basic activities might be extractive industries, such as coal mining for many towns in northern England, Wallonia, the Ruhr or Upper Silesia. They may be manufacturing industries such as cutlery and tool making in Sheffield, textile manufacture in Lille/Roubaix/Tourcoing on the French/Belgian border, motor vehicles in Wolfsburg (Germany), or electrical goods in Eindhoven (Netherlands). Transhipment can be a basic activity which led to the growth of the ports of Hamburg, Rotterdam and Antwerp at the mouths of important European rivers. In Cambridge higher education is a basic economic activity, as are financial services in the City of London.

The growth of basic industries leads to the expansion of non-basic economic activities – those that do not in themselves directly earn money from outside the area. Non-basic industries are of two types: productive activities that support and are integrated with the basic industries, and consumption or consumer activities that provide goods and services for the local population. Thus the growth of a port may lead to the development of chandlery, ship repair, insurance, legal and financial services that support the functioning of the port but do not themselves necessarily directly earn income from elsewhere. Of course, over the passage of time, some of these firms may expand to a point where they are capable of exporting themselves and become part of the basic economic infrastructure of the city in their own right. Consumer-focussed non-basic economic activity provides all the goods and services demanded by the local population: housing, nutrition, clothing, education, health services, local transportation and so on. The key point is that none of the jobs in these consumer-facing activities would exist without the basic industries providing the driving force for economic growth.

Economic structure is usually divided into three major sectors: the primary sector (agriculture, forestry and extractive industries such as mining and quarrying); the secondary sector (construction, manufacturing and engineering); and the tertiary sector (business and consumer services, ranging from financial and administrative services to retailing and personal services). Whilst many towns and cities may have grown historically to accommodate primary or secondary economic activity, today the economy of many urban areas is structured around some combination of secondary and tertiary activity. One of the biggest changes experienced by western cities since the 1960s has been the move towards ever greater dependency on tertiary activity.

The structure of a local economy can be measured by means of location quotients (LQ) which indicate an area's proportionate share of some economic activity compared with the (regional or national) average. A LQ greater than 1.0 indicates a relative concentration of that economic sector within the area and is considered to be part of the export or basic economic structure of the area. A very high LQ indicates industrial concentration, which might suggest the area has some strong comparative advantage in relation to that sector. Thus, it becomes possible to ascertain whether an area is heavily dependent upon specific economic sectors and, depending on the anticipated future for those sectors, whether some diversification of the local economic structure might be beneficial. Using this measure, Table 4.2 shows the contrasting economic structures of the cities of London, Liverpool, Sunderland and Cambridge. It can be seen that the key basic economic sectors in London are in the financial, insurance, information, communication, professional and property services, whereas in Liverpool public administration, health, and to a lesser degree, property services, education and tourism are the basic economic sectors. In Sunderland manufacturing remains the key export base sector of the local economy and in Cambridge there is an extreme bias towards education.

The LQ of 2.1 for the financial and insurance sectors in London reflects the locational advantages of London (and especially the City of London) in terms of skills, knowledge, professional networks, accessibility and so on for that economic sector. The LQ of 1.5 for the health sector in Liverpool reflects the city's historical strength in medicine, pharmaceutical and biomedical sciences, and makes it an attractive location for continued investment in those sectors. Similarly Sunderland's LQ of 1.8 for manufacturing shows its locational advantage for certain types of industrial and engineering activity, notably motor vehicles and IT. The LQ of 2.7 for education, 1.7 for information and 1.5 for professional and scientific services in Cambridge shows the impact of the historic growth and reputation of the University in attracting employment in related sectors.

The components of local economic change

The components of change in a local economy – growth or decline – can be measured using a technique known as shift-share analysis. The technique can be applied to different variables such as GVA or employment,

Table 4.2   *The economic structure of four UK cities*

Broad economic sector (or industry group)	London LQ	Liverpool LQ	Sunderland LQ	Cambridge LQ
Agriculture, Forestry & Fishing	0.0	0.0	0.0	0.0
Mining, Quarrying & Utilities	0.3	–	0.0	0.0
Manufacturing	0.3	0.5	**1.8**	0.3
Construction	0.4	0.6	1.0	0.4
Motor Trades, Wholesale, Retail	0.8	0.9	0.7	0.4
Transport & Storage (inc. Postal)	1.1	0.9	1.1	0.4
Accommodation & Food Services	1.1	1.1	1.0	1.0
Information & Communication	**2.0**	0.7	0.9	**1.6**
Finance & Insurance	**2.1**	1.1	1.1	0.4
Property	1.5	1.2	1.0	0.8
Professional, Scientific & Technical	1.7	0.9	0.4	1.5
Business Administration and Support Services	1.3	0.9	0.8	0.9
Education	0.9	1.1	1.0	**2.7**
Health	0.7	**1.5**	1.0	1.1
Public Administration	1.0	**1.7**	1.5	0.6
Other (inc. Arts, Entertainment)	1.1	1.1	1.1	–

Source: Calculated from data on location quotients by industrial sector, 2011, in Campos and Prothero (2012).

Note: Particularly significant export base sectors are **emboldened**.

on a sector by sector basis. Firstly, it examines the change that would occur if all the economic sectors in the local economy changed at the same rate as the national average. This is known as the national share (NS) or growth effect. Secondly, it measures the proportion of change that can be attributed to the particular economic structure of the city or region. If the local economy is well endowed with economic sectors that are nationally high growth industries (such as financial and professional services in the case of London) this will explain part of the reason for a high local growth rate. On the other hand, in a local economy where nationally slow growing or declining economic sectors are over-represented (such as manufacturing in Sunderland) this will partly explain the reasons for local decline or a slower than average rate of growth. This comparison is known as the industry mix (IM) or structural effect. Finally, there is a proportion of economic change that can be attributed to the characteristics of the city or region. This component identifies local economic sectors that are performing better than the national average for that sector. This indicates that the locality has particular characteristics (such as access to raw materials, availability or cost of labour or technology, access to markets, agglomeration economies and so on) which are advantageous to that economic sector. This is known as the regional shift (RS) or competitive effect. Thus shift-share analysis enables planners to separate national, industrial and local contributions when trying to understand and explain changes within a local economy. Table 4.3 gives an example of shift-share analysis applied to our four UK cities.

This analysis reveals that the performance of each of these cities is very different. London has a larger share of fast growing industries than the national average and has local or regional advantages that benefit the performance of its industrial base. Liverpool has a slightly larger share of growing industries than the national average but has local disadvantages that detract from the performance of its industrial base. Sunderland has a smaller share of growth industries than the national average but has local advantages that benefit the performance of the industries it does have. Cambridge is virtually identical to the national average in terms of the presence of growth industries but it does offer a

Table 4.3   *Shift-share analysis applied to change in GVA between 1995 and 2007 in four UK cities*

	National share (NS)	*Industry mix (IM)*	*Regional shift (RS)*	*Total change*
London	89.8	20.0	7.7	117.5
Liverpool	89.8	6.7	−14.6	81.9
Sunderland	89.8	−13.6	10.8	87.0
Cambridge	89.8	−0.1	29.4	119.1

Source: Oguz and Knight (2010); data from Appendix, table A1.

Note: Cambridge data is for Cambridgeshire CC.

very high level of local advantage which is most probably associated with the clustering and networking benefits in the higher education and scientific sectors that dominate the local economy.

Input-output analysis is a technique for measuring the relationships and interdependence between the different economic sectors within a local economy. It shows how the outputs from one sector can become the inputs to another sector and vice versa. The pattern of these relationships is usually expressed in terms of the monetary value of the exchanges and is presented as a matrix. A hypothetical example is shown in Table 4.4.

The absolute data shown in Table 4.4 can be turned into a set of coefficients to represent the relative strength of the relationships or linkages between sectors. These can then be used to forecast the total amount of economic growth that would be generated by growth in a particular sector: the multiplier effect. The following example of Liverpool's maritime sector shows how this can work in practice.

The maritime sector (which includes shipping companies, ship repair and maintenance, engineering, cargo handling, commodity agents and brokers, logistics, training and so on) is an important component of the Liverpool City Region (Merseyside) economy. In 2004/5 the sector contributed around £710m in direct GVA and £203m in indirect and induced GVA to the local economy, totalling between 5.0 % and 5.5 % of all GVA in the conurbation (see Table 4.5). Jobs in the maritime sector were found to be of high value, generating £34,600 per employee compared with about £26,000 for Merseyside in general. The locational advantages of the conurbation to the maritime sector included: the availability of staff, expertise and services; the proximity to ships and customers; and transport infrastructure (Fisher Associates, 2007).

Thus the overall size of the local economy can be measured in terms of output (GDP or GVA). The efficiency or productivity of the economy can be measured in terms of these measures per head or per hour worked. The structure of the economy can be explored by disaggregating it into economic sectors by using the standard industrial classification and the amount of employment or output per sector. This can be done at various levels of detail and can be expressed in terms of employment or output per sector. Economies can also be studied for their occupational structure: the proportion of professional, managerial, skilled and unskilled jobs in the economy. Activity rates and dependency ratios can be measured to determine how well the population is able to contribute to the economy; wage rates, income levels and purchasing power can be measured to determine how the local population benefits from such employment. Change (growth or decline) can be assessed by means of shift-share analysis to determine how much is due to industrial or locational factors. Finally, input-output analysis can be used to assess the multiplier effects

Table 4.4 *An example of an input-output matrix*

Inputs to: *Outputs from:*	*Primary sector*	*Secondary sector (manufacturing)*	*Tertiary sector (services)*	*Household consumption*	*Exports (from the local economy)*	*Total output*
Primary sector	2	10	8	12	4	36
Secondary sector (manufacturing)	1	15	5	6	12	39
Tertiary sector (services)	1	9	11	14	6	41
Household consumption	1	2	4	6	2	15
Exports (from the local economy)	3	15	7	1	-	26
Total inputs	8	51	35	39	24	157

Note: Figures are hypothetical and expressed in £m.

Table 4.5   *The impact of the maritime sector on the Merseyside economy, 2004/5*

Impact measure	Direct effects	Indirect/induced effects	Total impact
Output (£m)	1,974	560	2,534
Gross value added (£m)	710	203	913
Household income (£m)	543	155	698
Employment (FTE employees)	20,543	5,898	26,441

Source: Fisher Associates (2007).

across the local economy of growth or decline in any particular sector. A sound understanding of local economic structure is a prerequisite for planned interventions in local economic development. Further discussion of methods of local economic analysis can be found in the Cities Alliance's publication *Understanding Your Local Economy: A Resource Guide for Cities* (2007).

The questions for planners are: What should economic development policy be trying to achieve? and: How and at what spatial level should success be measured? Should success be measured in terms of increased output (economic growth) or in terms of output per head or per hour worked (economic efficiency)? Or should success be measured more in terms of the impact of change on local people: levels of income, wealth and purchasing power; activity rates, employment and dependency ratios? Other parties, such as land owners, might argue that rising property values are key indicators of economic success. Many environmental experts have argued that using increased output (GDP or GVA) as a measure of economic success is flawed because it takes no account of the social costs or environmental impact of economic activity. To compensate for this other measures have been devised, such as the Green GDP, which allocates a money value to such impacts as loss of biodiversity or climate change, or measures of waste production and environmental impact that can sit alongside conventional economic indicators (see, for example, Nordhaus and Kokkelenberg,1999; Lange, 2007; Li and Lang, 2010). Anther authoritative discussion of issues surrounding the measurement of economic and social progress is contained in the *Stiglitz Report* commissioned by President Sarkozy of France (CMEPSP, 2008), The question of spatial disaggregation is also important in measuring economic success: results for countries may hide great variation between regions; regional data may hide variation between cities; city-wide data may hide variation between districts and neighbourhoods. It cannot be assumed that a positive outcome in one location will trickle down to other locations.

The drivers of economic growth and change

Supply side drivers

In a market economy all firms are constantly seeking to maintain their competitiveness through increasing productivity, that is, reducing unit costs of production. This can be achieved through a number of different mechanisms including: investment (in more efficient machinery or by substituting machinery for labour); innovation (new methods of management, production, marketing or distribution); improving the skills of the workforce (to increase the quality and efficiency of output); enterprise or entrepreneurship (developing new business models or markets); responding to competition (the actions of other firms).

A key ambition of firms is frequently to increase output so as to obtain greater economies of scale such as greater specialization of labour, maximizing the output from fixed capital (machinery), area–volume relationships, or bulk purchasing economies. The shipping industry provides a good example of the benefits of economies of scale. In physics the cube-square law states that the volume of a container increases faster than the area of its sides. Therefore although larger ships cost more than smaller ships, the additional cost is more than offset by the additional cargo carrying capacity. Larger ships have also been found to be more fuel efficient and require fewer crew per ton of cargo than smaller ships. Thus, seeking economies of scale, shipping companies have tended to seek ever larger vessels. A period of particularly intense change was from the late 1960s to the 1980s with the emergence of large bulk carriers and container ships. These larger ships could not access older, smaller, shallower docks, usually in upstream locations, without considerable investment in dock infrastructure. It was commonly found to be cheaper to build new, larger docks downstream and to abandon the older facilities. The social cost and challenge to urban policy makers resulting from these changes was the problem of what to do about the derelict docklands.

Another mechanism to increase productivity is investment in technology. The cost of machinery and technology tends to decrease over time whereas the cost of labour tends to increase, so there is a constant imperative on firms to substitute technology for labour. There are many instances of this, from the advent of the spinning jenny and the steam engine in the early industrial revolution through to developments in the capabilities and use of computers and telecommunications in the late twentieth century. In many cases the impacts on the built environment have been profound. Staying with the example of shipping and port industries, the new technologies of palletization and containerization had a dramatic impact on the demand for dock labour. For example, between the 1950s and the 1980s, due to the use of these new technologies, throughput per berth in the Liverpool docks rose from 50,000 tonnes per annum to between 400,000 and 1,500,000 tonnes per annum. Furthermore, the output per unit of labour increased more than tenfold (Couch, 2003). The social cost and political challenge was how to respond to the falling demand for dock space and the rising unemployment of former dock workers that resulted from these changes.

Firms can also benefit from 'external' economies of scale which might provide advantages to a whole industrial sector or geographic area. For example, where there is a large group of firms in a similar industry concentrated in a particular location they may all be able to benefit from the availability of specialist services or specialized training at a local college or the benefits offered by networking and joint marketing. The size of the city can also provide economies of scale, known as agglomeration economies. For example, a larger city may provide a bigger local market for goods and services, a bigger pool of labour, a better range of business services, better communications and lower transport costs. In its *Local Growth* White Paper (BIS, 2010) the UK Government acknowledged that agglomeration economies – the concentration of people and businesses within a defined area – can have a big effect on economic performance:

> Many economists believe that agglomeration has been key in supporting growth in London, enabling it to play an increasingly prominent role on the world stage. This is being supported, for example through investment in high value transport projects and strategic approaches to planning, led by the Mayor. Such agglomeration effects may also help drive further growth in other areas, including cities and places with particular specialisms. (BIS, 2010, p. 7)

Firms will also seek to reduce costs through horizontal or vertical integration. Horizontal integration with other firms (competitors) in the same business increases the size of the company and its market share, leading to greater economies of scale. For example, the transatlantic shipping company White Star Line merged with its biggest British competitor, Cunard Line, in 1934 in order to better respond to the depression and the growing competition from other European and North American companies. However, by the 1960s further technological innovation – air travel – had effectively killed off the market for transatlantic passenger shipping. Similarly, in 1918 the successful Bank of Liverpool, which had a regional presence in the north of England having already taken over other local banks, merged with London-based Martin's Bank to create a bank of national standing. Its headquarters remained in Liverpool until in 1968 the bank was taken over by Barclays and its headquarters functions (including a number of highly skilled and highly paid jobs) moved to London. Each of these changes impacts on the number, type and location of jobs and on the amount and nature of development and the use of land.

Vertical integration occurs when firms seek to take over a number of stages in the production process. A much quoted example is that of the oil industry in which single firms might be responsible for oil exploration, extraction, transportation of crude oil, refining into petroleum and other products, transport to final distributors and ownership of petrol stations. Vertical integration is as much about control and security of supply as it is about cost reduction.

Another method of increasing productivity is to relocate production to a city or region that offers a better location or comparative advantage. Since the 1960s, labour costs have been a particularly influential factor in this regard. A substantial amount of industrial production has been moved from developed economies to the developing world: from the USA to Central and South America; from Europe to the Far East and more recently from Western to Eastern Europe. For example, in 2005 the motor vehicle manufacturers PSA Peugeot Citroën of France and Toyota of Japan combined to open a new factory, Toyota Peugeot Citroën Automobile Czech (TPCA), at Kolín in the Czech Republic to manufacture the new Citroen C1/Peugeot 107/Toyota Aygo. In 2014 Citroen's historic plant at Aulnay-sous-Bois, near Paris, was closed because of over-capacity. The example of the UK company Dyson illustrates the complexity of locational decisions in the increasingly globalized manu-facturing economy. Having established production in the small town of Malmesbury in Wiltshire some years earlier, in 2002 the company decided to move the manufacture of vacuum cleaners to Malaysia, with the loss of 800 UK jobs. The company claimed that the decision was not just about labour costs (although labour costs in Malaysia were around one-third of those in the UK); it also reflected proximity to suppliers, who were increasingly located in the Far East, and to the growing markets of South-east Asia and Australasia. But again the social costs of the decision were not borne by the firm. As trade unions pointed out at the time, it was difficult for the economy of a small town to absorb such a substantial level of job losses, although the company's research and development division did remain in the UK (BBC News Online, 2002).

It is not just the loss of jobs that is damaging to a local economy, it is also the particular loss of high status, high income jobs that can have an impact on civic leadership. During the nineteenth century local entrepreneurs endowed many British cities with civic, cultural, recreational or sporting facilities. In Liverpool the Walker Art Gallery was founded in 1873 with financial support from Andrew Walker, a local brewer. George Holt, owner of a local shipping line, was a major force in the founding of the University of Liverpool. In Birkenhead, shipbuilder John Laird established the Laird School of Art, the first public art school in the UK outside London. In Newcastle upon Tyne, Richard Grainger, a local builder and developer, was responsible for developing much of what is now the Grainger Town conservation area in that city. In Glasgow, Sir William Burrell, a local shipping magnate, gave his entire art collection to the city. Many of today's multinational corporate enterprises are more likely to sponsor a non-place-specific cultural or sporting event or programme rather than invest in a locality.

Demand side drivers

Changes on the demand side also influence economic activity. These changes may be cyclical or structural. Demand rises and falls cyclically in times of boom and recession. This in turn leads to the expansion and contraction of firms at different points in the economic cycle. The post-2008 economic crisis and recession led to a major downturn in production and a shake-out of less productive suppliers.

The GDP of the EU fell from €12,548bn in 2008 to €11,815bn in 2009 (around 6%) and only returned to previous levels in 2011 (Eurostat, 2014). The construction industry is particularly vulnerable to the effects of the economic cycle. Construction output in the EU fell by nearly 8% between 2008 and 2009 and continued to fall over the following four years. Housing construction was particularly affected. Between 2007/8 and 2008/9 annual housing completions in the UK fell by 18% and by 2010/11 output was 37% down (DCLG, *Live Tables on House Building*, Table 208, www.gov.uk/government/statistical-data-sets/live-tables-on-house-building (accessed 26.1.2015)). The consequences of this decline in output included massive lay-offs and unemployment in the construction sector, ranging from building workers to architects and even town planners. The impact also extended to reduced demand for a range of household goods from furniture and furnishings to kitchen and bathroom equipment. Another example can be seen in the motor industry. The Nissan car assembly plant in Sunderland, which had been hailed as the most efficient plant in Europe, reduced production from three shifts to two shifts at the end of 2008 and laid off some 1,200 workers. However, by 2010, with a good product range and growing demand within the UK and in export markets outside Europe, production levels were restored. The fall in demand had been a temporary consequence of the economic cycle. Not all firms can recover from these cyclical changes in demand. The recession caused many firms without the financial capacity to withstand even a temporary fall in demand, particularly in the construction and retail sectors, to close permanently with consequences for unemployment and vacant premises.

But changes in demand may also be structural, marking a more permanent shift away from particular products and towards others. For example, since the 1970s demand has moved from typewriters to personal computers; from film cameras to digital cameras; from record players to CD players and onwards to downloaded music. Firms producing goods in these sectors must respond or face extinction. One of the structural changes in demand that affected the economies of European countries from the 1970s was the permanent drop in demand for coal. Since the nineteenth century coal had been the main source of energy for power stations, industrial production, heating homes, powering maritime and rail transport. Gradually through the twentieth century electricity replaced coal as the energy source for manufacturing; oil, gas and nuclear energy replaced coal in many power stations; homes became centrally heated by gas, oil or electricity; and transport moved towards oil or electricity-based systems. At the same time, as coal reserves got more difficult to extract, the costs of coal mining were rising and cheaper imports were becoming available from Russia and elsewhere. In consequence, production of hard coal in the EU fell from 270m tonnes in 1973 to 100m tonnes in 1999, despite the eastward enlargement of the Union from 9 to 15 countries. Over the same period output in Germany fell from 144m to 44m tonnes, in France from 26m to 4.5m tonnes and in the UK from 130m to 36m tonnes (Eurostat, 2002). The number of deep mines in the UK fell from 261 to just 9. The effect of this permanent drop in output was to leave whole communities without an economic base, to make unemployed many that had previously been directly or indirectly employed in the coal industry as well as many more in the local non-basic economy. And there were environmental costs: much of the abandoned land was contaminated and in need of treatment, with mineshafts and slagheaps posing safety risks. The task of transforming the land and reinventing these local economies required substantial state intervention and planning.

Strategies for local economic development

Urban economies are changing. Many towns and cities in Europe, North America and elsewhere in the developed world, whose origins and development were based upon extraction, manufacturing or transhipment, find today that such industries have either vanished or employ a very small proportion of the local workforce. The economy of the post-industrial city is more likely to be based upon the service sector: financial services, governance, higher education, health care, leisure and tourism. These new growth sectors are often concentrated in city centres, heritage areas or mono-functional suburban campuses. Many former industrial zones are today being reused as areas of economic consumption: residential accommodation, retail and leisure complexes and urban parks.

Cities have become key drivers of regional economic performance. A study of 'competitive European cities' found no economically successful regions without successful cities at their core. Those that performed best had the best performing cities – and vice versa. Many successful European cities outperformed their national GDP per capita, with the factors leading to success identified as locally high educational attainment, innovation, social cohesion, connectivity and quality of life. Political capacity and the ability to take proactive and entrepreneurial policy decisions locally were also seen to be significant (Parkinson et al., 2004).

The infrastructure of a successful post-industrial city is therefore likely to include:

- good inter- and intra-regional accessibility by public and private transport;
- physical amenities and urban environments that support the post-industrial service-orientated economy (including attractive leisure-orientated central areas, event centres and so on);
- economic systems and skills to support such activity (including marketing and communications capacity);
- higher education, research, development and innovation capacity;
- social systems, including housing and neighbourhoods that support inclusion and diversity.

Some, such as Richard Florida (2002), have suggested that there is a new socio-economic group – the 'creative class', including skilled professionals in science, engineering, education, computing, the arts and media – who collectively make very significant contributions to local economic growth. Thus, according to this way of thinking, providing the right living conditions for this new class is seen as critical to city development in the post-industrial economy.

In an increasingly globalized world contemporary cities are ever more dependent upon attracting footloose service sector investment from external sources or developing their own potential for indigenous growth. Whichever their chosen route, and most cities choose both routes simultaneously, the requirements for economic growth are very different from those of the old industrial city. But the political recognition of the changing nature of urban economies is not always there. In many cities there remains a political desire to return to the days of the industrial city by trying to out-compete other locations by offering low rents, low taxes and relaxed planning regime. Writing about urban regeneration in Berlin, Colomb (2012) illustrates this conflict. The policy debate was between 'careful urban renewal' based upon endogenous, sustainable development or turning Berlin into a more globally competitive 'service metropolis'. Political choice favoured the second approach whereas in reality the city's economic regeneration has been based upon knowledge-intensive and creative industries. However, these sectors are threatened by public spending cuts, as she points out:

> On the one hand, public investments in infrastructure, police, healthcare, education, research are often argued to be fundamental to safeguarding or raising the attractiveness of the city to external investors and tourists. On the other, the hegemonic policy narrative of the 'city-in competition' and the 'city-as-enterprise' which underpins most forms of place marketing leads to strong attacks on public administration, public services and the public provision of social infrastructure. (Colomb, 2011, pp. 265–6)

Small and medium-sized enterprises (SMEs) play a particularly important role in the development of many local economies, stimulating competition and innovation and making a disproportionately large contribution to job creation. In the UK, for example, SMEs provided 59 % of private sector employment and 48 % of private sector turnover at beginning of 2013 (BIS, 2013). However, the growth and expansion of small businesses can be limited by internal constraints such as the ambition and ability of owners and by external factors, including access to finance and regulatory constraints. Nevertheless, supporting entrepreneurship, new firm start-ups and nurturing SMEs is recognized as playing a major role in economic development and has become an important dimension of policy in many countries.

> For a variety of reasons, promoting entrepreneurship enjoys support from governments at both ends of the political spectrum. Pro-entrepreneurship policies have been embraced as a means of increasing economic growth and diversity, ensuring competitive markets, helping the unemployed to generate additional jobs for themselves and others (rather than share existing work), countering poverty and welfare dependency, encouraging labour market flexibility, and drawing individuals out of informal economic activity. In short, an enterprise imperative has been charged with addressing a broad array of economic and social aspirations. (OECD, 2003, pp. 9–10)

A key element of the European Commission's strategy to promote growth has been the development of a range of policies to support SMEs, including particular support for women entrepreneurs, crafts and social economy enterprises. This support is embodied in the Small Business Act for Europe (2008) which aims to anchor the notion of 'Think Small First' in the policy making of member countries, and to promote SMEs by helping to overcome some of the barriers to growth (CEC, 2015).

Faced with the need to promote local economic development in the post-industrial era, cities need to devise a local economic development strategy that builds on a sound analysis of the present situation, the potentials of the area and consideration of alternative policies to reach the desired goals. Whilst such a process may be led by the public sector, whether local government or a single-purpose local economic development agency, the process will inevitably involve wider stakeholder participation, including local business and communities (Leigh and Blakely, 2013).

Success depends upon the ability to match what the locality has to offer, in terms of resources and comparative advantage, to the needs of contemporary industry and commerce, whether this means supporting the development of the existing local economy (indigenous growth) or encouraging inward investment from elsewhere (endogenous growth). The first stage in this process is to assess the current situation and forecast trends using the techniques discussed above. From this an analysis of the problems and potentials of the local economy can be established. A common method is to use a SWOT (strengths, weaknesses, opportunities, threats) analysis. Strengths and weaknesses are the internal characteristics of the local economy; opportunities and threats are external conditions or trends that may affect the local economy. Having completed the SWOT analysis, a strategy can be developed. This will attempt to build on local economic strengths, eliminate weaknesses, take advantage of external opportunities and become resilient in the face of external threats.

A typical local economic development strategy will include a number of layers. At the top will be a vision or mission statement establishing the general desired future for the area. Within this context, the strategy will set goals for specific economic outcomes, for example to build on existing local strengths, or to target inward investment, in particular sectors. These can then be developed into measurable objectives or targets, for example to double the size of the higher education sector within ten years; or to create a logistics park of at least 100 hectares. These objectives can then be translated into programmes and projects, and implementation arrangements agreed: what is to be done, when, by whom, at what cost, with what sources of funding? Thus final programmes of action might include selling municipal land to a university to facilitate expansion, agreeing with education providers to establish new logistics training programmes or using national or regional subsidies to collaborate with a private developer to speculatively lay out and equip a new logistics park in advance of user demand. The example of the local economic development strategy for the Dundee/Perth city-region illustrates this process in practice.

Local economic development, the example of TAYplan: economic outlook

In October 2013, TAYplan Strategic Development Planning Authority commissioned Oxford Economics to provide an economic outlook of the TAYplan (Dundee/Perth) economy. This included analysis of the current situation, including population, employment, sectoral structure,

---

Strengths

- Employment in tourism is predicted to grow by 11 % in the decade ahead. The sector will grow substantially in the short term on the back of hosting the Commonwealth Games and Ryder Cup.
- TAYplan's scenic attractiveness will encourage net in-migration to remain strong into the forecast period.

Opportunities

- House prices are forecast to grow over the coming decade; this will boost consumer confidence and expenditure in the area.
- Unemployment is expected to fall over the forecast period through the combination of job creation and a falling working age population.

Weaknesses

- Less developed professional services sector compared to the Scottish average. Professional services are predicted to be a key GVA growth driver in the future.
- Tourism is one of TAYplan's key growth areas for the future. Growth in this sector can be volatile and hard to forecast – often dependent on the weather.

Threats

- Employment within TAYplan is most heavily concentrated within sectors that have stagnant employment growth forecasts in the years ahead (agriculture, education and energy). Employment is not expected to achieve its 2008 peak.
- The upcoming referendum on Scottish Independence will create uncertainty.

Figure 4.1 *TAYplan economic SWOT analysis for 2014–2024*

Source: Based upon Oxford Economics (2014), p. 28.

Note: This analysis was prepared before the referendum on Scottish Independence in September 2014 which resulted in Scotland remaining within the UK.

productivity and the impact of global, macro and regional trends. From this analysis forecasts of future economic, employment, income and house price trends were produced along with an assessment of future housing needs. From these findings a SWOT analysis was produced (Figure 4.1).

The outcome of this analysis was that:

> The economic outlook for the medium term is quite positive. However, pressures on consumers and the government still weigh heavily on job creation prospects. The economic recovery will depend on the strength of the financial & business and tourism sectors ... and though Oxford Economics consider professional services likely to be the mainstay of such growth ... the possibilities in other sectors should not be discounted ... Population growth during the same period will be modest – underpinned by net in-migration in the TAYplan area. (Oxford Economics, 2014, p. 37)

In support of this policy, the Strategic Development Plan for the city region proposed, inter alia:

- to expand Dundee Airport and enhance principal railway stations and services;
- to focus the majority of the region's new development within its principal settlements, especially Dundee and Perth;
- to prioritize land release for all principal settlements using the sequential approach;
- to prioritize the reuse of previously developed land and buildings (particularly listed buildings).

The plan placed a lot of emphasis on improving the 'quality of place', including the incorporation and enhancement of existing natural and historic assets, not only as a contribution to a better quality of life for the region's people but also to improve its economic competitiveness as a place. This was argued to be particularly important in attracting footloose professional services and the tourist industry.

The plan identified the major locations for economic development:

> [as] the role of the further and higher education sector is central to growing the commercial value of research, particularly in life sciences, food, renewable energy and the games industry ... locations near to the region's universities and their relationships with business have potential benefits. (SPDA, 2012, p. 14)

And within the strategic framework established by TAYplan, the City of Dundee Local Development Plan elaborates these proposals in more detail. For example, by allocating employment land for research, development and professional services at carefully selected locations:

- Dundee Technology Park provides a substantive, high quality, Business Park location in the west of the city;
- Ninewells Medi-Park provides the opportunity for complementary uses to take advantage of synergies with medical and biological research and development at the hospital;
- Hawkhill Technopole, close to the University of Dundee, provides small scale 'incubator' opportunities for economic activities resulting as a spin off from research and development work at the University;
- The Creative Media District, near the City Centre and the University, already has a core of uses in the digital media sector and can provide innovative, low cost start up accommodation to encourage such uses (Dundee City Council, 2014, paras 5.21–5.24).

Local economic development: the impact of major cultural and sporting events

Major cultural and sporting events can make a significant contribution to local economic development. Obtaining the opportunity to run many of these events is frequently opportunistic and competitive and so cannot be planned with the same certainty as infrastructure investment or land use zoning. Nevertheless, events can be organized and designed to maximize local benefits. These benefits can be immediate or longer term and can range from direct capital investment to short and longer term revenue streams as well as changes to soft factors such as image and place marketing.

Whilst many cultural events (for example, art exhibitions, performances) make a contribution to image building and place marketing, few are of sufficient scale in themselves to generate significant measurable economic impacts, although multiple events, whether in series or in parallel, can increase the effect. An example of these would be the series of festivals run annually in Edinburgh (including the Edinburgh Festival, the Fringe, the Film Festival, Hogmanay and so on) which are said to benefit the Scottish economy by more than £300m of additional visitor expenditure annually (BOP Consulting, 2011). Another example would be the annual designation of European Capitals of Culture, which frequently provides the catalyst for capital investment (for example, in museums, galleries or performance venues), substantial revenue streams and a high level of place marketing (García, 2005; Palmer and Richards, 2007).

On the other hand, one-off mega-sporting events such as the football World Cup, Olympic Games or Commonwealth Games can have even more dramatic impacts. Estimating these impacts is a complex task, especially as one has to identify the spread of costs and benefits over time, space, organizations and social groups as well as accurately attributing these costs and benefits to the event in question or to other causes. For example, how much of the transport investment that has been provided in support of recent Olympic events would have happened anyway? That is, what would be the counter-factual situation?

The Sydney Olympic and Paralympic Games of 2000 were said to have generated A$3bn (Australian dollars) in business activity, A$2bn in post games sports expenditure and service contracts, A$6bn in local and regional infrastructure investment (including improvements to highways and the airport) and A$6bn in in-bound tourist expenditure (PWC, 2001). These are considerable benefits. In addition:

> For Sydney, New South Wales and Australia, the Sydney 2000 Olympic Games provided massive exposure and publicity to the world and in many cases a first or a renewed awareness of Australia. The business opportunities identified and the networks established internationally, particularly with the many thousands of business people who visited Australia during and prior to the Games, will continue to provide opportunities into the future for Australian business and trade, particularly in the Asia-Pacific region where Australia has a growing status as a stable and developed country with benefits to offer the region and the rest of the world wanting to do business there. (Locate in Kent, 2009, p. 6)

However, according to the *Independent* (19.8.2008) the cost to the public sector of staging the Olympics was far higher than originally estimated and resulted in a net cost to the New South Wales Government of A$1.5bn. It also took many years for a long term Olympic Park redevelopment plan to be realized. Although the park had become a tourist attraction and had allowed the city to host a number of international sporting and cultural events, it was several years before significant parts of the park were redesigned and transformed for residential and commercial development. A key lesson, which was learned in time for the London Olympics in 2012, was to plan early for the after-use of the site and legacy of the Games. See also Davidson and McNeill (2012) and Searle (2012) for contrasting views on the long term impact of the Sydney Games.

Policy responses: land use planning

Forecasting changes in employment and the demand for employment land

A fundamental role of planning systems in relation to economic development lies in the allocation of land. There are two sides to this: the provision of land in response to anticipated needs and the control and management of development proposals. As the UK Government stated in its National Planning Policy Framework:

> To help achieve economic growth, local planning authorities should plan proactively to meet the development needs of business ... planning policies should recognize and seek to address potential barriers to investment, including a poor environment or any lack of infrastructure, services or housing. In drawing up Local Plans, local planning authorities should set out a clear economic vision and strategy for their area which positively and proactively encourages sustainable economic growth; set criteria, or identify strategic sites, for local and inward investment to match the strategy and to meet anticipated needs over the plan period. (DCLG, 2012, para. 20)

The planning process that leads to land use allocations for economic development comprises a series of steps that start with an analysis of the current situation, estimates future needs and then makes appropriate land use allocations. This process has been codified in a number of documents, including the UK Government's *Employment Land Reviews: Guidance Note* (Environmental Resources Management, 2004) on which the following section is based.

The first step typically comprises a baseline study to assess the usefulness of the land allocated for industrial and commercial development in current plans: which sites should be retained and which sites might no longer be considered suitable (perhaps because of site constraints or changes in policy). The minimum data typically required for such an analysis includes site location, developable area, ownership, potential uses and constraints on development (physical and legal).

The second step is to assess future development needs, for example by monitoring planning permissions and the rate at which land has been developed in the recent past, and by more qualitative methods of property market analysis including consultation with stakeholders. Different economic sectors will be developing in different ways, at different speeds and will have different land requirements. As shown in Table 4.6, the *Guidance Note* identified ten distinct employment property market segments and types of site. Although this classification was drawn up in relation to the UK economy, its contents will resonate with planners in most developed countries.

The most straightforward method of assessing future employment trends and development needs is to project forward historic development trends. Whilst it is relatively simple to produce a running average of the take-up of land over recent years, this may not produce an accurate forecast of future requirements because it takes no account of any differences between previous and future economic circumstances.

Table 4.6   *A classification of employment property market segments and types of site*

1. Established or Potential Office Locations	Sites and premises, predominantly in city centres, recognized by the market as suitable for office development
2. High Quality Business Parks	Typically sites of 5–20 hectares currently or capable of being occupied by national or multinational firms, with high quality of buildings and public realm
3. Research and Technology/ Science Parks	Usually strongly branded and managed in association with academic and research institutions
4. Warehouse/ Distribution Parks	Large, often edge/out of town serviced sites located at key transport interchanges
5. General Industrial/ Business Areas	Industrial areas well suited for retention in industrial use; often with a mix of ages, qualities and site/building size
6. Heavy/Specialist Industrial Sites	Generally large sites already occupied by manufacturing or processing industries; often concentrated around historic hubs such as ports, riverside and docks
7. Incubator/SME Cluster Sites	Generally modern purpose built, serviced units
8. Specialized Freight Terminals	Sites for distribution or transhipment associated with specific ports, airports or rail links
9. Sites for Specific Occupiers	Sites adjoining existing established employers and principally intended for their use
10. Recycling/ Environmental Industries Sites	Can occupy premises in light industrial zones but often have substantial external storage requirements

Source: Adapted from Environmental Resources Management (2004), p. 41.

A more sophisticated approach is to develop a model of the local economy in order to forecast future economic trends in the locality and from that to produce an estimate of future land requirements. One well known example of such a model is that developed by Cambridge Econometrics (2015). Within the framework of national and regional trends, this model provides forecasts of local economic, labour market and demographic indicators (see Figure 4.2).

The next step is to translate employment forecasts into land requirements for each sector of the local economy. Economic forecasts are

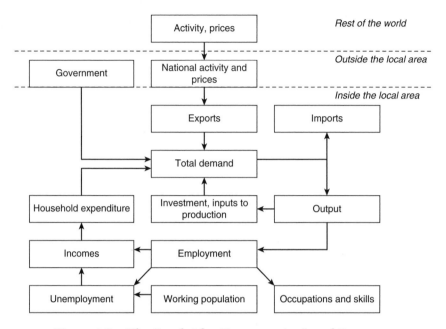

Figure 4.2 *The Cambridge Econometrics Local Economy Forecasting Model*

Source: Based upon Cambridge Econometrics (2015).

usually made and disaggregated by the Standard Industrial Classification (ONS, 2007). These groupings will not necessarily directly correspond with the classes of land use designated in development plans. For example, in England the planning system classifies uses as in Table 4.7. Typically, but not definitively, most forms of office employment will fall into classes A2 or B1; manufacturing will fall into class B2; warehousing and logistics into class B8.

Employment forecasts then need to be translated into floorspace and land use requirements. The amount of floorspace required to accommodate each worker varies substantially between different industries and firms. Nevertheless, some attempts have been made to calculate average floorspace requirements. For example, typical floorspace requirements per worker in the London region have been estimated as being 17.9 m² in offices, 31.8 m² in industrial premises and 40.1 m² in general warehousing (Environmental Resources Management, 2004).

Having established the total floorspace required for the forecast increase in employment, a further calculation is then needed to convert floorspace per worker into the amount of land required. Here it is necessary to use the concept of the plot ratio (the proportion of the site that is actually built on – calculated as the gross floorspace divided by the

Table 4.7   *Use classes in the English planning system, 2013*

A1	Shops
A2	Financial and professional services
A3	Restaurants and cafés
A4	Drinking establishments
A5	Hot food takeaways
B1	Business
B2	General industrial
B8	Storage or distribution
C1	Hotels
C2	Residential institutions
C2A	Secure residential institutions
C3	Dwellinghouses
C4	Houses in multiple occupation
D1	Non-residential institutions
D2	Assembly and leisure
Sui Generis	Uses that do not fall within any use class

Source: DCLG Planning Portal (www.planningportal.gov.uk/permission/commonprojects/changeofuse, accessed 22.1.2014).

land area). Again, there is great variation in practice but typical figures are a plot ratio of 0.35–0.45 for industrial areas, 0.4–0.6 for warehousing, 0.25–0.4 for business parks, and anything from 0.4 to 2.0 for city centre offices.

So, for example, if net change in manufacturing employment is forecast to be +3,300 jobs over the plan period, at a typical density of 34 m^2 per worker, a further 112,200 m^2 gross internal floorspace will be needed. At a plot ratio of 0.4, this gives a requirement for an additional 28.05 ha in use class B2 [General Industrial] (that is, each hectare of land is occupied by 0.4 hectares of floorspace). If the net change in employment in professional services is forecast to be +6,000 jobs over the plan period, at a typical density of 19 m^2 per worker, a further 114,000 m^2 gross internal floorspace will be needed. At a plot ratio of 0.3, this gives a requirement for an additional 38.00 ha divided between use classes A2 and B1.

Identifying additional employment land

Having quantified the amount of land required, the planner's task is then to identify which land should be zoned for development and what criteria should be used to respond to proposals from developers. This process involves identifying the need for land in each employment market segment, including the amount of land, plot sizes, location and other requirements. Potentially available and suitable land then has to be appraised, both in terms of market requirements and planning policy requirements (for example, sequential testing) and the selected sites identified and appropriately zoned in the development plan. Figure 4.3 shows an example of a sustainability appraisal methodology for selecting employment sites.

There are two constraints on this process. First, many of these criteria present difficulties in measurement, often requiring qualitative or subjective professional judgements. Second, the land that is allocated must, in the final analysis, suit the needs of the market. Thus, as well as meeting the criteria of sustainable development, the land must be suitable for development in terms of its location, shape, size, accessibility, adequacy of utilities and infrastructure, ownership and legal constraints. As the UK Government states: 'local planning authorities should plan proactively to meet the development needs of business and support an economy fit for the 21st century' (DCLG, 2012, para. 20).

Not all land that is going to be developed for employment uses will have been identified by planners in their development plan. Some other

---

The portfolio of sites was appraised using a set of 'sustainability indicators':

- accessibility to public transport;
- brownfield regeneration;
- social development;
- environmental amenity;
- jobs/workforce ratio; and
- distance travelled to work.

For each of the indicators the sites were graded according to how sustainable they were in each respect:

A strong and beneficial impact;
B beneficial impact;
C neutral impact;
D negative impact; and
E strong negative impact.

This methodology allowed particular weaknesses of sites to be identified and where actions could or should be targeted prior to a site being released for development.

Figure 4.3 *West of England Strategic Partnership (WESP) appraisal of strategic employment sites*

Source: Based upon RPS and Alder King (2013).

land might be brought forward and proposed for development by land-owners or potential users of the site. In the flexible UK planning system planners have to judge such proposals on their merits. Figure 4.4 provides an example of how such decisions might be made in one part of the United Kingdom.

These criteria mirror those used in the plan making process. To be permitted, proposals for economic development should be compatible with uses in the surrounding area, avoid environmental damage, including natural and built heritage, demonstrate that access, infrastructure and utility provision is suitable, and demonstrate a high quality of both functional and aesthetic design.

A proposal for economic development use ... will be required to meet all the following criteria:

(a) it is compatible with surrounding land uses;
(b) it does not harm the amenities of nearby residents;
(c) it does not adversely affect features of the natural or built heritage;
(d) it is not located in an area at flood risk and will not cause or exacerbate flooding;
(e) it does not create a noise nuisance;
(f) it is capable of dealing satisfactorily with any emission or effluent;
(g) the existing road network can safely handle any extra vehicular traffic the proposal will generate or suitable developer led improvements are proposed to overcome any road problems identified;
(h) adequate access arrangements, parking and manoeuvring areas are provided;
(i) a movement pattern is provided that, insofar as possible, supports walking and cycling, meets the needs of people whose mobility is impaired, respects existing public rights of way and provides adequate and convenient access to public transport;
(j) the site layout, building design, associated infrastructure and landscaping arrangements are of high quality and assist the promotion of sustainability and biodiversity;
(k) appropriate boundary treatment and means of enclosure are provided and any areas of outside storage proposed are adequately screened from public view;
(l) is designed to deter crime and promote personal safety; and
(m) in the case of proposals in the countryside, there are satisfactory measures to assist integration into the landscape.

Figure 4.4 *Development control criteria for economic development in Northern Ireland*

Source: DOE (2010), General Criteria for Economic Development.

Policy responses: transformation

In many cities recent decades have seen a decline in industrial employment that is unlikely to return. Many upstream and older docklands have fallen into disuse. Railway marshalling yards, freight depots and engine sheds have been abandoned as railway technology has changed. Urban electricity and gas power stations have closed down and much historic urban manufacturing industry has ceased operating or has moved elsewhere, either to more suburban locations or to other regions or countries where production costs are lower or markets more accessible. In these circumstances cities across the developed world have seen the appearance of swathes of vacant and derelict land, much of it contaminated with the residue of industrial processes. Yet this land represents a potentially valuable urban asset if it can be brought back into beneficial use.

At the same time many cities have seen a rising demand for land from new forms of economic activity with the expansion of the tertiary sector including retailing, information and communication activities, financial and administrative services, education, health, and public administration. Some cities have also become a focus for tourism and recreational activities. There has also been a rising demand for housing in cities.

The task therefore has been to transform the stock of vacant and derelict urban land into sites that are suitable for reuse to accommodate these alternative land uses. Transformation may involve a number of processes. In some cases it may be possible to recycle buildings and change them from their former use to some new purpose, for example in the conversion of former dockland warehouses to residential use. More often the task involves the removal of obsolete buildings and infrastructure and sometimes the decontamination of the ground before a site can be reused. The size and configuration of sites may not suit modern development requirements and a process of land assembly may be required to facilitate redevelopment. Utility provision (energy, water, sewerage, communications) may all require investment. The local transport system may need to be adapted to the new functions of the site.

The examples of Baltimore 'Inner Harbor' and the city of Dortmund are described below and provide examples of transformation and economic development in action.

Area transformation: Baltimore Inner Harbour

Baltimore is a large port city in the state of Maryland, USA. Based on the port and heavy industry, especially steel production, the city grew to a population high of 950,000 in 1950 but quickly declined in subsequent decades as much of the port fell into disuse and industrial restructuring took hold. As early as 1953, a report had revealed that population loss from the central city, caused by suburbanization, was devaluing central area land values by 10% a year and forecast that the city would be bankrupt within 10 years unless something was done to reverse these trends (Millspaugh, 2001).

Through the latter part of the 1950s plans for the redevelopment of the inner harbour area through public-private partnership were drawn up and approved. The initial response was the Charles Centre Redevelopment Plan (1958) which set the tone for the regeneration of the first 13 hectares of land. This initial plan had three ambitions: (a) to get prestigious office development along the main street (Pratt Street) facing the waterfront; (b) to develop apartment housing; (c) to develop the shoreline of the inner harbour as a public amenity (Millspaugh, 2003). One feature of the programme, that was unusual at the time but commonplace today, was that a number of older historic structures were retained and incorporated within the redevelopment area.

The project began to gather momentum by 1969 when the first major office investment, by a local insurance company, gave some credibility to the entire project. Spurred on by this, a number of national and international companies began to build offices in the area. In 1972 the flagship 28-storey World Trade Center was completed. Around the same time the City was investing in physical changes to the waterfront 'to make visible things happen, no matter how small or temporary, so as to make news and establish the Inner Harbor as a real, successful undertaking in the public consciousness' (ibid., p. 38). The street system was redesigned into wide boulevards enclosing a large area of parkland and a 10-metre wide promenade developed along the water's edge. Attracting housing investment proved more problematic. Apart from some housing for the elderly little was achieved until the City established a 'homesteading' programme, selling the shells of dilapidated terraced dwellings in the Inner Harbor West for $1 to local residents who would restore them. The scheme proved a great success and showed that there was a market for inner city 'walk-to-work' housing (ibid., p. 39). Subsequently, as confidence grew, more private housing developers were attracted to the area.

In the 1970s the redevelopment area was extended to include a further 97 ha of the Inner Harbor area to the south. A key catalytic event in the regeneration process was the arrival of the 'tall ships' in 1976 as part of the US bicentennial celebrations. For perhaps the first time, Baltimore was attracting tourists in numbers to visit the city. The Maryland Science Centre added to the attractions of the area. With support from an Urban Development Action Grant (gap funding) a new hotel, the Hyatt Regency Baltimore, opened in 1981. The National Aquarium was completed in the same year.

In 1980, a local developer, James W. Rouse, opened the retail and leisure complex – Harborplace. This proved to be the catalyst that provided the critical mass that generated an explosion in visitor numbers. By 1982 the area was estimated to be attracting 20 million visitors a year, of which one-third were tourists. Further redevelopment quickly followed. By this time a greater emphasis was being placed on leisure and tourism activities, with the completion of further hotels, restaurants and extensions to the promenade and public parkland. More recently the redevelopment effort moved on to Harbor East where further residential accommodation, hotels and retail space have been provided.

By setting out a clear vision and initiating the redevelopment programme the City was able to attract private investors to the area. By the millennium 75 % of all investment had come from the private sector (Millspaugh, 2001). There is no doubt that the programme revived the economy of the central city, transforming the former industrial economy based upon shipping and steel, to a post-industrial economy based upon services, leisure and tourism. The building of new forms of residential accommodation, suited to the needs of a modern, more fragmented society comprising more small adult households, ameliorated the problem of population loss. The decline in property values was staunched and a process of re-urbanization set in motion.

The regeneration of Baltimore's inner harbour has won many accolades, including those from the American Institute of Architects and the Urban Land Institute. Being one of the first cities to experience and successfully respond to economic restructuring, the Inner Harbor regeneration programme became a model that influenced the redevelopment and transformation of former industrial areas, and particularly waterfront areas, in cities across the world. Perhaps its biggest contributions to planning theory have been in demonstrating to households that the central city, especially when associated with waterfronts and landscaped public places, can be an attractive place to live; and in showing developers that investing in post-industrial economic activity, including housing and the leisure and tourism sectors, in such areas will yield a satisfactory return. However, it is also important not to claim more than has been achieved. Over a period of fifty years a large area of the inner city has been brought back into beneficial use and a process of re-urbanization has been facilitated. But it should not be forgotten that the city as a whole remains relatively poor with unemployment stubbornly high and nearly 20 % of the population living below the US poverty line in 2008 (US Census, 2011).

Area transformation: Dortmund

'Phoenix' was the name given to the Hoesch steelworks at Hörde about 5 km south of central Dortmund in the eastern Ruhr region of Germany. The works were divided between two sites on either side of Hörde town centre: blast furnaces were located at Phoenix West and steel mills in Phoenix East. In 1999 the plant closed, making thousands of workers redundant and leaving a 200 ha derelict site. But this site was only one of a number of similarly vast brownfield sites around the city, including a defunct steelworks and surplus canal wharfs north-west of the city centre, a third steelworks to the North-east, a derelict airfield and a former British army barracks.

The response of the City Council, working in association with the Land Government of North-Rhine Westphalia (NRW), was to seek to diversify employment and re-orientate the local economy towards high technology industries. One of first initiatives, dating from the 1960s, was the establishment of a new university with a strong technological focus on a large campus site in the south-west of the city. In 1985 this was complemented by the development, on an adjoining site, of a Technology Centre and Technology Park that could accommodate spin-off firms, research and development activities in advanced engineering and information technology. Today the park is virtually full with some 250 firms employing more than 8,500 people. Whilst not quantitatively compensating for the loss of former industrial jobs, these developments have gone a long way towards transforming the image of Dortmund as an investment location.

Through the 1990s Dortmund was included within the Emscher Park International Building Exhibition (IBA), which promoted the ecological and economic regeneration of the northern Ruhr region and included renaturization of the Emscher river, creation of a regional landscape park, celebration of industrial and cultural heritage, and investment in housing, industrial, commercial and leisure projects (Kunzmann, 2004). The lessons learned from this exemplary programme informed subsequent planning in the region.

Since 2000 the City Council, in partnership with other key stakeholders, has framed its economic development strategy under the banner of the 'Dortmund Project', focussing on supporting industrial development in selected sectors (notably in micro-technologies, logistics and so on) and increasing the attractiveness of the city for inward investment by strengthening 'soft locational factors' such as environmental quality, housing supply, leisure and cultural opportunities and promoting each of the large brownfield sites for a specific and appropriate purpose. Thus, for example, logistics are directed towards the harbour and offices towards Stadtkrone Ost (a former army barracks).

It was within this context that the future of the Phoenix complex was decided. The two sites are very different in character. Phoenix West is substantially flat and well connected, not too far from the existing university and the technology park, and was developed for manufacturing in the micro-electromechanical (MEMS) and IT sectors. Phoenix East is in a deep valley. It is here that a leap of imagination by the City Council led to the decision to create a 24 ha lake, to provide for water-based recreation and an attractive environment for new housing, particularly to increase the supply of higher quality private housing which was thought necessary to support growth in the new economic sectors. It also gave Dortmund a small taste of the sort of waterfront environment normally only found in former dockland or coastal locations. Between these two sites, in Hörde town centre, there was also investment in new buildings, improvements to the public realm and transport connections (see Figure 4.5).

The Phoenix regeneration programme is based upon an informal partnership between a number of different stakeholders. Ownership of the site passed from Hoesch to Dortmund City Council and then Phoenix East was transferred to Dortmunder Stadtwerke AG (DWS21), a utility company wholly owned by the City Council, while Phoenix West was acquired by the Landesentwicklungsgesellschaft NRW (LEG), a regeneration agency run by the NRW Land Government. Dortmund City Planners have been responsible for preparing the Bauleitplan (land use zoning plan) and for detailed Bebauungsplane (detailed site layout plans) for individual areas. A special short-life agency – Phoenix See Entwicklungsgesellschaft – a wholly owned subsidiary of DSW21, has been responsible for the development and marketing process (Tata, 2005).

The development of Phoenix East has been impressively quick. By 2014 the lake had been created. The south-west shore adjoining Hörde town centre had been given an urban feel with a pleasant promenade backed by new 4–6-storey blocks containing mixed residential, commercial and leisure uses. One historic building, the former headquarters of the steelworks, has been retained. Housing is being developed around the rest of the lake: high quality, lower density private housing to the north (with south-facing views over the lake) and higher density housing along the more accessible southern shore. A new area of parkland north of the lake connects with Phoenix West and extends to the existing Westfalen Park in the south of Dortmund (Biddulph, 2012).

Despite the MST factory opening in 2005, the development of Phoenix West has been much slower because the ambition to create a high technology engineering and IT manufacturing park of 115 ha had to contend with the impact of the post-2008 economic crisis. Overall the programme has benefitted from long term strategic planning and responds in high order to all the requirements of modern thinking about sustainable development and excellence in urban design (Biddulph, 2012). There is no doubt that this is a very expensive regeneration project but it is seen by both the City Council and the Land Government as a transformational flagship project that will not only provide a substantial development area for new industrial, commercial and residential investment itself but also make a major contribution to the continuing re-imaging of Dortmund and the Ruhr, which will have benefits across the region.

(a) Phoenix West

(b) Phoenix East

Figure 4.5   *Dortmund and the Phoenix regeneration area*

Sources: Plan drawn by A.L. Couch, based upon publicity material from Stadt Dortmund, available at www.phoenixdortmund.de/de/home/; photographs C. Couch 2016.

Note: The new uses for the two sites stand in contrast, with the flatter, more accessible Phoenix West given over to industrial development while Phoenix East is devoted to commerce, leisure and housing intended to attract the creative classes.

Alternative approaches to local economic development

'There is only one argument to have about the economy. It is about how this country is to grow' (Hutton, 2010). Few dare question this widely held assumption. The belief in economic growth has become so ingrained in the modern psyche that no mainstream political party has the courage to make the connection between economic growth and unsustainability (Meadows et al., 2005; Jackson, 2009).

> [However] economic growth, for so long the great engine of progress, has, in the rich countries, largely finished its work. Not only have measures of wellbeing and happiness ceased to rise with economic growth but, as affluent societies have grown richer, there have been long-term rises in rates of anxiety, depression and numerous other social problems. (Wilkinson and Pickett, 2009, p. 5)

It is clear what types of city and urban form the current economic model produces, the results are all around us. The evidence is within our towns and cities. Much research has been undertaken to envisage alternative 'sustainable cities', but what does the economic system required to deliver such visions look like?

In March 2009, the Sustainable Development Commission (SDC) published *Prosperity without Growth* which questioned the 'myth' of economic growth and assessed the consequences of growth, its failures and flaws, from inequality to environmental destruction. The report promoted a redefinition of prosperity, no longer based on measures of GDP but on human 'capabilities to flourish', where people fulfil their potential, live meaningful, purposeful lives and contribute to society. It concluded by setting out 12 steps to achieve a more sustainable economy that was not based on continual economic growth.

Many of these steps are beyond the scope of spatial planning but some do have implications for urban development. For example, Step 2 (Investing in jobs, assets and infrastructures) calls for increased employment in building and maintaining public assets; more investments in renewable energy, public transport infrastructure and public spaces; retro-fitting the existing building stock with energy saving and carbon saving measures; investing in ecosystem maintenance and protection, clean technologies and resource efficiency. Step 4 (Improving macro-economic accounting) highlights the shortcomings of using GDP as a measure of economic wellbeing and calls for the use of new measures that incorporate the social and environmental costs of change into the equation. And Step 8 (Strengthening human and social capital) argues that prosperity consists in part in our capabilities to participate in the life of society. Thus creating resilient and inclusive social communities is particularly important in the face of economic shocks. Such communities need investment in community assets such as green spaces, parks, libraries and museums and the capacity to take local planning decisions themselves (Jackson, 2009).

Examining the post-2008 economic crisis the SDC noted that many commentators were suggesting that economic recovery would require investment and that by targeting that investment carefully towards energy security, low carbon infrastructures and ecological protection would offer a number of benefits to society as a whole. These included reducing household energy bills, reducing reliance on imported energy, strengthening the resilience of energy supply, creating employment in the expanding 'environmental industries' sector, reducing carbon emissions, protecting valuable ecological assets and improving the quality of our living environment for generations to come (Jackson, 2009). It was argued that, by giving this kind of direction to local economic development, cities could not only see jobs created but a more sustainable and resilient economy than would be achieved through conventional or undirected growth.

But what should be the role of urban planning? It has been suggested that planning must be informed by these new economic models and should continue to envision the ideal city, or living environment, and backcast to understand the economic conditions required to achieve that ideal. Following this argument, planning can no longer be there simply to 'compensate for the externalities of capitalism' but should be at the epicentre of visioning better urban futures, posing questions, provoking debate and striving for places to be better than they already are. Working alongside communities, planners should then coordinate and enable the delivery of projects, in effect becoming the client and demanding more from developers (A. Couch, 2010).

An example of an alternative approach to economic development is provided by the recent growth of interest in urban agriculture.

Urban agriculture

In the UK there has been a long tradition of food production within cities, more so than in many continental European countries because of the lower density of urban development and prevalence of single family houses with gardens. This has manifested itself principally in the cultivation of fruit and vegetables in private gardens and allotments. At certain times, for example during the Second World War and with strong Government support, these gardens and allotments have made a major contribution to national food supply. Although such use has declined since that time, the potential in terms of land availability still remains.

In recent years there has been an emerging movement supporting 'urban agriculture' and the notion of 'continuously productive urban landscapes' (Viljoen, 2005). These ideas arise from the aim of sustainable development and the objectives of efficiently using urban land, localizing food production and reducing 'food miles' as much as possible. There are many aspects to urban agriculture. In addition to the fruit and vegetable cultivation mentioned above, activity can include arable farming and animal husbandry, natural (organic) and intensive methods of production. Production may be achieved by individuals, community or voluntary groups, cooperatives, private companies or large corporations. Products may be consumed by individual producers, exchanged, bartered, sold locally or offered on wider markets.

Cuba has become quite well known for its very well developed urban agricultural sector. Shortages of fuel and transport capacity have forced the country to turn towards urban agriculture. Today much of Havana's fresh food comes from farms and gardens in the immediate locality. This local food production also provides a valuable source of employment for many people. Detroit is one of a number of large cities in the USA where urban agriculture has become an important element of urban regeneration (Colasanti et al., 2012).

In the UK there have been some interesting developments. For example, the Middlesbrough Urban Farming Project was initially supported in 2007 with £4.1m from the Healthy Community Challenge

Figure 4.6   *'Incredible edible Todmorden': posters supporting the local environment and food awareness campaign*

Source: C. Couch, 2016.

Fund to tackle sustainable development, public health and eating issues via a programme of urban agriculture. The Middlesbrough 'town meal' became the focal point of an annual programme of growing and harvesting, a major public event and a vehicle for community participation (CABE, 2011a).

Since 2008 the town of Todmorden in West Yorkshire has had a community-led grow-your-own initiative known as 'incredible edible Todmorden' (Figure 4.6). The programme focusses on local food production and consumption and has transformed the way local people connect with food production and public green spaces. The aim is to make Todmorden self-sufficient in vegetables, orchard fruits and eggs by 2018, and ultimately to enable the town to locally source the majority of staple foods, including meat and dairy products (CABE, 2011b).

Conclusions

In a market economy all firms are constantly seeking to maintain their competitiveness. To achieve this they seek to increase productivity through economies of scale, use of new technologies, vertical or horizontal integration, or relocation. All of these changes impact on urban areas in one way or another. In one of the most obvious examples, owners have gradually increased the size of ocean-going cargo ships in order to benefit from the scale economies offered by larger ships. In consequence many of the smaller, upstream docks, found in estuarine ports such as Rotterdam or London, have been abandoned and become available for alternative uses. The use of new technologies has reduced demand for labour in many industries, perhaps none more so than in routine administrative, clerical and secretarial work where computers have replaced much of the human input, leading to unemployment but also rendering much former office space redundant and available for alternative uses. The search for integration, and the scale economies this brings, leads to the amalgamation of firms and the concentration of production and economic decision making in fewer places, with the consequence that industrial production is lost from the less favoured locations. This is also often associated with a centralization of decision making towards regional or capital cities. Relocation to a lower cost region or country is also an option for firms seeking to reduce labour costs, to be nearer raw materials or markets, or to benefit from some form of subsidy. All of these forces are constantly at work and directly influence the economic strength of towns and cities, the availability of employment and demand for land. They also indirectly impact on other sectors such as housing and retailing.

The process of planning for local economic development involves a number of stages, the first of which is to understand the present situation and to be able to forecast likely future changes. The absolute size of a local economy is usually measured in terms of its GDP. The economic health of an area can be assessed by using a combination of other measures: GDP per capita; activity rates; unemployment and dependency ratios and income levels. It is also important in the planning process to understand the structure of the local economy and its particular strengths in terms of industrial sectors. The location quotient (LQ) is a measure of the relative concentration of an economic sector in the area. Thus, for example, the City of London can be shown to have a great concentration (and strengths) in financial services, Cambridge in higher education, Sunderland in manufacturing.

The next stages in the local economic development planning process involve confirming the strengths and weaknesses of the local economy, and identifying external threats and opportunities (SWOT analysis), and forecasting future trends. Then a set of goals for future local economic development can be established, seeking to benefit from strengths, eliminating weaknesses and being flexible and robust in the face of threats and opportunities. Having established the goals, policies can be developed.

In general terms the infrastructure of a successful post-industrial city is likely to include good inter- and intra-regional accessibility; business agglomeration economies including good support systems (IT, marketing and so on); an attractive and efficient urban environment; strong higher education, research, development and innovation capacity; high quality and affordable housing in attractive neighbourhoods. Thus, not only must urban planning policies respond to the direct spatial needs of the economy for land and buildings but they must also ensure that this supporting and underpinning infrastructure is in place. In identifying suitable employment land, modern policy generally advocates a sequential approach that favours brownfield regeneration over greenfield sites; and sites compatible with surrounding land uses that minimize transport demand, energy use and environmental damage.

A large part of urban planning for economic development is concerned with the transformation of redundant former industrial areas into other productive uses. Sometimes this means their transformation into other employment land uses such as retailing, leisure or tourism; sometimes the next best use may be housing; and sometimes they may be transformed into non-money earning green infrastructure, either as part of a greening strategy or as a residual use. Thus in this chapter there are examples of the transformation of former docklands into areas dominated by leisure and tourism as in Baltimore, or the transformation of former steelworks to both new technology industry, green/blue infrastructure and residential uses as in Dortmund.

But there are alternative approaches to local economic development. There are many who do not accept that GDP provides an appropriate measure of the strength or health of a local economy and who call for new measures that take account of the impact of economic activity on the environment, health and quality of life of the population. The Sustainable Development Commission has proposed a new direction for economic development in the UK that puts less emphasis on conventional economic growth and more on investing in reducing energy consumption, renewable energy and improved public transport. Others are experimenting with new ideas such as urban agriculture.

In the modern economy towns and cities need to be competitive if they are to maintain their position in the urban hierarchy. To do this they must be efficient, well managed and provide a good business environment, broadly defined. In this context, town and city centres have specific characteristics and functions that make it worthwhile identifying them as distinct elements within the urban system that require more detailed treatment. Thus the next chapter looks at the changing function of urban centres and urban planning.

Chapter 5

Retailing, Central Areas and Urban Planning

Introduction

This chapter discusses trends in retailing and changes in the economic and cultural functions of town and city centres, and planning responses to the issues that arise from these changes. The discussion considers the evolving pattern of retailing, the revitalization of town and city centres, the control of retail and commercial development, and the new economy of urban centres. It is supported by case studies drawn from Liverpool, Bristol, London and Paris.

What are urban centres? They are difficult to define but they can be described. Most importantly, they are usually the main focus within a town or city for commercial activity, including retailing, especially comparison shopping, business and financial services and administration. They are frequently also the key location for civic and cultural activities including higher education, secondary health care, artistic and entertainment venues, places of worship, bars, restaurants and other meeting places. Urban centres commonly provide public transport hubs and interchange between long-distance and local services. Historic centres can also be a focus for tourism. And increasingly, urban centres are regaining a function as residential areas, especially for younger households (URBED, 1994).

The balance between these functions varies over time and from place to place. The suburbanization of population and employment, experienced by many cities in the latter half of the twentieth century, reduced the population dependent on city centres for work, shopping and leisure. This trend, combined with the growth in car ownership, stimulated the decentralization of a growing proportion of these activities to the urban periphery where the use of the motor car could be better accommodated.

Changing patterns of retailing

Whilst many western European cities saw a steady rise in average incomes and spending power through the 1950s, after a post-war boom in town centre investment, the seeds of incipient decline began to be sown in the 1960s. With the rise in motor car usage, increased traffic congestion in urban centres and following trends in North America there were growing pressures encouraging retail developments to move out of traditional city centres on to sites on the urban periphery where they could be better served by the road system and where the lower cost of land allowed the provision of bigger stores and large amounts of free car parking. Around Paris, for instance, a ring of large new out-of-town regional shopping centres were developed including Parly 2, near Versailles, Velizy 2 a little further east and La Belle Epine near Rungis, none of which are conveniently served by the Metro or RER services (Smith, 1973).

In the UK, where tough planning restrictions prevented much out-of-centre development until the regime was relaxed by the Thatcher Government in the 1980s, some developers tried to update town centres by inserting modern enclosed shopping centres within the existing urban fabric. Notable amongst these were developments by the Arndale Property Trust in a variety of cities in the late 1960s and 1970s. Schemes such as Cross Gates Arndale Centre in Leeds (1967), Wandsworth Arndale Centre (now Southside) (1971) and Manchester Arndale Centre (1972–79), provided a controlled and pleasant pedestrian environment, often with adjoining car parking.

Writing about this gradual decentralization of retail activity, Russell Schiller (1986) identified three 'waves' of retail change in the UK:

- the development of food superstores in out-of-centre locations from the 1970s;
- the development of out-of-centre retail parks aimed primarily at retailers of bulky goods such as DIY, furniture and carpets;
- the development of out-of-centre regional shopping centres for comparison goods retailers and leisure operators.

Some commentators subsequently identified an additional wave:

- further development of shopping centres, including designer and factory outlet malls (Fernie, 1995).

In their extreme form these out-of-town developments can form what is referred to as an 'edge city' in the USA. According to Joel Garreau an 'edge city' is a concentration of business, retail and leisure activity outside the traditional urban centre, typically on a ring road or major highway junction (1991). Whilst there are few true examples of edge cities in Europe, one example that comes close is the Cheshire Oaks development at the junction of two motorways (M53 and M56) near Chester (UK). Cheshire Oaks was developed on greenfield land adjoining the motorway

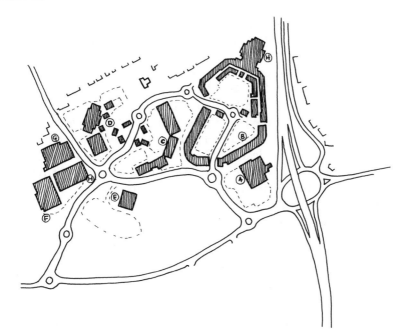

Figure 5.1 *Cheshire Oaks*

Source: drawn by A.L. Couch.

Note: A – Large 24-hour superstore; B – Designer outlet village; C – 'Big box' retailers;
D – Multiplex cinema, bowling alley and restaurants; E – Aquarium (regional attraction);
F – Large free-standing Marks & Spencer store; G – Private indoor sports and leisure club;
H – multi-storey car parks. In total the complex provides more than 4,000 car parking
spaces.

junction, starting in the 1990s with a large single-storey designer outlet
'village'. This was shortly followed by an adjoining 'big box' retail park,
an extension to the outlet village and a multiplex cinema and entertainment complex (Figure 5.1). Other nearby developments include a private
indoor sports and fitness centre, a large aquarium, several car show-
rooms, offices and a very large free-standing Marks & Spencer store. The
whole complex provides extensive car parking and whilst some local bus
services have been diverted to serve the area, traffic congestion has
become endemic at peak periods. There is also evidence to suggest some
adverse impact on retail provision in the nearby historic city of Chester.

There have been other changes in retail supply. In some countries,
notably the UK, relaxation of laws relating to opening hours has
permitted evening and Sunday trading which increased the amount of
retail supply (floorspace x opening hours) by perhaps 15–20 %. This
additional supply must continue to generate profit and so increases the
competitive pressure between retailers. Seeking economies of scale,

retailers have tended to require ever larger shop units. There has also been a concentration in store ownership as retailers seek the benefits of horizontal integration. For example, the Arcadia Group owns a wide variety of brands, each aimed at a different market sector, including: BHS, Burton Menswear, Dorothy Perkins, Evans, Miss Selfridge, Outfit (an out-of-town store), Topshop, Topman and Wallis. But there are counter-trends. Some of the larger supermarket chains have made great progress in reducing the cost base of smaller units (brands such as Tesco Express, Carrefour City), leading to inroads into the convenience store sector that was previously the domain of small independent retailers. And in some smaller centres strategies to support local markets and independent shops providing locally sourced food and craft products have met with some success.

There have also been changes in retail demand. Rising affluence and car ownership have increased consumers' choice of shopping centres. Urban centres that were previously considered to be too far apart to be a threat to each other are now in competition. This choice also extends to competition between urban centres and the various forms of decentralized retailing: retail parks; regional shopping centres; factory and designer outlets. A further trend is the growing synergy between increases in leisure activity and tourism and some forms of retailing.

Many central area populations have been in decline. Push factors have included reductions in local employment opportunities and slum clearance, while pull factors have included the attractions of the greater space and better environmental conditions provided by suburban living. Whatever the cause, the effect has been to carry yet more consumer spending away from central areas and towards the suburbs.

The first decade of the twenty-first century also saw the emergence and rapid growth of online internet-based retailing in which some retail activity is removed from any specific location. By December 2012, internet sales were 10.6 % of all retail sales in the UK, which was an increase of 15.5 % over the previous December (ONS, 2013). By 2013 online sales in the UK accounted for 80 % of music and video sales, 53 % of book sales, 42 % of electrical goods sales and over 14 % of clothing and footwear sales, but less than 6 % each in the DIY and gardening, furniture and floorcoverings, food, health and beauty sectors (Verdict, 2013). An associated trend is the emergence of 'click and collect' shopping. At the time of writing (2015) it is possible to see that these changes have led to rapid changes in urban centres, with retail space given over to music, books and electrical goods very much in decline. But the impact of internet and mobile phone technologies is still working its way through the retail system and further impacts are likely in the future.

With the integration and centralization of retail ownership, local supply chains became less important, leading to the closure of the local warehouses and workshops that might previously have been found on the periphery of the central area. These same forces, together with the advent of new technologies, reduced the need for clerks, typists and other office workers, leading to a decline in demand for traditional city centre office space. Many of the office buildings that had been erected in earlier periods have become obsolete and do not meet modern requirements, especially in terms of health and safety or their ability to accommodate IT and telecommunications systems at reasonable cost. By the 1980s the combination of these retail and commercial trends, along with increasing traffic congestion, deteriorating environmental quality, loss of sense of place and declining levels of personal safety, began to seriously threaten the economy and standing of many city centres, nowhere more so than in the shrinking and economically struggling cities of the north of England (Evans, 1997; Oc and Tiesdell, 1997).

Revitalizing the city centre

In the UK a new approach began to emerge towards the end of the 1960s. The first responses had little to do with retailing as such. Concerned about the deteriorating environment and loss of heritage in urban areas, the Government commissioned studies into the merits of conservation in four historic city centres: York, Bath, Chester and Chichester. Lord Esher's study of central York identified five objectives for the area: to make the commercial heart of the city competitive again; to eliminate decay, traffic congestion and noise so it would be an attractive place to live; to remove conflicting land uses; to conserve and enhance the historic character of the area; and to ensure that new buildings were of the highest architectural quality (Esher, 1968). This represented a major step forward in planning thought. The report provided a detailed study of what needed to be done to conserve and regenerate the historic city centre, eliminating the growing blight and the intrusion of traffic and transforming it into a more civilized place where tourists would want to linger and people would want to live.

Despite such forward thinking the decline of many centres continued through the 1970s as economic conditions worsened and social divisions grew. Clearly something had to be done. In 1984 Manchester City Council published a new plan for its city centre. The document noted a long run decline in the prosperity of the city centre, identifying the causes as emanating from a range of micro- and macro-economic, social and environmental trends. The plan also identified the importance of the enormous wealth and variety of economic, social and cultural activities that took place within the city centre, noting that the inter-relationships between these was what distinguished Manchester as the regional centre. The aim of the plan was to maintain and enhance the range of activities and to create a city centre that would be an economically sound, multi-functional, accessible place with a pleasant, safe environment.

> Although these aims are interrelated and for the most part, complementary, they may also at times be in conflict. A key task of the Plan is to resolve these conflicts ... More importantly, the Plan, in recognition of the close relationships between enhancing accessibility, activity and character has to ensure that the progress made on each of them adds up to a greater, more coherent whole. (Manchester City Council, 1984, p. 9)

This plan was one of the first in a series of 'rescue plans' for British city centres in the 1980s and 1990s.

Responding to the emerging concern for sustainable development, although focussed on the whole urban area, the European *Green Paper on the Urban Environment* (CEC, 1990) had some clear messages for the role and planning of European city centres. Whilst acknowledging that many cities, especially de-industrializing cities, were suffering the effects of structural economic change, and that modern communications permitted the decentralization of many economic activities, it was clear that much activity still required face-to-face contacts, which were best accommodated in the dense and accessible environment of city centres. The *Paper* supported the revitalization of European city centres and encouraged cities to plan for a higher density of urban development, mixed uses, heritage protection, environmental enhancement and better public transport.

In 1994 the UK Government published *Vital and Viable Town Centres: meeting the challenge*. This recognized the threat to town centres from out-of-town shopping and new forms of retailing, but also acknowledged that there were other, underlying causes arising from the shift towards a service-based economy and the growing ownership and reliance on motor cars that had increased mobility and consumer choice. The report called on local authorities to review the health of their urban centres and to develop strategies to improve their attractiveness, accessibility and amenity. This might be achieved through a variety of interventions including improvements to public transport and parking facilities; better design of streets and the public realm; development of key or vacant sites; increased personal security; the introduction of town centre management and strategies to market urban centres as retail and leisure destinations (URBED, 1994).

Other concerns included the fear that too many centres were losing their individual character and independence:

> the New Economics Foundation coined the term 'clone town' to describe a phenomenon which is transforming British high streets. Real local shops have been replaced by swathes of identikit chain stores that seem to spread like economic weeds, making high streets up and down the country virtually indistinguishable from one another. (Potts et al., 2005)
>
> the overall number of single outlet retailers has declined by nine per cent from 225,900 businesses in 1980 to 205,600 in 1991, and the decline is particularly pronounced in the food sector with the number of single outlet operators falling from 81,835 to 1980 to 56,440 in 1991, a decline of 31 per cent. (Tym, 2000)

Reviewing the vitality and viability, or health, of a town or city centre provides a baseline from which policy can be developed. Table 5.1 lists the indicators which can be measured and forecast over time to assess the health of a centre.

Planning urban centres and controlling retail and commercial development

The goal of sustainable development requires that urban planners recognize the importance of urban centres to their surrounding communities, protecting and promoting them according to their function in the urban

Table 5.1   *Town Centre Health Check indicators*

Diversity of uses
Proportion of vacant street level property
Commercial yields on non-domestic property
Customers' views and behaviour
Retailer representation and intentions to change representation
Commercial rents
Pedestrian flows
Accessibility
Perception of safety and occurrence of crime
State of town centre environmental quality

Source: Based upon DCLG (2014c), para. 5.

system. An important task is to define the hierarchy of centres within their areas and the functions expected of each layer in the hierarchy, and to define the boundaries of such centres. In many cities changing retail supply and shopping habits have modified the hierarchy of town, district and local centres. In many places there appears to have been a growing concentration of comparison goods shopping in the town or city centres, often at the expense of district centres. In local centres too the traditional parade of separate convenience shops (butcher, baker, greengrocer, newsagent and so on) has often been replaced by a single local supermarket. Thus planning authorities are faced with the dilemma of whether and how far to protect district and local centres from further change.

In order to maintain the integrity of a retail centre it is necessary to exercise planning control to avoid the loss of frontages and floorspace to non-retail uses and to ensure a diverse range of shops that reflect local needs and identity. The retention or re-introduction of retail markets is generally thought to enhance urban vitality. The planning system has a responsibility to allocate a suitable range of sites, including changes of use, to accommodate future needs for retail, commercial, civic, cultural, residential and other development within the town or city centre. In many centres, away from the core retail frontages, this may be achieved by adopting a flexible mixed use approach to land use zoning and the density of development. To protect the centre:

> Local planning authorities should apply a sequential test ... and require applications for main town centre uses to be located in town centres, then in edge of centre locations and only if suitable sites are not available should out of centre sites be considered. When considering edge of centre and out of centre proposals, preference should be given to accessible sites that are well connected to the town centre. (DCLG, 2012, para. 24).

Proposals for large retail, leisure and office development outside established centres need to be assessed for their impact on the vitality and viability of existing centres. The approach to assessing the impact of retail proposals is typically based on estimating the turnover of the proposed floorspace over a defined period of time compared with the estimated total turnover of competing stores in the catchment area. The amount and proportion of trade diverted to the proposed floorspace can then be calculated. The significance of the proposal will depend upon a range of factors including whether it is expected to draw deeply on trade from a small local area or have a shallower impact over a larger area, and whether it replicates or complements existing retail provision.

Policy for the future planning of an existing centre needs to be based upon knowledge of its current retail capacity. Figure 5.2 shows the

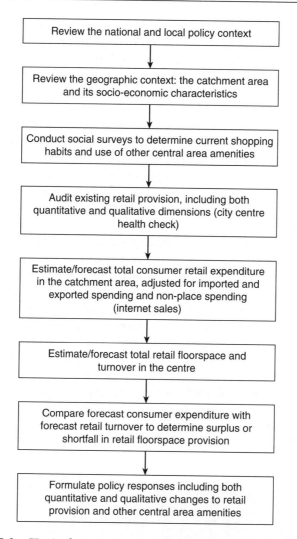

Figure 5.2   *Typical stages in a retail capacity study*

typical methodology for a retail capacity study which may often be extended to include analysis of the capacity of other central area facilities and amenities.

The first step is to consider the national, regional and local policy context insofar as they affect retail planning. Next there will be some analysis of local population and employment characteristics and trends, patterns of urbanization and transport provision. A household survey can be used to determine the inhabitants' current use of centres and shopping habits. Street surveys carried out in the centres under consideration will also help determine the catchment of the centre and the views of users about the centre and its health. These can be used to complement the professional audit of retail provision and the economic health of the centre. With this information, total current and forecast retail expenditure can be calculated and converted into floorspace with an estimate of current surplus or shortfall. Policy responses can then be devised.

Whilst recent changes in policy have protected and strengthened the position of many larger retail centres, the same cannot be said for district and local centres, especially in lower income areas. Much of their former comparison shopping has transferred to city centres, out-of-town locations or the internet and the purchase of most convenience goods has transferred to supermarkets. This has left many district and local centres, especially in lower income areas, with an oversupply of retail premises. Whilst some of these premises have found new uses as workshops, offices or even been converted into residential accommodation, the oversupply cannot be disguised. For example, in the Tranmere and Rock Ferry neighbourhoods of Birkenhead (UK), the local planning authority has since the 1980s pursued a policy of removing many of the obsolete nineteenth century shops with flats above that lined the main streets and replacing them with small purpose-built neighbourhood centres, reusing the cleared land to provide modern infill housing. Although the policy has been very effective in meeting the retail needs of the area and modernized the housing stock without gentrification, there is still a surplus of shops. Figure 5.3 illustrates the effect of the policy.

Figure 5.3   *Tranmere, Birkenhead, UK: retail change at the local level*

Source: C. Couch, 2016.

Note: The obsolete surplus nineteenth century shops with flats above are being demolished and replaced by small purpose-built neighbourhood centres.

The new economy of urban centres

But there have been other changes affecting urban centres in recent years: changes in the use of office accommodation; changes in tourism, leisure and cultural activity; and a rise in the number of people living in central areas.

Different cities have had different experiences in terms of office trends. Historically much of the office sector was located in central areas for convenience of access, both for employees and customers. Office functions frequently generated large numbers of clerical and administrative jobs and very high densities of employment per square metre of floorspace. More recently, employment in many 'back office' functions has declined, having been taken over by new technologies, and those that remain have moved to cheaper premises in more remote locations. This has tended to leave only certain sections of companies seeking accommodation in urban centres, for example the headquarters functions or functions that require high levels of personal interaction, such as financial and legal services. With the ever continuing trends towards horizontal integration and centralization of corporate ownerships, larger regional centres and capital cities (with greater agglomeration economies) have tended to gain office employment at the expense of smaller, more remote centres. Combined with the obsolescence of much of the older stock of existing office space, in terms of its ability to accommodate modern business practice and technologies, in some cities this has left a lot of office buildings requiring new uses.

Since the 1990s there has been growing evidence that cities in the UK and some other European countries have experienced a degree of re-urbanization after decades of counter-urbanization. A key element in this process has been the emergence of city centre living. From a few tentative developments in the early 1990s this became an established trend in the 2000s and made a significant contribution to the housing stock in many cities in the 2010s (Couch et al., 2009). According to Lever (1993) it was a combination of urban economic restructuring, demographic change and proactive urban policy that kick-started this phase of re-urbanization. More precisely, it has been argued that the emergence of city centre living has resulted from:

- an emerging supply of sites and premises (for example, obsolete offices and warehouses) for which more profitable uses did not exist;
- a demand for small urban dwellings arising from changes in household structure, notably the rising numbers of younger adults living alone or in small childless households;
- a demand for student accommodation arising from the growth in higher education;

- changes in public policy promoting city centre living as part of the aim of creating more 'vital and viable' city centres and as a contribution towards more sustainable cities. (Couch, 1999)

By the end of 2005 it was being suggested that the growth of city centre living was the most visible symbol of urban renaissance. The impact on city centre populations has been substantial, ranging from a modest 8 % increase between 1991 and 2001 in Birmingham, to over 30 % in Liverpool and over 60 % in both Bristol and Cardiff (Bromley et al., 2007; Couch et al., 2009). Most of the new city centre residents were young and single, and the level of turnover was much higher than in the rest of the housing stock (Nathan and Urwin, 2006). In many cities the resulting housing stock appears to be too homogeneous and marketed at too narrow a social group. Families are virtually absent from these developments because, compared with traditional inner urban housing, the stock tends to be relatively expensive and lacks the space, amenities and community facilities required for satisfactory family life. There is also potential for conflict between policies promoting city living and other policies promoting commercial activity and a vibrant evening and night-time economy which residents might find socially intrusive.

In order to achieve more sustainable and balanced city centre communities, policy makers need to reduce the amount of transience in the central area population and to encourage occupancy by a wider range of social groups. This suggests that planners need to adopt a more proactive and robust attitude to the control of city centre residential developments: dealing with residents' concerns about space, noise and amenity; providing more variety in dwelling size, form and cost; and making greater provision for the kind of facilities households would expect to find in more established residential neighbourhoods, including convenience shopping, health, welfare and recreational facilities. Such changes in policy would be likely to encourage more families into city centres, resulting in a more stable community with a longer term commitment to the area and reducing segregation between the city centre and traditional inner urban neighbourhoods. But it can be done. Figure 5.4 compares typical modern English city centre housing with a city centre housing development in Dortmund where a high density apartment development manages to accommodate all the necessary amenities for family life, with quietude and privacy within less than 300 m of the city's main central retail zone.

In the post-industrial economy, cultural, leisure and tourist activities have become important features in the revitalization of city centres. The reasons for the growth in these activities are associated with:

(a)   (b)

Figure 5.4   *City centre housing in (a) Germany and (b) the UK*

Source: C. Couch, 2016.

Note: (a) shows a city centre block in Dortmund equipped for family living. Most recent housing investment in UK city centres, typified by (b), is only suitable for small childless households.

- the rise in city-centre living;
- rising disposable incomes (although somewhat constrained since the post-2008 economic crisis);
- recognition by policy makers of the economic multiplier and job creation potential of the cultural and leisure sectors;
- the importance of place marketing in competition between cities and of a good 'cultural environment' in attracting the creative classes (Tallon, 2013).

Many cities have pursued explicit cultural regeneration strategies, encouraging investment in the hardware such as museums, galleries, theatres and concert halls, and staging events such as cultural festivals of various kinds. Being nominated for a year as a European Capital of Culture can bring enormous benefits to a city in terms of cultural investment, tourism, image creation and place marketing. When Liverpool was European Capital of Culture in 2008, the events generated a total income of over £130m, attracted 9.7 million additional visitors, transformed national and international media perceptions and left a long term legacy of enhanced cultural activity, an improved image of the city and continued growth in tourism (Garcia et al., 2010). The event also acted as a deadline for the completion of locally significant projects such as the Echo Arena and Convention Centre and the Liverpool One shopping centre.

Closely associated with cultural regeneration, urban tourism has also grown in importance in the economy of many city centres. There are two aspects to this. The first is business travel to conferences, seminars and exhibitions. For example, a number of German cities, such as Cologne and Leipzig, are well known for their 'messe' or trade fairs. Cologne has a long tradition as a trade fair city dating back to the fourteenth century. In the 1920s the city established its own trade fair company and designated a new messe site on the east bank of the Rhine opposite the city centre, accommodating many trade fairs during the inter-war years. Reopened and enlarged after the Second World War, Cologne Messe today annually attracts over 40,000 exhibiting companies and 2.6 million people to over 40 different events (Koelnmesse GmbH, 2014). The second factor stimulating urban tourism has been the growth of city breaks and leisure visits. On the back of rising disposable incomes and cheaper travel there has been a substantial rise in urban tourism based upon comparison shopping, the evening economy, sporting and cultural events, urban history and heritage. This has spawned growth in new hotel accommodation and tourist infrastructure which in turn have generated a need to market the city to fill the capacity created.

The economic impacts of urban tourism are substantial. There is a direct increase in employment at tourist destinations (historic buildings, event centres and so on) and in the hotel, catering and transport sectors. The income generated creates a multiplier effect stimulating further growth in the local economy. Tourism may also have an impact in increased spending on the local physical environment, both capital and revenue – to make the area more convenient, attractive and safer for visitors. There may also be benefits in terms of city marketing and improving the image of the city to potential external investors. However, there can be negative impacts such as changes in the local retail offer to favour demand from tourists and loss of locally accessible housing stock to demand for second homes, short lets and so on.

The case studies that follow examine different aspects of central area planning. In the first the overall regeneration strategy for Liverpool city centre is considered, while the second offers a more detailed look at Cabot Circus in Bristol, an example of the type of large-scale retail centres that have been inserted into existing city centres in recent years. The third case discusses a very different approach: the micro-management of properties and tenancies in Westminster to maximize central area building uses and returns. The final case contrasts the strategic out-of-centre developments at Canary Wharf in London and La Défense in Paris and their impacts on their respective cities.

Make no little plans: Liverpool Vision

Liverpool Vision was one of the first urban regeneration companies (URC) designated by the UK Government in 1999 in response to the proposal made by the Urban Task Force (1999). Unlike previous agencies such as urban development corporations, URCs had no substantial budgets or planning powers but were subject to local democratic control. They did not directly undertake development themselves but were to work in collaboration with stakeholders to develop a strategic regeneration plan and to identify and facilitate important development opportunities. The work of Liverpool Vision was to be focussed on the city centre.

Through the previous decades Liverpool had suffered a severe economic decline which left a legacy of high unemployment, vacant property, a depressed city centre economy and a neglected public realm. The retail centre had long since fallen from its position as one of the country's premier shopping centres. However, by the middle of the 1990s things were improving; nationally and locally there was economic growth. Following the lead established by the Merseyside Development Corporation and the Government's City Challenge initiative, European funding was supporting some important capital projects and the private development sector was, after many years of absence, beginning to take an interest in the city (Parkinson, 2008).

The role of Liverpool Vision was to build on these foundations and to attract and coordinate large scale investment in the city centre. The objectives of their strategic plan, completed in 2000, included:

- establishing a forward looking '21st century' economy;
- delivering a high quality and safe urban environment;
- exploiting the city centre's rich heritage;
- becoming a world class tourist destination;
- becoming (once again) a premier national shopping centre; and
- improving the image of the city.

The plan also included supporting the bid for European Capital of Culture (which was achieved in 2008), improving connectivity beyond the city centre, promoting community engagement and encouraging business development. It should be noted that this was not a comprehensive development plan in the convention of planning legislation but a sharply focussed strategy for the economic regeneration of a specific area. As such it might be criticized for some shortcomings, including the prioritization of economic growth over concerns about sustainability and some neglect of areas beyond the city centre (although the operational boundaries of the URC were later extended). Nevertheless the achievements of Liverpool Vision over the following decade were considerable (Figure 5.5).

The landscape of the Pier Head (the iconic heart of the Liverpool waterfront) was transformed. The old ferry terminal was rebuilt. British Waterways (now the Canal & River Trust) cut a new canal between the shoreline and the waterfront office buildings known as 'the three graces' to link the Leeds-Liverpool Canal with the Albert Dock. A new Museum of Liverpool, apartments and office buildings were developed on adjoining sites. A new commercial office district was created around the Princes Dock to the north of the Pier Head and much of the traditional commercial district turned into a live/work mixed use environment. To the south the former Kings Dock was redeveloped with hotels, an arena and convention centre. The retail core was extended with a

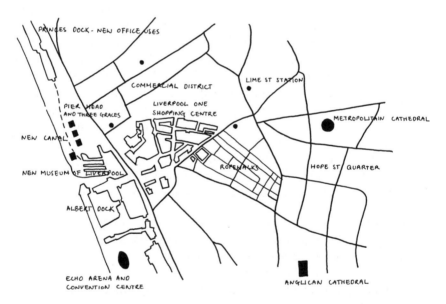

Figure 5.5 *The transformation of Liverpool City Centre*

Source: Drawn by A.L. Couch.

Note: The area illustrates contrasting approaches to urban regeneration: waterfront regeneration based on leisure and tourist developments around the Pier Head and Albert Docks; a single developer retail mega-project in 'Liverpool One'; the conversion of many former office buildings to residential use boosting city living in the commercial district; piecemeal organic regeneration based upon a multiplicity of small scale projects in the Ropewalks; and culture-led regeneration in the Hope Street Quarter.

private, nearly £1bn development by Grosvenor Estates, later known as 'Liverpool One'. Beyond this the city centre edge transition zone, known as the 'Ropewalks', continued to be regenerated in piecemeal fashion as a mixed use creative/leisure/residential quarter. A further 'high' culture area around St George's Hall, World Museum and Walker Art Galley benefitted from refurbishments and improvements to the public realm, as did the Hope Street quarter between the city's two cathedrals.

But what did Liverpool Vision itself contribute to this regeneration? According to Parkinson:

> two decades of economic and political challenges had ... created a culture of failure and low ambition ... Vision played a major part in changing attitudes and raising ambitions ... the change in developer and investor confidence in the city has been remarkable. (ibid., p. 49)

The strategic plan was also important in putting the city centre at the front of people's thinking and in mobilizing stakeholders. What the plan lacked in detail and precision it gained in clarity and purpose. Unlike the City Council with its severe financial constraints and competing demands on its spending, Liverpool Vision brought a different attitude, bridging the gap between the public and private sectors and using its knowledge of development finance and processes to lobby and negotiate with funding agencies and developers to deliver a clear programme of capital investment. Liverpool Vision also played an important role in coordinating development activity, ensuring synergies and collaborations and avoiding the dangers of fragmented or conflicting investments (Parkinson, 2008).

Extending the city centre: Bristol, Cabot Circus

Cabot Circus is a large mixed use redevelopment in part of Bristol's Broadmead shopping area. The scheme comprises 93,000 m² of retail space, a 2,600 space car park, 280 student bedspaces, 240 apartments, 20 affordable houses, a multi-screen cinema, restaurants, a 150 bedroom hotel and a site for future office development.

Broadmead was developed in the 1950s as a replacement for Bristol's war-damaged central retail area. With only one significant redevelopment since that time, in terms of national retail provision Bristol had fallen from 9th place in 1960 to 23rd in 2002. The centre was failing to offer the quality of facilities and environment that retailers and consumers had come to expect.

The Bristol City Centre Strategy was first published by the City Council in 1998 and updated in 2005. It aimed to provide a framework for guiding development in an area of significant change. Three key sub-areas were identified for planned investment. The first, Temple Quay, saw the development of a new office quarter with good pedestrian accessibility from the main railway station. The second, Harbourside, brought leisure, offices and residential accommodation to the derelict former docklands. The redevelopment of Broadmead represented the third key area of change (Figure 5.6).

The Council initially undertook research to establish the nature and scale of retail investment that would be required. The site, which lies to the east of the established Broadmead area, was identified and marketing took place in 1998–2000. Following the Council's consideration of alternative schemes, Land Securities (a property development company), working in collaboration with the City Council, prepared a masterplan and obtained outline planning permission. A compulsory purchase order to acquire the necessary land was also secured. Construction work proceeded quickly. A key task was the eastward diversion of the existing inner ring road to bring more usable land into the scheme. During

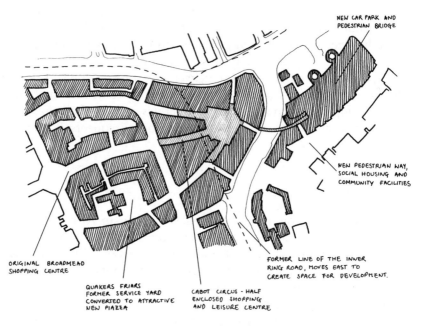

Figure 5.6 *Bristol: Cabot Circus*

Source: Drawn by A.L. Couch.

Note: The existing Broadmead shopping centre was extended by moving the inner ring road eastwards to provide a contiguous site for expansion. The resulting Cabot Circus enhances the environmental quality and amenities of the centre and adds significantly to its competitiveness.

construction as much waste as possible was recycled and many of the materials were locally sourced. There was a high degree of liaison and communication with local communities and other stakeholders. The development, which was completed in 2008, achieved an 'excellent' BREEAM rating. An original design feature was that the retail centre was not fully enclosed, as many earlier shopping centres had been, but comprised a series of pedestrian streets above which an artist designed roof was provided at high level to offer some protection from the worst of the elements.

The scheme has significantly enhanced the physical environment of the area, providing a mixed use redevelopment that meets the needs of contemporary stakeholders. Particularly successful are the three public spaces that have been created. Within the retail centre a multi-level space in the central atrium provides an attractive place for meeting, eating and relaxation. Within the existing Broadmead area the restored Quakers Friars buildings are situated in a square that has been transformed from a retail service yard into an elegant piazza surrounded by shops, restaurants and apartments. The community open space in the St Jude's area to the east has also been landscaped and provides for good integration between the scheme and the adjoining inner urban residential zone. Other links to adjoining areas have been made by improving access across the inner ring road and by opening up views to St Paul's church in nearby Portland Square.

A key issue that had to be overcome was the sheer complexity of the interests involved and the requirement for a sophisticated level of planning and collaboration between the City Council, the developers and other stakeholders. This was a transformational development that enhanced the functioning of the city centre and strengthened connections between the retail core and adjoining communities.

Managing mixed uses in the metropolitan centre: Westminster, Shaftesbury Villages

This example illustrates the important and perhaps surprising role that land owners can play in enhancing the quality of places and stimulating local economic development when they work to clear longer term objectives in close collaboration with the local planning authority and local stakeholders.

Shaftesbury PLC is a property company with significant holdings throughout the heart of London's West End. These holdings are located in specific areas or 'villages' with their own bespoke mix of uses and sense of community, and include Carnaby Street, Chinatown, Berwick Street, Seven Dials and part of Covent Garden. Through its successful management of these properties, working closely with the communities and developing an innovative and flexible planning strategy Shaftesbury has revitalized these areas, creating new jobs, new places to shop and eat and new homes. It has done this through incremental changes rather than comprehensive development, by developing close working relationships with all stakeholders including Westminster City and Camden Councils, and by seeing value in areas when others have not. Shaftesbury has worked with the same planning consultants (Rolfe Judd Planning) since 1991, building up a long term relationship of trust and shared goals.

Most of the villages are located within the Central Activities Zone (CAZ) of the London Plan and the CAZ of both Camden and Westminster. There are specialized planning policies for Chinatown and Covent Garden which are designed to protect and enhance the particular character and function of these areas. The overall objective of the CAZ is to strengthen and enhance the central area as being the focus within London for commercial, retail, leisure and residential uses. What Shaftesbury and Rolfe Judd have done is to emphasize the special mixed use character and function of certain areas within the West End, creating focal points for unusual mixes of uses within areas and individual buildings.

A demonstration of how Shaftesbury's investment has led to improvements in the physical environment is Carnaby Street. The fashion centre of the 1960s, two decades later it had become a shadow of its former self. By developing a retail strategy that supported young and up-and-coming designers over high street chains and by developing incubator units for start-up companies, Shaftesbury transformed the area into one of London's most vibrant and innovative fashion areas. This has been helped by investment in public realm improvements throughout the area, allowing a car-free environment with high quality surface materials and clear signage to attract visitors. The most striking change has been the development of Kingly Court from an isolated service area into a centre of fashion with a pedestrian courtyard at its heart (Figure 5.7). At ground floor level are restaurants and cafes creating a busy lively feel, while on the upper two floors is a mix of new start-up businesses on lower rents and flexible leases and small independent cafes.

Shaftesbury seeks where possible to reuse rather than redevelop its buildings. This has extended into the use of the floors themselves with flexible planning permissions allowing speedy re-letting of accommodation for a range of previously permitted uses, reducing the potential for void tenancy periods and improving commercial viability. This flexibility is most striking in Chinatown where Georgian and Victorian terraced properties can contain as many as four different uses within one building. Typically this might include a restaurant in the basement

Figure 5.7   London, Shaftesbury PLC: Kingly Court

Source: C. Couch, 2016.

Note: The mixed retail/leisure area of Kingly Court was created out of a former service yard.

and ground floor, retail on the first floor, offices on the second floor and residential accommodation on the top two floors. This creates a dynamic environment with activity on upper floors and means that the area can provide the range of functions that the local south-east Asian community require (banks, shops, hairdressers and so on) without detracting from the primary focus for the area which is restaurants.

All of the 'villages' are within Conservation Areas with a significant number of listed buildings. These are sensitive to adaptation and change. Supplementary Planning Guidance from Westminster City Council provides design advice on acceptable shop fronts, signage, etc. and on how the Council's land use policies can be flexibly applied to promote uses that will support the local community.

The success of the collaborative approach taken by Shaftesbury and their advisers and the local planning authorities, working with the local business and residential communities, can be demonstrated through the vibrancy of the villages, the growth in economic activity and the intensity of land use, whilst conserving the character of the areas and protecting the interests of the local community.

(a)

Figure 5.8 *(a) La Défense and (b) Canary Wharf*

Sources: (a) D.C. Couch, 2016; (b) C. Couch, 2016.

Note: (a) shows a view of La Défense from the eastern end of the Esplanade; (b) shows Canary Wharf with the Docklands Light Railway in the foreground.

The development of new peripheral centres: La Défense and Canary Wharf

Whilst much of planning thought advocates concentration on the development and protection of urban centres, there are situations where peripheral development can be both desirable and necessary. A comparison of the La Défense and Canary Wharf developments in Paris and London illustrates the issue (Figure 5.8).

La Défense is a very large planned concentration of offices and commercial activity to the west of Paris. It contains 3.5 million m^2 of office floorspace, including many company headquarters, and employs more than 180,000 people. Situated at the western end of the 10 km axis that runs from the Grande Arche in the heart of La Défense, through the Arc de Triomphe to the Louvre in central Paris, the complex is well served by public transport. It is on the east–west Réseau Express Regional (RER) ligne A and is the terminus for Metro ligne 1. It is also served by radial and tangential motorways.

(b)

Figure 5.8   *(continued)*

As long ago as the 1950s it had been decided to develop La Défense as an office centre and a special agency – the Etablissement Public d'Aménagement de la Défense (EPAD) – was set up. Early plans envisaged two rows of tall blocks around a central 'parvis' (square). By 1971 the RER connected the site to central Paris – a journey of around 15 minutes. Development slowed during the economic crisis of the 1970s but accelerated through the following decade with the building of many more office towers, the Quatre Temps shopping centre, hotels and some residential accommodation, culminating in the completion of the Grande Arche in 1989. Since then there have been further substantial developments and transport improvements.

Through a simple but robust plan for decentralizing office growth from Paris, concentrating a large amount of development within one major location and providing the basic infrastructure, including transport and utilities, the state has facilitated private sector investment in what has become Europe's largest purpose-built business district.

The development of La Défense is in marked contrast to that of Canary Wharf, an equivalent office complex in the London Docklands. Canary Wharf is about half the size of La Défense with around 1.5 million m² of office floorspace and employing about 100,000 people. But Canary Wharf grew out of a private sector initiative. Taking advantage of the regeneration already undertaken by the London Docklands Development

Corporation (LDDC) and the benefits provided by the Isle of Dogs Enterprise Zone, the Canadian property developers Olympia and Yorke began construction of the new business district in 1988, with the famous Canary Wharf tower (then London's tallest building – officially called One Canada Square) completed in 1991. Unfortunately the timing coincided with a crash in the property market and Olympia and Yorke went bankrupt. The complex was taken over by the Canary Wharf Group and has subsequently expanded considerably, providing extensive additional office and retail floorspace, residential accommodation and hotels.

Because this was a private initiative that did not relate to any existing strategic plan for London, or indeed any local plan for the area, the early years threw up a number of conflicts of interest. The transport system was particularly inadequate. The Docklands Light Railway (DLR), which had been initiated by the LDDC, did not have the capacity to cope with such a large development, neither was it connected into the rest of the London transport system. Through the 1990s the system was gradually improved and extended and in 1999 it was joined by an extension of the Jubilee underground line from central London to and through Canary Wharf (a journey time of 10 minutes). The Crossrail system (equivalent to the Parisian RER) will also have a station at Canary Wharf from 2018.

Both complexes provide a modern, efficient business environment and both contain some fine examples of modern business architecture. But whereas La Défense was essentially a greenfield development on the periphery of the city (albeit replacing some very low intensity development), Canary Wharf has been a redevelopment project, reusing the derelict docklands of the Isle of Dogs to great effect. However, perhaps the biggest difference lies in their relationship with the mother city. The development of La Défense has been enormously important in allowing Paris to meet international demand for office space and to maintain its position as a world city of the first order whilst protecting and conserving the fine architectural heritage and the mixed use character of the historic city centre. In contrast, the growth of Canary Wharf has had little impact in restraining the growth and redevelopment of office space in the historic City of London. It is hard to say whether this is because the commercial and financial services sectors have been growing faster in London in recent years or whether the Parisian planning system is more robust in defence of its historic environments.

Conclusions

The pattern of retailing continues to evolve. Traditional patterns of demand based upon the nuclear family using local parades of individual shops for the daily purchase of convenience goods and a larger centre for less frequent comparison shopping have long gone. Commentators have identified a series of 'waves' of change in retailing: the first was the arrival of the supermarket in convenience shopping; next came 'big box' retailers that moved the trade in household goods and appliances away from urban centres; later out-of-town regional shopping centres and designer outlets challenged the supremacy of urban centres for comparison goods; and today internet shopping is replacing a significant proportion of place-based retailing, particularly in sectors such as music, books and travel.

Through a combination of the impact of these changes in retailing, declining inner city employment, declining inner urban populations and deteriorating environmental conditions, many urban centres, particularly in the UK, went into decline. This prompted a rethink of policy. By the 1990s it was becoming clear that re-urbanization and a strengthening of existing urban centres were key components of sustainable urban development. Following publication of *Vital and Viable Town Centres: meeting the challenge* (URBED, 1994), the UK Government called on local authorities to review the health of their urban centres and to improve their attractiveness, accessibility and amenity.

As the importance of city centres in driving economic development in the post-industrial economy has been recognized and competition between cities has increased there has been a resurgence of investment in urban centres. Many have benefitted from heavy state-supported investment in infrastructure and the public realm, retail cores have been refurbished and developed, and centres have taken on new civic and cultural functions as well as being places of entertainment and living. Much of the expanding post-industrial economic activity (including IT, media and communications; financial and public services; hotels, catering and entertainment) fits well into central urban locations. Changes in population and occupation structures have boosted demand for city centre living, whilst economic restructuring has released former office and industrial premises for redevelopment.

Planning policies for urban centres have sought improvements to public transport and parking facilities; better design of streets and the public realm; increased personal security; development of key or vacant sites; town centre management and marketing; mixed use developments; an expanded evening economy; and living in the city. Furthermore, most planning systems today severely restrict the further growth in out-of-centre locations, employing sequential approaches to development control that give preference to development in existing centres and 'transit-orientated development' wherever appropriate.

The case study of Liverpool Vision illustrates the contributions that having some sort of coordinating agency can bring to the process of city centre regeneration. Cabot Circus and similar projects in other cities such as Victoria Square in Belfast show how accessible, modern, well-designed mixed use developments can boost the competitiveness of the city centre against competition from elsewhere. The study of central London shows that careful and sympathetic management of property with innovative approaches to leasing and planning control can not only enhance financial benefits to owners but also bring wider community benefits as well. In very different ways the out-of-town mega-developments at La Défense and Canary Wharf can also bring some benefit in terms of accommodating large scale growth whilst relieving commercial development pressures in the historic centres of expanding cities.

But the new found success of these larger urban centres has sometimes brought about a concentration and centralization of economic and cultural activity at the expense of weaker town, district and local centres. In consequence many of these centres, particularly in cities where the economy is stagnating or in decline, are faced with an oversupply of retail and commercial floorspace and an uncertain future in the urban hierarchy.

Chapter 6

Housing and Neighbourhood Issues in Urban Planning

Introduction

This chapter first considers the aims of housing policy and the scope for urban planning to intervene in the housing system. The first part of the chapter examines population trends and their relationship with household formation and housing requirements before going on to consider the provision of housing: what should be built and where should it be built? This is followed by two case studies that illustrate the planning and development of housing in different situations: new towns in China and a large new urban extension in the Netherlands. Following this, the chapter goes on to discuss issues around housing obsolescence and neighbourhood renewal before looking at two further case studies of area regeneration: housing refurbishment in an inner urban neighbourhood and remodelling an outworn peripheral social housing estate.

> Access to safe and healthy shelter is essential to a person's physical, psychological, social and economic well-being and should be a fundamental part of national and international action. The right to adequate housing as a basic human right is enshrined in the Universal Declaration of Human Rights and the International Covenant on Economic, Social and Cultural Rights. (*Agenda 21*, para 7.6)

Different countries express their aims for housing policy in different ways. Figure 6.1 illustrates the range of housing aims from selected European countries and demonstrates how the main expressed concerns of housing policy vary between countries. Most seem to adopt a preference for housing being provided by a well functioning market, yet recognize housing affordability as an important issue. Some countries see owner occupation as the preferred tenure and many recognize the importance of meeting consumer wishes and choices. Many countries have aims related to the control of housing location as a contribution to achieving more compact and efficient city

UK

'the government is helping local councils and developers work with local communities to plan and build better places to live for everyone. This includes building affordable housing, improving the quality of rented housing, helping more people to buy a home, and providing housing support for vulnerable people.'

Ireland

'the aim is to enable all households to have available an affordable dwelling of good quality suited to their needs, in a good environment and, as far as possible, at the tenure of their choice.'

France

'Housing policy … is predicated on the assumption that, in order for each person to be housed according to his/her wishes action must be taken on each link in the housing chain. This includes facilitating home ownership and stimulating private rental and social housing output.'

Belgium

'The aim is to promote home ownership and provide sufficient social housing.'

Netherlands

'the aim is to accelerate the restructuring of neighbourhoods and housing production, especially in cities; to achieve and maintain a sound, sustainable living climate; to tackle unsafe and run-down neighbourhoods and to

$\rightarrow$

Figure 6.1   *The aims of housing policies in selected European countries*

Source: UK, based on information on the DCLG website www.gov.uk/government/topics/housing (accessed 17.7.2014.); all other countries, based upon statements in Dol and Haffner (2010), Table 5.1.

forms. Of the countries considered here, only Germany makes any specific reference to tackling labour market issues and regional differentiation in housing, although these points are clearly of concern in a number of the larger countries.

Urban planning has two main contributions to make in relation to these aims:

- to facilitate housing provision and to influence the location and quality of housing constructed;
- to manage and coordinate responses to housing obsolescence and the socio-economic and environmental problems of residential neighbourhoods.

$\rightarrow$

prevent other areas from declining in this way; to promote home-ownership; to make city living more attractive for middle and higher income households and to ensure that housing is affordable.'

Denmark

'The main aim of the housing policy is – through a comprehensive supply of housing – to ensure that good and healthy housing is available to all of the population.'

Germany

'[the] task is to devise the range of housing policies necessary to address the increased regional differentiation of housing markets. At the same time, national housing policy has to make a reasonable contribution to the main political challenges like private retirement provisions by promoting owner occupied housing, reducing energy consumption, improving the living conditions for families with children in cities and stabilising the labour market.'

Poland

'The aim is to lower construction cost and improve the availability of financial resources; to ensure the expansion of housing for rental purposes provided both by the private and non-profit sectors; to improve the spatial mobility of the workforce through the potential of the existing housing stock; to revitalise urban areas; to provide support for municipalities as well as non-government organisations in respect of the provision of temporary accommodation.'

Figure 6.1 *(continued)*

In both cases the justification for intervention rests primarily on the need for the state to compensate for market failures in the housing sector: that is to say, the inability of the housing market to supply the appropriate quantity and quality of housing in the right place at the right time. Market failures in the housing sector are considerable. At the core of the problem lie a number of factors:

- there is a gap between the cost of housing and the ability of many households to meet these costs, which means that in many countries, especially in fast growing regions, it is necessary to offer some form of housing subsidy if the aim of adequately housing the population is to be achieved;
- the failure of the market to take adequate account of housing fitness means that the state has to set and regulate minimum standards of housing fitness and decency;

- the speed of societal changes, especially the nature of household formation, migration and changes in the location of demand, to which markets are often slow to respond and require state intervention to accelerate the resolution of problems.

Assessing general housing requirements

Control over the location and quality of housing was one of the earliest concerns of the modern planning system. As mentioned in Chapter 1, in many German towns, urban extensions were planned from the early nineteenth century. In the UK local building by-laws were used to control the quality and (indirectly) the layout of new housing from the middle of that century. The Housing, Town Planning, etc., Act of 1909 allowed British local authorities to control the location of development, land use and density in new suburbs. More recently, the proponents of sustainable development have argued for the importance of land use planning in controlling the location, density and form of housing in order to achieve more compact, energy efficient urban development that is less damaging to the natural environment (CEC, 1990; United Nations Conference on Environment and Development, 1992; DoE, 1994).

The process of determining the number of dwellings required in an area is methodologically straightforward but in practice it is almost impossible to make an accurate assessment of future requirements or to implement policies that will precisely achieve the necessary supply of dwellings.

The process begins with projections of population change. The projected population is then converted into numbers of households of different types and sizes. From this the required number, type and sizes of dwellings can be calculated. On the other side of the equation the existing stock of dwellings and its attributes (size, type, location, and so on) are projected forwards, adjusting for anticipated gains and losses. The difference between the dwellings required and the projected dwelling stock can then be considered and policies devised to respond to the anticipated shortfall or surplus. The process is illustrated in Figure 6.2.

Most population projections use the cohort component method. Starting with the baseline population, annual adjustments are made for anticipated net migration in each age group (the difference between inward and outward migration), minus the number of deaths and plus the numbers of births during the year. These adjustments depend upon assumptions about fertility, mortality and migration rates, usually based upon past trends and expert opinion.

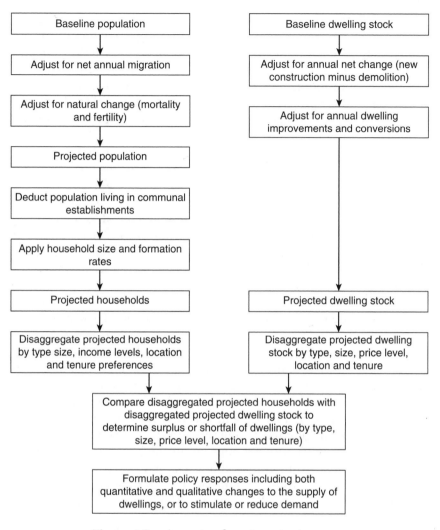

Figure 6.2 *Assessing housing requirements*

Household projections take the projected population as their starting point. Having deducted that proportion of the population expected to be living in communal establishments such as care homes, the remaining projected population is divided into private households of different types: one person households; two or more person adult households; families with children and so on, and by income levels. This is done by applying past trends and expert opinion on household formation rates and household size. These trends are influenced by both economic and cultural factors.

Projecting the future dwelling stock will also take as its base the existing stock, its characteristics and condition, adjusting for anticipated annual changes in terms of gains and losses and changes in the character of the stock such as changes in tenure. The projected future stock, disaggregated by location, tenure, type, and size and price level can then be compared with the projected numbers of private households, also disaggregated by type, size, income levels and so on to identify dwelling surplus or shortfall.

Because of the law of large numbers, projections such as these are usually more accurate at the national level than at the regional level, and regional projections are more accurate than local ones. What may appear to be a balance between supply and need or demand at a national or aggregate level may hide major imbalances in individual localities, or in particular tenures or price levels, or in relation to particular household needs. Thus, it is important that policies to deal with dwelling surplus or shortfall are similarly disaggregated and contain sufficient variety of response.

However, any estimate of tenure requirements or 'affordable housing' requirements must inevitably be based upon some normative view of what role the state should have in intervening in or taking over from the housing market. This will be based upon political choices made in particular places at particular times. In the UK in 2015 calculating the need for affordable housing is the responsibility of local authorities. In France, since 1991, the Government has sought to secure a greater 'solidarité' and social mix of housing tenures in urban areas by obliging most communes in the larger agglomerations to provide at least 20 % social housing. In the Netherlands there has historically been a strong tradition of social housing provision, which peaked at 38 % of the total dwelling stock in 1990 but had declined to 32 % by 2008, although still amongst the highest in Europe (Dol and Haffner, 2010).

The population of the EU is likely to increase slowly over the coming years (see Table 2.1, p. 59). However, there is considerable variation in the expected population change in individual countries. Whilst the populations of some countries, such as Ireland and the UK, were continuing to grow in the mid-2010s, others such as Germany and Poland were experiencing long run population decline. The ways in which the components of population change – natural change and migration – interact and affect total population change can vary substantially between one location and another. Such changes in population pose major challenges for planners: growing populations will require an expansion in national housing stock in order to be accommodated whereas shrinking populations may result in surplus housing which may become under-occupied or even abandoned.

In 2012 Germany and France had somewhat older populations than the EU average whilst Poland and Ireland had significantly younger populations. However, in terms of future trends in old-age dependency the UK is in a more stable situation than many other European countries, notably the Netherlands, where the population is still expected to grow but to age rapidly, and Poland, where the projection is for both population decline and a very rapid increase in the old-age dependency ratio. An increase in the old-age dependency ratio poses two problems: the first concerns the provision or modification of the housing stock to meet the needs of an ageing population and the second concerns the question of how this provision is to be financed with a declining proportion of the population economically active.

There are also great variations between localities in terms of household formation rates and average household size, which have an important influence on projections of housing need. Thus Ireland and Poland, with an average household size of 2.8 persons per household (pph) require only 357 dwellings to accommodate each 1,000 population; France and the UK, with an average household size of 2.3 pph, require 435 dwellings per 1,000 people; whilst Germany, with an average household size of only 2.1 pph, requires 476 dwellings per 1,000 people. This has significant resource implications for the countries and cities concerned. The size and form of dwellings required will also vary with household size and composition. Larger households with more children are more likely to seek single-family houses, whereas single or two-person adult households are more likely to be satisfied with apartment living. This has implications too for the density and compactness of the city.

It is also important to understand that housing need is not the same as housing demand. Just because a population needs housing does not mean that the market will supply that housing. Housing need is a normative concept based upon society's view on how much and what type of housing is required for a given population, whereas housing demand is an economic concept referring to the amount of housing consumed at a particular price. Therefore the term 'housing requirements', referring to a combination of need and demand, is sometimes used, for example, when considering both private market and affordable or social housing (Bramley, 2010).

A difficult question facing governments concerns the extent to which they should intervene in housing markets and plan to meet perceived housing requirements. After each of the world wars many European countries had such severe housing shortages that their governments faced political imperatives to intervene in housing supply either by direct action or through subsidy mechanisms. In most cases, after a number of years, the housing situation eased and governments gradually lessened their involvement.

The UK government requires local planning authorities to adopt a top-down approach to the assessment of housing requirements (DCLG, 2014a). The starting point is the national household projections for the next ten years which are updated by the government every two years. Whilst such updating is inevitable as social and economic circumstances continuously evolve, it does make for very unstable foundations for assessing the local housing situation. It can take longer than two years to prepare an urban development plan and when combined with a planning horizon of, say, 11–15 years this can easily lead to plans being based upon woefully inaccurate projections of local housing requirements.

In many urban areas the key driver of changes in housing requirements at the city-regional level is likely to be that of employment trends. Employment growth will attract inward migration and employment decline will stimulate outward migration. But more locally, housing demand is driven by a calculated trade-off between housing costs, transport costs and local amenity, so in all but the smallest and most self-contained urban areas, employment is likely to generate commuting from other localities. In the case of major cities such as London or Paris, this can often stimulate housing demand at considerable distances from the source of employment. This suggests, on the one hand, that a level of regional coordination is required in making local assessments of housing requirements but, on the other hand, there is considerable scope for modifying and guiding the location of housing provision to minimize commuting, maximize convenience and minimize environmental damage and energy use. There will also be some scope for directing employment to accessible locations that use land efficiently and minimize commuting. But employment is not always the key driver. In popular retirement areas, such as seaside towns and spas, housing demand is more driven by environment, reputation and price than by the availability of local jobs. In such locations there may also be a demand for second homes that has only the loosest connection with the source of the demand (the first home).

Today, most housing in European countries is provided by the private sector. This means that there is a much weaker relationship between the assessment of housing requirements and actual dwelling provision. Local planning authorities can assess how many dwellings, in what locations and of what types are needed but they cannot directly control any of these three elements. Developers will build dwellings only in such numbers, locations and types as are profitable. Thus in times of high employment and plentiful cheap mortgages, housing production will increase and in times of recession and restrictions on lending, housing production will decline. Such changes may affect particular locations or types of dwelling unevenly. For example, as shown in Table 6.1, in the

Table 6.1   *Annual housing completions in London and other regions, selected years*

	London	South-east Region	North-west Region
2005/6	18,810	28,210	20,620
2009/10	20,370	24,440	10,340
2011/12	20,000	22,280	9,580
2011/12 completions as a % of 2005/6 completions	106.3 %	79.0 %	46.5 %

Source: DCLG, *Live Tables on House Building*, Table 232; www.gov.uk/government/statistical-data-sets/live-tables-on-house-building#discontinued-tables (accessed 29.5.2015).

post-2008 economic crisis, housebuilding in the UK was cut back far less in London and the South-east than more depressed regions such as the North-west.

An important contribution to understanding the nature of housing supply came from a review conducted for the UK government by the Treasury economist, Kate Barker. Although published in 2004, much of its analysis applies with even greater force in the post-2008 period of economic crisis and while the focus is the UK, many of its recommendations resonate across other countries.

In the decades prior to 2008 housing demand had been increasing, driven by demographic trends and rising incomes yet, particularly in the UK, housing construction rates had been slow to respond. After 2008 this situation worsened as bank lending to both developers and consumers became difficult to obtain and, despite continuing need, the supply of new dwellings shrank. Although there was some recovery in housing production, supply continued to lag even further behind demand in the regions where growth was most quickly regained, notably London, leading to rapid price rises in those regions.

A further problem is that owner occupied housing is not only perceived as a utility good (providing a home) but also as an investment good (providing a return on investment). This perception also stimulates housing demand in regions and cities where prices are already rising, so further inflating prices. As economies strengthened after the 2008 crisis, London and a number of other European cities where the markets were seen to be secure have attracted a considerable amount of inward investment from foreign purchasers acquiring dwellings for their investment value – regardless of whether they were to be owner occupied, privately rented to tenants or left vacant. Such activity can create an additional distortion of local housing markets and be a complicating factor in assessing local housing requirements.

All of this has added to the kind of volatility in the housing market identified by Barker. She argued that housing affordability in the UK had worsened between economic cycles; that rising prices were leading to a redistribution of wealth from those outside the housing market to existing homeowners; that regional differentials in price rises restricted the mobility of labour and constrained productivity. She also suggested that simply increasing total supply was only part of the story. Dwelling location, type and size matter and planning has an important role in ensuring that towns and cities develop as valued and sustainable communities. Thus she recommended that, in making plans and planning decisions, planners should make better use of information about prices and preferences, and that the planning process should have greater certainty and speed, though not at the expense of good decisions. Central to achieving change was the need to allocate more land for development, whilst still ensuring protection for the most (environmentally or agriculturally) valuable land (Barker, 2004).

Following Kate Barker's recommendations the UK Government suggested that housing need assessments should be adjusted to reflect market signals. These include such matters as dwelling prices, rents, affordability ratios, overcrowding and rates of development, which would all be taken into account in assessing the number of dwellings and the amount of land required (DCLG, 2014a). This is all very well, but market circumstances can change very quickly. Whilst increases in the rate of housing development tend to be slow to accelerate, decreases can be very rapid, as in the post-2008 economic crisis when UK housing output fell by around 20 % within one year. This makes such adjustments very difficult to incorporate within a development plan.

Housing costs vary considerably between countries and between cities and regions. Table 6.2 illustrates the difference between the level of dwelling prices and the ability of households to afford them. Denmark has the most expensive dwellings and these costs appear to impose a heavy burden upon the population, with 27.6 % of the population spending more than 40 % of their total disposable income on housing. France and Belgium have the lowest average dwelling prices and amongst the lowest rate of housing cost overburden. Ireland represents an interesting case where, although prices are high, household incomes are also high and households are significantly larger than in Denmark, so the housing cost burden is pushed down. It should also be remembered that, whilst a country may have a reasonable national balance between housing supply and demand, the situation in individual regions or cities may be very different. For instance, there are considerable differences

Table 6.2   *Dwelling prices and costs, selected European countries*

	Average price of existing dwellings (2009) (euros)	Percentage of population experiencing 'housing cost overburden' in densely populated areas (2010)
UK	256,000	17.8
Ireland	275,000	5.1
France	175,000	7.2
Belgium	173,000	10.9
Netherlands	238,000	14.6
Germany	–	16.2
Denmark	293,000	27.6
Poland	–	11.5

Sources: Average price based on data from Dol and Haffner (2010), Table 4.5; housing cost overburden rate based on data from Eurostat, table tessi165 (Housing cost overburden rate by degree of urbanisation).

between Wallonia and Flanders in Belgium; between the former East Germany and the western Länder in Germany; between London and the rest of the UK; and between Paris and the rest of France.

Groups with specific housing requirements

Housing for older people

The ageing of the populations in most western countries presents one of our greatest housing challenges. In 2015 there were 96.7 million people in the EU aged 65 or over (18.9 % of the population). By 2050 this will have increased to 147.5 million (28.1 % of the population) (Eurostat, 2015). The composition of the elderly population is also changing with a greater proportion of single person elderly households, the frail elderly (over 80 years) and the disabled.

Much current thinking seeks to facilitate and encourage elderly people to remain in their own homes, within their own communities for as long as possible. Allowing older people to choose where and how they live, to remain economically active, to be involved with friends and family, makes both financial sense and leads to a more inclusive society. The provision of suitable housing for older people reduces pressure on the extended family, social care and health services (DCLG, 2011).

For reasons of failures in housing fitness, heating, internal layout and equipment and the local environment, too much of the existing housing stock is unsuitable for occupation by older people, especially the frail elderly. According to Age UK (2006) if older people are to remain living independently, housing must be suitable for all stages of life, with new housing readily adaptable to meet changing needs as occupiers become older. Specifically they advocate that all new homes should meet the Lifetime Homes Standards (DCLG, 2008) and that elderly persons should have access to the range of housing, health and care services they need in order to remain in their own homes.

Not only is there a need to adapt existing homes and neighbourhoods to meet the needs of the elderly, there is also a requirement for additional purpose-built accommodation including sheltered housing, residential care and nursing homes. Sheltered housing allows for independent living, typically a managed group of flats or small bungalows, to buy or rent, with a warden and some communal facilities such as a residents' lounge or gardens. Residential care homes provide rented accommodation, usually single rooms, meals and personal support for the frail elderly. Nursing homes additionally provide nursing and medical care for the extremely frail and bedridden.

An approach to a more communal style of living that is emerging in Germany, Denmark and elsewhere is that of multi-generational housing developments. Typically comprising blocks or groups of low rise apartments, usually rented from a housing company, these developments contain amenities that are useful to all inhabitants (communal rooms, gardens, bicycle storage, perhaps a laundry). However, they are managed in such a way as to ensure that the apartments are occupied by a mix of generations that can offer mutual social support, for example in babysitting for the young or shopping for the elderly, as well as informal social interaction. Given Germany's ageing population, the high proportion of single-person households and tradition of apartment renting this would seem to offer an approach to housing that that reflects more historic patterns of living and might be usefully copied elsewhere.

It is not only the dwelling that needs to be elderly-friendly; it is also the surrounding neighbourhood. Many older people feel trapped in their own homes or are put off enjoying their neighbourhood because of their perceptions of the local environment. Seemingly minor issues such as poor paving, lack of benches or toilets can become significant psychological deterrents. The resulting social isolation can impact on both mental and physical health with consequent costs for the rest of society (DCLG, 2008). Bevan and Croucher (2011) have identified the requirements for a 'lifetime neighbourhood' that is both functional and attractive with regard to the needs of older people. These include:

- supporting and empowering residents to participate in the management of their neighbourhood;

- creating walkable environments, which are safe, attractive, well signed, convenient and well maintained;
- providing local greenspace, including parks, gardens and allotments for both passive and active enjoyment;
- providing accessible local services and amenities, including local shops with a good range of products (for example, access to fresh food).

Not only does such provision serve a useful purpose for older people, it creates safe, sociable and convenient neighbourhoods that benefit everyone. But this is not just about planning new neighbourhoods: most of the neighbourhoods that will be occupied by the elderly in 30 or 50 years time already exist, so much of the concern is about retro-fitting to ensure that existing neighbourhoods meet 'lifetime neighbourhood' objectives (Bevan and Croucher, 2011).

Housing for students

Another group of people who have particular housing needs are students. They are typically young, single, on modest incomes and in occupation for only a part of the year. The requirement for student housing is often concentrated in a few specific areas near to higher education facilities. Whilst some student accommodation is provided on campus developments around universities, much is located within the general community, either in purpose-built blocks or within the ordinary housing stock.

'Studentification', the impact that high concentrations of students can have on a neighbourhood, has both negative and positive aspects. On the one hand, students can increase demand for car parking, reduce demand for family services and schools and cause excessive noise and environmental damage. On the other hand, the presence of students can stimulate local economic activity, bring a cultural vibrancy and help populate previously low demand neighbourhoods. Whilst many planning authorities try to manage these areas through, for example, limiting the number of houses in multiple occupation (HMOs), there is a trend for students to prefer purpose-built accommodation with better facilities and security than the more traditional shared accommodation. In consequence, developers have responded and many cities have brought in policies specifically to control this type of housing (Universities UK, 2006).

Typical of these policy responses is Leicester City Council's Supplementary Planning Document on Student Housing (Leicester CC, 2012). The policy is intended to ensure that any proposal demonstrates that new student accommodation is needed; is of appropriate size and scale; in suitable locations; includes appropriate facilities and management arrangements; and does not have an unacceptable cumulative impact on existing neighbourhoods.

Where and what to build?

Local planning authorities need to plan for a mix of dwelling locations, types, sizes and tenures, based on current and future demographic trends, market trends and the needs of different groups in the community. With regard to location, Patrick Abercrombie, writing in the 1930s, argued that planning should 'allow the citizen to go to and from work with the least loss of time and energy' (Abercrombie, 1933, p. 104). This suggests proximity between homes and workplaces and provision for accessibility by means that minimize energy use: walking, cycling and public transport. Even at the height of the era of modernist planning in the USA, F. Stuart Chapin argued that: 'Living areas should be located in convenient proximity to the work and leisure-time areas where there are nearby transit and thoroughfare routes to insure easy access ... [and] in easy walking distance of accessory community facilities' (Chapin, 1965, p. 371). As shown in Figure 3.6 (p. 120) Richard Rogers and his colleagues (*Towards an Urban Renaissance*, Urban Task Force, 1999) favoured raising housing densities around transport hubs and urban centres.

The achievement of more sustainable urban development requires more compact cities and higher net residential densities, especially around public transport hubs, but the question arises as to how high a density should be expected. Through the twentieth century the most typical density for peripheral residential development around British cities was in the range of 20–30 dwellings per hectare (dpha) and somewhat higher around many European cities. But the need for more sustainable development suggests a need to increase this. Planning consultants Llewelyn-Davies advocate densities that could be well over 200 dpha, mostly flats, in central areas; perhaps 50–100 dpha, mixed terraced housing and flats, along urban transport corridors; and 30–50 dpha, detached and linked houses, in more suburban locations (Llewelyn-Davies, 2000). But what seems reasonable and achievable will depend upon the geographic characteristics of individual urban areas. In Westminster (London), for example, the average density of completed schemes increased from 177 dpha in 2002 to 194 dpha in 2006/7 (Westminster City Council, 2007a). The redevelopment in the ZAC Cathédrale in Amiens included housing at around 75 dpha (see Chapter 8). In Utrecht's Leidsche Rijn urban expansion the target was 37 dpha (Gemeente Utrecht, 1995).

In general, modern planning theory suggests that planners should prioritize the reuse of previously developed land within urban areas, including the conversion of existing buildings to residential use and bringing empty homes back into use, before considering the development of greenfield sites. The potential of existing urban areas to accommodate additional housing is often considerable. Based upon the report *Tapping the Potential* (URBED, 1999), a range of opportunities could be explored, depending upon the structure and form of the area being considered:

- Sub-division of existing housing – not only have many larger nineteenth century homes now been sub-divided into flats, in areas of high demand an increasing number of two-storey terraced dwellings are successfully subject to horizontal sub-division into a ground-floor and an upper-floor flat.

- Flats over shops – since the 1990s there have been initiatives such as 'Living over the shop' (LOTS) to reuse of the floorspace above shops as flats, especially in inner urban areas. However, despite the substantial number of dwellings that could be created, the idea has encountered a number of technical difficulties and lacked appeal to private market providers.

- Empty homes – the 'natural' vacancy rate for urban housing appears to be around 3%. In many areas of structural decline in housing demand, especially in 'shrinking cities', much higher rates have been recorded and there are difficulties in getting this stock re-occupied. However, where higher vacancy is the result of market friction, disrepair, or local environmental reasons, there may be scope for bringing empty homes back into use.

- Reuse of previously developed vacant and derelict land and buildings – as industrial use of urban land has declined so these sites have provided a valuable source of housing land. However, the conversion costs can be high in comparison with greenfield sites, especially where there is contamination that needs remediation.

- Intensification of existing areas and the redevelopment of existing housing – there has been some intensification in the use of existing residential land, particularly in the opening-up of 'backlands' and in building on parcels within excessively large gardens and incidental open spaces. However, the UK Government discourages the inappropriate development of residential gardens, for example where development would cause harm to the local area. The redevelopment of existing housing at higher densities can be effective, particularly in areas of declining demand for larger family dwellings and rising demand for smaller apartments. Figure 6.3 shows such a redevelopment in Bebington in north-west England where four large detached houses were replaced with a development of seventy apartments on a site well served by public transport and close to community facilities.

- Conversion of commercial buildings; numerous city centres have seen a declining demand for commercial floorspace, often in buildings of architectural or historic interest. Over the last twenty years much of this space has been successfully converted into residential accommodation.

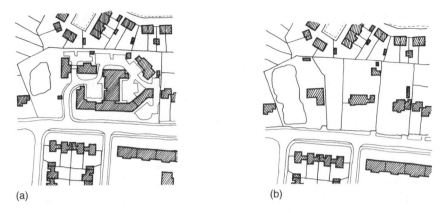

(a)   (b)

Figure 6.3   *Redevelopment and intensification of development on existing residential land: Bebington*

Source: Drawn by A.L. Couch.

Note: Plan (a) shows the apartment blocks containing more than seventy flats, built on the site of the former detached houses shown in (b).

The shortfall in new housing that cannot be accommodated within the urban area through any of these means will have to be provided on new sites. By dividing this shortfall by the appropriate density the area of land required for development can be determined. The next task is to select the most appropriate sites for development.

According to the advice given by the UK Government (DCLG, 2014a) the process should generally begin with the identification of a broad range of possible sites and locations. The development potential of sites and locations will be determined by their fit with planning policies and the economic viability of development. This will be influenced by:

- physical limitations or problems such as access, infrastructure, ground conditions, flood risk, hazardous risks, pollution or contamination;
- potential impacts such as the effect upon landscapes including landscape features, nature and heritage conservation;
- appropriateness and likely market attractiveness for the type of development proposed;
- contribution to regeneration priority areas;
- environmental/amenity impacts experienced by would-be occupiers and neighbouring areas (DCLG, 2014a, para. 19).

Whilst much housing development will be provided by incremental additions to the urban area, sometimes when substantial amounts of housing are required, the supply of new homes can be best achieved through planning for larger scale development, such as extensions to existing towns or cities or new settlements that follow the principles of Garden Cities.

The UK Town and Country Planning Association (TCPA) has been a consistent advocate of planned new towns and the notion of garden cities. In April 2014 the UK Government announced that 'Communities with ideas for a new generation of garden cities will receive support from the government to turn their ambitions into reality' (DCLG and others, 2014). In response the TCPA welcomed the announcement and set out a number of principles to which it felt a garden city should adhere. Many of these principles reflect modern conventional thinking about sustainable urban development. However, a key additional element proposed by the TCPA is to capture the increase in land values created by the development in order to repay infrastructure costs and provide a portfolio of assets which can be managed in perpetuity for the benefit of the community. This would require the acquisition of land at, or near, current use value by a community-based organization with effective planning and land assembly powers (TCPA, 2014).

The next two sections examine the concept of new towns and urban extensions in an international context: new towns around Shanghai in China and the Leidsche Rijn urban extension in Utrecht, Netherlands.

The Garden City revisited or not? Shanghai's New Towns

Since the 1960s Shanghai has developed auxiliary or satellite towns to accommodate urban expansion. Following the economic reforms of the 1990s the metropolis has grown rapidly, its population rising from around 13 million in 1990 to over 23 million in 2010. In 2001 the 'One City, Nine Towns' plan was announced with the aim of moving from a highly centralized city to a more polycentric structure through the development of one new city (Songjiang) and nine new towns in the surrounding area. Some local townships were also to be expanded. It was felt that this approach would go some way towards meeting Shanghai's need to expand whilst simultaneously spreading the benefits of economic growth into the hinterland and protecting the surrounding countryside from urban sprawl (den Hartog, 2009). Complementing this strategy, within the central city of Shanghai the so-called 'double increase and double decrease' policy was designed to decrease the heights and densities of new building projects whilst increasing the amount of green and open spaces within the city. This had the effect of pushing real estate developers towards the more outlying municipal territory. Supported by state investment in transport infrastructure and municipal land acquisitions, new town development corporations were established and masterplans prepared (Wang, 2010). According to the approach adopted in Shanghai, the first step in developing a new town lay in local economic development: providing jobs that would attract new inhabitants. Infrastructure also had to be provided ahead of housing construction. Hence the up-front capital costs of new town development could be very high.

Much of the responsibility for the planning and design of each new town was given to western planning agencies. The new city is situated about 35 km west of Shanghai adjoining the historic town of Songjiang. The original masterplan, devised by the UK-based consultants Atkins, envisaged the new city accommodating 500,000 inhabitants, although this was revised upwards in a policy review. The masterplan was based upon a grid structure of roads and a network of green and blue infrastructure separating the new city into residential, employment, higher education, commercial and cultural zones. The layout is spacious: main roads are 35 to 50 m wide and lined with 10 to 20 m of landscaping along each side. A central feature of the new city is a 300 m-wide green spine. In all, one-quarter of the area of the city comprises green or blue infrastructure. The first phase of development (2000–2003) concentrated on infrastructure, environmental works and employment zones. Only then was the main bulk of the housing development begun. There are intended to be nine residential zones, each accommodating 50–80,000 inhabitants and typically subdivided into a number of neighbourhoods which each comprise communities of 2,500–4,000 people. Figure 6.4 shows typical new housing in the area. Retail and social facilities are planned on a similar hierarchy (Zhou, 2010).

The main function of the new city was to accommodate overspill population from central Shanghai, to become an administrative, economic and cultural centre for the district, and a major location for the expansion of higher education. The historic town of Shanghai is a local tourist destination and subject to strong environmental protection policies. Although the new city is linked back to Shanghai by motorway and rapid transit connections, the intention was that it, like the original conception for the British new towns, should be relatively self-contained, providing homes and jobs for its population rather than being a dormitory town for Shanghai. In addition to conventional industrial zones, a major employment location is the new university district, which accommodates more than 70,000 students in a number of important higher education institutions. One of the most well known residential quarters in the new city is Thames Town, which was designed to mimic the physical structure and environment of an English market town. It was originally intended to provide attractive homes for up to 10,000 middle class inhabitants, predominantly in low density single-family houses, but in reality many of the dwellings have been purchased for investment or

Figure 6.4.   *New housing in China*

Source: M. Cocks, 2016.

Note: All the blocks are aligned north–south in accordance with feng shui tradition.
Despite the high density, the blocks and surrounding environment are well designed with
plenty of green infrastructure and a road system that facilitates cycling.

use as second homes. It has also been criticized for being too socially
segregated from the rest of the city and its low density is seen by some as
an inappropriate underuse of scarce building land (Wang, 2010). Zhou
(2010) praises the success of the new city development in being implemented at great speed and more or less in accordance with the original
plan but comments that the zoning is too rigid, leading to a segregation
of land uses as well as social groups and 'a lack of urban vitality ... the
new city is not designed on a human-friendly scale' (pp. 282–4).

Nevertheless, despite this and other criticisms about the amount of
affordable housing provided, the overall impact of the new town development programme has changed the urban landscape of Shanghai,
decentralizing the overcrowded central city, providing good quality
dwellings for the expanding population and creating new economic
focal points. Although the 'one city nine towns' strategy contains some
recognizable elements of the garden cities concept, the scale and density
of development are very different from the European experience. One
can also see nuances of Le Corbusier's Radiant City in the ideas of
spreading urban density to better balance traffic flows and freeing up
ground-level space for circulation and recreation.

Developing a large new settlement: Utrecht, Leidsche Rijn

In 1988 the former Dutch Ministry of Housing, Spatial Planning and the Environment (VROM) responded to rapidly increasing housing need by proposing the construction of over 450,000 new dwellings between 1996 and 2005. The policy, known as Vierde Nota Ruimtelijke Ordening Extra (VINEX), envisaged the building of a number of large new housing areas as close as possible to existing urban settlements, thus using and supporting existing physical and social infrastructure, minimizing the need for travel and limiting the impact on open land (the green heart of the Randstad).

Leidsche Rijn, a 2,560 ha extension of Utrecht, intended to accommodate 30,000 dwellings, was the largest of the schemes proposed under VINEX. Started in the mid-1990s, by 2014 around two-thirds of the scheme had been completed. The area lies to the west the existing city but is separated from it by the broad Amsterdam-Rijnkanaal and the A2 (Amsterdam–Utrecht–Eindhoven) motorway. These barriers are to be overcome by building a number of new bridges across the canal and placing part of the motorway in a tunnel to minimize impact and improve permeability.

A draft masterplan was drawn up in 1994 and following a period of public debate the definitive Leidsche Rijn masterplan was adopted in 1995. Unlike a development plan, the masterplan had no legal status and was not binding. It represented an agreed approach between the municipal authorities concerned and it provided guidelines for the more detailed planning of individual neighbourhoods. An agreement between the national government and the municipalities concerned set out the size of the housing programme, public transport provision, programme and funding arrangements.

The masterplan was based on three concepts: compactness (and proximity to the existing city), durability (balancing ecological and economic needs) and identity (taking account of the character of different areas). The plan (see Figure 6.5) proposed a series of residential neighbourhoods developed around a central park (Máximapark), with a 'town centre' in the north-east and industrial zones to the north and south of the development area. The circulation system runs between these neighbourhoods providing a hierarchy of urban and local distributor roads and cycle paths. The area is bisected by the existing Utrecht–Gouda railway and additional stations have been opened to serve the area. Development is intended to be sustainable and durable, with substantial investment in environmental protection and energy management. Water management is very important with rainwater being retrieved, either from the ground or in open water, and retained for reuse. Many of the new neighbourhoods are connected to the city's district heating system, saving energy and reducing emissions.

Implementation of the scheme was divided into a large number of smaller projects to encourage variety in urban form and design, including

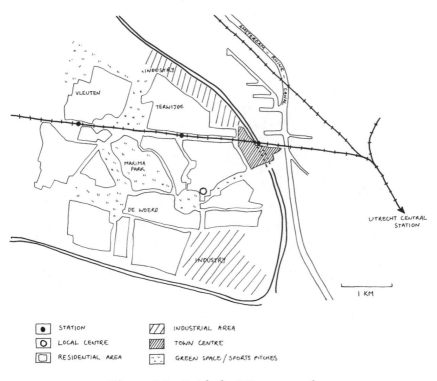

Figure 6.5 *Leidsche Rijn masterplan*

Source: Drawn by A.L. Couch.

variations in residential densities, building styles and heights, varying proportions of public and private greenspace and varying proportions of social and private housing within individual zones (although the overall target was 30 % social housing). Higher density housing was to be concentrated around railway stations and neighbourhood centres. Another basic principle was to retain as much of the old rural structure of dykes, roadways and farm buildings as possible. Two existing villages, De Meern and Vleuten, were incorporated into the development.

Parkwijk and Hoge Weide are typical residential neighbourhoods. Much of the Parkwijk was completed quite early in the development process and comprises two parts separated by a strip of parkland (Princess Amalia Park), a busway and a canal. The area to the south of the park was the first to be occupied and contains more higher density housing, including some high rise apartments, much of which is let as social housing. North of the park housing is mainly in the form of single-family owner occupied houses (Figure 6.6). A small local neighbourhood shopping centre opened in 2004. Hoge Weide is a more recent neighbourhood comprising 1,300 dwellings on 30 hectares of land (43 dpha)

(a)

Figure 6.6   *Leidsche Rijn: contrasting styles of housing*

Source: C. Couch, 2016.

Note: There is a contrast in housing styles between (a) which recalls the Dutch tradition of brick-built urban housing, with large windows and frontages giving directly onto the pavement, and (b) which reflects a more rural Dutch vernacular.

adjoining the proposed Leidsche Rijn Centre. Housing is divided 70:30 between low and high rise at a range of price levels. The scheme also includes some office space, a school and other community facilities. The design incorporates an existing watercourse, a medieval road and some retained farm buildings. A pattern of green routes based on the old river valley separates the neighbourhood into three smaller zones.

The layout of the Máximapark in the centre of Leidsche Rijn was the outcome of a competition held in 1997. The winning design by the architects West 8 provides a 50 ha core of woodland, watercourses, green areas and playgrounds surrounded by a meandering four kilometre long pergola. Beyond this lie playing fields and sports facilities. The park is seen as an important counterbalance to the residential character of the rest of the area.

The post-2008 economic crisis has impacted on the development of the area. Whilst by 2014 many of the residential neighbourhoods had been completed, some 10,000 dwellings and the proposed town centre, intended to be the commercial and cultural heart of the scheme, had yet to be built. Also, less employment had been provided in the area than was

(b)

Figure 6.6 *(continued)*

envisaged in the masterplan. Situated at a very accessible point in the Randstad, not only are residents able to commute to jobs in Utrecht but Rotterdam and The Hague are both less than 45 minutes away. Thus whilst the internal design may encourage short trips and favour cycling and walking, the location favours longer distance travel to work. Although physically close to Utrecht city centre (2 km at its nearest point) the city feels more distant, with the canal, motorway and open spaces creating a psychological barrier. Further connections are proposed and these will be important in binding the old and new parts of the city together.

Despite the protestations as to variety in design, many of the neighbourhoods have a uniformity about them, possibily because of similarity in scale and simply because they are new. Like many British new towns there seems to be some tension between the relatively high net residential densities that pertain within the neighbourhoods and the large open spaces between them, some of which feel more like barriers than useful greenspace. The plan makes claim to a wide variety of land uses: residential, community, commercial, industrial, green and blue infrastructure. Yet, perhaps partly because much employment has been pushed to the edges, much of the area feels like a rather monofunctional housing estate, although this lack of mix may be tempered when the Leidsche Rijn centre is completed.

Nevertheless, it is important to remember that this is a very large new settlement. To have built it at all is an impressive achievement. By and large the overall planning and detailed design is well conceived and meets its own aims of compactness, durability and identity. The test will come in the future when construction is over and the landscaping is mature. Two key questions will then need to be answered: has the new town been bound together with the old city into a single whole and do people of all social groups continue to find it an attractive, desirable and affordable place to live? In other words, has it become a sustainable community?

Housing obsolescence and neighbourhood renewal

Housing becomes obsolete when its economic life has expired and decisions are taken about whether it should be refurbished, or replaced. As shown in Figure 6.7, the economic life of a dwelling can be considered

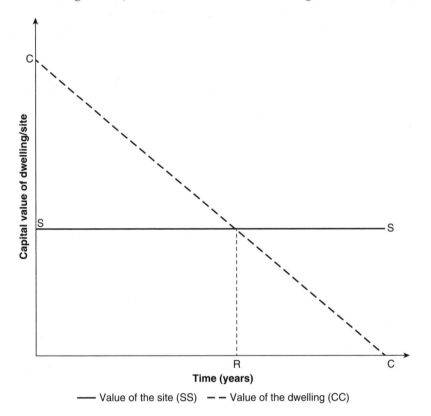

Figure 6.7   *The economic life of a dwelling*

Source: Based upon Goodall (1972), p. 209.

Note: When first completed the value of the dwelling is at its highest and declines over time. When it falls below the value of the site, at point R, market forces would suggest redevelopment.

as the period of time over which the capital value of the building exceeds the capital value of the cleared site (Goodall, 1972). Sometimes these decisions are taken by the market but frequently they are the subject of state intervention and outside of this context there is no definable 'physical' lifespan for a dwelling. Thus it is not possible to make a statement such as 'typical European dwellings have a physical lifespan of 100 years', because it simply is not true. In many older settlements, especially in southern Europe, there are dwellings built in medieval times that are continuing to provide satisfactory homes, yet in some large cities, especially in the UK, numerous multi-storey apartment blocks built in the 1960s were demolished within less than 40 years of their construction. Thus the timespan in Figure 6.7 may be decades or centuries. Where demand is high the economic life is likely to be extended, where it is weak the lifespan may be shorter. However, this assumes that the price of the site (land) does not vary. In an expanding city, especially one in which outward expansion is restricted by planning regulations, the price of land may rise, with the effect of shortening the life of the dwelling as it becomes profitable to redevelop the site more intensely or for a different use. In a shrinking city the price of land may fall and the life of the dwelling extend, possibly indefinitely.

The problem arises when the market shows no economic desire to replace or improve older housing even though it may have become unfit and no longer be providing a decent home. Concepts of fitness are politically defined determinants of housing need. For this reason most governments feel obliged to intervene in the housing market at a point when the dwelling has become unfit according to their definition, even though the market shows no desire to act. Whether this intervention takes the form of clearance and replacement or renovation and improvement depends upon policy preferences prevailing in that location and at that time.

The different arguments in favour of housing clearance and redevelopment on the one hand or housing refurbishment and area improvement on the other hand are summarized in Table 6.3.

There are many other factors that may also have an influence. In England the typical nineteenth century terraced housing still found in many inner urban neighbourhoods is often in multiple single ownerships, physically attached to adjoining dwellings and with a footprint perhaps 4 m by 8 m. These factors make it very difficult for the market to demolish and replace a single dwelling. Decisions must be taken on the future of a group of dwellings, possibly a whole terrace, to make redevelopment feasible. This usually requires some form of state intervention. This is one reason why British policy has favoured housing renovation rather than clearance over much of the past 40 years. Contrast this with the situation in many German and central European

Table 6.3   *Housing renewal: clearance or improvement?*

Clearance and redevelopment	Housing refurbishment and area improvement
• Creates efficient modern, higher value residential areas • Destroys embodied value in existing dwellings, streets and infrastructure • Eliminates mixed uses, damaging local economies • Changes local townscape, removes landmarks • Leads to tenure change • Creates and exacerbates spatial social segregation and encourages gentrification • Removes cheap and easy access housing stock, exacerbating homelessness • Imposes high costs on movers • Breaks up existing communities • Traumatic process	• Retains much of the inefficiency of existing dwelling structures and area layouts • Retains embodied value • More gradual change allowing communities time to adjust • Retains local amenities and employment opportunities • Retains current townscape and landmarks • Retains tenure and social mix, gentrification less likely • Retains cheaper housing stock • Less costly to occupiers, more affordable for local communities • Less traumatic process

cities where much of the equivalent housing was built in the form of separate multi-storey tenement blocks of rented apartments. These blocks might have a footprint 15 m by 20 m, typically in the ownership of a single landlord with the physical and economic capacity to make decisions on refurbishment or demolition without the need for assistance from the state. Figure 6.8 illustrates these two forms of inner urban development.

In the UK, since the late nineteenth century the traditional method of tackling obsolete housing was to initiate programmes of slum clearance. In the wake of economic crises in the late 1960s and growing criticism of the clearance and redevelopment process, policy shifted towards housing renovation and area improvement. Official (MHLG, 1966) and academic studies (for example, Needleman, 1965) demonstrated the feasibility and economic benefits of housing renovation; there was growing disillusionment with the design and quality of some replacement dwellings (for example, high rise flats, remote locations). In addition, many supposedly obsolete neighbourhoods contained communities that were long-standing, close-knit and with features of local social and economic life that were thought worthy of retention.

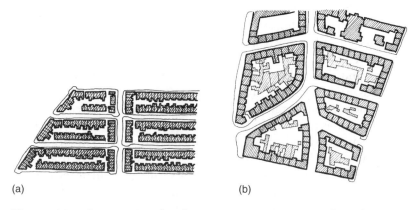

(a)   (b)

Figure 6.8   *Contrasting development patterns in British and German inner urban neighbourhoods*

Source: Drawn by A.L. Couch.

Note: The streets in the British example (a) comprise small, two-storey single-family terraced houses with small front areas and backyards with rear access via alleyways. The dwellings are usually built with shared party-walls. The street blocks in the German example (b) are bounded by tenements, usually four to six storeys high and constructed as separate but contiguous buildings. Historically the rear courtyards were gradually infiltrated by workshops and other one or two storey buildings.

One of the difficulties in moving from clearance to improvement was how to convince owners that it was worth investing in their properties. They faced two linked uncertainties: whether their property might be included in a clearance scheme at some future date and even if not, whether they would recoup the value of their investment. The solution adopted in the UK under the Housing Act, 1969 was to create General Improvement Areas (GIAs) within which there was a presumption in favour of housing retention, evidenced by raised subsidies to home-owners to assist with housing renovation and crucially, local authority investment in area improvements such as traffic calming, landscaping and amenities, confirming their own faith in the future of the area. This policy of subsidized housing renovation complemented by area improvement initiatives gathered momentum and became the principal method for dealing with obsolete housing over the next twenty years.

The early 1970s saw a similar shift in policy in the Netherlands. One early and influential experience was in the Dapperbuurt area of Amsterdam where local residents rejected the city council's comprehensive redevelopment proposals, arguing that they were happy in the area and did not want the overspill housing or higher rents that were the inevitable outcome of comprehensive renewal. After a struggle the city council came to accept a process of more gradual renewal through street level community participation (Community Forum, 1987).

In Rotterdam in 1974 the city council established a vigorous renewal programme to tackle housing and environmental problems in the worst parts of the city. Eleven urban renewal areas were designated, comprising 60,000 dwellings, in which the objectives were to improve the quality of buildings and the environment whilst retaining the character of neighbourhoods and continuing to provide housing within affordable rent limits. Much of the detailed decision making was devolved to project teams within the renewal areas. These teams included local community representatives advised by experts funded by the city. The presence of these locally-based experts enabled the City Council proposals to be professionally evaluated by the community and gave them the capacity to develop credible alternatives. The resulting quality of area renewal in Rotterdam demonstrated that a substantial and sustained process of community participation in urban renewal would work to the benefit of all parties and was not something for city councils to fear but something to embrace as a means of producing better urban planning (Couch, 1990).

Multiple deprivation and area regeneration

During the 1970s it became clear in many cities that it was not sufficient to tackle housing obsolescence alone. Many of these communities were also simultaneously suffering from other problems including poverty, poor health, low educational attainment, and job insecurity. But what was the cause of this multiple deprivation? Was it the result of a 'culture of poverty' (as many had argued in the nineteenth century) which could be tackled through education and social integration? Was there a 'cycle of deprivation' in which poverty led to a spiral of poor housing, poor health, inadequate education and insecure employment which had to be broken at some point? Were there 'managerial' or 'resource distribution' issues within central or local government which, if fixed, would in turn help fix deprivation? Or were there deep rooted structural issues in the capitalist economy that made urban deprivation inevitable? (Lawless, 1979).

In 1969 the UK Home Office launched a series of action-research Community Development Projects (CDP). Probably against the expectations of the government, the CDP produced a series of strongly argued reports clearly locating much of the cause of urban poverty in recent changes in the economic structure of cities, the inadequacies of central and local government responses and, more fundamentally, in the workings and imperatives of the capitalist system (Loney, 1983). In 1972 the Department of the Environment commissioned three major Inner Area Studies (in Birmingham, Lambeth and Liverpool) in order to better understand the issues involved. They concluded that economic change was indeed one of the fundamental causes of urban deprivation (Shankland, 1977).

In the event the then Labour Government recognized the scale and severity of urban deprivation and responded with a coordinated approach that included the setting up of partnerships between central and local government under the Inner Urban Areas Act, 1978, quadrupling funding for urban regeneration and bending mainstream funding and policies in favour of the inner areas. But the policy was short-lived. On winning the 1979 General Election, the Conservative Government led by Margaret Thatcher favoured a different approach, with more central government intervention and partnership, not between government and local authorities but between government and the private sector and a focus on economic (property-led) regeneration. However, support for housing renovation and the physical improvement of inner urban neighbourhoods continued and were actually strengthened.

In (West) Berlin in the 1980s there was growing criticism of comprehensive urban redevelopment which was seen as being too advantageous to speculative developers and big housing companies, supporting their strategies to demolish the old, low rent, low profit dwelling stock without equivalent community benefits. This led to a debate on the future of housing regeneration policy which included ideas about tenant-led modernization and new forms of ownership. On the ground this discussion led to and was stimulated by an emerging squatting movement, occupying not just single apartments but whole blocks.

The example of Berlin's Kreuzberg district is illustrative. The area had been developed in the late nineteenth century as a dense, working class residential district. It had been badly damaged in the Second World War and after 1961 Kreuzberg found itself on the edge of the western city adjoining the Berlin Wall. As a consequence the area fell into sharp decline. Between 1965 and 1975 redevelopment corporations bought up property, demolished dwellings and rehoused tenants. Cleared sites were redeveloped in the manner of large housing estates on the edge of the city. However, by the mid-1970s there was strong resistance to the removal of existing tenants from their familiar neighbourhoods and the policy was changed. A new phase of renewal preserved the outward appearance of streets. Interior blocks were demolished and densities reduced. Some dwellings were refurbished to modern standards and where replacement building took place it was in sympathy with existing building lines and building form. By 1980 squatters were renovating vacant dwellings to demonstrate an alternative future for the neighbourhood and by the end of the decade, after political changes within the Berlin City Government, a new approach of 'careful urban renewal' was emerging. This more sensitive approach, which formed a large component of the Berlin International Building Exhibition of 1989, involved a high level of community participation, consolidated the existing housing stock, reused vacant properties and supported community and local business development (Bodenschatz, 2008; Couch et al., 2011).

Back in the UK, the late 1980s and much of the 1990s saw attention being paid to the renovation of run-down social housing estates. In an era of emerging housing surplus in many cities outside London, dwellings on some of these estates were becoming increasingly hard to let. Criticism was levelled at estate and dwelling form as well as the poor quality of construction, maintenance and management. Remedial action, undertaken under an Estate Action programme or, in a few cases, through Housing Action Trusts (HATs), saw widespread demolition of unpopular housing, especially multi-storey apartments, the installation of new management regimes and changes to housing tenure, including the insertion of pockets of new private housing. The Liverpool Housing Action Trust (LHAT) was one such example. By 1993 many of Liverpool's tower blocks were obsolete and LHAT took over responsibility for 67 of the 71 blocks. There was little demand for renovated tower blocks and this made refurbishment uneconomic, in most cases leaving demolition as the only solution. Tenant participation played a major role in LHAT decision making, from strategy to detailed design and project management. Falling demand and changing household structures meant that less replacement housing was needed. As a consequence most rebuilding comprised lower density, low rise accommodation (Couch, 2003).

In France too, the state of social housing was causing concern. However, in contrast with the inner city focus which framed the debate in the UK, the concentration of urban problems in French cities lay in the large peripheral social housing estates. Although there were some physical and design issues, most of the problems were socio-economic in nature. Since the French government launched its Politique de la Ville (City Policy) after riots in the Lyon suburb of Venissieux in 1981, an array of policy innovations have sought to ameliorate the seemingly intractable social issues of these social housing neighbourhoods. In 1982 the government funded a programme of local economic and social development, Developpement Social des Quartiers (DSQ), to be implemented by communes. It was also in this period that there was a significant decentralization of powers from the central state to regions and communes, including increased powers over town planning for local communes. By 1988 a new idea of Contrats de Ville (Town Contracts) was being tried. This was a broader approach setting local problems within a city-wide perspective in which the local authorities and the state worked together in partnership to implement a multiple-year programme of integrated urban development. One of the problems was that the provision of social housing was spatially concentrated in a few communes. Following further social unrest, the 1990s saw attempts to strengthen the idea of solidarity within urban areas and develop a more even spatial distribution of social housing and a better social balance by obliging most communes within the larger urban agglomerations to provide at least 20 % of the stock as social housing (Hall and Hickman, 2002).

In the UK there was growing concern that regeneration policy was too centralized and too fragmented between departments, agencies and funding sources. John Major's Government (1992– 1997) established a national regeneration agency for England (English Partnerships), and set up regional offices of government to better coordinate programme delivery and to simplify funding into a Single Regeneration Budget (SRB). The SRB included a funding stream for which local partnerships (usually comprising local authorities in a new 'facilitating' role, together with other local agencies) could bid for funding for regeneration programmes and projects that reflected locally determined priorities. A typical programme was that of the North Liverpool Partnership. With the aim of tackling the area's social deprivation, the area received £21.9 million of funding from the SRB for a six year programme of economic development, social development, housing and environmental improvements; the programme levered in other funds worth £138 million (Couch, 2003).

The UK's New Deal for Communities (NDC) was set up by the Labour Government in 1998, with the aim of tackling multiple deficits in the most deprived neighbourhoods by providing the resources to tackle problems in an intensive and coordinated way. The target was to achieve convergence between these neighbourhoods and the rest of the country. Thirty-nine partnerships were established, and some £2 billion of central government funding was allocated to the problem. Policies were aimed at five key themes: creating jobs; reducing crime; improving educational attainment; improving health; and tackling problems with housing and the physical environment. The innovative characteristics of the policy were a long term (ten year) commitment to deliver real change, community involvement, partnership with key agencies and 'joined-up thinking'. Broadening the approach of the NDC, in 2001 the Government published a national strategy, *A New Commitment to Neighbourhood Renewal*, intending that within ten to twenty years no-one should be seriously disadvantaged by where they live (ODPM, 2001a). The idea was to combine the activities of relevant agencies in a 'joined-up' holistic approach to solving the inter-related problems of unemployment, crime, low educational attainment, poor health, and housing and the local physical environment.

In Germany the fall of the Berlin wall in 1989 and the reunification of Germany in 1990 changed the spatial structure of the country, the landscape of planning and the priorities for urban and regional development. In the early 1990s much of the Federal Government's funding for urban regeneration became concentrated in the east; consequently federal support for regeneration programmes in the western Länder fell sharply. What also became clear during these years was that many cities in the east were rapidly losing population; they had become 'shrinking cities' (Turok and Mykhnenko, 2007). Similar but less dramatic problems were also emerging in the older industrial cities of the west. In consequence the government extended its support for urban regeneration to cities in need across the country. Known as 'Die Soziale Stadt', the aim was to counteract the widening socio-spatial rifts in cities by fostering participation and cooperation and a new integrative approach to urban development in Germany as a whole. This led to projects and interventions being developed across several policy fields at the same time (for example, housing improvement, community development and environmental improvements) as well as coordination between public and other agencies. The approach focussed on a range of physical and social issues including employment, education and training, sport, the local environment, housing and social integration.

In former East Germany much of the housing stock built in the postwar period comprised prefabricated public sector multi-storey housing (Plattenbau). By the end of the 1990s demand for this type of housing was plummeting and very high levels of vacancy were appearing. In consequence in 2002 the Federal Government started the Stadtumbau Ost programme. The question was how to execute very substantial reductions in the unpopular prefabricated housing stock of eastern cities whilst minimizing the damage to existing urban structure and fabric and supporting the remaining traditional urban housing. Again it became apparent that there were continuing problems associated with population ageing and decline in a number of western German cities and so in 2004 the programme was extended as Stadtumbau West. The actions supported included urban restructuring and the reuse of derelict land and buildings and investment in physical, social and cultural infrastructure (Bodenschatz, 2008).

The European Commission too was taking an interest in neighbourhood renewal. As a part of its obligations to regional development the Commission developed an Urban Community Initiative (URBAN I) that ran from 1994 to 1999 to enable urban areas in crisis to design innovative, integrated neighbourhood renewal measures. In all, some 118 urban areas took part in the initiative. Encouraged by the results, the approach was continued as Urban II (2000–2006), financed by the European Regional Development Fund (ERDF), for sustainable development in the troubled urban districts of the EU. The aim was to promote new strategies and share knowledge on economic and social regeneration in troubled urban areas. Some 70 urban areas took part in the programme. Their problems included high levels of unemployment, poverty, social exclusion, anti-social behaviour, precarious demographic trends and poor environment conditions. The actions funded through the programme included improving living conditions, for example by renovating buildings and creating green areas; creating jobs, for example in environment, culture, and services to the population; and integrating the less-favoured social groups into the education and training systems.

For example, in Århus, Denmark, in the neighbourhoods of Gellerup, Hasle and Herredsvang, problems included high unemployment, low income levels, immigration, 'ghettoism', drug abuse and crime. Yet the neighbourhoods also contain an abundance of green areas, a well-organized environmental and public transport system, a strong sense of community and a considerable amount of affordable housing. Key actions therefore included improving the labour market capacity and skills in new technologies; measures to tackle crime and drug abuse; as well as the promotion of community involvement and the integration of ethnic minorities. And in the Nordstadt district of Dortmund, Germany, a high density, predominantly working class inner urban district of 55,000 people, the community's problems were related to the phasing-out of the coal mining and steel industries, in which many inhabitants had formerly been employed. Poverty and social exclusion were wide-spread. The programme focussed on three priorities: (i) improving the quality of the physical urban environment, focusing on public spaces in housing areas; (ii) supporting the local economy, in particular strengthening local businesses through counselling and investment support, promoting the area, as well as stimulating entrepreneurship, employment pacts, and local business networks; (iii) stimulating grassroots initiatives and structures by local inhabitants, in particular integration of groups at risk of being socially excluded.

Between 2003 and 2011, cities in the North and Midlands of England benefitted from a programme of Housing Market Renewal (HMR). This was to be a 15-year programme, but the post-2008 economic crisis and public spending cuts led to its termination in 2011. The UK Government had acknowledged what appeared to be a serious and growing issue of rapidly falling demand and housing market failure affecting a number of inner urban areas. The idea was to reduce the quantity and improve the quality of housing supply in these problematic neighbourhoods. By March 2011, HMR had invested £2.2bn nationally, with a further £1bn of leveraged investment from public and private partners resulting in the clearance of 30,000 properties, the refurbishment of 108,000 more and the completion of 15,000 new homes (Audit Commission, 2011). From its inception, HMR was controversial. Criticisms included: questions about the evidence base behind the programme (Townsend, 2006); that it represented a middle class view of the housing market, seeing it as an investment to be 'consumed', rather than the more trad-itional working class perception of a form of 'shelter', a 'place to live' (Allen, 2008); that it conflicted with the New Deal for Communities (NDC) initiative by questioning the sustainability of communities and neighbourhoods and removing their ownership and control of the regeneration process, and that the goal of HMR shifted over time from a specific concern with low housing demand to a broader economic regeneration agenda (Ferrari and Lee, 2010).

The two case studies that follow illustrate the complexities of neighbourhood renewal in two contrasting contexts: an older, predominantly private, terraced housing area in Gateshead (UK) and an obsolete social housing estate in Dublin (Ireland).

Area regeneration in Gateshead, Bensham and Saltwell

Bensham and Saltwell is a diverse and multicultural inner urban neighbourhood in Gateshead which was included in the Bridging Newcastle Gateshead (BNG) Housing Market Renewal (HMR) Pathfinder Area. The neighbourhood was recognized by the Council as one of the key areas in the borough that could benefit from HMR funding due to its location close to the regional centre and its ability to create a distinctive and sustainable place to live for a variety of households and lifestyles.

In the view of the Council the housing market in Bensham and Saltwell was failing because of the limited choice and poor quality housing in which vulnerable socio-economic groups tended to live. Whilst vacancy was not excessively high, dwelling prices were low in the private sector and turnover high in the social sector. Housing disrepair and environmental decay blighted the area and detracted from its sustainability. Many people who could move elsewhere, whether owner occupiers, social or private tenants, were choosing to do so, leading to a spiral of decline. Many who remained experienced multiple forms of social exclusion, including above average levels of unemployment and below average levels of educational attainment, health and wellbeing.

Within this context the Bensham and Saltwell Neighbourhood Action Plan was devised in 2005 to meet the specific regeneration needs of the community: the lack of housing choice; the poor condition of many homes; the very hard street environments and the lack of green infrastructure. The plan recommended that work be carried out to improve confidence in the area and improve the sustainability of homes. It included proposals for the selective demolition of some smaller units, some new building, and conversion of some properties to accommodate larger households, creation of new and improved open spaces, improvements to neighbourhood facilities and amenities, a neighbourhood management scheme and better regulation of the private rented sector. But the most substantial element of the plan was for a Block Improvement Scheme to transform 1,300 of the neighbourhood's terraced properties.

This programme was delivered over a phased four-year period. The Council worked with residents during a series of consultation events to agree the works that would most improve the area. The Block

Improvement Scheme aimed to tackle three specific issues affecting the housing market in the neighbourhood: perceptions of the area, the visual appearance of housing; and the condition and management of privately rented housing.

After a full inspection of properties, residents were offered advice and financial assistance to remedy problems that made their homes unsatisfactory. The scheme offered tailored support for the private rented sector to ensure landlords could participate. This required landlords to implement a property improvement plan, bringing homes they owned up to an 'accreditation standard' and to join the Gateshead Private Landlords Association (GPLA). GPLA members then received financial assistance towards the costs of the Block Improvement Scheme and could access a range of free services from the Council.

The most striking element of the Block Improvement Scheme was the visual change it introduced into the neighbourhood. This comprised a range of external improvements including: new front boundary walls built with locally sourced materials; garden treatments to introduce more greenery to front gardens; painted stonework to front elevations in smart neutral colours to blend with the architectural style of the neighbourhood; renewed front doors and replacement windows to complement the age and style of properties; installation of smart black rainwater pipes to trim the roofs and walls of properties. These improvements were made to entire streets and dramatically changed their appearance. The once run-down and weather-beaten terraces were transformed into revitalized streets boasting coordinated frontages and classic finishings. Figure 6.9 illustrates the nature of the area and the changes achieved.

The success of the project was evident from residents' feedback that showed over 90 % satisfied or very satisfied with the works and a similar proportion feeling that the scheme had had a positive or very positive impact on their property. Overall, the scheme made a substantial difference to the Bensham and Saltwell community. Streets have been completely restored to reclaim their architectural heritage. Residents were encouraged to shape the programme from the start and benefitted from substantial financial and advisory support. This commitment to community engagement and the high quality of design solutions resulted in a scheme that made a significant physical impact on the neighbourhood, improving the sustainability of the community for future generations.

However, another aspect of the programme, the proposed demolition of some 440 smaller properties, proved more controversial and provoked strong objections from the Saltwell and Bensham Residents Association, supported by the national pressure group, SAVE Britain's Heritage (Saltwell and Bensham Residents Association, 2014). This illustrates the politically difficult nature of much planned intervention in housing renewal areas.

(a)

Figure 6.9   *Area regeneration: Gateshead, Bensham and Saltwell*

Source: C. Couch, 2016.

Note: Photograph (a) shows a very fine refurbished terrace of housing in Bensham; (b) shows one of the (relatively few) sites cleared during the HMR programme and still awaiting redevelopment in 2015 due to the impact of the post-2008 economic crisis.

Remodelling an outworn social housing estate: Dublin, Ballymun

The Ballymun Housing Scheme in Ireland was first developed in the mid-1960s as a large social housing estate on the northern periphery of the Dublin conurbation. The estate included more than 2,600 (mainly high rise, system-built) flats and around 400 houses. However, 'no sooner did construction work begin than the realities of the under-budgeted, under-planned and poorly designed estate became apparent to the [Dublin] Corporation' (Somerville-Woodward, 2002, p. 39). In particular, the town centre was inadequate and there was a lack of community and recreational facilities (Power, 2000).

Social as well as physical problems emerged and by the 1970s the more mobile tenants began to leave. Through the next two decades the estate experienced similar socio-economic and housing management problems and suffered the same stigmatization as many other large peripheral social housing estates built in the same period across Europe.

(b)

Figure 6.9 *(continued)*

By this time the UK Government was pursuing its Estate Action programme to revitalize poorly designed and poorly managed social housing estates. In the Netherlands the huge Bijlmermeer housing complex, accommodating nearly 100,000 people outside Amsterdam, had to be substantially remodelled to reduce the number of high rise apartments and reduce the 'ghettoization' of the area by improving tenure and social mix. In France the policy of Developpement Social des Quartiers similarly sought to tackle social exclusion in problem social housing estates outside French cities.

It was becoming clear that some equivalent form of state intervention would be needed in Ballymun. A Ballymun Housing Task Force was established in 1987 and began a process of dialogue between residents, the Corporation and other agencies. The 1993 Craig Gardner report outlined a number of possible approaches to housing renewal and argued strongly in favour of tenant involvement in the decision making process. By 1996 it had been decided that the solution to the area's problems lay not in refurbishment, which had become prohibitively expensive, but in demolition and redevelopment of the entire stock of high rise flats, a decision which would affect the lives of some 18,000 inhabitants. Thus in 1997 Dublin Corporation set up Ballymun

Regeneration Limited (BRL) 'to facilitate community consultation, and to develop and implement a masterplan for Ballymun's regeneration' (Somerville-Woodward, 2002, p. 59).

Following an extensive consultation programme and adopting an integrated and strategic view of Ballymun and its surroundings, the masterplan was completed in 1998. It sought to provide for the physical, social, environmental and economic regeneration of the area; to address critical social problems (poverty, drug abuse and so on); to create a sustainable new urban environment; and to change the image of Ballymun projected to potential investors and residents. The masterplan proposed to achieve this through:

- redeveloping the high rise blocks and replacing them with low rise housing;
- enhancing the identity of the five neighbourhoods that comprised the estate and providing new neighbourhood centres;
- providing properly landscaped parks and open spaces;
- creating a new 'town centre' based around a traditional 'high street' including retail, commercial and civic facilities;
- improving public transport, education and other services (Ballymun Regeneration Limited, 1997 and 2008).

Figure 6.10 gives an indication of what has been achieved on the estate in terms of housing renewal.

Reviewing the success of the programme, Kintrea and Muir (2009) argued that whilst significant progress had been made in delivering new housing, community and commercial facilities and improving the local environment, less had been achieved in terms of integrating the area with the rest of the Dublin conurbation and ending 'the socio-spatial segregation of one the largest deprived populations in Ireland' (p. 103). Although this may be true, it seems a little harsh on those responsible for planning and implementing one of the biggest regeneration schemes in Ireland who have no control over the nature of the political and institutional system in which they find themselves working. This was a holistic plan to tackle a difficult and interconnected set of social, housing and environmental problems on a comprehensive basis, with many agencies and local people working collaboratively to create a much more pleasant, liveable and sustainable community than existed previously. It shows how well planned and resourced interventions can improve many aspects of the local environment and the lives of local people, but it also shows the limits of urban planning, which does not have the capacity to tackle the wider ills of capitalist society in general.

Conclusions

The United Nations acknowledges access to adequate housing as a basic human right. This suggests that governments have fundamental obligations to ensure, either by direct action or other means, that there exists an appropriate housing supply to meet the needs of their populations. Urban planning can contribute to this goal through guiding and controlling the location and quality of new housing, by compensating for market failures in the housing sector (for example, meeting housing needs not provided for by the market) and by managing and coordinating responses to neighbourhood socio-economic and environmental problems.

In some countries and regions populations are growing, sometimes very fast, whilst in other regions populations are in decline and cities are shrinking. Each brings a different set of planning problems. In growing cities a key issue is to estimate the number and characteristics of new dwellings that will be needed and to determine where they should be built. In a command economy this is a reasonably straightforward process in which the state pulls all the levers to provide land and to finance housebuilding, as was the case with much social housing built in Western Europe after the Second World War. However, if most housing is to be provided by the market, as is the case in much of Western Europe today, then this becomes a much more complex process.

Planners can make an attempt to calculate housing requirements but they have very little influence over housing demand or private housing supply. Whilst rented housing provides a utility good (location, quality of accommodation and amenities) for which there is a certain level of demand, owner occupied housing provides both a utility good and an investment good (yielding a certain level of profit over time). Thus demand for owner occupied housing is influenced not only by location, quality of accommodation and amenities but also by the rate of return to the owner compared with other dwellings and other forms of investment. This increases the volatility of demand for owner occupied housing, leading to, for example, the 'low demand' crisis that faced some northern UK cities around the millennium, or the example of 'excess' demand for housing and price inflation in inner London as investors sought safe and profitable investment goods some ten years later.

To attract private investment housing must generate a return at least as high as alternative investment opportunities. And within the housing development industry the chances of a particular housing scheme being built depends upon its profitability compared with other projects the developer might be considering. Thus, for example, since the millennium there has been a shift in housing supply away from the less profitable peripheral regions to the more profitable markets of London and the South-east.

(a)

Figure 6.10   *Remodelling an outworn social housing estate: Dublin, Ballymun*

Source: C. McCorkell.

Note: The austere blocks from the 1970s (a) have been replaced by low rise dwellings at a more human scale (b).

One of the primary goals of contemporary urban planning is to achieve more compact cities and to reduce urban sprawl. The example of Shanghai shows how one of the world's major cities is approaching this problem. The development of Leidsche Rijn near Utrecht provides a model of a well connected compact, sustainable urban extension, but even here some of the benefits of higher densities are lost, because inhabitants travel so far for employment.

Further, the goal of urban compaction can create a tension between the need to provide land upon which the private sector is willing to build and the desire to intensify the use of urban land and restrict peripheral development on green fields. Having said this, the experience of British urban regeneration from the late 1970s until the 2010s showed that some elements of housing demand, such as that from a growing number of smaller adult households, would accept more central housing locations and that private developers, previously reluctant to build within existing urban areas, adopted strategies that made such investment profitable.

In static or declining regions housing surplus can be the main issue facing urban planners. This too presents difficult choices. The economic life of a dwelling depends upon there being a continuing demand that maintains its value above that of the site upon which it sits. Left to the

(b)

Figure 6.10 *(continued)*

market, the housing stock in a declining city is likely to become fragmented, with less popular neighbourhoods entering a spiral of housing obsolescence, vacancy, environmental and social deterioration and decline. The problem is to manage this decline so that the housing stock remains fit and in use, neighbourhoods and communities remain 'sustainable' and property values do not suffer volatile change. The example of Bensham and Saltwell demonstrates how this can be done in a neighbourhood that is essentially sustainable but needs some intervention and subsidy to support the process of area management. In Ballymun, the deterioration of the housing stock and the state of the neighbourhood was so far gone that there was little alternative to large scale renewal. But again, working with local stakeholders and through a regeneration company a remarkable turnaround has been achieved.

Whether planning new neighbourhoods or regenerating existing ones, modern planning theory (ODPM, 2003) suggests that a sustainable community will be one which provides a flourishing local economy; community engagement in decision making; a safe and healthy local environment, with good provision of local amenities and public services; well designed and flexible buildings and spaces that minimize the use of resources; a mixture of dwelling types and tenures supporting a range of household sizes, ages and incomes; high quality green and blue infrastructure; good public and private transport systems; a diverse local culture and a sense of place.

Chapter 7

Placemaking: Urban Design and Conservation in Urban Planning

Introduction

Through the Leipzig Treaty (2007) the European Union acknowledges the importance of high quality public spaces, urban landscapes and architecture in the living conditions of urban populations, as well as their role in attracting knowledge industry businesses, a qualified and creative workforce and tourism. The treaty argues for the creation of a 'baukultur' in European cities. 'Baukultur is to be understood ... as the sum of all the cultural, economic, technological, social and ecological aspects influencing the quality and process of planning and construction' (CEC, 2007, p. 3). The UK Government also attaches great importance to the design of towns and cities, seeing good design as a key aspect of sustainable development and indivisible from good planning (*National Planning Policy Framework*, paras 56–57).

The process of planning and designing the physical form of cities, neighbourhoods, individual sites, streets and public spaces is known as urban design. 'Urban design is about creating a vision for an area and then deploying the skills and resources to realise that vision' (Llewelyn-Davies, 2000, p. 12). The purposes of urban design include:

- ensuring the good functioning of areas and developments in terms of the efficient and effective use of land and buildings, safety, access and circulation;
- creating attractive physical environments that are aesthetically pleasing and generate a sense of place and respond to local character and history.

This chapter introduces a number of aspects of urban design, starting with a discussion of the main concepts and techniques used in the analysis of townscape. This is followed by some consideration of the principles of urban design, and its implementation through design guidance and the use of design and access statements. Two examples of contemporary urban design are then considered: St Anne's Square, Belfast, and the ZAC de la Cathédrale in Amiens. The importance of green infrastructure is discussed and illustrated through a case study of the development of new parks and public spaces in Paris. Finally the chapter moves on to examine the protection and conservation of urban heritage, using case studies of conservation in a world heritage site, Warsaw's Stare Miasto, and an industrial neighbourhood, Birmingham's Jewellery Quarter, before reaching conclusions.

The image, character and aesthetic quality of urban places

Urban planning invariably involves change: the extension or redesign of the physical fabric of urban areas. These developments, redevelopments, refurbishments or conversions can make the area function better or worse and they can make the area look better or worse. In this context 'function' refers to the way the city works as a physical unit – efficiency and effectiveness in the use of land and buildings and of the infrastructure of the city. The 'look' of the city refers to the degree to which the physical environment is aesthetically legible and pleasing to the eye. Urban design is a process of responding to these two issues when making decisions about the location and physical manifestation of investment in the built environment: the adaptation of building and engineering operations to functional and aesthetic ends.

In the development and redevelopment of cities a process of urban design has always been implied. Historically the process has sometimes been conscious, grandiose and comprehensive, for example in the development of the classical city, the bastide towns, and parts of Georgian London or Haussmann's Paris. But in many more instances the process has been unconscious, implicit and piecemeal. Most towns and cities throughout history have grown in this organic fashion. Frequently the functional and aesthetic results of this process justified few criticisms until these places began to be overwhelmed by sudden accelerations in the rate of urbanization, such as followed the industrial revolution, or the intrusion of non-local materials, building methods or investors without local awareness or sympathy.

Many architects, planners and other concerned authors have written about the design of urban areas, either to interpret, explain and evaluate the existing city or to offer prescriptive solutions to the problem of designing urban areas in modern circumstances and to meet modern needs. Here the contributions of a few of these writers are considered in order to introduce some of the key ideas and developments in contemporary thinking about urban design.

Writing about the 'image of the city' Kevin Lynch (1960) suggested that perceptions of the city as a physical entity are conditioned by and

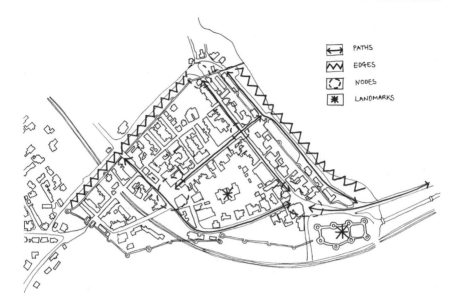

Figure 7.1 *Paths, edges, districts, nodes and landmarks*

Source: Drawn by A.L. Couch.

Note: The plan shows the historic centre of the town of Conwy in North Wales. The edges of the district are clearly defined by the town walls and harbourside. The main paths through and around the central area meet at various nodes. The most important node is that outside the castle with a significant secondary node on the western edge of the district. The castle represents a major landmark, visible from both within and beyond the town. In contrast, the parish church provides a secondary landmark, only visible from its immediate surroundings.

interpreted through the existence of five elements: paths, edges, districts, nodes and landmarks (Figure 7.1). He argued that in extending or redeveloping the city urban design should build upon and enhance these elements. A path is a route through the city chosen by the individual. It does not necessarily conform to the patterning and hierarchy of paths shown on a map. The individual's image of the city is determined by his or her chosen path (route) and mode of transport: home to work by train; home to local shops by bicycle; home to school on foot. Collectively the most important paths are those used by most people. Edges are the physical boundaries of districts or neighbourhoods formed by such elements as highways, green spaces, walls or shorelines. For Lynch edges are not as dominant as paths but nevertheless are important organizing features in the townscape. Districts are contiguous zones with identifiable and similar socio-economic or physical characteristics and distinguishable from other zones. Extreme examples would be the historic cores of many European cities such as the 'vieille ville' in French cities or the 'altstadt' in Germany where the tightly enclosed, intense development of the aged core is self-evidently a different place from its more open, extensive, modern surroundings. But every city can be subdivided into districts. Visitors to London can easily identify the physically and economically different districts of Bloomsbury, Whitehall, Kensington or Hampstead. Nodes are places, often at the junction of paths or places of interchange between travel modes, that can be entered and passed through. They provide reference points for journeys through the city. Landmarks are another type of reference point but these are not generally entered, they are external to the viewer. In London, for example, Big Ben and St Paul's are both distant and local landmarks, although in a relatively flat city with many high buildings these are not particularly strong landmarks when compared with, say, the Eiffel Tower in Paris. Landmarks need not simply be high buildings: the main railway station in Amsterdam is an essential orientating feature in that city and the Puy de Dôme (a hill outside Clermond-Ferrand in France) dominates the western skyline of the city. And within a district a landmark might be a much smaller feature in the townscape: a corner building, a statue or a tree.

People need paths, edges, districts, nodes and landmarks in order to understand the physical structure of the city, to find their way around and to get to know and enjoy the city. Urban planning decisions that increase the legibility of the city by clarifying paths, emphasizing landmarks or maintaining edges increase people's understanding, appreciation and enjoyment of the city as a physical entity. Decisions that remove a commonly used path or a well recognized landmark are doing a disservice to the community, making it more difficult for people to relate to the city and increasing their alienation from it.

Gordon Cullen is a key figure in the evolution of the understanding and analysis of townscape. His concern is about the relationships between the physical elements of the city.

> There is an art of relationship just as there is an art of architecture. Its purpose is to take all the elements that go to create the environment: buildings, trees, nature, water, traffic, advertisements and so on, and to weave them together in such a way that drama is released. (Cullen, 1971, pp. 7–8)

He refers to three concepts that stimulate our visual reaction to the city environment: 'serial vision', the idea of 'place' and the 'content of places' (Figure 7.2). Serial vision refers to the way we experience the city. We do not normally see the city from a static perspective but from a dynamic perspective, that is, as we move through it. An implication of serial

Figure 7.2 *Townscape: scale, style and character*

Source: C. Couch 2016.

Note: This ensemble of five buildings in Amiens, from different eras and in different styles but illustrating 'variety within the same kind, variety within an established rhythm, variety ... within a broad unity of character' (Sharp, 1968, p. 13).

vision is that the city falls into two elements, the present view and the emerging view, and each has to be taken into account in this dynamic approach to townscape analysis and urban design.

Cullen's second concept was that of place – somewhere that can be entered, experienced and departed from. Once the city is divided into identifiable places (streets, squares and so on) that one is either in, not in, entering or leaving, it becomes possible to talk of 'here' and 'there' and, as Cullen points out, '[s]ome of the greatest townscape effects are created by a skilful relationship between the two' (ibid., p. 10).

With the content of places Cullen is concerned with the fabric of the urban environment including its colour, texture, scale, style, and character. Most cities are a jumble of building types, styles and ages. Yet this organic growth has not been as diverse as we might think (at least until these places became overwhelmed by sudden accelerations in the rate of urbanization or the intrusion of non-local materials, building methods or investors without local awareness or sympathy). There was an unconscious, unspoken 'agreement to differ within a recognised tolerance of behaviour' (ibid., p. 11). This variety evolved within an overall unifying set of rules or criteria that provided the framework for organic growth. That framework set the conventions in the colour, texture, scale and style that came to dominate building in that particular town. Where one convention might be broken (for example, colour or materials) the building would probably still conform to other conventions such as proportion, scale and style and remain recognizable as part of that town (and no other). So the fabric of the town was not homogeneous but a heterogeneous interplay of 'this and that'.

> Thus we have motion, position and content, or to put it another way: serial vision, here and there, this and that ... all that remains is to join them together into a new pattern created by the warmth and power and vitality of the human imagination ... This is the theory of the game, the background. In fact the most difficult part lies ahead, the Art of Playing. (Cullen, 1971, p. 12)

Writing in 1968 at the culmination of more than 30 years of scholarship in urban design, Thomas Sharp commented that 'never before have there been so many different influences for change operating upon [towns] at the same time. And never before has the tempo of possible change been so swift' (1968, p. 1). Whilst Sharp was writing towards the end of a period in which massive slum clearance, town centre redevelopment and the influence of the 'modern movement' had been dominant, and before the conservation movement had become established, his arguments retain some validity today. He expresses a concern that new building within existing towns and cities should accept and be designed within the discipline imposed by the existing urban fabric, both in terms of the scale and character of existing buildings and the rhythm and perspective of existing streets and spaces. As Cullen does, he suggests that what makes historic, organically evolved towns aesthetically interesting is often variety in building form and materials but 'variety within the same kind, variety within an established rhythm, variety ... within a broad unity of character' (Sharp, 1968, p. 13).

Cullen and Sharp were amongst a number of theorists who started to challenge the 'modernist' approach to urban planning in which designers looked for standardized, rational comprehensive solutions to city form. They were at the beginning of a 'postmodern' philosophy that sought to recognize the importance of locality and context in a more contingent and responsive approach to urban design. Taking these ideas forward, Bentley et al. (1985) conceived the notion of 'responsive environments' as a technique for urban design. Their approach considers seven different components of a responsive environment: permeability, variety, legibility, robustness, visual appropriateness, richness and personalization (Figure 7.3).

Reflecting the ideas of Lynch, they suggest that the first requirement of a district or neighbourhood is that it should be accessible, that is to say, as permeable as possible to ease movement to and through the area. So the first stage in the design is to create permeability through designing the overall layout of routes and development blocks. But permeability itself is of little use until there is greater variety in building uses. Whilst

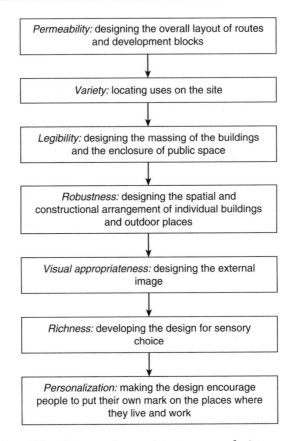

Figure 7.3. *Responsive environments: a design process*

Source: Based upon Bentley et al. (1985), p. 11.

it is useful to be able to find a number of ways through an area in order to reach other dwellings, it becomes more meaningful if there are useful destinations (other uses such as shops, schools and workplaces) at the end of these routes, hence variety is important. Creating variety occurs in that stage in the design process that allocates land uses to sites. People need to be able to find their way around the area in order to benefit from this variety and permeability, they need to be able to read the city in the sense of being able to easily identify what type of area they are in, what sorts of buildings they are looking at, to recognize features (landmarks) and routes (paths). The city should be legible. Designing the massing of buildings and the enclosure of public spaces determines legibility. A responsive environment is also one that is designed to be sufficiently robust to withstand socio-economic change. In fact 'flexibility' is probably a more accurate term. By way of example a contrast may be drawn between the flexibility of a nineteenth century terraced house and a flat in a multi-storey block. The terraced house can be used as a single dwelling, sub-divided into flats, partly or wholly converted into a shop, office or workshop. The flat in a multi-storey block has no such flexibility in use. Robustness and flexibility emerge from the spatial and constructional arrangements of individual buildings and outdoor spaces. Visual appropriateness refers back to the visual cues given by the physical appearance of the area – the 'character' discussed by Cullen and Sharp. It is about designing the external image of the building. Within the context of visual appropriateness, richness is about details in the design of facades, roofs and floorspace. Finally, personalization is about providing scope in the design for the individual owner or occupier to apply their own personal stamp through decorating and 'garnishing' their own buildings or spaces (Bentley et al., 1985).

More recently Rob Krier is representative of a number of authors who have theorized a postmodern approach to the design of urban spaces (Krier, 2006). His approach to urban design, expressed through the philosophy of his firm, KK Urbanism-Architecture-Landscape, is to build upon traditional methods of spatial composition in which buildings are components of the urban fabric and in which this fabric defines the urban spaces. His designs strive to respect conventions and traditions and historical contexts, building upon existing street patterns as well as traditional building types and facades.

Contemporary approaches to urban design

Whilst urban design has always been a major component of urban planning in many countries, in the UK, where the emphasis has historically been on land use planning, interest in urban design waned in the face of the economic crises of the 1970s and 1980s. However, by the 1990s there was a renaissance of concern. English Partnerships (the regeneration agency for England) published useful guidance in *Time for Design* (1996) and the *Urban Design Compendium* (Llewlyn-Davies, 2000), and the Urban Task Force provided a design-led approach to urban policy in their report *Towards an Urban Renaissance* (1999). Between 1999 and 2011 the Commission for Architecture and the Built Environment (CABE) advised the UK Government on architecture, urban design and public space in England. Its principal task was to influence and improve design decisions in relation to the built environment. Amongst its many publications was the seminal guide to better urban design: *By Design* (CABE, 2000). Its purpose was to promote higher standards in contemporary urban design, with a central message that: 'careful assessments of places, well-drafted policies, well-designed proposals, robust decision-making and a collaborative approach are needed ... if better places are to be created' (CABE, 2000, p. 8). The similarity of the views emerging from these documents makes it possible to establish a number of key principles for contemporary urban design. Thus, there is some consensus around the ideas that:

- Urban centres should provide safe and attractive environments in which to work, shop, recreate and live. They should also be public transport nodes, ranging from access to national rail services in city centres to local bus services in neighbourhood centres. Mixing of uses within a centre or a neighbourhood can assist convenient access to facilities, reduce travel-to-work distances, increase vitality, visual stimulation, social interaction and personal safety (with more 'eyes on the street') and facilitate sharing of infrastructure (for example, car parking) and energy efficiency (for example, through CHP). Mixing of uses only need be avoided where there is genuine conflict (for example, in terms of traffic generation or noise pollution).
- As far as possible streets should be lined with 'active frontages' which maintain vibrancy and interest on the street and spread activity and surveillance across different times of day. Public paths and spaces need to be functionally safe, well maintained and managed to encourage their use and avoid anti-social behaviour and crime. There should be a clear distinction between public and private space and all spaces should have a clear sense of ownership and responsibility.
- The layout of residential neighbourhoods should facilitate access to local facilities and amenities through walking and cycling. The street network should be permeable and facilitate movement in many directions. Mixing dwellings types, sizes, ages and tenures increases social mix and diversity within neighbourhoods.

A series of objectives for urban design were set out in *By Design* (CABE, 2000) and are shown in Table 7.1. Thus, whether preparing design guidance ahead of development, or responding to development proposals, planners should test the form of development against the objectives of good urban design. Again, the similarity of the ideas and concepts with those of earlier writers can be seen.

Design control: the role of density, design guidance, design and access statements

The concept of density can be used in a number of ways in urban planning. 'Urban density' usually refers to the population per unit of area for a city (for example, Liverpool: population 440,000/area 111.8 km^2 = 3935 ppkm^2). The density of a neighbourhood may be measured in terms of population, dwellings or habitable rooms. This may be expressed

Table 7.1 *Objectives and issues in urban design*

Topic	Objective
Character	– a place with its own identity;
Continuity and enclosure	– a place where public and private spaces are clearly distinguished;
Quality of the public realm	– a place with attractive and successful outdoor areas;
Ease of movement	– a place that is easy to get to and move through;
Legibility	– a place that has a clear image and is easy to understand;
Adaptability	– a place that can change easily;
Diversity	– a place with variety and choice.

These objectives should then be applied to the choices made by designers about the form their development might take. The key aspects of development form defining the layout, scale, appearance and landscape of a place include:

Aspect	Design issue
Layout: urban structure	– the framework of routes and spaces that connect locally and more widely, and the way developments, routes and open spaces relate to one another;
Layout: urban grain	– the pattern of the arrangement of street blocks, plots and their buildings in a settlement;
Landscape	– the character and appearance of land, including its shape, form, ecology, natural features, colours and elements, and the way these components combine;
Density and mix	– the amount of development on a given piece of land and the range of uses - density influences the intensity of development, and, in combination with the mix of uses, can affect a place's vitality and viability;

(continued)

Table 7.1 *Objectives and issues in urban design (continued)*

Scale: height	– scale is the size of a building in relation to its surroundings, or the size of parts of a building or its details, particularly in relation to the size of a person – height determines the impact of development on views, vistas and skylines;
Scale: massing	– the combined effect of the arrangement, volume and shape of a building or group of buildings in relation to other buildings and spaces;
Appearance: details	– the craftsmanship, building techniques, decoration, styles and lighting of a building or structure.
Appearance: materials	– the texture, colour, pattern and durability of materials, and how they are used.

Source: Based upon CABE (2000), pp. 15–16.

as 'gross residential density' (including land used for roads, schools, retail centres and so on) or 'net residential density' (the density of a housing area and incidental open space plus half the width of adjoining roads). Net residential density is the most commonly used measurement of density in relation to the planning and design of residential areas. However, another useful measurement is that of the 'plot ratio' (also called 'floor space index'). This is the ratio of the floor area of a building to the area of the land on which it is situated and is useful in measuring or controlling the intensity of development, especially in mainly non-residential areas. Figure 7.4 sets out examples of comparative density measurements expressed in habitable rooms, dwellings per hectare (dpha) and plot ratios for a range of different densities. In the residential quarters of central London or Paris, densities might exceed 200 dpha. Typical areas of inner city terraced housing in the UK might be in the order of 60–80 dpha, inter-war suburbs 20–30 dpha.

It has been calculated that the minimum net residential density to support a good suburban bus service is around 45 dpha, and in more central areas 60 dpha will sustain a tram service (Llewelyn-Davies, 2000). Achieving a more compact city suggests higher net residential densities but this does not necessarily mean 'town cramming' or an

High	
>300 habitable rooms per hectare >100 dwellings per hectare >1:1 plot ratio	
Medium 100–200 habitable rooms per hectare 30–50 dwellings per hectare 0.3–0.5:1 plot ratio	
Low <100 habitable rooms per hectare <30 dwellings per hectare <0.2:1 plot ratio	

Figure 7.4 *Comparison of net residential densities*

Source: C. Couch, 2016.

over-reliance on high rise apartment blocks. Net residential densities of up to around 50 dpha can be built as two-storey terraced housing with modest gardens and up to 70 dpha can be achieved with a mixture of houses and three- or four-storey flats. Only at densities above this does some high rise housing become necessary (MHLG, 1962).

Having said this, there are many examples of innovative housing layouts that achieve higher densities whilst still maintaining low rise and functionally efficient yet humane designs. At Borneo-Sporenburg in the Amsterdam dockland, architects West 8 designed a development of

2,500 low rise dwelling units at a density of 100 dpha. The design was based upon a new interpretation of the traditional Amsterdam canal houses with ground-floor accessed three-storey houses incorporating patios and roof gardens. By repeating the basic type with subtle variations in configuration and appearance an animated yet immensely liveable residential environment has been created (www.west8.nl/projects/all/borneo_sporenburg/, accessed 9.6.2015).

However, many would subscribe to the view that medium rise, medium density buildings (of about 3–4 storeys) can provide a sufficiently high density to maximize convenience and efficiency whilst minimizing perceptions of overcrowding. Residential areas developed at such densities:

- reduce urban sprawl, the costs of land acquisition and site infrastructure;
- provide a robust form that allows for changes in use over time;
- form terraces or low-rise flats, the most cost effective building form in housing;
- increase energy-efficiency and the ability to be orientated for passive solar gain;
- avoid costs of lifts and other services;
- can provide 'lifetime homes' readily adaptable for the elderly or disabled (Llewelyn-Davies, 2000, p. 48).

The purpose of design guidance is to permit a planning authority to articulate its advice to potential developers on the basic design principles it would expect to see applied to a particular type of development, or a particular location, having undertaken its own analysis of the character, form and design requirements. Thus, local design guidance is likely to be more detailed and its content will be more contingent on locality than the general statements found in publications such as *By Design*.

Thus, for example, the City of Birmingham's *Bournville Design Guide* explains that any changes should retain the character of the area, noting that:

Bournville inspired the Garden City Movement of the early 20th century ... The village has a rural feel, although it is only four miles from Birmingham City Centre. Its parks and recreation grounds create green spaces which are an important part of the area's special character. The village is largely made up of traditional brick built houses, many of them semi-detached. They are grouped in informal patterns which helps create a sense of community. (Birmingham City Council, no date)

In contrast, Cotswold District Council states that:

> A first class modern design for a building will be preferable to a poor
> copy of a past style. Original modern designs should, however, reflect
> the existing distinctive Cotswold style. The Cotswold style is easily
> recognisable – steep pitched roof with ridge tiles and coping, tall
> chimneys, symmetrically balanced design with evenly spaced windows
> surrounded by stone. There are no barge boards or eaves fascias.
> (Cotswold District Council, 2000, p. 4)

Design and Access Statements (DAS) are used in the UK planning system
as a means by which potential developers can explain how their proposed
development represents an appropriate response to the site and its
setting. The DAS should explain the principles and ideas that have
shaped the design and will set out the use, amount, layout, scale, landscaping and appearance of the development.

The DAS will specify the proposed land and building uses and the
amount of development: the number of dwelling units or floorspace for
other uses. A site plan will show the proposed layout including the
disposition of buildings (their form, scale and massing); access routes for
pedestrians, cycles and vehicles; open spaces and their landscaping.
There will usually be some consideration of the appearance of the buildings and other physical features, including their architectural style, scale,
massing, materials, colours and so forth.

The DAS will also contain an appraisal and evaluation of the context
of the development and its appropriateness, both in terms of the local
physical environment, social and economic conditions and planning
policies. It will explain how the proposal has responded to this context
and how local community stakeholders have been involved in this
process.

For the local planner receiving a development application the task is
to evaluate the proposal, asking such questions as:

- Does the statement contain a full assessment of the site and its phys-
  ical, social and economic conditions and relevant planning policies?
- Have the developers responded to the concerns of community
  stakeholders?
- Are the proposed uses, amount and density of development
  appropriate?
- Is the layout appropriate and does it make efficient and effective use
  of the space?
- Is the design of buildings appropriate both functionally and aesthetically?
- Is the landscaping appropriate?
- Are the access arrangements satisfactory?

(a)

Figure 7.5   *Urban placemaking: Belfast, St Anne's Square*

Photographs © WDR & RT Taggart.

Note: The ground and first floors are given over to commercial and leisure uses with living accommodation above (a). The public space is frequently used for events such as arts festivals (b).

The following two case studies illustrate good design in the creation of new urban places: a new mixed-use development and public realm at St Anne's Square in Belfast and a new urban quarter between the city centre and the River Somme in Amiens.

Designing new urban places: Belfast – St Anne's Square

St Anne's Square is a mixed-use development located in the heart of Belfast's historic Cathedral Quarter conservation area (Figure 7.5). The scheme comprises a new public piazza, a number of cafe/restaurant units, a hotel, fitness suite, more than 100 residential units and a multi-storey car park. The overall site masterplan was designed by WDR & RT Taggart. Design work began in 2006, with planning permission obtained in 2007 and completion achieved in late 2010. The plan included space for a new arts centre to be delivered by the Department of Culture, Arts & Leisure. This was subject to an international design competition and opened in 2012 as the Mac Arts Centre.

The new piazza has been designed to align symmetrically with the major axis of the adjacent Cathedral, provide a new heart to the Quarter and link into the existing pedestrian network to improve permeability. The piazza itself is surrounded by active commercial frontage at ground

(b)

Figure 7.5 *(continued)*

level and has been kept largely unobstructed to accommodate outdoor events such as street theatre. A new piece of public art terminates the axial view into the square from the Cathedral.

The design process was informed by design guidance from the Northern Ireland Department of the Environment (DOE) relating specifically to the Cathedral Quarter Conservation Area. The design team worked closely with the DOE conservation officer to ensure guidelines were interpreted as accurately as possible.

The scheme has enhanced the physical environment of this previously run-down area by providing a well designed complex of buildings that works within the European tradition of placemaking, creating clearly defined streets and squares, adopting the traditional built forms and the palette of materials found in the historic fabric of the area. From the outset, the plan was not to import a sculptural architecture that would contrast with its surroundings but to view the scheme as an extension of the older fabric – both spatially and in terms of established pedestrian movement patterns – and of adding to the identifiable character of the conservation area. During the planning and design process, public consultations were staged at outline, detailed and final design stages. The local arts umbrella organization and other organizations were consulted separately. These processes resulted in broad local support for the scheme, with letters of support being sent to the planning department urging approval.

The mixed use nature of the development and the inclusion of residential units reduce travel demand, whilst the use of local building materials and craftsmanship reduces haulage and helps sustain the local economy. The scheme makes use of sustainable urban drainage and buildings have been designed to minimize energy use. The provision of this new, purpose-built, family-friendly space for Belfast encourages the coming together of the City's diverse communities. In particular the space has acted to introduce the arts community to a wider population and facilitates a major venue for the annual Belfast 'Festival of Fools'.

It is anticipated that the scheme will have a significant regenerative effect on the redevelopment of other vacant or underused sites in the vicinity. With this in mind, a wider masterplan was also devised to demonstrate how these further sites could be developed in spatial and land use terms, including the substantial precinct of Belfast Cathedral. In this way, the St Anne's Square project could be viewed as an important and central element of a larger vision for the area.

Creating a new urban quarter: Amiens, ZAC de la Cathédrale

In France a Zone d'Aménagement Concerté (ZAC) is a development or redevelopment area designated by the state and subject to its own specific detailed planning and implementation procedures. It allows the public authority detailed control over the planning, design and implementation of the area. Amiens cathedral is one of the most historic and important in France. It lies between the city centre and the River Somme but since the Second World War much of its immediate surroundings had been in a poor state. In 1992 the district north of the cathedral was designated a ZAC with the aim of reconstructing the area as a mixed-use zone of private and social housing, commercial and civic uses.

The initial redevelopment concept was designed by Bernard Huet (whose earlier work had included the realization of the Parc de Bercy in Paris). The design was completed after his death by his firm Ville et Architecture. The first aim of the design concept was to ensure continuity, harmony and balance between the different projects that comprised the ZAC and to maintain an ongoing aesthetic dialogue with the cathedral, in terms of design typologies, access and views. The second aim was to provide spatial continuity between the city centre and the traditional (now somewhat gentrified) working class quarter of Saint Leu on the north bank of the Somme.

Opposite the west front of the cathedral lies a terrace of four buildings of vastly different ages and designs, yet the effect is harmonious, providing 'variety within an established rhythm, variety ... within a broad unity of character' (Sharp, op. cit.). The square or parvis in front of the Cathedral is maintained and framed by a combination of existing and new buildings. Running along the contours down the slope towards the river are a series of terraced building blocks, the uppermost of which comprises a mixture of commercial and public amenities on the ground floor with offices and apartments on the three upper floors. The scale, height, colour and proportions of these well mannered new buildings contrast perfectly with the imposing scale and richly detailed facade of the ancient cathedral. Punched through these blocks at right angles are cross ways that allow pedestrians to permeate down to the next level where a new view is suddenly revealed: an elongated public space with a central tree-lined water feature running its whole length. Beyond this is another contour-hugging row of terraced houses, less imposing and smaller in scale than the upper row. Again pedestrian ways punch through the buildings and over a small tributary of the Somme to another narrow parallel street. Here smaller dwellings, including some original buildings, hug the banks of the stream whilst on the other side new university faculties have been built. Beyond this, approaching the Somme, the project moves from redevelopment to conservation of the riverside warehouses and workshops, connecting across the river to the Saint Leu quarter beyond (Figure 7.6).

The ZAC de la Cathédrale provides a lesson in the integration of new buildings into an historic environment: from the grandeur of the cathedral in the south to the Saint Leu district in the north; how to blend redevelopment with conservation; and how to develop on the side of a hill without losing a sense of scale or enclosure.

Green and blue infrastructure and their importance

The natural environmental elements, including water features, which are found within urban areas are frequently referred to as the green and blue infrastructure of the city. According to the European Commission: 'Green Infrastructure can be broadly defined as a strategically planned network of high quality natural and semi-natural areas with other environmental features, which is designed and managed to deliver a wide range of ecosystem services and protect biodiversity in both rural and urban settings' (CEC, 2013b, p. 7). As such it includes land within the urban boundary in agricultural or horticultural use, parkland, cemeteries, sports fields, local wildlife sites, allotments, street trees, hedges and landscaping, and private gardens, and even green roofs and walls. Blue infrastructure includes streams, rivers, ponds and lakes, reservoirs, canals, docks and harbours. This green/blue infrastructure can be defined by type (for example, grassland, woodland, stream), by function (for example, wildlife habitat, informal recreation area), and by benefit (for example, flood alleviation, quality of life, health and wellbeing). It can also be assessed in terms of its land or development value – that is to say, the opportunity cost of protecting it from development (Mell, 2012).

(a)

Figure 7.6 *Designing a new urban quarter: Amiens, from the cathedral to the Somme*

Source: C. Couch, 2016.

Note: Photograph (a) shows the new buildings in the Cathedral square (or parvis); Photograph (b) shows a secondary, greener place lower down the slope towards the River Somme. The design of the whole area provides a harmonious connection between the central city, the Cathedral and the St Leu quarter to the north.

Green infrastructure is a resource and asset which can contribute to the delivery of a sustainable city through:

- maintaining biodiversity by providing habitats and corridors for flora and fauna – in many cities the major wildlife habitats are already protected through various local, national or international designations such as Sites of Special Scientific Interest (UK) or Ramsar sites (defined by the Convention on Wetlands of International Importance, 1971 – Ramsar is the town in Iran where the treaty was signed);
- combating climate change through the absorption of carbon dioxide and other air pollutants into tree cover and vegetation and by mitigating urban heat island effects through evaporative cooling;
- reducing the need for urban drainage by absorbing rainfall into vegetation and permeable surfaces, so reducing the volume and rate of rainwater run-off and the risk of surface water flooding;
- improving the health of urban populations by providing space for outdoor sports, recreation and contact with nature, and by contributing to improved air quality;

(b)

Figure 7.6 *(continued)*

- facilitating local food production through allotments, gardens and urban agriculture;
- providing a resource for environmental education;
- retaining the heritage or aesthetic value of urban open spaces and views;
- creating attractive environments and improving the image and marketability of a city, thus supporting inward investment and economic growth.

It is important to plan for the protection, enhancement and creation of green infrastructure. A modern urban planning policy towards green infrastructure is likely to include provision for a high level of protection from development, especially those areas that offer a significant contribution in terms of the above benefits. The planning system can also contribute to the enhancement of green infrastructure in various other ways that might include requiring development proposals to contribute to the city's green infrastructure resource, either on site or by a contribution to improving nearby assets by, for example:

- preserving trees and other natural features on development sites;
- linking existing green spaces (for example, through hedgerows or landscaping alongside highways and footpaths) to provide wildlife corridors;
- opening and renaturizing culverted watercourses to contribute to amenity and biodiversity;
- using sustainable urban drainage systems (SUDS);

- providing green roofs or walls;
- improving the recreational function of open spaces (including accessibility and personal safety);
- addressing local deficiencies in provision for outdoor sports and recreation.

Greening the city: new parks in Paris

By the 1980s it was becoming clear that substantial parts of Paris were in need of redevelopment. There were many obsolete buildings. The population density was very high, with most inhabitants living in apartments. Despite the broad boulevards there was a lack of public open space and particularly a lack of green spaces, especially in the historic working class districts. At the same time a number of large tracts of land that had previously been in use for industrial purposes were becoming vacant and falling into dereliction. If Paris was to continue to compete as a world city it would require considerable public investment into its infrastructure and environment, whilst conserving its historic character. For these reasons, during the next two decades, considerable sums were spent on public transport, infrastructure and housing. There were new and improved rail (RER and Metro) and tram lines, and major programmes of housing redevelopment using the mechanism of the ZAC to demolish outworn dwellings and build modern replacements, often at a higher density. An even greater number of dwellings benefitted from property renovation combined with local environmental improvements. And there were major public works to update the cultural facilities of the city including the opening of the Musée d'Orsay, the extension of the Louvre, the Opera Bastille, and the Stade de France.

As part of this programme of modernizing the city the need to increase the amount of green infrastructure was recognized. In consequence, since 1984 a dozen new parks have been created. One of the first was the 7.4 ha Parc George-Brassens, located on the site of a former slaughterhouse and fish market in the south of the city. The park provides valuable greenspace in an area where it was previously lacking. Its design retains the clock tower from the old fish market and incorporates lawns, a lake and winding paths in an informal layout. The Parc de Belleville which opened on a hillside site in the east of the city in 1988 performs a similar function, providing a green lung in the historically poor and very dense Belleville neighbourhood.

The Parc de la Villette and the Parc André Citroën, which both opened in the early 1990s, were much bigger projects. Villette was the site of former abattoirs and wholesale meat markets in the extreme north-east of the city. This 35.5 ha site was redeveloped to provide the parkland setting for a number of new cultural facilities, including a science museum, a concert venue and a conservatoire of music. The site is flat and the formal design of the park was intended to create space for activity and interaction, although it might be criticized for lacking intimacy and being limited in its contribution to ecology. The Parc André Citroën is of a similar size but occupies the site of the former Citroën car manufacturing plant in the extreme south-west of the city on the left bank of the River Seine. The park is divided into formal and informal zones. There is a large lawn, two enormous greenhouses containing exotic plants, and a series of six small gardens, each with its own landscape theme. Around the southern and western edges of the park some land was sold off for the development of up-market apartment blocks.

The 13 ha Parc de Bercy lies on the right bank of the Seine just to the east of the city centre on the site of former wine warehouses (Figure 7.7). The design retains some of the old wine depot in the south of the site as a recreational and retail zone. To the east adjoining land has been redeveloped as a combination of social and private apartments and at the northern end of the site a multi-purpose indoor arena has been built. The design of the green space has been sub-divided into three themed areas: a meadowland of lawns shaded by tall trees; a romantic garden including water features;

(a) (b)

Figure 7.7 *New green infrastructure in Paris: (a) Parc de Bercy and (b) Parc André Citroën*

Source: D.C. Couch, 2016.

Note: The new apartment blocks, part social, part private, along the north side of the Parc de Bercy (a), whose landscape design is more intimate and less formal than the Parc André Citroën (b).

and an area of flowerbeds. A new footbridge across the Seine links it to the Bibliothèque Nationale de France which also opened in the 1990s.

Other novel additions to the green infrastructure of the city include the Promenade Plantée (1993) and the Jardin Atlantique (1994). The former is a 4.7 km long high-level green walkway along the track of an abandoned railway line that ran from the Bastille to the eastern suburbs. The Jardin Atlantiqueis a giant 3.4 ha 'green roof' on top of the Montparnasse railway terminus and comprises a central lawn surrounded by smaller gardens and modern sculpture. A more recent addition to the greenery of the city is the Promenade des Berges de la Seine which opened in 2013. The park makes use of a strip of land 2.3 km long formerly used for a highway that ran alongside the river, and includes sports facilities, playgrounds and even floating gardens.

It is rare for cities to allow the reuse of high value land for uses that bring little or no financial gain. But taking a more strategic view, these public investments have not only had the social benefit of significantly increasing the amount of green infrastructure and contributing to the city's sustainability but will also have enhanced the competitive image of the city with long run benefits for the whole economy of the conurbation.

Urban conservation

Often the work of the planner in relation to urban design is as much about the protection of existing townscape as creating new environments. The UK Government calls on planning authorities to develop positive strategies for the conservation and enjoyment of the historic environment and to 'recognise that heritage assets are an irreplaceable resource and conserve them in a manner appropriate to their significance' (DCLG, 2012, para. 126).

Much of the philosophy of urban conservation that underpins practice in the UK and other countries today can be found in the work of Roy Worskett (1969). For Worskett urban conservation comprised two parallel concerns:

- identifying the historic buildings and archaeological features of the area and establishing principles governing their preservation;
- assessing the townscape qualities of the area and establishing a visual discipline for the design of changes to the physical environment.

It was through the amalgamation of these two strands of activity that conservation policy could be formed. The development of the visual discipline would include consideration of the relationship between the area and its surrounding townscape or landscape; the impact of high buildings and the protection of skylines; the maintenance of those qualities of design, space and layout that represented a local discipline; and the exploitation of opportunities to enhance the visual appearance of the area through new building, renovation or landscaping.

Contemporary advice on the management of conservation areas in the UK still follows this basic premise and suggests that conservation areas can be enhanced by:

- preparing an audit or character appraisal of those buildings, structures and features which make the area special;
- preparing special Development Briefs for sites that are identified as detracting from the character or appearance of the area;
- ensuring that new buildings harmonize with or complement their neighbours in scale, style and use of materials;
- making environmental improvements, for example by reinstating historic paving materials, sympathetic landscaping and planting, or removing unsightly elements such as hoardings;
- integrating road signs and markings as far as possible with the character of the street;
- controlling the position and design of advertisements and shop signs;
- ensuring that traffic safety and control measures harmonise with the landscape;
- making grants available for the repair of buildings (English Heritage, 2014).

The following two case studies illustrate contrasting urban conservation situations: the Stare Miasto World Heritage Site in Warsaw, Poland, and the quasi-industrial Jewellery Quarter in Birmingham, UK.

Conservation in a World Heritage Site: Warsaw, Stare Miasto

Since the World Heritage Convention in 1972 the United Nations Educational, Scientific and Cultural Organization (UNESCO) has taken the view that:

> cultural and natural heritage is among the priceless and irreplaceable assets, not only of each nation, but of humanity as a whole. The loss, through deterioration or disappearance, of any of these most prized assets constitutes an impoverishment of the heritage of all the peoples of the world. Parts of that heritage, because of their exceptional qualities, can be considered to be of 'Outstanding Universal Value' and as such worthy of special protection against the dangers which increasingly threaten them. (UNESCO, 1972, para. 4)

National governments have a duty to protect and conserve such property in accordance with UNESCO guidelines. A World Heritage Fund is available to support the protection of properties at risk. There are ten possible criteria under which the UNESCO World Heritage Committee will consider listing properties for protection. Some of the most important ones relevant to urban conservation are that the property represents a masterpiece of human creative genius; an outstanding example of a type of building, architectural or technological ensemble or landscape which illustrates a significant stage in human history; or 'an outstanding example of a traditional human settlement ... which is representative of a culture' (UNESCO, 2013, p. 20).

An exceptional example of an historic urban area listed by the World Heritage Committee is the Stare Miasto or old town in Warsaw, Poland. The Stare Miasto was first established in the thirteenth century. At the heart of the town was the Market Square, where regular fairs were held. Other significant buildings included the fourteenth century royal palace, later remodelled in the baroque style, and the fifteenth century Cathedral of St John. Further streets and squares completed a remarkable urban ensemble representing an almost complete span of vernacular and architectural styles from the thirteenth to the twentieth century.

However, following the Warsaw Uprising of 1944, more than 85 % of Warsaw's historic centre was destroyed by Nazi troops. After the end of the war, faced with the choice of redevelopment in a contemporary style or restoration, the citizens of Warsaw, supported by the new Polish government, began a campaign to reconstruct and restore the Stare Miasto in its historic (pre-war) urban and architectural form.

> The reconstruction included the holistic recreation of the urban plan, together with the Old Town Market, the town houses, the circuit of the city walls, as well as the Royal Castle and important religious buildings. The reconstruction of Warsaw's historical centre was a major contributor to the changes in the doctrines related to urbanisation and conservation of urban development in most of the European countries after the destruction of World War II. Simultaneously, this example illustrates the effectiveness of conservation activities in the second half of the 20th Century, which permitted the integral reconstruction of the complex urban ensemble. (UNESCO listing citation, available at http://whc.unesco.org/en/list/30, accessed 11.6.2015)

Thus the UNESCO listing not only recognizes the beauty and magnificence of this historic urban composition but also the process of restoration and its contribution to the theory and practice of urban conservation in the late twentieth century.

Conservation in an industrial quarter: Birmingham, Jewellery Quarter

According to Birmingham City Council:

> In an age of volume house builders, multiple retailers, fast food chains and nationally based leisure groups there is an inevitable sameness about new development across the country. Against this background our historic buildings, traditional street patterns and urban landscapes provide a local distinctiveness vital to our sense of place and of belonging. (Birmingham City Council, 1999)

There is a tendency in urban conservation to concentrate on the protection of the most important buildings and structures of architectural or historic interest. However, this does not provide a complete picture of urban heritage. In reality even the finest buildings existed within the context of a complete urban environment and supported by the urban economy and society of the period of their construction. Thus to truly understand and benefit from urban heritage it is necessary to respect and conserve some of the more ordinary and vernacular elements of the urban fabric where they represent a particular aspect of the economy or society. There are some 30 Conservation Areas in Birmingham intended to protect the special character of each area. One of the Conservation Areas that is particularly representative of an ordinary, yet remarkable, element of the urban fabric of the city is the Jewellery Quarter, which contains one of Europe's best surviving groups of historic buildings devoted to the manufacture of jewellery and metal goods (Figure 7.8).

Having established the strategic planning principle of 'Regeneration through Conservation' the City Council prepared a character appraisal and management plan to protect and enhance the unique character of the Jewellery Quarter (Birmingham City Council, 2002). But conservation areas are not preserved in aspic; they are not museums but continue to be working elements within the urban economy. They have to evolve and absorb some new development. Therefore in 2005 the City Council published a design guide that would provide architects and others with the Council's view on the acceptable design parameters for new developments, be they conversions, extensions or new buildings. The purpose of the guidance was not 'to stultify development but rather to promote sensitive new design of high quality which demonstrates a sympathetic and contemporary response to the unique historic context of the Jewellery Quarter Conservation Area' (Birmingham City Council, 2005, p. 4).

Figure 7.8   *A Conservation Area: Birmingham, Jewellery Quarter*

Source: C. Couch, 2016.

Note: The area presents a limited palette of traditional materials, generally red brick with brick, stone or terracotta details and blue grey slate. The private external space is provided by narrow rear yards, usually paved in blue brick.

Specifically the *Design Guide* makes a number of observations:

- The topography of the Jewellery Quarter allows good views within, into and from the area and enhances the vistas along its streets. In any new design therefore it is important to establish how and from where the proposed development will be seen.
- The Jewellery Quarter has a clear hierarchy of streets. Any site is defined by its location within this pattern. New development should reflect the local hierarchy in scale, massing and architectural detail.
- The dense urban grain of the Jewellery Quarter creates a strong sense of enclosure. The clear division between public and private space is emphasized by the views allowed through cart and carriage entrances into yards and courts.
- The close urban grain of the Jewellery Quarter is particularly distinctive and should be retained and wherever necessary enhanced by new development.
- New buildings should respect the urban context of the site in height and scale. New development should not generally attempt to match the height of adjacent buildings precisely but should maintain the subtle variety of roofline characteristic of the area.
- One of the defining characteristics of the Jewellery Quarter is the limited palette of traditional materials, generally red brick with brick, stone or terracotta details and blue grey slate. Window frames are

timber or metal. These materials should be used in new development to reflect local context and create a harmonious street scene.

- Architectural detail should always be an integral part of the design of any new development in the Jewellery Quarter and should never be considered as an afterthought. The primary frontage should be the focus of architectural display with secondary buildings given a simpler treatment.
- Private external space in the Jewellery Quarter was traditionally provided by narrow rear yards, usually paved in blue brick. New development should reflect this tradition.
- In a commercial area such as the Jewellery Quarter signage can make a significant contribution to local character.
- Security in the Jewellery Quarter, where valuable goods are being manufactured and sold, is clearly an issue of great importance. A balance must be struck between preserving the character and appearance of the conservation area and providing appropriate security.

With the status of a 'supplementary planning document' the *Design Guide* can be used by the City Council in their development management processes. Proposals that ignore these design requirements are unlikely to gain planning consent.

Conclusions

Urban design is that element of urban planning concerned with ensuring the good functioning of areas and developments in terms of the efficient and effective use of land and buildings, and creating attractive physical environments that are aesthetically pleasing, safe, accessible, generate a sense of place and respond to local character and history.

Too many urban areas suffer from urban sprawl, inappropriate development and poor quality in the physical environment. Most planning systems today recognize that 'good design is a key aspect of sustainable development (and) is indivisible from good planning' (DCLG, 2012, para. 56). There is a need for planners to intervene in the design of new development and to protect and enhance existing urban areas because, as in economics, the market only takes account of the financial costs and benefits to the individual developer and ignores the wider social and environmental costs of development. Design controls oblige developers to take account of the impact of their development on its surroundings both in terms of visual impact and the functioning of the wider area.

Some elements of physical urban form can be assessed through quantitative measurement. For example, the density of development can be calculated in terms of residential densities or plot ratios; the mix of land uses can be discussed in terms of the proportions of floorspace or amount of land devoted to each use; the provision and amount of walkways, cycle ways and roads can be considered in terms of their length, travel times or capacity. However, measuring the character and aesthetic qualities of an area or building relies on qualitative techniques. Kevin Lynch provided the foundations of a method for assessing the structure and legibility of an area using the simple concepts of nodes, edges, paths, districts and landmarks. Cullen explored our visual reaction to the urban environment in terms of the ideas of 'serial vision', 'place' (here and there) and the 'content of places' (this and that). Sharp explained how many aesthetically pleasing historic environments display variety within established rhythms and a broad unity of character. The architecture of individual buildings can be discussed in terms of the building's function, age, architectural style, scale, proportions, materials, colour, and relationships with other buildings and spaces.

Achieving the goals of sustainable development requires urban development:

- to be compact, normally containing a mixture of uses, with vital and viable urban centres that meet the needs of inhabitants;
- to be visually attractive, respecting the local building vernacular, local architectural and cultural heritage, and to protect important views and vistas;
- to be constructed so as to minimize the consumption of energy and natural resources;
- to provide good permeability and connectivity within the area and to surrounding areas, with well proportioned streets and enclosed spaces that respect and integrate with existing hierarchies and give primacy of movement to walkers and cyclists over that of the motor vehicle;
- to minimize the intrusive effects of extraneous noise, air pollution, fear of crime and anti-social behaviour;
- to be well provided with green and blue infrastructure that will provide places for outdoor recreation and relaxation, local food production, natural habitats, pollution absorption, flood alleviation and urban temperature reduction.

Wherever possible existing buildings will be retained, reused or renovated. The cultural and economic value of the built heritage of the area will be recognized with buildings and other features of architectural or historic interest protected and conserved. Within a process of planning for sustainable development urban conservation should not be seen as an 'extra' or a 'branch' of planning: it is the sustainable way of approaching the regeneration and renewal of urban areas.

Chapter 8

Mobility, Accessibility and Urban Planning

Introduction

There is a symbiotic relationship between land use and transportation. Traffic is generated and journeys are made in relation to the nature and disposition of land uses. That is to say, different land uses generate and attract different amounts and types of traffic. This in turn generates pressure for investment in transport infrastructure and systems: for short journeys – footpaths and cycle routes; for longer journeys – roads, parking facilities and public transport. On the other hand, investment in transport generates demand for land use change and development at accessible locations that can take advantage of the infrastructure and systems provided, for example near motorway junctions, airports, railway stations and on bus routes.

The relationship between land use and traffic generation was first postulated by two American investigators, Mitchell and Rapkin (1954). They provided the theoretical basis for the development of the mathematical land use and transportation models that came to shape US and, later, UK and European transportation planning in the 1960s. At that time traffic congestion was seen as the dominant concern and the solutions were thought to lie in increasing highway capacity and speeding traffic flow. Car ownership and usage were rising quickly whereas the use of public transport, cycling and walking were in decline. Although, in the UK, a government report, *Traffic in Towns* (Buchanan, 1963), did recognize that the capacity of existing urban areas to absorb traffic was finite and that, at least in the bigger cities and in historic areas, some restraint would be necessary, it was not until the end of the decade, through the work of activists such as John Thompson (1969) and the London Motorway Action Group, that these ideas were seriously challenged.

Gradually, policy shifted as the huge financial and environmental costs of expanding urban highway capacity were recognized and as the environmental lobby was increasingly able to demonstrate the damaging role played by traffic in consuming non-renewable energy resources, polluting the atmosphere, causing noise and visual intrusion and accidents (Banister, 1993; Whitelegg, 1993; Tolley, 1995).

It became accepted that policy should be less focussed on improving mobility (the physical movement of people and goods by various modes of transport) and more concerned with accessibility (the ability to obtain goods and services and reach destinations). Increased mobility, unless on foot or by bicycle, imposed social and environmental costs, whereas what individuals required was efficient and equitable access to destinations, for work, shopping and leisure. Similarly, what firms needed was efficiency in access to and delivery of goods and services.

This chapter looks at the impact of transport on urban areas before going on to discuss methods of planning that provide for accessibility whilst mitigating such impacts, including contemporary views about best practice in the use of road space, parking and the design of streets. The chapter then explores the relationships between transport investment and urban regeneration and provides case studies of local improvements to highways and streets in Southend-on-Sea and planning for cycling in Lambeth (London). Finally, there is a look at the mechanisms for transportation planning and a case study of the Local Transport Plan for the West Midlands.

The impact of transport infrastructure and systems

The consumption of land

Transport infrastructure and systems have a significant impact on land use. In England between 1989 and 2011 some 46,350 ha of land changed to transport or utility use, although the annual rate reduced in the following years (DCLG, 2014). Roissy, Charles de Gaulle Airport near Paris covers an area approximately 8 km × 4 km: some 32.28 km^2 of former farmland, equivalent to one-third of the whole of the area covered by the Ville de Paris itself. The Port of Rotterdam covers 126.03 km^2, over one-third of the whole municipal area of the city (325.79 km^2) (Port of Rotterdam, 2014). The M25 London Orbital motorway consumes well in excess of 1,000 ha of land over its 188 km route and the land contained within the junction between the M6 and the M62 motorways in north-west England encompasses around 100 hectares (enough land to build 4,000 dwellings).

The building of urban motorways, which was an outcome of the 'predict and provide' approach to highway planning in the 1960s, has been very intrusive in the urban landscape. One of the most notorious examples was the building of 'Westway' – an extension of the M40 motorway towards central London. This elevated highway passed within only 4 m of bedroom windows of some housing in North

Kensington, causing widespread public opposition. The road also left a swathe of wasteland at ground level. In 1971 local inhabitants formed the North Kensington Amenity Trust to take over and reuse this land for community use. Eventually the combined impact of spiralling costs and public opposition brought a halt to such schemes (see Duncan and Bartlett, 1992).

Transport infrastructure can itself become a barrier to local movement. One such example is Byrom Street/Scotland Road in Liverpool. Formerly an important and well known commercial high street providing a retail and social hub for the north Liverpool community, today it is a six-lane highway that forms part of the city's inner ring road. Not only does it convey a large volume of fast-moving traffic (much of which regularly exceeds the legal speed limit), the former pattern of dense mixed-use urban neighbourhoods has been destroyed, many hectares of valuable urban land have been consumed and a major barrier to local movement has been created between the residential communities of Vauxhall to the west and Everton to the east. There are only three safe pedestrian crossings in more than 1 km of road (see Figure 8.1).

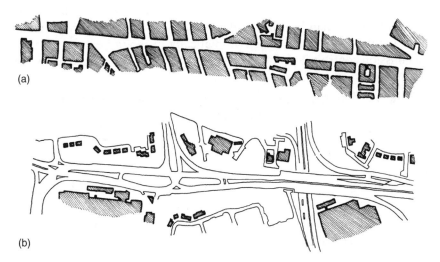

Figure 8.1   *The impact of major highways in urban areas: Liverpool, Scotland Road in (a) the 1920s and (b) 2014*

Source: Drawn by A.L. Couch.

Note: The tightly enclosed urban high street shared by communities on both sides in the early twentieth century (a) has become a wide open space containing a busy highway that separates the two communities (b).

Energy consumption, pollution, noise, visual intrusion and accidents

Energy consumption for transport purposes represents a large proportion of all energy used by final consumers. Transport energy use in Europe peaked before the 2008 economic crisis and has subsequently declined. This appears to be partly due to improved energy efficiency within the transport sector but mainly due to the impact of recession on the demand for transport. However, despite this reduction transport energy use actually increased as a proportion of total energy use over this period (Table 8.1).

Transport also has a major impact on air pollution, although the situation is improving across most types of pollution in most European countries. Carbon dioxide (CO_2) is the most important greenhouse gas causing global warming. As shown in Table 8.2 emissions fell between 2006 and 2012 in all sectors except transport because the growth in traffic outstripped energy efficiency gains in vehicle design. Without the economic downturn growth could have been even bigger (Table 8.2).

Nitrous oxides (NO_x) are toxic to plants and cause breathing difficulties in humans. Transport is the main source of nitrous oxides. However, emissions have fallen in recent years, mainly as a result of tighter emission controls and fuel standards. Volatile Organic Compounds (VOCs) are one of the main sources of ground level ozone, toxic to plants and damaging to human health. Road transport remains a major source of VOCs but volumes have fallen dramatically in recent years as a result of emission controls. Sulphur dioxide (SO_2) is toxic and a major cause of

Table 8.1   *Transport energy consumption in Europe (thousand tonnes of oil equivalent)*

	2006	2012
Road transport	307,388.2	287,542.9
Railways	7,296.4	6,994.1
Domestic air travel	6,693.9	5,509.7
Other (including international air travel)	55,680.2	51,671.0
Total transport final energy consumption	377,058.7	351,717.7
Transport as a proportion of total gross inland consumption	20.6%	20.9%

Source: Eurostat, Energy statistics, table nrg_100a (Simplified energy balances – annual data), (accessed 28.1.2015).

Table 8.2   *The contribution of transport to greenhouse gas*
emissions in Europe

	2006		2012	
	Total emissions (1,000 tonnes CO_2 equivalent)	*Proportion of emissions deriving from all transport modes*	*Total emissions (1,000 tonnes CO_2 equivalent)*	*Proportion of emissions deriving from all transport modes*
Greenhouse gas emissions	5,311,631	18.4 %	4,678,812	19.1 %

Source: Eurostat Greenhouse Gas Emissions (source: EEA) Table [env_air_gge] available at: http://appsso.eurostat.ec.europa.eu/nui/show.do?dataset=env_air_gge&lang=en (accessed 15.6.2015).

acid rain. Road vehicles and railway (steam) trains were once major sources of sulphur dioxide but emissions have fallen substantially since the 1970s (Table 8.3).

Another problem associated with mobility is that of noise intrusion. One pioneering policy in this field is the Westminster Noise Strategy

Table 8.3   *The contribution of road transport to air pollution in*
Europe

	2006		2012	
	Total emissions (tonnes)	*Proportion of emissions deriving from road transport (%)*	*Total emissions (tonnes)*	*Proportion of emissions deriving from road transport (%)*
Sulphur oxides	9,201,175	0.30 %	5,376,508	0.13 %
Nitrogen oxides	13,817,909	34.1 %	10,723,295	31.0 %
Non-methane VOCs	8,661,179	18.9 %	6,793,224	12.4 %
Particulates	2,206,102	13.9 %	1,988,766	11.9 %

Source: Eurostat Air pollution (source: EEA) Table [env_air_emis] available at:
http://appsso.eurostat.ec.europa.eu/nui/show.do?dataset=env_air_emis&lang=en.

(Westminster City Council, 2009). They suggest that the typical noise level generated by a busy urban street is 78–85 db(A) (decibels – the relative loudness of sound as perceived by the human ear), whereas the desirable noise level should be no more than 55 dB LAeq (the average sound level over a period of time) on balconies and outdoor living areas, 30–40 dB LAeq in a residential living room and 20–30 dB LAeq in a bedroom. Unpleasant noises can be annoying but loud noise, especially if prolonged, can damage hearing and impact upon other aspects of physical and psychological health.

Traffic noise derives from two sources: the vehicle's motor and the interface between the vehicle and the road surface. Recent innovations in road surface design have proved quite effective in reducing noise. The noise level is also dependent upon the amount and mix of traffic, its speed and level of congestion. Urban railways can also generate high levels of noise, with diesel engines tending to be noisier than electric engines.

Airports are another source of intrusive urban noise. The UK Government regards 57 dB LAeq over a 16-hour period between 07:00 and 23:00 as the limit beyond which 'significant community disturbance' would occur. Taking the example of London City Airport, in granting permission the planning authorities restricted airport development and operation so as not to exceed this level within a defined distance of the airport. The 57 dB LAeq noise contour runs approximately 2 km beyond the ends of the runway and 400 m on either side. In 2009 the Airport operators agreed with Newham Council to draw up a draft *Noise Monitoring and Mitigation Strategy (NOMMS)* whose provisions included: monitoring and provision of data on aircraft noise and tracking for aircraft departures and arrivals, ground noise, encouraging airline operators to use quiet operating procedures, restricting the times when aircraft movements may occur (usually 06:30–22:00), the number of flights and the type of aircraft permitted, provision of noise barriers and sound insulation for badly affected existing buildings.

The paraphernalia of road traffic infrastructure causes considerable visual intrusion into the urban scene. This can be seen in the structures of road systems, such as flyovers and bridges, in traffic signage, road markings and car parking facilities. And the volume of traffic itself can be an impediment to the visual enjoyment of townscape. Figure 8.2 illustrates such examples of visual intrusion. The planning system can contribute to the reduction of visual intrusion through influencing the design of, or even necessity for, highway structures and signage and the control of vehicular access to sensitive areas.

Accidents are one of the most unwelcome side effects of mobility. In the UK there were 28 road deaths per million population in 2013 which, whilst still too high, is only around half of the rate a decade earlier. For comparison, the equivalent figures were 41 in Germany, 50 in France,

Figure 8.2 *Visual intrusion of road traffic and infrastructure*

Source: C. Couch, 2016.

Note: The little used flyover cuts across the view of the listed building destroying the visual unity of the street.

and 87 in Poland (Department for Transport statistics: Table RAS52001 International comparisons of road deaths: number and rates for different road users: by selected countries, 2012 and 2013 (provisional), accessed 28.1.2015). In most European countries the accident rate is decreasing, with fewer fatalities and serious injuries being incurred. But the pattern is not even. The countries of north-west Europe have a better record than those in the south or east. The reasons are complex, with climate, topography, degree of urbanization, historic levels of infrastructure investment and driving habits all playing a part. But the planning system can assist in accident reduction by avoiding conflicts between land use and transportation through the imposition of speed limits, traffic control systems and traffic calming measures, especially in residential areas.

Planning for accessibility and mitigating the impact of mobility

In the words of the US Federal Highway Administration:

> Coordinating (or integrating) land use and transportation planning and development are commonly considered today as one facet of 'smart growth', sustainable development, new urbanism, or other

similar concept. These share policies, principles, and strategies intended to preserve and even enhance valued natural and cultural resources and facilitate 'healthy', sustainable communities and neighborhoods. These approaches also tend to foster a balance of mixed uses (including housing, educational, employment, recreational, retail, and service opportunities) which recognize the importance of spatial or geographic proximity, layout, and design of those uses. (US Federal Highway Administration, 2013)

And the UK Government has argued that:

Land use planning has a key role in delivering the Government's integrated transport strategy. By shaping the pattern of development and influencing the location, scale, density, design and mix of land uses, planning can help to reduce the need to travel, reduce the length of journeys and make it safer and easier for people to access jobs, shopping, leisure facilities and services by public transport, walking, and cycling. (ODPM, 2001b, para. 3)

The contemporary planning agenda is concerned with transport in two ways: mitigating the impact of mobility and planning for accessibility. So the aims of urban planning in this regard might be summarized as:

- encouraging better accessibility rather than mobility;
- creating the city of fewer and shorter journeys;
- shifting modal split in favour of walking, cycling and the use of public transport;
- minimizing the environmental and social impact of movement.

Modal split

Modal split is the proportion of journeys made by different modes of transportation. The concept may be applied to passenger trips (usually measured as percentages of individual trips) or freight (usually measured by volume or weight). In passenger transport modal split is influenced by a number of factors including city size and structure, topography, public policy and investment in different transport modes. Figure 8.3 compares a number of European cities to illustrate the impact of some of these factors. Brussels, Berlin and London are all capital cities. London, which is much larger than the other two has, as expected, the lowest level of car usage and the highest use of public transport. Liège, Dortmund and Liverpool are all regional cities. Liège has by far the highest level of car usage but Liverpool has a high level of public transport usage and walking for the size of city. Leuven, Münster and

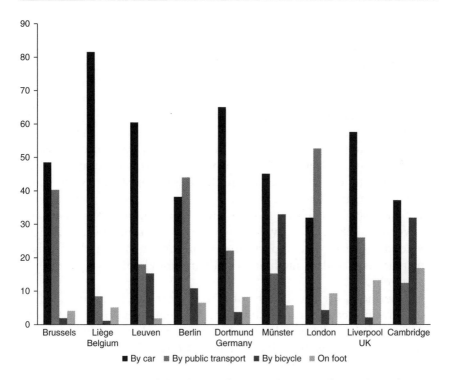

Figure 8.3 *Modal split on the journey to work in selected European cities*

Source: Based upon Eurostat (2014b).

Note: Data for Belgium and the UK are for 2011, Germany for 2012.

Cambridge are smaller university towns. Leuven is heavily car-dependent; Münster and Cambridge both display high levels of cycle usage. Cambridge has the highest proportion who walk to work of any of these cities.

Looking specifically at medium-sized European cities Santos et al. (2013) found that modal split was influenced by a number of factors: car use increased with car ownership and GDP per capita; the proportion of journeys by public transport increased with population, GDP per capita and number of buses but decreased with fare increases; the proportion of journeys by bicycle increased with the length of the cycle network. Thus modal split could be influenced by both charging – reducing bus fares increases ridership – and investment policies. For example, they suggested that reallocating road space as cycle lanes is relatively inexpensive and likely to increase the proportion of journeys to work by bicycle.

Urban form and density

There is strong evidence that lower urban densities encourage longer transport trips and greater use of the motor car than higher urban densities. Writing in 1989, Kenworthy and Newman compared gasoline consumption in a sample of cities across the world. They demonstrated a remarkably strong correlation between urban density and gasoline consumption. In the very low density cities of the USA per capita consumption was highest. In the somewhat denser cities of Australia with better public transport systems, consumption was around half that of the US cities and for the European cities the figure was halved again. The best results came from some of the very dense cities of Asia: Singapore, Tokyo and Hong Kong (Newman and Kenworthy, 1989). This evidence provides a strong motive for the development of more compact cities to minimize the length of urban transport trips and to facilitate a shift in modal split away from the motor vehicle.

Furthermore, greater use of public transport can be encouraged by concentrating generators of heavy transport demand at locations near to public transport hubs, with land uses that generate less transport demand located elsewhere, as illustrated in Figure 3.6 (p. 120).

Since the 1990s these ideas have been promoted through the concept of 'transit orientated development' (TOD), which has become popular with urban planners in the USA and elsewhere. Similar to the concept advocated by Rogers et al., the idea is to concentrate high density mixed use residential and commercial development around transit stops (light rail, tram or bus) to encourage the use of public transport. It is generally thought that public transport is most likely to be used if stops are located no more than 400–500 metres from trip origins and destinations.

From the early 1990s the Dutch Government advocated its well known ABC policy. Type A locations were sites with a high level of accessibility by public transport, such as major railway and metro stations, and considered suitable for activities with a high intensity of employment (for example, offices) or visitors (for example, retail centres or higher education). Type B were sites with both good public transport and highway accessibility, such as suburban stations near motorway junctions, considered suitable for less intense urban uses where both vehicular and public transport access was required. Type C were sites located near motorway junctions but without good public transport access, considered suitable for activities that required good vehicular access such as logistics and industrial activities with a low density of employment. Whilst the policy has not been as successful as originally hoped in directing investment, the country has seen policies favouring

TOD and a substantial concentration of investment in office developments and other high intensity land uses (for example, higher education, high density housing) near to major railways, such as the central stations in The Hague and Rotterdam.

An example of this approach can be found in Krier's work as master planner for the high density, mixed use De Resident redevelopment project in The Hague. The area forms a link between the high rise buildings of the new business district around The Hague Central Station and the low rise traditional townscape of the historic city core. The aim of the development was to strengthen The Hague's position as an international institutional and business centre, and was designed to provide 115,000 m² office space in four large towers, residential blocks containing 315 apartments, 4,500 m² retail space and an intricate network of streets and public spaces. The area is crossed by two main pedestrian and cycle routes that intersect in a horseshoe-shaped square in the centre of the scheme (Figure 8.4).

(a)   (b)

Figure 8.4 *High density development near (a) The Hague Central Station and (b) Rotterdam Central Station*

Source: C. Couch, 2016.

Note: Photograph (a) shows the Muzentower in the De Resident development adjoining The Hague Central Station, designed by Rob Krier and his firm. Photograph (b) shows high density office development on the Weena, adjoining Rotterdam Central Station at the north end of the pedestrianized Lijnbaan.

Provision of local facilities

In a sustainable community basic local facilities should be available within easy walking or cycling distance of most homes. That is to say, all residential neighbourhoods should be equipped with provision for local shopping, leisure and community facilities (Barton et al., 2010). This in turn suggests that neighbourhoods have to be of sufficient density to generate an adequate support population within a walkable catchment area of the local shops and community facilities.

Historically in the UK it was a relatively easy planning task to estimate the population required to support a two-form entry primary school and design the neighbourhood at an appropriate density to ensure that all children were within 10 minutes' safe walking distance of the school. In the planning of new towns in the 1950s the reasoning would have gone something like the following calculation. A two-form entry primary school could accommodate 60 children starting at the school each year (30 per class). A birth rate of 60 children a year would have been generated by a population of about 6,000 people. At an average household size of around 2.8 people this population would have required around 2,143 dwellings. In order to accommodate this population within a 10-minute walk of the school (at a child's pace, about 500 m), the net residential area of the neighbourhood would be about 80 hectares. To accommodate 2,143 dwellings this area would have to be developed at an average density of about 27 dwellings per hectare – the typical density of residential neighbourhoods in British new towns in the post-war period. In many planning books of the time (for example Keeble, 1964) and in new town masterplans such calculations were commonplace.

Today such calculations can still be made in some circumstances but social changes have made the situation much more complex. In the first place, societies have become much more diverse since the 1950s. There is much greater variation in household size and composition with many more childless households and greater social mix within many communities, making estimates of birth rates and numbers of children within particular localities increasingly difficult to predict. Secondly, several UK Governments have permitted and indeed encouraged greater parental choice over the schools which their children attend, and fewer children today automatically go to their local neighbourhood school. Whether this choice is based upon perceived educational quality, curriculum, social class or faith, the result is that many children are travelling well beyond a convenient walking distance to their schools. This has had implications for the transport system because many of these longer journeys to school are made by car. This is in direct contrast to the ambitions of an integrated transport strategy that seeks to reduce car use and encourage walking and cycling.

There are similar conflicts within the health system where, for reasons of economies of scale and improved primary health care, local doctors are increasingly encouraged to join larger group practices or district health centres. Similarly in secondary care, local general hospitals are being replaced by more concentrated specialist provision in fewer centres. The result in each case is to decrease the local accessibility and require longer journeys to access services.

In some areas it has become difficult to sustain a good range of local shopping provision. In extreme cases 'food deserts' have emerged. Typically these are low income communities with low levels of car ownership whose spending power is insufficient to sustain an adequate range of retail provision. Local shops close and the remaining outlets often charge inflated prices and fail to offer sufficient choice, especially in fresh food. The problem can be particularly prevalent in some peripheral social housing estates. One such estate, Speke, some 12 km from the centre of Liverpool, had been planned in the inter-war period for a population of 25,000 with its own district centre and a number of local shopping parades. From the 1970s the population began to decline and age, and became increasingly impoverished. The local shopping parades declined from 5–6 shops each down to only one convenience shop or even none. Major retailers pulled out of the district centre leaving only a handful of shops providing for basic needs. The ensuing vacancy led to problems of anti-social behaviour and environmental degradation around the centre. The City Council's solution was to demolish most of the former district centre and to develop a new centre based around a large supermarket at a location closer to the edge of the estate and accessible from one of the main highways into the city, but still served by local buses and within reasonable walking distance of most of the population. By attracting sufficient external trade from the highway to make the development financially viable, the problem of local retail provision was ameliorated.

Continuing with the idea of land uses that generate heavy transport demands being easily accessible by all forms of transport, especially public transport, in many countries modern planning policy places strong restrictions on the location of developments such as large retail complexes. Typical of these is the requirement of the UK Government that local planners should apply a 'sequential test' to development proposals whereby applications for main town centre uses should be located in existing centres and only if suitable sites are not available should out of centre sites be considered. Even then preference should be given to accessible sites that are well connected to the town centre (DCLG, 2012, para 24).

The use of road space, parking and the design of streets

Efficiency in the use of urban road space

It is well known that the demand for urban road use is such that traffic will tend to increase to meet the supply of road space available. Thus building new urban roads tends to reduce travel time/cost and increase demand until the road space that has been created is full and the advantage has been lost. But the reverse argument also has some validity. By reducing the amount of road space the amount of road traffic is reduced and there may be some change to other modes of transport. The supply of road space can be managed by both physical prohibitions and by road pricing. Control over road space can include:

- the complete or partial prohibition of vehicles from a 'pedestrianized' street, such as major shopping streets or other leisure or tourist destinations with high concentrations of pedestrian flow;
- restricting the direction of flow of traffic along a street;
- restricting the street, or particular lanes, to specific users, such as buses, cyclists or delivery vehicles;
- controlling the flow and volume of traffic through traffic light systems;
- controlling the volume of traffic through road pricing, such as the London 'congestion charge'.

In London since 2003 most motor vehicles entering the central congestion charge zone during the working week pay a fee (£11.50 in 2014). Measuring the effect of the congestion charge is complex but it seems to be the case that the total volume of traffic within the zone has reduced by 10–15% with some slight increase in traffic and parking outside the charging perimeter. The greatest benefit has been in the increased provision of bus and cycle lanes, improvements in the reliability and speed of bus services, significantly increased bus patronage and cycle use. However, it is difficult to attribute these changes directly to the charge because other factors such as population increase and overcrowding on the underground railway system have also been influential.

A motor vehicle is generally only useful for a journey if it can be parked at its destination. For many years urban planners have realized that by providing or controlling parking they can influence the pattern of urban road use. The management of car parking can include both physical prohibitions and pricing. Controls over car parking can include:

- the amount of space provided, to facilitate or discourage parking in certain locations, such as prohibition parking in narrow streets or on dangerous corners;

- limiting the use of spaces by time, such as allowing short-stay parking to facilitate retail trade, or allowing parking only after working hours to support the evening economy;
- limiting the use of space by user, such as permitting parking of vehicles for the disabled, or for residents only;
- by pricing parking spaces, such as setting the charging regime to encourage short-term users in a close to a shopping area, with a long-term parking pricing regime for commuter parking at a more distant location.

Many cities, especially popular tourist destinations with historic centres, have established 'park and ride' provision to encourage casual visitors to leave their vehicles on the periphery of the city and to access the central area by public transport. York is a good example of a city where an outer by-pass and 'park and ride' system has been combined with powerful restrictions on central area car parking and an extensive pedestrianized city centre to create an environment in which use of the motor vehicle has been brought under a reasonable degree of control (see Figure 8.5).

The design of streets

Modern thinking about the design of streets aims to give priority to pedestrian and cycle movements, creating safe and secure layouts which minimize conflicts. Figure 8.6 shows the new priorities in a modern housing development, Vauban in Freiburg, Germany. The

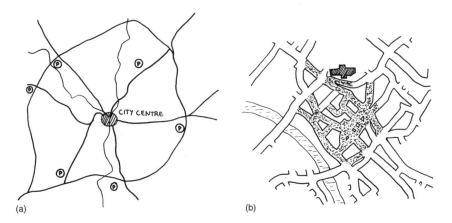

Figure 8.5 *Car access and parking facilities and restrictions: York*

Source: Drawn by A.L. Couch.

Note: Map (a) shows the location of 'park and ride' sites around the outer ring road; map (b) shows the pedestrianized city centre streets where most motor vehicles are prohibited.

Figure 8.6 *Designing the modern main street: Freiburg, Vaubanallee*

Source: C. Couch 2016

Note: Pedestrian and cycle access on the left, tramlines in the centre, and restricted motor vehicle access and a footpath on the right; note also the permeable surface surrounding the tram tracks.

street accommodates a broad, safe pedestrian and cycle path, tram tracks on a sustainably drained green surface, a two-lane road that allows motor vehicle traffic restricted access to the estate and a broad footpath.

In its *Manual for Streets* (2007) the UK Department for Transport (DfT) advises that new developments should be integrated into the existing movement system. Whilst there should be a hierarchy of distributor and local access roads to exclude unnecessary through traffic, the street should be the focus of movement in a neighbourhood. History has shown that the perimeter block is an effective structure for residential neighbourhoods, working well in providing convenient, safe routes for movement, making quality places and using land efficiently. Too many housing developments built since the 1960s have departed from traditional arrangements, often creating layouts that lack legibility, use land inefficiently and lack convenience for pedestrians, cyclists and bus users.

The street systems of existing neighbourhoods can be – and many have already been – redesigned to exclude through traffic (eliminating 'rat-runs') and to slow the passage of vehicles by introducing traffic calming measures, thereby increasing pedestrian safety and local environmental quality. Traffic speeds can be restricted to 20 mph (30 kph) in residential areas. The creation of Home Zones (pioneered as 'woonerf' in the Netherlands, and in many British General Improvement Areas in the 1970s) attempts to claim the street back from the motor vehicle and make it a safe and pleasant place for local people, especially children.

Transport investment and urban regeneration

Urban transport investment can have a significant impact on local property values and urban regeneration. In Rotterdam, the former dockland area of Kop van Zuid lies on the south bank of the River Maas opposite the city centre. During the 1970s these upstream docks became redundant and the whole area fell into disuse. By the 1980s, with the post-war city centre redevelopment virtually complete, the city council was seeking further sites to meet demand from commercial property developers, and by 1991 a new plan to provide for expansion of the city centre south of the Maas in Kop van Zuid had been devised. However, the area suffered from very poor accessibility from the city centre. Road access involved a 3 km easterly detour across a bridge onto an island then a series of swing bridges back to Kop van Zuid. A metro line from Rotterdam Central Station passed under the area but there was no station. It was therefore decided to build a new road bridge and metro station to provide a direct link from the city centre. The Erasmus Bridge was completed in 1996 and incorporates a roadway, bus lane and tramlines, cycle track and pedestrian walkways (Figure 8.7). The new metro station opened the following year, bringing the heart of the regeneration area within 4 minutes of the city centre and 8 minutes of Central Station. The effect was to kick-start the redevelopment process. In the vicinity of the metro station a large office and retail compex, theatre and technical college were quickly developed. Nearby the transformation of the former headquarters of the Holland-America shipping line into a luxury hotel stimulated further regneration.

In 1999 the London Underground Jubilee Line Extension (JLE) was opened. It runs from Westminster, passing beneath the Thames, through London Bridge Station, the riverside districts of Southwark and Bermondsey, back across the Thames to the Isle of Dogs and Canary Wharf, then northwards to Stratford. The impact of this investment on the regeneration of nearby districts in south-east and east London was the subject of a number of impact studies.

Perhaps the first point to note was that the need to improve access to Canary Wharf was one of the key reasons for constructing the JLE on this route. Conversely, without the JLE much of the subsequent development around Canary Wharf and the Isle of Dogs might not

Figure 8.7   *Transport investment to stimulate regeneration: Rotterdam,*
the Erasmus Bridge

Source: C. Couch, 2016.

Note: The bridge forms an important connection between the city centre and the south
bank of the River Maas, supporting the regeneration of the Kop van Zuid area.

have happened as quickly – if at all (Eyers and Jones, 2004). Indeed,
another study attributes an increase in land values around Canary
Wharf of some £2 billion over the period 1992 to 2002 to the opening
of the JLE (Jones Lang LaSalle, 2004).

The districts of Southwark and Bermondsey have historically been
amongst the most socially deprived in London. The JLE transformed the
accessibility of this area, reducing lengthy bus journeys to central
London to a few minutes by Underground. The impact has been considerable. Employment around the stations east of London Bridge has
increased faster than for London as a whole and the area has seen an
upsurge in housing investment. However, whilst this has increased the
employment and residential capacity of London as a whole, it is a moot
point whether the local population in these districts have benefitted to
the same extent. There remains some degree of mismatch between the
skills of the traditional population and the nature of the new employment opportunities (Eyers and Jones, 2004). And the housing investment
is gentrifying the area, pushing the prices or rents of new and refurbished
property beyond the means of local people. Jones Lang LaSalle (2004)
estimated that the JLE raised land values in the immediate vicinity of the
new Southwark Station alone by £800 million between 1992 and 2002.
Thus it can be seen that there are substantial but complex relationships
between transport investment and urban regeneration.

Local improvements to highways and streets: Southend-on-Sea

Southend-on-Sea is a large Essex town and seaside resort on the Thames Estuary. It has a population of more than 175,000 and with only one strategic primary route (A127) providing access to the town, it had long suffered high levels of traffic congestion. In 2010, with financial support from central government, the Borough Council developed the Better Southend programme to resolve a number of interlinked traffic problems along the primary road into the town and in the central area (see Figure 8.8). Their proposals represent the implementation of previously approved policies within the adopted Southend Core Strategy and Southend Local Transport Plan (Southend-on-Sea Borough Council, 2010).

Historically the Progress Road junction on the primary route at the entrance to the town had caused lengthy traffic queues, together with delays on side roads, especially at the peak period and summer weekends. Using only land within the highway boundaries, the junction approaches were widened and modern traffic signals installed, along with electronic message signs, journey-time cameras and webcams. The result was a reduction in queueing traffic and improved safety and accessibility for cyclists and pedestrians. New landscaping, coordinated street furniture and banners enhanced the junction as a visual 'gateway' to Southend.

Figure 8.8 *Highway and street improvements in Southend-on-Sea*

Source: C. Couch, 2016.

Note: Southend, City Beach. Relatively low cost junction and highway improvements have dramatically reduced the impact of traffic and produced a much improved public realm and safer pedestrian environment.

The second scheme – at Cuckoo Corner, some 2 km further along the route into the town – was designed to alleviate heavy congestion caused by the lack of capacity in the existing roundabout. Retaining the round-about but combining computerized 'metering' of traffic entering the junction with modern traffic light systems that minimized 'intergreen' time, the project created a more efficient and safer junction. Improvements to the junction allowed the introduction of bus priority measures and improved cycle and pedestrian accessibility, and were also seen as crucial to releasing nearby land for housing development and expanding a local industrial estate.

A little further on, the route enters the town centre alongside the Southend Victoria railway station. At this point an existing roundabout junction between the primary route and local streets visually and physically severed the station from the heart of the town centre, creating an unfavourable image for arriving passengers and an unsafe environment for pedestrians and cyclists. By converting the roundabout to a signal controlled junction, the scheme permitted the development of new bus stops directly adjoining the station and released a substantial area of land for a new hard-landscaped public space, providing an attractive and much safer pedestrian connection between the station and the town centre.

One kilometre further on, the road reaches the beach just east of the town centre. The beach-front road, Marine Parade, was a wide dual carriageway carrying more than 14,000 vehicles over a 12-hour period, which created a poor environment and separated the beach from the town. The scheme involved reduction of the road width to a single carriageway, a significant increase in public open space and improved pedestrian and cycle links to the town centre. Combined with new lighting, reduced street clutter and landscaping that reflects natural movement patterns, the scheme provides a pedestrian-orientated environment more in keeping with needs of the leisure and tourism activities that the Borough Council sought to accommodate at this location.

Collectively, these four linked schemes have created a more sustainable environment, reduced traffic congestion and its associated fuel consumption and air pollution, improved accessibility and safety for pedestrians and cyclists and enhanced the local townscape and landscape. And, importantly, the programme was devised within a framework provided by the Core Strategy and Local Transport Plan.

Planning for cycling: London, Lambeth

According to Lambeth Council, 'A place that is good to cycle in is a place that is good to live in' (Lambeth LB, 2013). The Council's aim is to make Lambeth London's most cycle-friendly borough. Whereas the Mayor of London has a target for 5 % of all trips to be made by bicycle by 2026, the Borough's target is 6 % of all trips by 2020. The reasons for wanting to stimulate cycle use are that it is a very convenient mode of urban transport for short trips; it reduces congestion, being much more space-efficient than cars; it is healthy and pollution free; and it is socially inclusive because it is cheap to provide.

Thus the Borough's cycling strategy aims to:

- Create safe and attractive streets for cycling through a mix of measures including a borough-wide 20 mph speed limit; allocating more road space for cycling and walking and giving greater priority to cycling; converting some one-way streets to two-way for cycling; removing railings and kerbs where they impede convenient local access by bicycle; and opening up cycle routes through parks and public open spaces.
- Encourage and enable a greater range of people to cycle through cycle hire schemes; by providing free cycle training and information for individuals; and developing a network of cycle routes where women, young people and older people feel safe enough to cycle. Routes are to be coherent, direct, safe, attractive and comfortable with secure cycle parking provided at both ends of the trip.
- Reduce through traffic on residential streets and, away from main roads, make a presumption in favour of local access and amenity.
- Improve road user behaviour and bicycle awareness through information, training and enforcement.

But the Council recognizes that there are some difficulties to overcome in implementing such a strategy, including the poor perception of cycling amongst many people, antagonism between road users, local objections and lack of political will, cost and the availability of finance.

The mechanisms for transportation planning

A development plan provides the means by which urban planners can determine a pattern and density of development that will best support the use of sustainable modes of transport. The transportation impact of population and economic change will be taken into account in the plan making process. At the strategic level this is likely to include the location and size of major growth zones and large scale facilities and their supporting transport infrastructure. At a local level this is likely to be concerned with the use of specific plots of land, and the form, density and accessibility of development.

It is an important part of the planning process for planners to be able to assess the traffic impact of proposals. For smaller development proposals a simple Transport Statement may be sufficient whilst for larger developments a full Transport Assessment will be necessary (DCLG, 2014b). A Transport Statement will typically audit and appraise the proposed development against existing conditions, measuring the proposed land use and scale of development, access arrangements, a quantitative and qualitative assessment of likely trip generation and modes of travel, parking and servicing arrangements and the impact of construction traffic.

A Transport Assessment is a more comprehensive and systematic process that sets out the transport issues relating to a proposed development and identifies measures to deal with the anticipated transport impacts of the scheme. Generally improvements to accessibility and encouragement to use sustainable travel are expected to take precedence over measures to increase traffic capacity or increase the use of vehicles. Transport Assessments, and to a lesser extent Transport Statements, are required to identify the impact on the entire transport system in the vicinity of the development. This means that 'person trips' by all modes of transport to/from the development should be considered and not just vehicle trips on the local road network. In major developments the Transport Assessment is likely to be accompanied by a Travel Plan containing a package of measures tailored to the transport needs of the development, aimed at increasing travel choices and reducing reliance on the private car. For example, a travel plan might include initiatives to encourage car-sharing, subsidized use of public transport, cycle parking and changing facilities.

Typical of the development management policies relating to the accessibility requirements for a development proposal are those contained in the City of York Local Plan (City of York, 2014). These suggest that a new development will only generally be permitted where it is in a location and has an internal layout that gives priority to the needs of pedestrians, cyclists and users of public transport, or through obligations, conditions and other provision, can give such priority. Such development is also expected to provide safe, convenient, direct access to local amenities and facilities, and to connect with the wider area through high quality and frequent public transport services.

Local transport plans

Although not directly concerned with land use or spatial planning, Local Transport Plans (LTP) form an important part of the transport planning process in England. LTPs are prepared by strategic transport authorities in England (county councils, unitary authorities, passenger transport authorities and London boroughs). The purpose of the LTP is to plan for the future provision of transportation in the area concerned so it will contain both strategic policies and implementation programmes. They will comprise a baseline report on the current situation, forecasts of future trends, objectives for future transport provision, transport policies, an implementation programme and outline funding bids to achieve the objectives. LTPs are about the integration, coordination and delivery of local transport systems, including highways, rail, bus and other services, and are subject to a Strategic Environmental Assessment.

A good example of local transport planning is that undertaken by the Passenger Transport Authority for the West Midlands (Centro). The strategic objectives of the Centro LTP for the period 2011–2026 include:

- prioritizing interventions which will have greatest economic benefit;
- enhancing the efficiency and reliability of local transport networks for the movement of people and freight;
- improving safety and security;
- promoting low carbon corridors and Smarter Choices to influence travel behaviour;
- developing an integrated public transport network, including Smartcards and technology-led information (Centro, 2011).

The implementation plan provides a mechanism for integrating contributions from a number of agencies with different transport responsibilities. The local authorities are responsible for various highway improvements, traffic management schemes, on and off street parking and road safety measures. The contribution of Centro itself includes extensions to the Midland Metro (tram) system, development of bus interchange and park & ride facilities and the coordination of public transport services provided by various local bus companies and train operating companies. The (national) Highways Agency undertakes motorway and trunk road management and enhancement, while Network Rail is responsible for the management and development of the rail network and principal stations.

Specific schemes range from the strategic 'mega-projects' to local improvements. One of the biggest projects involved the redevelopment of Birmingham New Street railway station between 2009 and 2015. The station opened in 1854 and was rebuilt in the 1960s, but by the millennium passenger numbers had increased so much that it was operating beyond its capacity and was in need of redevelopment. In 2009 work began on the £600m New Street Gateway scheme to provide a new station concourse, more than three times bigger than the old concourse, improved and more accessible platforms, a new station facade and better links to and through the station for pedestrians (Network Rail, 2014). At the other end of the scale, a congested highway roundabout at

Burnt Tree Island between Dudley and Sandwell was replaced by a new traffic-light controlled junction to improve traffic flow and increase pedestrian safety.

Conclusions

Transport planning has an important role to play in facilitating sustainable development but also in contributing to wider sustainability and health objectives (DCLG, 2012, para. 29). The transportation system impacts upon urban areas in a number of ways:

- large amounts of land are required for transportation networks, especially rail and road systems and the parking of motor vehicles;
- transport infrastructure can be very intrusive, for instance creating barriers between urban districts;
- traffic can significantly reduce the environmental quality of busy streets, causing noise, visual intrusion and air pollution which in turn reduce the value of adjoining properties;
- the transportation system uses considerable amounts of energy with the motor car being particularly inefficient in this regard;
- use of motor vehicles is associated with many unnecessary deaths and injuries to other road users, particularly cyclists and pedestrians.

Key objectives of urban planning are to reduce the need for travel and to shift modal split away from the motor vehicle. Land use planning can influence transport demand and modal split through the location and intensity of development. The mixing of land uses and the locating of amenities and services which are in daily use in close proximity to their users can reduce travel demand. However, in modern societies there is often a tension between the pressures on service providers, such as hospitals, schools and retailers, seeking economies of scale and the desire of urban planners to provide services locally. The more compact and dense the city the less the need to travel and the shorter intra-urban journeys will be on average. Shorter journeys are more easily accomplished by cycling or walking than longer ones. Balancing uses that generate high levels of travel demand across a network, in terms of space and time, can improve its efficiency, ameliorating peaks and troughs in demand.

In addition to distance travelled, modal split can be influenced by many factors including pricing and quality. Raising road and car park prices can have a significant deterrent effect on motor car use. Public transport use is influenced by both price and the quality of service (in terms of frequency, reliability, vehicle quality and so on). Usage by cyclists and walkers is increased where safe and convenient routes are provided.

It is clear that urban transport investments, including new connections, railway stations or tramlines, can have a significant effect on urban regeneration, as in the case of the Erasmus Bridge in Rotterdam. Conversely, major urban regeneration schemes can stimulate transport investment, as in the case of Canary Wharf in London.

The design of urban areas should incorporate layouts that maximize access and the opportunities for safe and convenient movement by all in society, including the elderly and disabled. This means giving priority to the needs of pedestrians, cyclists and those using public transport over those using motor vehicles and minimizing conflicts between traffic and other transport infrastructure users. Any development that is likely to generate significant amounts of traffic should be subject to a Transport Assessment or Transport Statement in order to allow planners to consider the impact of proposals and alternative means of providing for the required movement of people or goods. Such developments should also produce a Travel Plan showing how the need for travel will be addressed in a sustainable manner.

Chapter 9

Conclusions: A Future for Urban Planning

The evolving urban planning agenda

Modern town planning emerged around the beginning of the twentieth century as various countries began to establish a legal basis for intervention. This led to the founding of professional organizations, academic programmes and a growing body of literature and professional discourse. Initially the majority of planners were architects, surveyors or civil engineers by original training, although it took a scientist, Patrick Geddes, to establish the basic tenets of planning method: 'survey – analysis – plan' (Geddes,1915). In that era planning was principally concerned with land use and the physical structure of cities. Planners offered two principal and distinct utopias for urban living in the twentieth century: one, perhaps favoured more in the UK, was based upon Ebenezer Howard's notion of the low density 'garden city' bringing together the best of town and country; the other, initially more favoured in continental Europe, was based upon the ideas of Le Corbusier and the modern movement, using technology to build high density, efficient and healthy cities.

Writing in the 1930s, Patrick Abercrombie argued that the goal of planning was to achieve 'beauty, health and convenience' in the design and layout of the city (1933, p. 104); that is to say, a visually attractive, healthy and efficient urban environment. Despite and to some extent because of the Second World War, the 1940s saw rapid advances in planning thought: in ideas about regional planning; the need for comprehensive town planning; and in the redesign and reconstruction of war-damaged city centres and urban quarters. Despite the influence of the garden cities movement on the design of new towns in the UK, it was modernism that held most sway in the post-war years. But by the 1960s there were challenges to these functional approaches to land use and transportation planning and a new postmodern philosophy emerged, calling for more sensitive urban planning based upon a growing recognition of urban social issues, the conservation of urban heritage and natural environments and the restraint of traffic. Urban planning was evolving and becoming increasingly informed by the social as well as the technical sciences.

294

From the 1970s, increasing globalization, economic restructuring and the decline of many traditional urban economies brought the issue of local economic development and regeneration onto the urban planning agenda. But others were looking at the consequences of industrial development in another way, with a growing awareness of the immense environmental damage and the inequalities brought about by unrestrained economic growth. The *Brundtland Report* defined the need for 'sustainable development' that would 'meet the needs of the present without compromising the ability of future generations to meet their own needs' (Brundtland, 1987). By the 1990s it was recognized that urban planning could contribute to this agenda through supporting greener, more compact, better designed and more energy efficient cities. By the millennium, as the impact of climate change became clearer, arguments favouring the planning of more sustainable urban environments were only strengthened.

In terms of economic development, some cities may be blessed with and can exploit economic sectors that are nationally or internationally growing. Other cities may need to diversify their economic structures before they can grow. And indeed, some cities in already prosperous regions may feel that they are at their economic capacity, with full employment, strong local demand for goods and services and high dwelling prices. In these circumstances the planning response might be to restrain further economic growth.

Many city centres, particularly in larger cities, have seen substantial investment in their urban fabric in recent years and are performing well. But to some extent this is a result of a centralization of retail and leisure activity in major centres at the expense of smaller town and district centres. In these other cases planners may face a difficult choice between planned shrinkage or a battle to restore the fortunes of the smaller centre against the trends of retail concentration and changing patterns of consumption.

The dichotomy in housing is typically between areas where demand outstrips supply and vice versa. Closely related to the economic fortunes of the city, the planning choices are limited. In areas of high demand, whilst the planning system can release land and support some intensification in the use of land, in a market economy there is little that can be done by urban planners to influence the rate of construction, the type, size, affordability or tenure of dwellings produced. In areas of low demand, the policy choice lies between reducing supply, which is often locally politically fraught, or struggling to increase demand against economic trends.

On many indicators, the environment of most urban areas has improved substantially over recent decades. Cities are better planned and land used more efficiently. Transport systems have improved and the needs of pedestrians and cyclists taken into greater account. More buildings of architectural or historic interest are protected from change or demolition. There are many more conservation areas. The majority of new buildings are better designed in terms of functionality and energy efficiency, if not always in their visual appearance.

But problems remain. There is a legacy of buildings, particularly those constructed in the 1960s and 1970s and especially in the housing sector, that have not proved to have the length of economic life that was anticipated when they were built. Most were designed in good faith, were well received at the time they were built and thought to offer good solutions. But, for various reasons including cost-cutting, inadequacies in the construction process, building management, maintenance, or for reasons of social change, too many of these buildings and neighbourhoods became obsolete too quickly. This imposed a burden on subsequent generations who had to deal with the costs of refurbishment or, often, demolition and replacement. It is also unfortunate because the experience has tarnished the wider image of planning and design from that era. At the micro scale this has led to unfairly critical condemnation of many buildings whose only fault was to have become unfashionable. At the macro scale it has provided ammunition to those who wish to criticize the whole profession and the very concept of planning.

The key aims of contemporary transport planning are to reduce the environmental impact of transport systems, and to maintain and improve accessibility whilst reducing the need for travel and shifting modal split away from use of the motor vehicle. The symbiotic relationship between land use and transportation means that decisions about the use and intensity of use of land can play an important role in achieving these aims, and conversely transportation investment decisions can contribute significantly to sustainable urban development.

Since the millennium many newly designed urban quarters, places and buildings have embraced the sustainable development agenda in terms of social inclusiveness, energy and transport efficiency and natural resource management. However, the environmental quality of too much of the urban fabric is still inadequate, especially in obsolete inner city neighbourhoods, poorly maintained social housing estates, retail and warehouse parks and traffic-dominated highway zones.

The nature, limitations and future of urban planning

Today, in most countries the range and complexity of stakeholders involved in urban change inevitably leads to a governance-based approach to public decision making and an inclusive and collaborative style of urban planning. However, whilst this might mean that many planning decisions are taken through negotiation and consensus building it has to be recognized that there are absolute limits to this approach. There are inherent conflicts between economic growth and the environment, between the desires of the individual and the needs of society, and there are social costs of economic activity which are not borne by the market. These can only be dealt with through legal controls. Urban planning has a duty to be transparent, to manage externalities, to adopt the precautionary principle and to operate in favour of the societal needs.

Urban planning is evidently a multi-faceted and multi-scaled process and as such requires variety and subtlety in developing and implementing solutions to urban problems. Responses need to be based upon a multi-disciplinary understanding of the socio-economic and environmental forces affecting urban areas, the nature of governance, policy making and implementation, and the normative goals of sustainable development. These can be considered at different levels of analysis from the long term strategic or macro level down to the short term tactical or micro level. At the macro level are the geopolitical paradigms and trends that shape urban societies such as globalization, the nature of capitalism and its accounting systems, political ideologies and climate change.

Globalization and a general reduction in transport costs have increased the amount and speed of flows of capital and labour between countries and cities. It has brought cities closer in terms of their economic, social and cultural interrelationships but has increased competition between cities for footloose investment and created new activities in city marketing and image building. Competition has brought benefits to many cities in terms of environmental improvements and developments in physical and social infrastructure as they seek to gain an entrepreneurial edge over rival cities. On the other hand, competition inevitably creates losers as well as winners and other cities, perhaps in less competitive locations or with a poorer image or less dynamic political leadership, have not benefitted from the same level of improvement and have been left with outworn infrastructure and surplus land, buildings and even populations.

Even in successful cities the benefits are not evenly distributed, with existing land and property owners typically gaining most from the increased demand for urban space, whilst tenants and incomers are more likely to be worse off. In market economies all firms are constantly seeking to improve their productivity. Technological innovation has been particularly important in this regard. Whether in manufacturing or service provision the ownership, configuration, means and location of production and markets of firms are continuously evolving. At one time this might have led to changes within a locality; today such changes can be global in their reach. Decisions taken in one city can affect workers, firms and cities thousands of miles away.

Climate change and natural resource depletion represent another set of global, macro issues impacting upon cities and requiring policy response. Climate change is threatening cities in different ways. In many coastal cities sea level rise may result in inundation; in other cities excessive heat or food or energy shortages may be the issue. Some of the problems can be resolved through physical investments but urban life style changes will also be important in reducing the threat or ameliorating the impact of climate change.

Similarly urban planning can make a contribution to reducing demand for energy and natural resources and reduce the ecological footprint and environmental damage caused by urban development and lifestyles. The compact city may be thought a desirable goal but there are opposing forces that must be taken into account. Around London, for example, the re-zoning of land from agricultural to residential use can easily increase its value one hundred-fold. The financial pressure for urbanization and urban sprawl is obvious. At the same time, excepting the period of the post-2008 economic crisis, real incomes are continuously rising and increasing the level of demand for housing space, goods and services and transport, all of which increases pressure for urbanization.

But urban planning cannot tackle the root causes of environmental degradation or the excessive exploitation of energy and other natural resources. That requires policy change at the highest level, for example in changing macro-economic accounting systems to take account of the social and environmental costs of production and development.

Within this macro context national governments create their own institutional, fiscal and regulatory environments which support particular forms of urban planning or particular goals for urban planning depending upon their own political ideologies and inclinations. Some, as shown in Chapter 3, support multi-tiered planning systems ranging from the national, through the regional to the local level. Some rely more on reactive and regulatory processes to mediate the use of space, whilst others like to be more proactive and interventionist in urban transformation and placemaking. Some have strong goals relating to such matters as sustainable development and spatial equality whilst others try to use the planning system to promote the short term benefits of economic growth over environmental protection. The planning system cannot determine macro-political priorities; it can only work within the prevailing political hegemony, although it can point out the social and environmental costs of political choices.

Within these contexts, the circumstances of the individual town or city become significant in determining the shape of the planning agenda and the scope for intervention. Location and geography, history, demography, socio-economic circumstances and governance arrangements will all be important influences.

It is frequently suggested that core cities are likely to grow and prosper more than peripheral cities. The idea is that core cities, such as those in the golden triangle of European economic and political power, between London, Paris and Frankfurt, have access to larger markets and are more likely to receive investment than more remote cities. There is certainly some evidence to suggest that cities that are already national or regional capitals are benefitting from agglomeration economies and the processes of economic concentration and centralization. It is many of these cities that are seeing the fastest economic growth in their respective countries. But there is also evidence of growth in other cities, even some quite remote from the European heartlands, such as Dublin and Lisbon. This suggests that local meso level circumstances can be influential. In the post-industrial economy in which proximity to raw materials and markets are of declining importance, there are a number of factors that can stimulate economic growth in a locality, such as successful local growth coalitions, local entrepreneurialism, local environmental conditions or quality of life.

History and heritage can represent a burden or an opportunity for growth. Derelict and contaminated land detracts from the urban image and imposes a heavy cost burden on the regeneration of urban areas. On the other hand, the presence of historic buildings and physical or social heritage, for example, can form the basis for growth based upon the leisure and tourism sectors. Events can also be used as a catalyst for growth.

At the micro level it is the decisions of individual households and firms and other actors, such as individual landowners or service providers, that will influence what actually happens in a city. It is individual households who, according to their own analysis of costs and benefits to them, decide whether to buy or rent a dwelling and whether to invest in housing maintenance, repairs or refurbishments, or to spend money in local shops. It is individual firms who are well or poorly managed, who increase productivity and prosper or who struggle to compete and flounder, which invest in new premises or leave a legacy of dereliction. It is individual landowners who decide to hold onto their land or to sell, to protect their land from development or to seek development.

The populations of many cities are becoming more diverse in terms of social structure, race, nationality, culture and religion. There is increasing social spatial segregation as income and cultural differences manifest themselves in housing choices, creating both high and low income ghettos: exclusive suburbs, urban villages and gated communities for the rich; run-down inner city neighbourhoods or remote peripheral social housing estates for the poor. But there is also increasing social segregation between age groups and household types, with the young and childless adults concentrated in and around city centres while families seek out the suburbs and ex-urban villages. The wealth gap between rich and poor is widening and in many cities social exclusion is an increasing problem, whether these cities are growing or shrinking.

There are serious demographic challenges facing many cities, especially in Europe, where ageing, falling household size and shrinking inner urban populations are putting increased pressure on support services while the funding and provision of such services becomes ever more problematic. Even in growing cities, it seems to be an increasingly common truth that urban economic growth is failing to provide sufficient, secure, well paid employment to sustain social progress and is leaving too many people economically inactive or forced into insecure, low wage jobs, especially in the service sector. In shrinking cities these problems are simply exaggerated.

In growing cities where housing demand outstrips supply, prices and rents are likely to rise faster than incomes, leaving the poorest struggling to find adequate accommodation. The rising costs of travel and access to services tend to reduce the mobility of those on the lowest incomes and increasingly exclude them from important aspects of urban life. In growing cities this occurs though gentrification that pushes the poor towards the urban periphery. In shrinking cities this is likely to manifest itself through housing and neighbourhood obsolescence while the economics of austerity force reductions in spending on social welfare.

To some extent planning systems can ameliorate these problems, encouraging housing production or refurbishment, transforming and reusing brownfield lands, creating urban forms that reduce the need to travel and facilitating modal shift towards lower cost cycling and walking and public transport. Programmes of urban regeneration can reduce the stigmatization of areas, improve local amenities and environments including, to some extent, 'designing out crime'. However, for the most part social exclusion results from fundamental inequalities in societies that need to be addressed at a more strategic political level than can be achieved through urban planning.

The speed and scale at which these changes can occur increase the instability of local economies and the vulnerability of cities to change beyond their control. Cities need somehow to become more resilient: more robust to withstand change and more flexible to accommodate change. This suggests that the cities of the future will have to be built in such a way that they can recover quickly from natural shocks such as flooding or storm damage. Cities need to become diverse in their economic structures and offer the widest possible range of agglomeration economies so as to be able to absorb the impact of socio-economic shocks and economic restructuring. They need to provide housing and residential areas that are flexible, inclusive, social places that can efficiently and safely accommodate people at different stages of life, different household types and income groups, different cultures and lifestyles. They need to maintain a physical environment that minimizes impacts on energy and natural resources whilst respecting and protecting urban heritage.

But, reflecting the views of the EU in *Cities of Tomorrow* (CEC, 2011), these problems can be turned into opportunities if cities:

- exploit their diversity as a source of innovation to promote economic development that can fully support social participation and inclusion;
- change in the ways they are constructed and managed to become more elderly-friendly and family-friendly, as well as places of tolerance and respect;
- become more energy efficient, greener and healthier, with attractive neighbourhoods and green spaces, not just to reduce their impact on the environment but to increase their competitiveness and liveability, so they must be redesigned to reduce the need for internal movement and encourage walking, cycling and the use of public transport over the motor vehicle;
- evolve city governance systems to become more flexible, contingent, inclusive and participative, more holistic and better coordinated, both vertically and horizontally.

So, what can be concluded about the modern urban planning agenda? How has it evolved and changed over the last century? Reinterpreting Abercrombie's views on planning, it is possible to suggest that his notion of creating 'beauty' might be widened to include not just architecture but the conservation of built heritage and the protection and enhancement of green and blue infrastructure. His notion of 'health' could be understood to mean not just human health but also the social health of communities and the broader environmental health of the planet. 'Convenience' can be interpreted at a number of spatial scales from the energy efficiency of compact urban forms to neighbourhoods where all have safe access to the facilities and services they require. The goals of urban planning remain surprisingly unchanged and continue, as Abercrombie said more than eighty years ago, to be about the creation and maintenance of urban 'beauty, health and convenience'.

Bibliography

Abercrombie, P. (1933) *Town and Country Planning*, 3rd edn, London: Oxford University Press.

Abercrombie, P. (1945) *The Greater London Plan 1944*, London: HMSO.

Adams, D. and Watkins, C. (2002) *Greenfields, Brownfields and Housing Development*, Oxford: Blackwell.

Age UK (2006) *Housing Choices for Older People: a discussion paper*, London, Age UK.

Allen, C. (2008) *Housing Market Renewal and Social Class*, London: Routledge.

Allen, R.C. (2009) *The British Industrial Revolution in Global Perspective*, Cambridge: Cambridge University Press.

Allmendinger, P. (2002) *Planning Theory*, Basingstoke: Palgrave.

APA (American Planning Association) (2014) *About Planning/What is Planning*, available at: www.planning.org (accessed 22.9.2014).

Ash, J. (1980) 'The rise and fall of high rise housing in England', in C. Ungerson and V. Karn (eds) *The Consumer Experience of Housing*, London: Gower.

Ashton, J. (1989) 'Liverpool: creating a healthy city', in D. Seedhouse and A. Cribb, *Changing Ideas in Health Care*, London: John Wiley & Sons.

Ashton, T.S. (1997) *The Industrial Revolution, 1760–1830*, Oxford: Oxford University Press.

Atkinson, R. and Moon, G. (1994) *Urban Policy in Britain: the city, the state and the market*, Basingstoke: Macmillan.

Audit Commission (2011) *Housing Market Renewal: housing programme review, March 2011*, London: Audit Commission.

Australian Government (2011) *Our Cities, Our Future: a national urban policy for a productive, sustainable and liveable future*, Canberra: Department of Infrastructure and Transport.

Balchin, P.N., Bull, G.H. and Kieve, J.L. (1995) *Urban Land Economics and Public Policy*, 5th edn, Basingstoke: Macmillan.

Ballymun Regeneration Limited (1998, updated 2007) *Masterplan*, Dublin: Ballymun Regeneration Limited.

Banister, D. (1993) *Transport: the environment and sustainable development*, London: Spon.

Barker, K. (2004) *Delivering Stability: securing our future housing needs (Barker Review of Housing Supply)*, London: HM Treasury.

Barker, K. (2006) *Barker Review of Land Use Planning*, London: HMSO.

Barlow Commission (Royal Commission on the Distribution of the Industrial Population) (1940) *Report of the Royal Commission on the Distribution of the Industrial Population* (Cmnd 6153), London: HMSO.

Barton, H., Grant, M. and Guise, R. (2010) *Shaping Neighbourhoods for Local Health and Global Sustainability*, 2nd edn, London: Routledge.

BBC News Online (2002) 'Dyson to move to Far East' (5.2.2002). Available at:. http://news.bbc.co.uk/1/hi/business/1801909.stm (accessed 3.6.2014).

BDP (2008) *Heslington East Campus, Master Plan and Strategic Design Brief*, University of York.

Bentley, I., Alcock, A., Murrain, P., McGlynn, S. and Smith, G. (1985) *Responsive Environments: a manual for designers*, London: Architectural Press.

Bernt, M. Cocks, M., Couch, C., Grossmann, K., Haase, A. and Rink, D. (2012) *Policy Response, Governance and Future Directions, Shrink Smart Research Brief No.2*, Leipzig: Helmholtz Centre for Environmental Research.

Bevan, M. and Croucher, K. (2011) *Lifetime Neighbourhoods*, York: Centre for Housing Policy at York University and London: Department for Communities and Local Government.

Biddulph, M. (2012) *Steelworks to Lakeside: strategy, water and landscape for the post-industrial city*, academia.edu.

Birmingham City Council (no date) *Bournville Village: Conservation Area and Design Guide*, Birmingham City Council.

Birmingham City Council (1999) *Regeneration through Conservation*, Birmingham: Birmingham City Council.

Birmingham City Council (2002) *Jewellery Quarter Conservation Area Character Appraisal and Management Plan*, Birmingham: Birmingham City Council.

Birmingham City Council, with English Heritage (2005) *Jewellery Quarter Conservation Area, Design Guide*, Birmingham: Birmingham City Council.

BIS (Department for Business, Innovation and Skills) (2010) *Local Growth: realising every place's potential*, Cm 7961, London: The Stationery Office.

BIS (Department for Business, Innovation and Skills) (2013) *SMEs: the key enablers of business success and the economic rationale for government intervention, BIS Analysis Paper Number 2*, London: Department for Business, Innovation and Skills.

Bodenschatz, H. (2008) 'Von der stadterneuerung zum stadtumbau', *Informationen zur Raumentwicklung*, 11(12): 661–5.

BOP Consulting (2011) *Edinburgh Festivals Impact Study*, Edinburgh: BOP Consulting.

Bramley, G. (2010) *Estimating Housing Need*, available at: www.gov.uk/government/publications/estimating-housing-need (accessed 1.11.2014).

Breheny, M. (1997) 'Urban compaction: feasible and acceptable?', *Cities*, 14(4): 209–17.

Bromley, R.D.F., Tallon, A.R. and Roberts, A.J. (2007) 'New populations in the British city centre: evidence of social change from the census and household surveys', *Geoforum*, 38: 138–54.

Brundtland, G.H. (1987) *Our Common Future: Report of the World Commission on Environment and Development*, Oxford: Oxford University Press.

Buchanan, C. (1963) *Traffic in Towns*, Harmondsworth: Penguin in association with HMSO.

Burnett, J. (1986) *A Social History of Housing, 1815–1970*, 2nd edn, London: Methuen.

CABE (Commission for Architecture and the Built Environment) (2000) *By Design: urban design and the planning system, towards better practice*, London, DETR.

CABE (Commission for Architecture and the Built Environment) (2011a) *Middlesborough Urban Growing*, available at: http://webarchive.national archives.gov.uk/20110118095356/http://www.cabe.org.uk/case-studies/middlesbrough-growing (accessed 11.6.2015).

CABE (Commission for Architecture and the Built Environment) (2011b) *Incredible Edible Todmorden*, available at: http://webarchive.national archives.gov.uk/20110118095356/http://www.cabe.org.uk/case-studies/incredible-edible-todmorden (accessed 11.6.2015).

Cambridge Econometrics (2015) *The Local Economy Forecasting Model*, available at: www.camecon.com/SubNational/SubNationalUK/Modelling Capability/LEFM/LEFMOverview.aspx (accessed 24.3.2015).

Campbell, S. and Fainstein, S.S. (eds) (2003) *Readings in Planning Theory*, 2nd edn, Oxford: Blackwell Publishers.

Campos, C. and Prothero, R. (2012) *The Spatial Distribution of Industries*, London: Office for National Statistics.

Carson, R. (1962) *Silent Spring*, New York: Houghton Mifflin.

CEC (Commission of the European Communities) (1990) *The Green Paper on the Urban Environment*, Brussels, Commission of the European Communities.

CEC (Commission of the European Communities) (1999) *European Spatial Development Perspective: towards balanced and sustainable development of the territory of the EU*, Luxembourg: Office for Official Publications of the European Communities.

CEC (Commission of the European Communities) (2007) *Leipzig Charter on Sustainable European Cities*, Brussels: Commission of the European Communities.

CEC (Commission of the European Communities) (2010) *Europe 2020: a strategy for smart, sustainable and inclusive growth*, available at: http://eur-lex.europa.eu/LexUriServ/LexUriServ.do?uri=COM:2010:2020:FIN:EN:PDF (accessed 22.5.2015).

CEC (Commission of the European Communities) (2011) *Cities of Tomorrow: challenges, visions, ways forward*. Brussels: Directorate General for Regional Policy.

CEC (Commission of the European Communities) (2013a) *Building a Green Infrastructure for Europe*, Brussels: Commission of the European Communities.

CEC (Commission of the European Communities) (2013b) *The European Union Explained: a healthy and sustainable environment for future generations*, Brussels: Directorate General for Communication.

CEC (Commission of the European Communities) (2015) *Enterprise and Industry: small and medium-sized enterprises (SMEs)*. Available at: http://ec.europa.eu/enterprise/policies/sme/index_en.htm (accessed 9.4.2015).

Centro (2011) *West Midlands Local Transport Plan (2011–2026)*, Birmingham: Centro.

Chadwick, G.F. (1971) *A Systems View of Planning*, Oxford: Pergamon Press.

Chambers, N. et al. (2004) *Scotland's Footprint*, Oxford: Best Foot Forward.

Chapin, F.S. (1965) *Urban Land Use Planning*, Urbana: University of Illinois Press.

Cherry, G. (1972) *Urban Change and Planning: a history of urban development in Britain since 1750*, Henley on Thames: G.T. Foulis.

CIRIA (2013) *Water Sensitive Urban Design in the UK: ideas for built environment practitioners*, London: CIRIA.

Cities Alliance (2007) *Understanding Your Local Economy: a resource guide for cities*, Washington, DC, The Cities Alliance.

City of Baltimore (2006) *Live, Earn, Play, Learn: Baltimore City's Comprehensive Master Plan*, Baltimore: Department of Planning.

City of York (2014) *Draft Local Plan, York*.

CMEPSP (2008) *Report by the Commission on the Measurement of Economic Performance and Social Progress (The Stiglitz Report)*, available at: www.stiglitz-sen-fitoussi.fr (accessed 24.3.2015).

Colasanti, K., Hamm, M.W. and Litjens, C.M. (2012) 'The city as an "agricultural powerhouse"? Perspectives on expanding urban agriculture from Detroit, Michigan', *Urban Geography*, 33(3): 348–69.

Colomb, C. (2012) *Staging the New Berlin: place marketing and the politics of urban reinvention post-1989*, London: Routledge.

Community Forum (1987) *A Tale of Three Cities*, Birmingham: Community Forum.

Cooney, E.W. (1974) 'High flats in local authority housing in England and Wales since 1945', in A. Sutcliffe (ed.) *Multi-Storey Living: the British working class experience*, London: Croom Helm.

Copenhagen City Council (1947) *Regional Plan for Greater Copenhagen*, Copenhagen.

Copenhagen City Council (2011) *Copenhagen Climate Adaptation Plan*, short version (English) available at: http://international.kk.dk/artikel/climate-adaptation (accessed 10.11.2014).

Cotswold District Council (2000) *The Cotswold Design Code*, Cirencester: Cotswold District Council.

Couch, A. (2010) *Planning without Growth*, unpublished MCD dissertation, University of Liverpool.

Couch, C. (1990) *Urban Renewal: theory and practice*, Basingstoke: Macmillan Education.

Couch, C. (1999) 'Housing development in the city centre', *Planning Practice and Research*, 14(1): 69–86.

Couch, C. (2003) *City of Change and Challenge: urban planning and regeneration in Liverpool*, Aldershot: Ashgate.

Couch, C., Fowles, S. and Karecha, J. (2009) 'Reurbanisation and housing markets in Central Liverpool', *Planning Practice and Research*, 24(3): 321–41.

Couch, C., Karecha, J., Nuissl, H. and Rink, D. (2005) 'Decline and sprawl: an evolving type of urban development observed in Liverpool and Leipzig', *European Planning Studies*, 13(1): 117–36.

Couch, C., Leontidou, L. and Arnstberg, K.O. (2006) 'Introduction', in C. Couch, L. Leontidou and G. Petschel-Held (eds) *Urban Sprawl in Europe: landscapes, land-use change and policy*, Oxford: Blackwell Publishing.

Couch C., Leontidou, L. and Petschel-Held, G. (eds) (2007) *Urban Sprawl in Europe: landscapes, land-use change and policy*, Oxford: Blackwell.

Couch, C., Sykes, O. and Börstinghaus, W. (2011) 'Thirty years of urban regeneration in Britain, Germany and France: the importance of context and path dependency', *Progress in Planning*, 75(1): 1–52.

Cullen, G. (1971) *The Concise Townscape*, London: Butterworth Architecture.

Cullingworth, B. and Caves, R.W. (2014) *Planning in the USA: policies, issues and processes*, London: Routledge.

Danish Ministry of the Environment (2007) *Spatial Planning in Denmark*, Copenhagen: Ministry of the Environment.

Danish Wind Energy Association (2015) *Denmark Sets World Record in Wind – Again*, available at: www.windpower.org/en/news/news.html#737 (accessed 27.5.2015).

Davidson, M. and McNeill, D. (2012) 'The Redevelopment of Olympic Sites: examining the legacy of Sydney Olympic Park', *Urban Studies*, 49(8): 1625–41.DCLG (2012, updated) 'Live tables on house building, Table 208, permanent dwellings started, by tenure and county'. Available at: www .gov.uk/government/statistical-data-sets/live-tables-on-house-building (accessed 26.1.2015).

DCLG (Department for Communities and Local Government) (2008) *Lifetime Homes, Lifetime Neighbourhoods*: a *national strategy for housing in an ageing society*, London: DCLG.

DCLG (Department for Communities and Local Government) (2011) *Laying the Foundations: a housing strategy for England*, available at: www.gov.uk/ government/publications/laying-the-foundations-a-housing-strategy-for-england—2 (accessed 29.12.2014).

DCLG (Department for Communities and Local Government) (2012) *National Planning Policy Framework*, available at: www.gov.uk/government/ publications/national-planning-policy-framework--2 (accessed 5.9.2014).

DCLG (Department for Communities and Local Government) (2014a) *Planning Practice Guidance: Housing and economic development needs assessments*, available at: http://planningguidance.planningportal.gov.uk/blog/ guidance/housing-and-economic-development-needs-assessments/ (accessed 30.10.2014).

DCLG (Department for Communities and Local Government) (2014b) *Planning Practice Guidance: Travel plans, transport assessments and statements in decision-taking*, available at: http://planningguidance.planningportal.gov. uk/blog/guidance/travel-plans-transport-assessments-and-statements-in-decision-taking/ (accessed 28.8.2014).

DCLG (Department for Communities and Local Government) (2014c) *Planning Practice Guidance: Ensuring the vitality of town centres*, available at: http://planningguidance.planningportal.gov.uk/blog/guidance/ensuring-the-vitality-of-town-centres/ensuring-the-vitality-of-town-centres-guidance/ (accessed 20.1.2015).

DCLG, Deputy Prime Minister's Office, The Rt Hon Nick Clegg, The Rt Hon Eric Pickles and others (2014) 'Government offers support for locally-led garden cities'. Press release, 14 April 2014. Available at: www.gov.uk/ government/news/government-offers-support-for-locally-led-garden-cities (accessed 29.5.2015).

DECC (Department of Energy and Climate Change) (2014) *Historical Coal Data: coal production, availability and consumption 1853 to 2013*. Available at: www.gov.uk/government/statistical-data-sets/historical-coal-data-coal-production-availability-and-consumption-1853-to-2011 (accessed 25.9.2014).

Deltacommissie (2008) *Working Together with Water: a living land builds for its future*, Den Haag: Deltacommissie.

den Hartog, H. (2009) 'Shanghai New Towns: searching for community and identity in a sprawling metropolis', *Proceedings of The New Urban Question – urbanism beyond neo-liberalism*, 4th International Conference of the International Forum on Urbanism (IFoU), Amsterdam/Delft.

DETR (Department of the Environment, Transport and the Regions) (2000) *Our Towns and Cities: The Future: delivering an urban renaissance (Cmnd 4911)*, London: TSO.

DfT (Department for Transport) (2007) *Manual for Streets*, London: Thomas Telford.

DoE (Department of the Environment) (1976) *Inner Urban Policy*, London: Press Notice 835 (17 September 1976).

DoE (Department of the Environment) (1990) *This Common Inheritance: Britain's Environmental Strategy*, London: HMSO.

DoE (Department of the Environment) (1994) *Sustainable Development: the UK Strategy*, London: HMSO.

DoE (Department of the Environment) (1996) *Planning Policy Guidance 6, 'Town Centres and Retail Developments'*, London: Department of the Environment.

DOE (Department of the Environment (NI)) (2010) *Policy Statement 4: Planning and Economic Development*, Belfast: Department of the Environment (NI).

DOE (Department of the Environment (NI)) (2013) *Northern Ireland Community Planning Foundation Programme: preparations in advance of 2015*, Belfast: Department of the Environment (NI), Local Government Policy Division.

Dol, K. and Haffner, M. (eds) (2010) *Housing Statistics in the European Union*, The Hague: Ministry of the Interior and Kingdom Relations.

Duncan, A. and Bartlett, L. (1992) *Taking on the Motorway: North Kensington Amenity Trust 21 years*, London: Kensington and Chelsea Community History Group.

Dundee City Council (2013) *Strategic Environmental Assessmen: Environmental Report for the Proposed Dundee Local Development Plan*. Dundee.

Dundee City Council (2014) *Dundee Local Development Plan*, Available at: www.dundeecity.gov.uk/sites/default/files/publications/CD_LDP_written_statement_Dec13.pdf (accessed 28.5.2015).

ECTP-CEU (European Council of Spatial Planners) (1985) *Founding Charter*, Brussels: ECTP.

EEA (European Environment Agency) (2006a) *The Changing Faces of Europe's Coastal Areas*, Copenhagen: European Environment Agency.

EEA (European Environment Agency) (2006b) *Urban Sprawl in Europe: the ignored challenge*, Copenhagen: European Environment Agency.

EEA (European Environment Agency) (2013a) 'Highest recycling rates in Austria and Germany – but UK and Ireland show fastest increase', Press Release, 13 March 2013.

EEA (European Environment Agency) (2013b) *Land Take Data (CSI 014/LSI 001)*, Copenhagen: European Environment Agency.

EIA (Energy Information Administration) (2014) *International Energy Outlook 2014*, Washington DC: US Department of Energy.

Engelen, G., Uljee, I., Gobin, A., Van Esch, L. and van der Kwast, H. (2005) *Supporting Strategic Plan Development in Flanders*, Mol: Flemish Institute for Technological Research.

English Heritage (2014) *Conservation Area Guidance*, London: English Heritage.

English Partnerships. (1996) *Time for Design*, London: English Partnerships.

Environmental Resources Management (2004) *Employment Land Reviews – Guidance Note*, London: Office of the Deputy Prime Minister.

Esher, L. (Lord) (1968) *York: a study in conservation*, London: HMSO.

Etzioni, A. (1973) 'A "third" approach to decision-making', in A. Faludi (ed.) *A Reader in Planning Theory*, Oxford: Pergamon Press.

EUKN (2005) *National Urban Policy of Poland*, available at: www.eukn.eu/ e-library/project/bericht/eventDetail/national-urban-policy-of-poland/ (accessed 19.9.2014).

European Parliament, Directorate General for Internal Policies, Policy Department A: Economic and Scientific Policy (2014) *Mapping Smart Cities in the EU*, available at: http://www.europarl.europa.eu/studies.

Eurostat (2002) *50 years of the ECSC Treaty Coal and Steel Statistics*, Luxembourg: Office for Official Publications of the European Communities.

Eurostat (2009) *Eurostat Table lan_lcv_art – Land covered by artificial*; available at: http://appsso.eurostat.ec.europa.eu/nui/show.do?dataset=lan_lcv_ art&lang=en (accessed 11.6.2015).

Eurostat. (2013a) *EUROPOP2013: population projections at the national level*, EUROSTAT; available at: http://appsso.eurostat.ec.europa.eu/nui/ show.do?dataset=proj_13npms&lang=en (accessed 19.1.2015).

Eurostat. (2013b) *Eurostat Yearbook*; available at: http://epp.eurostat.ec. europa.eu/statistics_explained/index.php/Europe_in_figures_-_Eurostat_ yearbook (accessed 7.1.2014).

Eurostat (2014a) 'Tables: GDP and main components – current prices' [nama_ gdp_c], and 'Government revenue, expenditure and main aggregates' [gov_10a_main], available at: http://appsso.eurostat.ec.europa.eu/nui/show. do?dataset=nama_gdp_c&lang=en (accessed 3.12.2014).

Eurostat (2014b) 'Transport – cities and greater cities', Table [urb_ctran], available at: http://appsso.eurostat.ec.europa.eu/nui/show.do?dataset=urb_ ctran&lang=en (accessed 11.6.2015).

Evans, A.W. (2004) *Economics and Land Use Planning*, Oxford: Blackwell.

Evans, S.R. (1997) *Regenerating Town Centres*, Manchester: Manchester University Press.

Eversheds (2015) *New EU Directive on Environmental Impact Assessment*, Eversheds. Available at: http://www.eversheds.com/global/en/what/articles/index.page?ArticleID=en/Real_estate/New_EU_Directive_on_Environmental_Impact_Assessment (accessed 7.4.2015).

Eyers, T. and Jones, P. (2004) *The Jubilee Line Extension Impact Study: main findings and lessons for future appraisal of major public transport investments*. Paper from The Association for European Transport Conference held in Strasbourg, France on 4–10 October 2004.

Faludi, A. (1973) *Planning Theory*, Oxford: Pergamon Press.

Fernie, J. (1995) 'The coming of the fourth wave: new forms of out-of-town retail development', *International Journal of Retail and Distribution Management*, 23: 4–11.

Ferrari, E. and Lee, P. (2010) *Building sustainable housing markets: lessons from a decade of changing demand and Housing Market Renewal*, London: Chartered Institute of Housing.

Ferreira, A. Sykes, O. and Batey, P. (2009) 'Planning Theory or Planning Theories? The Hydra Model and its implications for planning education', *Journal for Education in the Built Environment*, 4(2): 29–54.

Fincher, R. and Iveson, K. (2008) *Planning and Diversity in the City: redistribution, recognition and encounter*, Basingstoke: Palgrave Macmillan.

Fischer, T.B. (2007) *The Theory and Practice of Strategic Environmental Assessment: towards a more systematic approach*, London: Earthscan.

Fisher Associates (2007) *The Maritime Sector on Merseyside: economic impact study, final report*, Liverpool: Mersey Maritime.

Fishman, R. (1982) *Urban Utopias in the Twentieth Century: Ebenezer Howard, Frank Lloyd Wright and Le Corbusier*, Cambridge, MA: MIT Press.

Florida, R. (2002) *The Rise of the Creative Class: and how it's transforming work, leisure, community and everyday life*, New York: Perseus Book Group.

Freestone, R. (2010) *Urban Nation: Australia's planning heritage*, Collingwood: CSIRO Publishing.

Freiburg im Breisgau (2014) *Approaches to Sustainability: Green City Freiburg*, Stadt Freiburg, available at www.fwtm.freiburg.de (accessed 6.11.2014).

Galster, G., Hanson, R., Ratcliffe, M.R., Wolman, H., Coleman, S. and Freihage, J. (2001) 'Wrestling sprawl to the ground: defining and measuring an elusive concept', *Housing Policy Debate*, 12(4).

García, B. (2005) 'De-constructing the City of Culture: the long term cultural legacies of Glasgow 1990', *Urban Studies*, 42(5/6): 1–28.

García, B., Melville, R. and Cox, T. (2010) *Creating an Impact: Liverpool's experience as European Capital of Culture*, Liverpool: University of Liverpool and Liverpool John Moores University.

Garreau, J. (1991) *Edge City: life on the new frontier*, New York: Anchor Books.

Gaudie, E. (1974) *Cruel Habitations: a history of working class housing 1780–1918*, London: Allen & Unwin.

Geddes, P. (1915) *Cities in Evolution*, London: Williams & Norgate.

Gemeente Utrecht (1995) *Master Plan Leidsche Rijn*, Utrecht: Gemeente Utrecht.

Gibson, M.S. and Langstaff, M.J. (1982) *An Introduction to Urban Renewal*, London: Hutchinson.

Gideon, S. (1967) *Space, Time and Architecture: the growth of a new tradition*, 5th edn, Cambridge, MA: Harvard University Press.

Glasson, J., Therivel, R. and Chadwick, A. (2012) *Introduction to Environmental Impact Assessment*, 4th edn, London: Routledge.

Goodall, B. (1972) *The Economics of Urban Areas*, Oxford: Pergamon.

Gordon, P. and Richardson, H.W. (2000) 'Defending urban sprawl', *The Public Interest*, 139: 65–71.

Greenpeace USA (2014) *Global Warming and Energy*, Greenpeace USA; available at: www.greenpeace.org/usa/en/campaigns/global-warming-and-energy (accessed 25.1.2015).

Hall, P. (1975) *Urban and Regional Planning*, Harmondsworth: Pelican.

Hall, P. and Tewdwr-Jones, M. (2011) *Urban and Regional Planning*, 5th edn, London: Routledge.

Hall, S. and Hickman, P. (2002) 'Neighbourhood renewal and urban policy: a comparison of new approaches in England and France', *Regional Studies*: 36(6): 693–6.

Hallock, J.L., Wu, W., Hall, C.A.S. and Jefferson, M. (2014) 'Forecasting the limits to the availability and diversity of global conventional oil supply: validation', *Energy*, 64: 130–53.

Halton Borough Council (2013) *Halton's Local Plan: core strategy*, Widnes: Directorate of Policy, Planning and Transportation.

Harloe, M. (ed.) (1977) *Captive Cities: studies in the political economy of cities and regions*, London: Wiley.

Harvey, D. (1973) *Social Justice and the City*, London: Arnold.

Healey, P. (1997) *Collaborative Planning*, London: Macmillan.

Heseltine, M. (2000) *Life in the Jungle*, London: Hodder & Stoughton.

Hiorns, F. (1956) *Town-building in History: an outline review of conditions, influences, ideas, and methods affecting 'planned' towns through five thousand years*, London: Harrap.

Hirsch, R.L., Bezdek, R. and Wendling, R. (2005) *Peaking of World Oil Production: impacts, mitigation, and risk management*, Science Applications International Corporation/US Department of Energy, National Energy Technology Laboratory.

Hobsbawn, E.J. (1968) *Industry and Empire: an economic history of Britain since 1750*, London: Weidenfeld & Nicolson.

Hohenberg, P.M. and Lees, L.H. (1985) *The Making of Urban Europe, 1000–1950*, Cambridge, MA: Harvard University Press.

Howard, E. (1898) *To-morrow: a peaceful path to real reform*. London: Swan Sonnenschein. Republished as: Howard, E. (1902) *Garden Cities of Tomorrow*, London: Swan Sonnenschein.

Hutton, W. (2010) 'This country's renewal is being betrayed by cheap, paltry politics', *The Observer* (11.4.10).

IAIA (International Association for Impact Assessment) (2009) *What Is Impact Assessment?*, Fargo, ND: IAIA.

Imrie, R. and Thomas, H. (1999) *British Urban Policy and the Urban Development Corporations*, London: Sage.

IPCC (Intergovernmental Panel on Climate Change) (2007) 'Summary for policymakers', in *Climate Change 2007: impacts, adaptation and vulnerability*. Contribution of Working Group II to the Fourth Assessment Report of the Intergovernmental Panel on Climate Change, Cambridge: Cambridge University Press.

IPCC (Intergovernmental Panel on Climate Change) (2013) 'Summary for policymakers', in *Climate Change 2013: the physical science basis*. Contribution of Working Group I to the Fifth Assessment Report of the Intergovernmental Panel on Climate Change, Cambridge: Cambridge University Press.

Jackson, T. (2009) *Prosperity without Growth? The transition to a low carbon economy*, London: Sustainable Development Commission.

Jacobs, J. (1961) *The Death and Life of Great American Cities*, New York: Random House.

John, P. (2001) *Local Governance in Western Europe*, London: Sage.

Jones Lang LaSalle (2004) *Land & Property Value Study: assessing the change in land & property values attributable to the Jubilee Line Extension*, London: Transport for London (TfL).

Keeble, L. (1964) *The Principles and Practice of Town and Country Planning*, 3rd edn, London: Estates Gazette.

Kintrea, K. and Muir, J. (2009) 'Integrating Ballymun? Flawed progress in Ireland's largest estate regeneration scheme', *Town Planning Review*, 80(1): 83–108.

Knapp, W. (1998) 'The Rhine-Ruhr area in transformation: towards a European metropolitan region?', *European Planning Studies*, 6(4): 379–93.

Koelnmesse GmbH (2014) *Koelnmesse since 1924*, available at: www.koelnmesse.de (accessed 27.11.2014).

Korn, A. (1953) *History Builds the Town*, London: Lund Humphries.

Krier, R. (2006) *Town Spaces: contemporary interpretations in traditional urbanism*, Basel: Birkhäuser.

Kunzmann, K.R. (2004) 'Creative brownfield redevelopment: the experience of the IBA Emscher Park initiative in the Ruhr in Germany', in R. Greenstein and Y. Sungu-Erylmaz (eds) *The Use and Reuse of Urban Land*, Cambridge: Lincoln Institute of Land Policy.

Lange, G.-M. (ed.) (2007) 'Special issue on environmental accounting: introducing the system of integrated environmental and economic accounting SEEA-2003', *Ecological Economics*, 61(4): 589–724.

Lambeth (London Borough of) (2013) *Lambeth Cycling Strategy*, London Borough of Lambeth; available at: http://lambeth.gov.uk/parking-transport-and-streets/cycle-strategy (accessed 11.1.2015).

Lawless, P. (1979) *Urban Deprivation and Government Initiative*, London: Faber & Faber.

Le Corbusier (1935, republished 1964) *La Ville Radieuse: éléments d'une doctrine d'urbanisme pour l'équipement de la civilisation machiniste*, Paris: Editions Vincent, Freal.

Leicester City Council (2012) *Student Housing Supplementary Planning Document*, Leicester: Leicester City Council.

Leigh, N.G. and Blakely, E.J. (2013) *Planning Local Economic Development: theory and practice*, 5th edn, London: Sage.

Lever, W.F. (1993) 'Reurbanisation – the policy implications', *Urban Studies*, 30(2): 267–84.

Li, V. and Lang, G. (2010) 'China's "Green GDP" experiment and the struggle for ecological modernisation', *Journal of Contemporary Asia*, 40(1): 44–62.

Lindblom, C. (1973) 'The science of "muddling through"', in A. Faludi (ed.) *A Reader in Planning Theory*, Oxford: Pergamon Press.

Liverpool City Council (1993) *Liverpool City Centre Plan*, Liverpool: Liverpool City Council.

Llewelyn-Davies (2000) *Urban Design Compendium*, London: English Partnerships, The Housing Corporation.

Lloyd, M.G. and Peel, D. (2012) 'Planning reform in Northern Ireland: Planning Act (Northern Ireland) 2011', *Planning Theory and Practice*, 13(1): 177–82.

Locate in Kent (2009) *Economic Impacts of Olympic Games*, West Malling: Locate in Kent. Available at: www.locateinkent.com.

Loney, M. (1983) *Community against Government: the British Community Development Project, 1968–78: a study of government incompetence*, London: Heinemann.

Lord, A. (2012) *The Planning Game*, London: Routledge.

Lynch, K. (1960) *The Image of the City*, Cambridge, MA: MIT Press.

McCarthy, J. (1998) 'Reconstruction, regeneration and re-imaging: the case of Rotterdam', *Cities*, 15(5): 337–44.

McLoughlin, J.B. (1969) *Urban and Regional Planning: a systems approach*, London: Faber & Faber.

Manchester City Council (1984) *Manchester City Centre Local Plan*, Manchester: Manchester City Council.

Mason, P. (2014) 'What makes a perfect city?', *The Guardian, G2 Section*, 25 August 2014.

Meadows, D., Meadows, D. and Randers, J. (1972) *The Limits to Growth: a report of the Club of Rome's Project on the Predicament of Mankind*, London: Earth Island.

Mell, I. (2012) *Green Infrastructure: concepts, perceptions and its use in planning – developing green infrastructure planning in the UK, Europe and North America*, Colne: LAP Lambert Academic Publishing.

MHLG (Ministry of Housing and Local Government) (1962) *Residential Areas: higher densities*, London: HMSO.

MHLG (Ministry of Housing and Local Government) (1966) *The Deeplish Study: improvement possibilities in a District of Rochdale*, London: HMSO.

Mills, E.S. and Hamilton, B.W. (1984) *Urban Economics*, 3rd edn, Glenview, IL: Scott, Foresman.

Millspaugh, M. (2001) 'Waterfronts as catalysts for city renewal', in R. Marshall (ed.), *Waterfronts in Post-Industrial Cities*, London: Spon Press.

Millspaugh, M. (2003) 'The Inner Harbor Story', *Urban Land*, April: 36–41.

Mitchell, R.B. and Rapkin, C. (1954) *Urban Traffic: a function of land use*, New York: Columbia University Press.

Morris, A.E.J. (1979) *History of Urban Form: before the industrial revolutions*, 2nd edn, London: Godwin.

Mumford, L. (1961) *The City in History: its origins, its transformations, and its prospects,* London: Secker & Warburg.

Nairn, I. (1955) *Outrage,* London: Architectural Press.

Nathan, M. and Urwin, C. (2006) *City People: city centre living in the UK,* London: Institute for Public Policy Research.

Needleman, L. (1965) *The Economics of Housing,* London: Staples Press.

Network Rail (2014) *Birmingham New Street Redevelopment,* available at: http://www.networkrail.co.uk/aspx/6222.aspx (accessed 11.6.2015).

Nevin, B. (2001) *Liverpool's Housing Market Research Programme, 1999/2001: a review of the main findings and policy recommendations,* Birmingham: Centre for Urban and Regional Studies, University of Birmingham.

Newman, P. and Thornley, A. (1996) *Urban Planning in Europe,* London: Routledge.

Newman, P.W.G. and Kenworthy, J.R. (1989) 'Gasoline consumption and cities: a comparison of U.S. cities with a global survey', *Journal of the American Planning Association,* 55(1): 24–37.

NFB (National Federation of Builders) (2006) *Response to the Barker Review of Land Use Planning,* available at: www.builders.org.uk/resources/nfb/000/304/336/barker.htm (accessed 23.9.2014).

Nielsen, R. (2006) *The Little Green Handbook: seven trends shaping the future of our planet,* New York: Picador.

Nordhaus, W.D. and Kokkelenberg, E.C. (eds) (1999) *Nature's Numbers: expanding the national economic accounts to include the environment,* Washington, DC: National Academy Press.

O'Connor, J. (1973) *The Fiscal Crisis of the State,* New York: St James Press.

O'Neill Associates (2010) *The RTPI Planning Awards, Submission of University of York Heslington East Campus Design Brief including Masterplan,* York: O'Neill Associates.

Oc, T. and Tiesdell, S. (1997) 'The death and life of city centres', in T. Oc and S. Tiesdell (eds), *Safer City Centres: reviving the public realm,* London: Paul Chapman.

ODPM (Office of the Deputy Prime Minister) (2001a) *A New Commitment to Neighbourhood Renewal,* London: TSO.

ODPM (Office of the Deputy Prime Minister) (2001b) *Planning Policy Guidance Note 13 Transport,* London, TSO.

ODPM (Office of the Deputy Prime Minister) (2003) *Sustainable Communities: building for the future,* London: TSO.

OECD (Organisation for Economic Co-operation and Development) (2003) *Entrepreneurship and Local Economic Development: programme and policy recommendations,* Paris: OECD.

Oguz, S. and Knight, J. (2010) 'Regional economic indicators: with a focus on sub-regional gross value added using shift-share analysis', *Economic and Labour Market Review* 4(11): 64–105.

Oliver, L., Ferber, U., Grimski, D., Millar, K. and Nathanail, P. (2005) *The Scale and Nature of European Brownfields,* CABERNET (Concerted Action on Brownfield and Economic Regeneration). Network) Working Paper. Available at: www.cabernet.org.uk/resourcefs/417.pdf (accessed 23.9.2014).

ONS (Office for National Statistics) (2007) *UK Standard Industrial Classifica-tion 2007*, available at: www.ons.gov.uk/ons/guide-method/classifications/current-standard-classifications/standard-industrial-classification/index.html (accessed 25.9.2014).

ONS (Office for National Statistics) (2013) *Statistical Bulletin Retail Sales, December 2012*, London: ONS.

ONS (Office for National Statistics) (2014) *Indices of Deprivation across the UK*, London: ONS. Available at: www.neighbourhood.statistics.gov.uk/dissemination (accessed 19.1.2015).

Oxford Economics (2014) *TAYplan Economic Outlook*, Dundee: TAYplan SDPA.

Page, E. and Goldsmith, M. (1987) *Central and Local Government Relations*, London: Sage.

Palmer, R. and Richards, G. (2007) *European Cultural Capital Report*, Arnhem: Association for Tourism and Leisure Education (ATLAS).

Parkinson, M. (2008) *Make No Little Plans: the regeneration of Liverpool city centre 1999–2008*, Liverpool: Liverpool Vision.

Parkinson, M., Clark, G., Hutchins, M., Simmie, J. and Verdonk, H. (2004) *Competitive European Cities: where do the core cities stand?*, London: Office of the Deputy Prime Minister.

Parkinson, M. et al. (2012) *Second Tier Cities in Europe: in an age of austerity why invest beyond the capitals?*, ESPON and European Institute of Urban Affairs, Liverpool John Moores University.

Peiser, R. (2001) 'Decomposing urban sprawl', *Town Planning Review*, 76(3).

PIA (Planning Institute Australia) (2014) *Become a Planner*, available at: www.planning.org.au (accessed 22.9.2014).

Pickvance, C. (1976) *Urban Sociology: critical essays*, London: Tavistock.

Pitt, M. (2008) *Learning Lessons from the 2007 Floods*, London: Cabinet Office.

Planning Advisory Group (PAG) (1965) *The Future of Development Plans*, London: HMSO.

Port of Rotterdam. (2014) *Port Statistics*, available at: www.portofrotterdam.com/en/Port/port-statistics/Documents/Port-statistics-2013/index.html#18 (accessed 26.8.14).

Potts, R., Simms, A. and Kjell, P. (2005) *Clone Town Britain: the survey results on the bland state of the nation*, London: New Economics Foundation.

Power, S. (2000) 'The development of the Ballymun housing scheme, Dublin', *Irish Geography*, 33: 199–212.

Punter, J.V. (1989) 'France', in H.W.E. Davies (ed.), *Planning Control in Western Europe*, London: HMSO.

PWC (2001) *The business and economic effects of the 2000 Sydney Olympics, a collation of evidence,* Sydney, NSW: DSRD.

Quality Assurance Agency for Higher Education (2008) *Subject Benchmark Statement for Town and Country Planning*, Gloucester: Quality Assurance Agency for Higher Education.

Ren, X. (2013) *Urban China*, Hoboken, NJ: Wiley.

RPS and Alder King (2013) *Strategic Employment Sites in the WESP area, for South West of England Regional Development Agency and West of England Strategic Partnership (June 2013)*.

Ruimte Vlaanderen (1997) *Ruimtelijk Structuurplan Vlaanderen*, Brussels: Department van de Vlaamse Overheid.

Rydin, Y. (2003) *Urban and Environmental Planning in the UK*, Basingstoke: Palgrave Macmillan.

Rydin, Y. (2010) *Governing for Sustainable Urban Development*, London: Earthscan.

Saltwell and Bensham Residents Association (2014) *No to Demolition in Saltwell and Bensham*, available at: www.sbresidents.org/ (accessed 1.1.2015).

Santos, G., Maoh, H., Potogiou, D. and van Brunn, T. (2013) 'Factors influencing modal split of commuting journeys in medium-size European cities', *Journal of Transport Geography*, 30: 127–37.

Schiller, R. (1986) 'Retail decentralisation: the coming of the third wave', *The Planner*, 72(7): 13–15.

Schmitt P. (2013) 'Managing urban change in five European urban agglomerations: key policy documents and institutional frameworks', in A. Eraydin and T. Tasan-Kok (eds), *Resilience Thinking in Urban Planning*, Dordrecht: Springer.

Schumacher, E.F. (1973) *Small is Beautiful: a study of economics as if people mattered*, London: Blond & Briggs.

Scottish Government (2009) *National Planning Framework for Scotland*, Edinburgh: Scottish Government, Directorate for the Built Environment.

Searle, G. (2012) 'The long-term urban impacts of the Sydney Olympic Games', *Australian Planner*, 49(3), 195–202.

Searle, G. (2013) '"Relational" planning and recent Sydney Metropolitan and City strategies', *Urban Policy and Research*, 31(3): 367–78.

Shankland, G. (1977) *Inner Area Studies: Liverpool, Birmingham and Lambeth: summaries of consultants' final reports*, London: Department of the Environment.

Sharp, T. (1968) *Towns and Townscape,* London: John Murray.

Sitte, C. (1889) *City Planning According to Artistic Principles*, Vienna.

Smith, B.A. (1973) 'Retail planning in France', *Town Planning Review*, 44(3): 279–306.

Somerville-Woodward, R. (2002) *Ballymun. A History: volume 2, c.1960–1997 Synopsis*, Dublin: Ballymun Regeneration Limited.

Southend-on-Sea Borough Council (2010) *Better Southend,* available at www.bettersouthend.com (accessed 30.2.2014).

SPDA (Strategic Planning Development Authority for Dundee, Angus, Perth and North Fife) (2012) *Strategic Development Plan 2012–2032*, Dundee: TAYplan SPDA.

Stadt Dortmund (2014) *Bebauungsplan EV 148 – Wohnsiedlung Am Eckey*, Dortmund.

Stewart, C. (1964) *A Prospect of Cities: being studies towards a history of town planning*, London: Longmans.

Stouten, P. (2010) *Changing Contexts in Urban Regeneration: 30 years of modernisation in Rotterdam*, Amsterdam: Techne Press.

Stübben, J. (1907) *Der Städtebau*, 2nd edn, Stuttgart: Alfred Kroner Verlag.

Sutcliffe, A. (1981) *Towards the Planned City: Germany, Britain, the United States and France 1780–1914*, Oxford: Basil Blackwell.

Tallon, A.R. (2013) *Urban Regeneration in the UK*, 2nd edn, London: Routledge .

Tang, W.-S. (1997) 'Urbanization in China: a review of its causal mechanisms and spatial relations', *Progress in Planning*, 48(1): 1–65.

Tata, L. (2005) *Learning in Urban Regeneration: the case of Phoenix in Dortmund*. Paper to Regional Growth Agendas Conference at the Aalborg University, Aalborg, Denmark.

Taylor, N. (1998) *Urban Planning Theory Since 1945*, London: Sage.

TCPA (Town and Country Planning Association) (2014) *The TCPA Garden City Principles*, London: TCPA.

TCPA and FOE (Town and Country Planning Association and Friends of the Earth) (2010) *Planning for Climate Change – guidance and model policies for local authorities*, London: TCPA.

Teitz, M. (2002) 'Progress and planning in America over the past 30 years', *Progress in Planning*, 57(3–4): 179–203.

Thompson, J.M. (1969) *Motorways in London*, London: Duckworth.

Tolley, R. (ed.) (1995) *The Greening of Urban Transport: planning for walking and cycling in Western cities*, Chichester: Wiley.

Townsend, T. (2006) 'From inner city to inner suburb? Addressing housing aspirations in low demand areas in NewcastleGateshead', UK, *Housing Studies*, 21(4): 501–21.

Tudor Walters Committee (1918) *Report of the Committee to Consider Questions of Building Construction in Connection with the Provision of Dwellings for the Working Classes in England and Wales, and Scotland*, Cmnd 9191, London: HMSO.

Turok, I. and Mykhnenko, V. (2007) 'The trajectories of European cities 1960–2005', *Cities*, 24: 65–182.

Tym, R. and Partners (2000) *Secondary Shopping: Retail Capacity and Need: a scoping paper*, London: National Retail Planning Forum.

UK Green Building Council (2015) 'Retrofit domestic buildings', available at: http://www.ukgbc.org/resources/key-topics/new-build-and-retrofit/retrofit-domestic-buildings (accessed 27.5.2015).

UK Meteorological Office (2012) *Climate Services, Case Studies: urban heat islands*, available at: www.metoffice.gov.uk (accessed 2.7.2014).

UN (United Nations) (2011) *World Urbanisation Prospects, 2011 Revision, File 6*, United Nations Department of Economic and Social Affairs, Population Division.

UNESCO (United Nations Educational, Scientific and Cultural Organisation) (1972) *World Heritage Convention*, Paris: UNESCO.

UNESCO (United Nations Educational, Scientific and Cultural Organisation) (2013) *Operational Guidelines for the Implementation of the World Heritage Convention*, Paris: UNESCO.

United Nations Conference on Environment and Development (1992) *Agenda 21: The Rio Declaration on Environment and Development*, New York: United Nations.

United States Department of Agriculture (1997) *National Resources Inventory*, available at: www.nrcs.usda.gov/wps/portal/nrcs/main/national/technical/nra/nri/ (accessed 1.9.2014).

Universities UK (2006) *Studentification: a guide to challenges, opportunities and good practice*, London: Universities UK.

Unwin, R. (1909) *Town Planning in Practice: an introduction to the art of designing cities and suburbs*, London: Fisher Unwin.

Urban Task Force (1999) *Towards an Urban Renaissance*, London: E&F Spon.

URBED (Urban and Economic Development Group) (1994) *Vital and Viable Town Centres: meeting the challenge*, London: Department of the Environment.

URBED (Urban and Economic Development Group) (1999) *Tapping the Potential: best practice in assessing urban housing capacity*, London: DETR.

US Census Bureau (2011) *Poverty Level by City*, Table 707, available at: www.census.gov/compendia/statab/2011/tables/11s0707.pdf (accessed 12.1.2015).

US Federal Highway Administration (2013) *Land use planning*, available at: www.fhwa.dot.gov/planning/processes/land_use/ (accessed 4.8.2014).

Vandevyvere, W. and Zenthöfer, A. (2012) *The Housing Market in the Netherlands, Economic Papers 457*, Brussels: European Commission.

Verdict (in association with SAS) (2013) *How the UK Will Shop: 2013*, London: Verdict Research.

Viljoen, A. (ed.) (2005) *Continuously Productive Urban Landscapes: designing urban agriculture for sustainable cities*, London: Architectural Press.

Vlaamse Overheid (2012) *Flanders in 2050: human scale in a metropolis? Spatial Policy Plan, Green Paper*, Brussels.

Wang, L., Kundu, R. and Chen, X. (2010) 'Building for what and whom? New town development as planned suburbanization in China and India', in M. Clapson and R. Hutchison (eds), *Suburbanization in Global Society*, Bingley: Emerald.

Ward, S. (1994) *Planning and Urban Change*, London: Paul Chapman.

Welsh Government. (2004) *Wales Spatial Plan – People, Places, Futures*, Cardiff: Welsh Government.

Westminster City Council (2007a) *Controlling Housing Density*, London: Westminster City Council.

Westminster City Council (2007b) *Unitary Development Plan*, London: Westminster City Council.

Westminster City Council (2009) *Westminster Noise Strategy 2010–2015*, London: Westminster City Council.

Whitelegg, J. (1993) *Transport for a Sustainable Future: the case for Europe*, London: Belhaven Press.

WHO (World Health Organisation) (1998) *Health Promotion Glossary*, Geneva: World Health Organisation.

Wilkinson, R. and Pickett, K. (2009) *The Spirit Level: why more equal societies almost always do better*, London: Penguin.

Williams, K. (2004) 'Reducing sprawl and delivering an urban renaissance in England: are these aims possible given current attitudes to urban living?', in H.W. Richardson and C.B. Chang-Hee (eds), *Urban Sprawl in Western Europe and the United States*, Aldershot: Ashgate.

Worskett, R. (1969) *The Character of Towns*, London, The Architectural Press.

Wu, F. (2015) *Planning for Growth: urban and regional planning in China*, London: Routledge.

Xu, J. and Chung, C.K.L. (2014) '"Environment" as an evolving concept in China's urban planning system', *International Development Planning Review*, 36(4): 391–S412.

Yeh, A.G.O. and Wu, F.L. (1999) 'Urban planning issues in China', *Progress in Planning*, 51(3): 165–252.

Zhou, J. (2010) 'Urban development and management in Songjiang New City', in H. den Hartog (ed.), *Shanghai New Towns: searching for community and identity in a sprawling metropolis*, Rotterdam, 010 Publishers.

Index